Women and Men in Society

Charlotte G. O'Kelly

Providence College

D. VAN NOSTRAND COMPANY
New York • Cincinnati • Toronto • London • Melbourne

Dedication

To Seth, Adam, and Robin

The cover shows a wedding party outside the Church of San Sebastian, La Paz, Bolivia. Photo by United Nations/Rothstein.

D. Van Nostrand Company Regional Offices:
New York   Cincinnati

D. Van Nostrand Company International Offices:
London   Toronto   Melbourne

Library of Congress Catalog Card Number: 79-65546
ISBN: 0-442-25794-5

Published by D. Van Nostrand Company
135 West 50th Street, New York, N.Y. 10020

10 9 8 7 6 5 4 3 2 1

Preface

The central theme of this book is that, although the roles of women and men vary widely from society to society, gender roles can be explained by social variables. Sexual stratification is a multifaceted phenomenon not amenable to simplistic or monocausal explanations. Furthermore, since the determinants of women's and men's positions differ in differing social circumstances, it is necessary to study a wide range of contemporary and historical societies. I have, therefore, located gender roles and sexual stratification systems in their social contexts and related them to the wider social institutions and ecological and economic circumstances of hunting and gathering, horticultural, pastoral, agricultural, industrial, capitalist, and socialist societies.

Other books on gender roles, sexual stratification, and women's studies have focused on gender roles only in modern industrial society or are case studies of specific societies. Little material has been available to help the student synthesize this vast, wide-ranging literature. Furthermore, writers tend to stay within the traditional boundaries of their disciplines: "exotic" preindustrial peoples for anthropology, modern society for sociology, past societies for historians, economic institutions and behavior for economists, political institutions and behavior for political scientists, individuals in modern society for psychology. In addition, most books examine only "woman's place" with little or no reference to "man's place" in society.

I have attempted to bridge these gaps and cross these boundaries by approaching the subject matter of women and men's positions in society from an interdisciplinary, cross-cultural, historical perspective. I have brought together from the various social sciences material that is relevant to understanding why women and men have held various positions in different types of societies.

Chapter 1 deals with the problem of sexism in social science and the negative effects this has had on the development of theories of women and men in society. Chapter 2 examines a number of attempts to explain the development and evolution of sexual stratification. I have given particular attention to Frederick Engels' early theoretical efforts and to contemporary writers who remain in this tradition of evolutionary, materialistic theories of gender roles.

In Chapters 3 through 10 I use the theoretical insights presented in

Chapter 2 to analyze the positions of women and men in different societies. Chapter 3 describes and analyzes gender roles in several simple hunting and gathering societies noted for their sexual egalitarianism. Chapter 4 deals with horticultural societies which exhibit both high and low degrees of sexual egalitarianism. In Chapter 5 I discuss variations among nomadic pastoral peoples.

In Chapter 6 I use historical sources to examine patterns and changes in sexual stratification in the agrarian societies of ancient Greece and Rome and medieval Europe. I analyze contemporary underdeveloped societies in Chapter 7 with particular attention to Mexico, India, and Iraq.

The impact of the rise of capitalism and the industrial revolution on women and men in society is treated in Chapter 8, which discusses the United States and England from 1700 to 1920. The continuing effects of industrialization on sexual stratification in the United States from 1920 to 1980 are explored in Chapter 9. In Chapter 10 I examine industrialization in the context of socialist society in the USSR and on the Israeli kibbutz.

Chapter 11 summarizes the general conclusions of this comparative and historical analysis of women and men's positions in society. This chapter points to the implications of these conclusions for the future of gender roles and sexual stratification.

The book is appropriate for women's studies courses and for sociology, anthropology, psychology, economics, political science, and history courses dealing with gender roles and sexual stratification. The book's emphasis on family structures makes it suitable for courses on the family in departments of sociology. Its emphasis on economic and class structures and sexual stratification makes it useful in social stratification classes. The focus on societal evolution and cross-cultural and historical comparisons makes the book appropriate for courses in social change. It can also be used in introductory sociology courses to introduce students to the study of gender roles and to the comparative, evolutionary, institutional approach in social science. Teachers of general social science courses will also find the interdisciplinary, comparative approach relevant to their needs.

I would like to thank the following people for their help in the preparation of this book: my husband and colleague, Larry S. Carney, my colleagues Susan Spiggle and Mary Anne Sedney, and the reviewers, who provided useful criticism and advice. Special thanks go to Ann Marie Palmisciano, who in addition to her work as my research assistant prepared the indexes. Thanks also go to Jean Jackson for her help in typing the many drafts of the manuscript, to my publisher, Judith Joseph, and to my editor, Elaine Krause. I am especially grateful to my son Seth, who was born during the course of the book's preparation and cooperated fully with my work, and who attended my lectures at the age of two weeks, accompanied me to libraries, and slept peacefully in my study.

Contents

1

Social Scientific Views

What women do is perceived as household work and what they talk about is called gossip, while men's work is viewed as the economic base of society and their information is seen as important communication. Kinship studies are usually centered on males, marriage systems are analyzed in terms of the exchanges men make using women to weave their networks . . . . These are all instances of deeply rooted male orientation which makes the anthropological discourse suspect.

Rayna Reiter, *Toward an Anthropology of Women*

In modern society, science is enshrouded in the myth of objectivity. People believe that scientific investigation is carried out without reference to values or prejudices. The scientist, so the myth goes, searches for the truth using objective, value-neutral research methods. Although such objectivity may be the ideal for science, it is not the reality. Scientific investigation and the development, refinement, and testing of scientific theories are social phenomena. Like other social phenomena, they are subject to the influence of social forces such as tradition, conventional wisdom, existing frames of reference, power relationships, and social movements. The scientific treatment of gender roles and the study of women provide clear examples of the nonobjective, social-contextual nature of scientific theory and research.

The scientific treatment of women and the nature of gender roles has until very recently been largely a reflection and justification of the surrounding society's sexual stratification system, sexual division of labor, and ideology of women's place. Just as the civil rights movement exposed and challenged the racist treatment of black Americans in the social and natural sciences, feminist movements have exposed and challenged sexism in science.

Sexism pervades all of our sciences and all levels of science. Every field of science is male dominated. Women are both numerically underrepresented in the scientific professions and concentrated in the lower ranking, less prestigious, less influential scientific institutions, fields, specialties, and positions. Furthermore, the universities, research institutes, and research grant foundations that provide the necessary settings and funds for scientific work are controlled largely by men.

Male experiences and masculine viewpoints have influenced the decisions concerning what is important to research. For example, research on contraception has focused on controlling female fecundity rather than male fecundity, and research on aggression and dominance has concentrated on the effects of the male hormone testosterone to the near exclusion of other potentially important non-male hormones.

The male viewpoint has also been reflected in methods of research. Studies based on all-male samples have often been discussed as "human responses," "human behavior," or "human characteristics," while studies based on all-female samples are assumed to reflect not human but merely female characteristics. These samples are usually considered hopelessly biased until males are included.

Moreover, scientific journals and the scientific book publishing industry have similarly been in the hands of males who make the important decisions about what is worthy of being published and what is not. Often this has meant that issues of importance to women, issues related to some analysis of women's bodies and lives, or works that challenge accepted beliefs and institutions have been considered too trivial or biased for scholarly publication.[1]

THE TRADITION OF SEX BIAS IN THE SOCIAL SCIENCES

Masculine domination has been the rule in all sciences, but this book is concerned primarily with the masculine domination of social science and the consequent biases in the social scientific treatment of women and gender roles in society. A masculine bias has been evident since the very inception of social science. One sign of this bias has been the exclusion of women and gender roles from study by most social scientists. Another result is that social scientific considerations have been colored by pre-existing sexist beliefs about the "natures of women and men" held by scientists as well as by the public. These theories, and even the data amassed to "prove" these theories, have served to justify the status quo in gender roles. Science has often been used as an instrument of social control, telling women and men what their roles are and predicting terrible consequences if they deviate from their appropriate roles—terrible consequences for the deviants, for their families, and often for society as a whole.

Early European Sociologists on Women and Men in Society

The early sociologists were clearly influenced by the gender role stereotypes of their time. In the nineteenth century, males were presented as the naturally dominant, aggressive, and masterful sex, the rightful leaders of the society. Females were seen as passive, innocent and pure, the natural mothers, and the subordinates of males. The females' proper place was the home and hearth. The founders of sociology in Europe and America incorporated these views into their works if they dealt with women or gender roles at all.

Auguste Comte.   Comte was one of the founders of European sociology. In his four-volume work, *System of Positive Polity,* he laid out his views of the perfect society. He dealt with questions of woman's nature and her proper roles in society. His ideas are unabashedly sexist. Comte saw women as the mental and physical inferiors of men. "In all kinds of force, whether physical, intellectual or practical, it is certain that Man surpasses Woman, in accordance with the general law prevailing throughout the animal kingdom." [2] However, females, according to Comte, surpassed men in the areas of emotion, love, and morality.

In Comte's view of society, women should not be allowed to work outside the home, to own property, or to exercise political power. Their gentle natures require that they remain in the home as mothers tending to the early moral education of their children and as wives tending to their husbands' emotional, domestic, and sexual needs.

Comte was an active opponent of the feminist ideas and social movements that accompanied the equalitarian debates evolving out of the American and French revolutions. According to Comte, sexual equality would only endanger women socially and morally. Women would necessarily lose out in competition with men for society's resources. Comte argued that progress would result only from rendering the female's "life more and more domestic; to diminish as far as possible the burden of out-door labour; and so to fit her more completely for her special office of educating our moral nature."[3] Women were, in short, to be "the pampered slaves of men."[4]

Herbert Spencer.   Herbert Spencer's position on woman's proper place in society underwent a major transformation between the publication of *Social Statics* in 1850 and the publication of Volume One of his *Principles of Sociology* in 1897. In *Social Statics* he devoted an entire chapter to the defense of women's legal and political rights.[5] He challenged the practice of male domination in marriage, regarding it as an unnecessary barbarism which interfered with the development of true affection. He similarly analyzed other popular arguments in favor of female subordination and found them unacceptable.

The changes in his thought on this subject were great. The chapters devoted to women in his *Principles of Sociology* no longer refer to women's freedom or rights; they are entitled "The Status of Women" and "Domestic Retrospect and Prospect." He no longer argued that sexual equality is possible. Instead he asserted that the status of women improved immeasurably with the development of Western civilization and might improve even more in the future. But he maintained that a certain minimum of female subordination must remain because males are naturally more forceful and females are more emotional and maternal.[6] Although he was committed to the laissez-faire ideal of free and open competition (which in *Social Statics* he argued should be extended to women), Spencer declared in *Principles of Sociology* that it would be "mischievous" to allow women to pursue education for careers in business, the professions, or politics. Their proper place is in the home. "If women comprehended all that is contained in the domestic sphere, they would ask no other."[7] If women do persist in asking for something other than the domestic sphere, they should not be allowed to have it because female participation in the public domain would retard progress. Spencer predicted that female subordination would continue indefinitely into the future.

Comte and Spencer, although sexist in their treatment of gender roles, did include the subject in their analysis of society. Most early sociologists did not. Traditional conceptions of gender roles, in particular the idea of women's domestic role, were so deeply embedded in society that most saw no need to examine them. Western concepts of gender roles have been accepted as natural and largely immutable.

Nineteenth-Century Social Evolutionists

Spencer's work was both influenced by and influential on the work of other nineteenth-century social evolutionists, including those allied with the growing field of anthropology. The late nineteenth century was a period of great intellectual concern with the origins of society in general and the origins of kinship and marriage systems in particular. A great deal of data on diverse and seemingly strange cultures was brought back to Western Europe and the United States by missionaries and travelers. Social evolutionary theories attempted to account for these different social forms by considering them to be in less developed stages in the evolution of society, inferior to the practices and society of the Western world.

The debate over kinship and marriage systems often led the social evolutionists into discussions of gender roles and the nature of the sexes. However, these debates and investigations were all heavily biased by Victorian sexual morality and by the belief that Western civilization represented the highest human physical, cultural, and social development. Thus, the appropriateness of the highly sex-segregated and sexually stratified society of nineteenth-century Europe was not questioned by these scholars. On the contrary, their abhorrence of other gender role arrangements led them to characterize such systems as savage and inferior.

Matrilineality and Patrilineality.   One of the areas of concern during this period was the historical primacy of matrilineal kinship systems, which trace descent only through the mother's blood line. Writers such as Johann Bachofen, John McLennan, John Lubbock, and Lewis Henry Morgan [8] argued that the earliest stage of human social life was characterized by sexual promiscuity and lack of control over sexuality. Since females in such early societies had sexual intercourse with more than one male, no one could be certain of a child's paternity. Therefore, descent could be reckoned only through the female line.

Because these writers so thoroughly accepted the naturalness of patriarchy, male dominance, and patrilineality (the practice of reckoning descent through the father's line), they saw matrilineality as a reversal of patriarchy. That is, they believed that matrilineality would automatically give rise to matriarchy or female dominance. This is an incorrect assumption. Matrilineality has been widely practiced in the history of human society, but there is little evidence for the existence of truly matriarchal societies at any time.

The social evolutionists believed that male dominance and patrilineality were higher principles than matrilineality. Matrilineality was seen as a violation of the natural order. They argued that the greater strength, cunning, and sexual desires of the early males were used to bring women under male control. Monogamy arose out of this situation in order to allow males to ensure the known paternity of children and thereby to substitute patrilineal descent for matrilineal. This was accompanied by a transference from female gods to patriarchal religions and the growth of civilization in general.

The theories of early anthropology reflected and reinforced Victorian gender roles. Women were presented as more moral than men, less interested in and less driven by sexual passion, weaker, less intelligent, and generally inferior to men. Female domination in any form, even the female focus of a matrilineal kinship system, was seen as unnatural and inferior to male domination.

Ironically, the works of the social evolutionists have been used, in particular by socialist writers, to advance feminist perspectives and theories. Beginning with Frederick Engels, feminist writers dropped the sexist assumptions concerning the natural inferiority of females and elaborated on the ideas of early practices of primitive communism, sexual promiscuity, and matriarchy.

Frederick Engels.   The only breath of fresh air for feminists in these early works on gender roles and family life came in the work of the socialists. Frederick Engels wrote *The Origin of the Family, Private Property and the State*[9] during this period and was significantly influenced by the works of the social anthropologists. As a socialist, however, he was highly critical of Victorian capitalist society, and his work does not attempt to justify Victorian family structure, sexual stratification system, or gender roles. Unlike other nineteenth-century scholars, Engels denied the biological basis of sex roles and analyzed the sexual stratification system as a system of male exploitation of females based on male control of private property under capitalism. Since it was a criticism of nineteenth-century capitalist society, Engels' theory of the evolution of society did not present the gender roles of that society as the highest form of civilization. Rather, Engels looked to a socialist future in which the power of private property would be overthrown and equality would be achieved between the sexes as among all individuals in his vision of the classless society.

Engels presented a positive view of primitive non-capitalist communal society in which males and females supposedly related to each other as equals. Since females were not economically dependent on males in this early stage, partners could be chosen on the basis of mutual love and attraction. During this stage of "savagery," or what we call today hunting and gathering societies, private property and state level government did not exist. Property was owned communally by the clans and shared within them. There was no need for centralized institutions for the maintenance of law and order. Everyone contributed to the welfare of the group, and women and children were not dependent on men. All members of the clan were equal.

Drawing upon Morgan, Engels theorized that "group marriage," which involved sexually non-exclusive, non-possessive, non-permanent loose pairings, characterized savagery. This supposedly gave way to the more permanent "pairing marriage" of the second stage of development: "barbarism" or what we would refer to as hoe agriculture or horticultural societies. More restrictions were placed on pairing marriage because the clan was now an important property-holding body and had a vested interest in making and maintaining marriage alliances with other clans. Therefore, the clan tried to cement marriage relationships through the exchange of property (dowries and bride-prices) and through intervention to keep the couples from separating when conflicts arose. Like the other evolutionists, Engels believed that matrilineality would have characterized the first two stages but that eventually it would give way to patrilineal descent systems, the patriarchal family, the subordination of women and children to the father, and the organization of government (the state) as an institution to maintain the power of the wealthy males over poor males, women and children.

Unlike his contemporaries, Engels explained the transition from matrilineality to patrilineality not on the basis of the naturalness or progressiveness of male dominance, but on the economic power of some males under the new system of individually owned private property. Engels hypothesized that males became the owners of the domesticated livestock. Instead of belonging to the matrilineal clan as a whole, livestock for some reason was the sole property of individual males. This first private property conflicted with the communal principle, undermined the clan organization, and eventually led to the demise of the clan.

Since males supposedly owned the livestock, they would have, according to Engels, resisted the practice of matrilineal inheritance. Engels was not entirely unaffected by the ideas of his age, for he saw it as somehow natural for males to want to pass their property on to their sons rather than to their sisters' children as the matrilineal principle would dictate. To the extent, therefore, that males violated the matrilineal principle by passing their cattle on to their children, they weakened the matrilineal clan. Furthermore, the power to buy and control the labor of others which private wealth gave to a few undermined the egalitarian, communal society and led to the development of the state with its law, police, soldiers, court systems and so on, designed to protect the private wealth of the few from the poor. The governmental machinery thus maintained and strengthened the power of the male property holders.

Matrilineal descent was replaced by patrilineality. Egalitarian male-female relationships gave way to the patriarchal family, the sexual double standard, prostitution, and the subjection of women. Chastity and monogamy were enforced on wives to ensure the paternity of the male's heirs. But sexual freedom was allowed to males wealthy enough to buy or support several wives or to buy the sexual favors of unattached women—thus the development of prostitution. Engels held that the economic dependence of women forced them to sell themselves either as wives or as whores. Truly affectionate, loving marriages were no longer possible under capitalism because women had to depend on their relationships with men for economic support. Women had become just another form of private property.

Because Engels' theory conflicted with established beliefs and practices, it was largely rejected in the Western world until segments of the current feminist movement revived it in an attempt to counter the still dominant sexist theories of gender roles and woman's place.

The Early Psychologists

The first psychologists were relatively unconcerned with gender roles and the nature of the sexes, especially the female. However, as in anthropology and sociology, the incorporation of evolutionary theory into psychology in the late nineteenth century necessitated a consideration of the female. Consequently, study of the psychology of gender roles was undertaken. These early psychologists held that gender roles and male dominance were biologically based and essentially immutable. As Stephanie Shields points out, three major topics dominated this early psychology of gender roles: the attempt to prove the lesser capacity of the female brain; the attempt to prove the evolutionary insignificance of the female with the variability hypothesis; and the attempt to prove the innate character of the Victorian feminine role with the maternal instinct concept.[10] In this manner nineteenth- and early twentieth-century psychology gave "scientific" backing to the contemporary cultural stereotypes of women and men.

Female Intellectual Inferiority.   A great deal of scholarly attention was devoted to proving the superiority of the male brain in relation to the female brain.[11] At first brain size was thought to be an important factor in intelligence and the lighter average weight of female brains compared with the average weight of male brains was used as "proof" of the lesser intelligence of females. However, as further data became available disputing the relationship between brain size and intelligence, and when it was discovered that relative to body weight, the female brain is actually larger than the male brain, this line of reasoning was abandoned. But the search continued for other kinds of deficiencies in the female brain. Psychologists were so certain of the inferiority of the female brain that they accepted any evidence supporting the inferiority hypothesis and rejected as irrelevant or incorrect data which refuted it. It was believed that the female was less intelligent, more primitive than the human male, more ruled by instinct and emotion. And of course this greater intelligence meant that human progress was attributed to males, not females.

The Variability Hypothesis.   Psychologists also drew heavily on Charles Darwin's variability hypothesis, using it to "prove" the evolutionary importance of the male and the corresponding irrelevance of the female.[12] Darwin theorized that for natural selection to operate in evolution, individuals of the species had to vary on the trait in question. Adaptive variations could then be selected for and maladaptive variations selected out over the generations. Shields notes that this theory inspired great attention to the study of individual differences and differences by sex. Males were "proved" to be the more variable sex and, therefore, the progressive sex in evolution. Scientists pointed to the dominance of men in areas of high achievement and to the disproportionate numbers of men among the mentally defective as evidence of greater variability in males than in females.

Maternal Instinct.   Females were believed to be superior to males only in their ability to nurture the young and psychology attributed this to instinct.[13] Males were supposedly instinctively protective of females and children, but females were the only true nurturers. Similarly, instincts were used to explain the "innate submissiveness" of the female and her "coyness" in courtship.

Although based on faulty methodology, biased data, and unproved assumptions, these views of women dominated scientific and lay thought for decades. Even the early behaviorist psychologists who rejected instinct theory and biological explanations of human behavior in favor of environmental or social causes were slow to reject biological theories of gender roles.[14] The behaviorists were unconcerned with female psychology or gender roles. Therefore, as the psychoanalytic theory of gender roles was developed and elaborated by Sigmund Freud and his students, it became the dominant theory of sex differences and female nature in psychology.

Sigmund Freud and Psychoanalytic Theory.   Freud developed his theories of gender roles and the nature of the sexes in the late nineteenth and early twentieth centuries as part of his wider consideration of the power of the unconscious and the importance of sexuality in human psychological development. It is generally recognized that his views on women and gender roles reflect and reinforce the highly patriarchal Victorian society of Freud's time. He accepts male dominance and female dependence as natural to human beings. The healthy adult female desires little more than the opportunity to play the wife and mother roles.

The developmental process necessary to achieving a healthy adult personality is a complex and painful one for both males and females. Freud recognized that human beings are sexually responsive from infancy. The infant responds sexually first to the mother's breast (the oral stage) and later to its own excretionary functions (the anal stage). As a young child develops, the genitals become more important foci of sexuality. According to Freud the young boy is very proud of his penis while the young girl thinks she has been castrated or that a penis will eventually grow on her.

At about the age of three the young boy enters the Oedipal stage, in which his love for the mother takes on a more explicitly sexual component. The son is jealous of the father for possessing the mother and supposedly wants to kill the father and take his place as the mother's husband. However, the son also fears the father and is terrified that the father may castrate him in revenge for sexually desiring the mother (castration complex). To resolve this Oedipal complex successfully the young boy must learn to repress his sexual desire for the mother and to identify with the father so that when he grows up he will be a powerful male and be allowed to possess a woman of his own. According to Freud, this transference from the mother to the father is a painful and fearful process. It is so painful, in fact, that the boy can deal with it psychologically only by repressing all memory of it and repressing his sexual desires until puberty. Thus, as the Oedipal complex is resolved, the boy enters a latency stage in which it appears that he has no sexual longings at all.

The Electra complex which little girls supposedly undergo differs in important respects from the Oedipus complex. Freudian theory states that the daughter realizes that she does not have a penis. She does not, however, correspondingly recognize that she has a vagina, nor does she feel any pride in female genitalia. The girl envies males and desires a penis. Like the son, the daughter would like to possess the mother sexually, but since she has no penis she cannot hope to do so. She comes to resent her mother who also has no penis and blames her mother for having castrated her (castration complex). The daughter transfers her desire for the mother to a sexual desire for the father. In order to resolve the Electra complex, the daughter must eventually replace her desire for a penis and her desire for her father with the desire for a baby, in particular for a male baby with the long-sought-after penis.

Freud theorized that this transference from penis envy to the desire for motherhood entailed the transference of sexual responsiveness from the clitoris to the vagina. Hence, the clitoral orgasm was described as an infantile sexual response. The healthy adult woman should experience only vaginal orgasm. (William Masters and Virginia Johnson's research on human sexuality found this to be physiologically incorrect. The vagina has few nerve endings; the clitoris is the physiological locus of orgasmic response in women.[15])

The concept of penis envy is also related to Freud's concept of feminine narcissism. Freud asserted that because the female is embarrassed by her inferior clitoris she attempts to compensate for that inferiority with her entire body. Therefore, she is much more vain and concerned with her personal appearance than the male. Penis envy also results in the female's greater sense of jealousy than the male, derived from her original envious reaction to the male's penis. This envy impairs the female's sense of justice, rendering her less capable than males of making fair and impartial judgments. This is related to Freud's belief that women do not develop as strong a superego as males do. The superego refers to our conscience and our ability to control our impulses, desires, and egotistical yearnings. It develops in males as the boy learns to control or suppress his desire for his mother. The girl, however, is not as stringently required to suppress her desire for the father. Since she does not have to develop the same degree of control over her Electra complex desires, she never develops the same strength of character that the male does. But Freud also believed that the resolution of the Electra complex was more likely to be incomplete than the resolution of the Oedipus complex. Therefore, women are more likely than men to develop into inadequate adults and to exhibit pathological symptoms.

The portrait of men and women derived from Freudian psychoanalytic theory is one of clear male superiority and female inferiority. The male is strong and active with a highly developed superego and sense of justice. The female is passive, narcissistic sexually immature, masochistic, jealous, with a weak superego, an inadequate sense of justice, and prone to psychological pathology. The healthy woman who avoids the worst psychological pitfalls of her sex does so only through an identification with her wife and mother roles symbolized in vaginal orgasm.

Psychoanalytic theory has been revised by many of Freud's students, but its basic principles are still widely accepted by modern Freudians. Its view of women has been influential among therapists and the general public. Psychoanalytic theory has been potent in keeping women in their place. Women who have attempted to break out of or rebel against the passive feminine role of wife and mother have often been told they suffer from penis envy and are attempting to castrate males. The psychological distress of women has been treated by telling them they must adjust to the feminine role. Inability to experience vaginal orgasm has been attributed to inadequate psychological development. Psychoanalytic theory focuses on the individual woman and the supposedly internally generated causes of her misery. Therefore, it calls attention away from the social context of her symptoms. The feminine role itself has only recently come under scrutiny by psychoanalysts as a possible source rather than cure for the woman's problems. Science again has been used to justify the status quo in gender roles.

Early American Sociologists

Sociology as developed in the United States perpetuated many of the sexist assumptions of the European social scientists. It is not surprising that a conservative committed Social Darwinist such as William Graham Sumner would consider the subordination of women the result of women's innate inferiority. (Social Darwinists argued that "you get what you deserve." If a person is rich and powerful, that is proof that he or she is superior. Since women are subordinate to men, they must be inferior to men.) But even those who argued most strongly against Social Darwinism in favor of environmental explanations clung to accepted sexual stereotypes. Socialist theories such as Engels' were largely rejected or ignored.

Among the early American sociologists, the subjects of gender roles, sexual stratification, and the natures of the sexes were given extensive treatment only by Lester Frank Ward and W. I. Thomas.[16] These men greatly influenced the development of sociology in the late nineteenth and early twentieth centuries. They were both liberals who actively opposed the conservative doctrines of the Social Darwinists. They supported sexual equality and in their writings on women attempted to transcend the sexist beliefs of their day, to present a social explanation of women's position in society, and to justify efforts toward social change in the area of gender roles. However, they too resorted to biological explanations and psycho-biological differences between the sexes to explain gender roles and sexual inequality and they denied any validity to the demands of militant feminists.

Ward, for example, outlined the inequities suffered by women in dress, duties, education, and law. He pointed out that male dress was for utility, but female dress was ornamental and restricted activity. Ward supported functional unisex styles for males and females. In his discussion of the sexual division of labor, he attempted to draw upon historical and cross-cultural data. He noted that contemporary custom requiring that women remain in the home doing domestic chores was not universal. According to Ward, in primitive societies and among the lower classes, women often do most of the physical work done indoors or out. Furthermore, he argued that it was unhealthy for women to be confined in the home. Instead both men and women should engage in a variety of tasks not segregated along sex lines. Yet Ward's and Thomas's pleas for the equality of the sexes coexisted with their opposition to most programs which would have bettered the condition of women. Their theories of the origins and maintenance of sexual stratification were highly sexist. Like the social evolutionists, they traced our gender roles back to the dawn of civilization and the primitive stage of human development and relied on the theory of natural selection to explain the processes of change which led to male domination.

According to Ward, males are innately more aggressive and highly sexed than females. Males have a stronger, more constant sexuality. Females are passive, shy, and timid, and have weaker, more cyclical sexual drives and, therefore, resist male sexual advances. Among early human beings females could successfully resist male sexual advances most of the time. Females controlled their own sexuality. But the male's drive for sexual release is so strong that he must win in this courtship struggle. Since human beings have much greater intellectual capacities than other animals, human males could use these skills to persuade females to give sexual favors. Males then resorted to reason, persuasion, and trickery in courtship. They also promised females rewards if they would give in to male sexual demands. In this process males further developed and enhanced their capacities for reason and imagination, while females allowed their intellectual capacities to lie in disuse. According to Ward, "Superior cunning, i.e., sharper wits, may be regarded as a secondary sexual character as much as the tusks of the boar or the spurs of the cock." [17]

According to the laws of natural selection, those males who developed their intellectual powers were more likely to reproduce than those who did not, hence males gradually improved their genetic intellectual capabilities while females did not. The intellectually gifted female was no more likely to reproduce than her ungifted sister. In fact, the intelligent female could probably better resist male trickery and avoid reproducing her superior genes in future generations of females. Hence natural selection would not work in favor of female intelligence.

In addition to sexual passion, Ward held that males are also motivated by strong passions for property ownership. These were the important forces in shaping the sexual stratification system. Women became the possessions of men like any other object of consumption. "Woman at once becomes property, since anything that affords its possessor gratification is property. Woman was capable of affording man the highest of gratification, and therefore became property of the highest value." [18] The institution of marriage developed as an institution for regularizing the transfer of ownership of women. Women were also forced into domestic service for men through the operation of these same passions for sex and property. "The passage from sexual service to manual service on the part of women was perfectly natural. If woman were man's property for sexual purposes, he would certainly claim that she was also for all other purposes, and thus we find the women of most savage tribes perform the manual and servile labor of the camp." [19]

Ward viewed female reproductive processes as extremely debilitating. Childbearing supposedly saps both physical and intellectual strength. He refers to menstruation as the "curse" and describes it as a "laborious and debilitating process" [20] which developed not for the advantage of females but rather to allow males uninterrupted sexual access to females not possible in species with a single rutting season.

W. I. Thomas also depicted primitive man as an active, highly sexed creature and primitive woman as relatively inactive and sexually passive. Thomas described woman as being closer to plant life than animal life in her natural state. Females constitute a lower form of life "intermediate between the child and the man." [21] In Thomas's theory natural selection again favored the active male who had to exercise force and cunning in hunting for food and protecting the passive and stationary women and children. Although women and children formed the core of primitive human society, men ruled it. Ward and Thomas both reasoned that females probably dominated the first social groups because strong mother-child ties were the basis for the first groups. But because of their passive, stationary, plantlike natures, women could not maintain control over active, aggressive males: "Nature obviously started out on the plan of having woman the dominant force, with man as an aid; but after a certain time there was a reversal of plan, and man became dominant and woman dropped back into a somewhat unstable and adventitious relation to the social process." [22]

In modern society women are largely irrelevant to the important social processes. Through natural selection man developed into a higher form of being and supplanted woman as the dominant force in human society. Females remained inactive, undeveloped, and trivial. According to Thomas, females are still controlled by the maternal instinct and other instincts which make them want to please the men on whom they depend. Furthermore, since the development of morality requires great intellectual capacity, women must be watched over and controlled by males or they will easily allow themselves to become dissipated and degraded. And because females are so simple-minded and weak, men have developed a contempt for women and prefer the company of other males in sex-segregated institutions such as men's clubs and fraternities.

After their lengthy and detailed analyses of women as frivolous, petty, and inferior creatures, Ward and Thomas attempted to demonstrate their liberal support of sexual equality by saying that women can overcome their limited evolutionary development by expanding their intellectual capacities through education. Disuse had led to degeneration. Thus, both Ward and Thomas called on women to improve themselves; after they did so, society would open the avenues of advancement to them. Neither called on society to institute active programs of change to alleviate women's subordination. Both say this subordination is the result of the female's failure in the evolutionary development of intelligence. The solution consists of bringing females up to male standards, and this, they believed, would take a long time. They ignored the importance of institutional barriers to women in education and competition for power and privilege. They opted instead for gradualist policies that would not challenge the status quo of male domination.[23]

CONTEMPORARY MAINSTREAM PERSPECTIVES IN SOCIAL SCIENCE: SOCIOLOGY

The issues which had been debated by the social evolutionists, early European and American sociologists, and early psychologists ceased to be of concern as the last embers of feminism died out in the 1920s. For over three decades a male sociology existed which "did not necessarily have great relevance for women." [24] Sociology was, and to a surprising degree still is, characterized "by the naive, unconscious, taken-for-granted unexamined acceptance by sociologists of the idea that sociology as developed by men is the one and only sociology worth bothering with, that society as men experience it is the only society worth researching, that the topics men sociologists are concerned about—especially power, mobility, conflict—are the only kinds worth pursuing." [25] It was not until well after the re-emergence in the 1960s of strong feminist movements in the Western world that women's and gender role issues re-emerged in sociology.

It was not, however, that feminist perspectives were unavailable to sociologists.[26] As Arlene Daniels has pointed out, Gunnar Myrdal's treatment in 1944 of women as a minority group analogous to black Americans was ignored, as was Helen M. Hacker's article on the same subject published in 1951. Simone de Beauvoir's monumental work on women, The Second Sex, first published in 1949, had little impact on sociology. And while Betty Friedan's The Feminine Mystique swept the nation as a best seller in the late 1960s, it did not sweep sociology. The feminist perspective did not significantly affect the discipline until the early 1970s. But since then the feminist viewpoint has led to an analysis of the masculine biases in sociology and to a redirection of research, publishing, and teaching to include wider treatments of women and gender roles.

Women in Sociology

An examination of masculine biases in sociology must begin with a consideration of the representation of women in the field. The American Sociological Association's Committee on the Status of Women published such a study of the profession in 1973.[27] The committee found that women held only 12 percent of the faculty positions in graduate sociology departments and received only 21 percent of the Ph.D. degrees granted in 1971. Furthermore, women were concentrated in lower ranks and in the less prestigious universities and colleges. They were more likely than males to be in part-time and non-tenure track positions. Women were underrepresented in the powerful positions in the national association, among the journal editorial boards, and as department chairpersons. Moreover, the Committee found that women were subjected to many forms of discouragement and discrimination, from the admissions processes for graduate programs to the granting of full professorships. In short, although there was evidence that some changes were underway to improve the position of women, sociology in the 1968–1972 period was still very much a male-dominated field.

Other writers have outlined the ways in which this male domination manifests itself in sociological research. They have charged that women have remained invisible in much sociological work. Ann Oakley, for example, compares the *sociological visibility* of women with the actual *social presence* * of women in the different subfields of sociology.[28]

Sociology of Occupations and Work

In the study of occupations and work, women's sociological visibility has been far below their social presence. Women make up about 40 percent of the paid labor force in the United States and Great Britain, and this figure has been increasing steadily for decades. Yet studies of work have until recently often excluded females entirely or treated women's work as a deviation from the appropriate female roles of wife and mother. For example, Peter Blau and Otis Dudley Duncan's award-winning book *The American Occupational Structure* excluded the female labor force from considera-

---

* *Sociological visibility* is the extent to which women are discussed and researched in the various sociological specialties. *Social presence* is the actual participation of women in different social arenas.

tion.[29] In addition, Glen and Weiner's study of the social backgrounds of sociologists arbitrarily excluded female sociologists from their sample.[30] One of their conclusions was that it is regrettable that so few sociologists come from rural backgrounds. They lamented this loss of a useful perspective to the discipline. Yet as Pauline Bart points out, they showed no concern for the fact that the female perspective might be a valuable one for the profession and did not study the women who are in the profession.[31]

Oakley notes that if women are studied at all in occupational research they are usually asked "Why do you work?"[32] It has been assumed that it is not "natural" for women to work, but that men must work. Thus unemployed males, but not females, are asked "Why aren't you working?" Furthermore, working women have often been treated as a social problem. For example, many sociologists have blamed family problems and juvenile delinquency on working mothers.[33] Concern has been voiced over the supposed "maternal deprivation" suffered by children of working mothers. However, little credence has been given to the analogous concept of "paternal deprivation" suffered by children of fathers who work outside the home.

Similarly, sociology has helped to perpetuate the myth that women are not seriously committed workers, that their primary roles are those of wife and mother and this necessarily interferes with career orientation. Oakley also charges that sociologists until recently have accepted the industrial folklore that women have a greater tolerance of boring repetitive work without subjecting this to empirical verification.[34] Furthermore, sociologists have focused their research on men's work and either ignored women's work or treated it in a highly stereotypical manner. Industries with a high concentration of females—food manufacture, textiles, clerical and sales, teaching, nursing and domestic labor—have received less research attention than industries dominated by male workers, such as the automobile industry which has been intensely researched.[35]

Research and general texts on working-class jobs have rarely dealt with working-class women. Pamela Roby reviewed a sample of occupational and industrial sociology textbooks and found

> Women are not integrated into their discussions of unions, working conditions, vocational choice, work assignments, alienation, automation, etc. Women's concerns about maternity leave, child care, the work environment, the process of breaking into traditional male occupations, fighting for equal pay for equal work, breaking through union barriers, opening up apprenticeships to women, and other matters . . . were not mentioned . . . .[36]

Oakley's own work along with that of Helena Lopata begins to fill perhaps the largest gap of all in occupational sociology: the study of housework and the housewife as a work role and occupation rather than as an aspect of the feminine role.[37] And Louise Kapp Howe published a study of women's work which includes such occupations as waitress, beautician, and office worker.[38]

Sociology of Education

Work done in the area of sociology of education overlaps with the area of occupational sociology in its treatment of the teaching profession. The sexism apparent in both fields of research, however, has resulted in important research gaps regarding teachers. First, little work has been done on the role of teachers because it is a female-dominated occupation. Second, the professional aspect of the teacher's role has been ignored because researchers have been blinded by the sexist assumption that these female workers are not primarily professionals, but rather are wives and mothers who also do some work as teachers. Sara Lightfoot suggests that this literature sustains negative stereotypes of the teacher and that sociologists "do not seem to be interested in the teacher's conception of her work, her professional goals, and her maturation."[39]

Social Stratification

Much of what has been said about the sociology of occupations can be repeated for the field of *social stratification*.* Women again have been sociologically invisible until recent years. Studies of stratification hierarchies have treated females only as appendages of males. Acker notes that six questionable assumptions justifying the exclusion of women underly stratification theory.

1. The family is the unit in the stratification system.
2. The social position of the family is determined by the status of the male head of household.
3. Females live in families; therefore, their status is determined by that of the males to whom they are attached.
4. The female's status is equal to that of her man, at least in terms of her position in the class structure, because the family is a unit of equivalent evaluation.
5. Women determine their own social status only when they are not attached to a man.
6. Women are unequal to men in many ways, and are differentially evaluated on the basis of sex, but this is irrelevant to the structure of stratification systems.[40]

* *Social stratification* is the study of social ranking systems such as social classes, racial and ethnic hierarchies, and sexual hierarchies.

As Acker points out, these assumptions are unfounded. Many people do not live in families. Not all families have male heads. Moreover, the percentage of the population not living in families and the percentage of female-headed families is increasing.[41] The family may no longer be (if it ever was) a homogeneous unit in class status. Given the unstable nature of the modern nuclear family, it is dangerous to treat the nuclear family as the unit of stratification analysis or as a unit of equivalent evaluation within a stratification hierarchy. Members of the same family may not occupy the same status in society. In particular, the female members of a family may have a lower social status than the males.

Furthermore, women are not completely without status-enhancing resources of their own, resources which sometimes differ from those of their husbands and fathers. Women do own wealth, earn incomes, and have educational attainments and occupational skills. It cannot simply be assumed without corroborating empirical research that women's resources are the same as their fathers' and husbands'. Such discrepancies in class or status have been studied only for the effects differences between husbands and wives have on marital stability and happiness.

Even more basic to the field of social stratification is the fact that sexual stratification systems were taken for granted in sociology and largely unstudied until feminists undertook to study them. The concepts of social stratification have excluded consideration of sexual stratification and its impact on other stratification hierarchies. According to Dorothy E. Smith, concepts of class have been derived from the male worlds of work and power, and these obscure other aspects of class. Smith points out that the role of housewife intersects with other institutions in our society and is important for maintaining our stratification system:

> Housework, for example has a managerial or organizational aspect that articu-
> lates the family unit to the bureaucratic, educational, professional and retailing
> organizations (e.g., welfare, school, dentist, supermarket, etc.) so as to complete
> the cycle from production to subsistence . . . . The wife of the journalist is not
> necessarily doing the same "work" as the . . . wife of a garbage collector.[42]

There are now, however, a few studies on social stratification which do include women and sexual stratification in their analyses.[43]

Political Sociology

Given the fact that political sociology covers the social domain with the greatest masculine mystique, politics, it is not surprising that women have been sociologically invisible in this field. According to Thelma McCormack, certain assumptions have served to exclude women as research topics in political sociology: [44]

1. Women's social roles prevent them from actively participating in the political arena.
2. Women are tied to familial roles.
3. Male political activity is the norm against which female participation is judged.
4. Men and women share the same political reality and, therefore, differences in political participation are due to the different attributes of men and women.
5. The appropriate political activity for women is far removed from power, is locally oriented, and is a leisure pursuit rather than a career.

In political sociology women have been most often studied in relation to their voting behavior. Yet women have been placed in a double bind in these studies. When women vote differently from men, it has been assumed they are deviants and are wrong. When they vote the same as men, it has been interpreted as women having no independent political judgment.[45]

Women's efforts to obtain power are also filtered through gender role preconceptions. For example, until recently the early women's movement received little attention in the study of political social movements despite the large numbers of people involved, the international scope of the movement, its impact on society, the violence and excitement it aroused, and its colorful heroines and heroes. On the other hand, the Women's Christian Temperance Union (WCTU) and its fight for prohibition had greater sociological visibility. The WCTU and its prohibition crusade was a more "appropriate" movement for women. These ladies using their virtue to raise the moral standards of the country fit gender role stereotypes. They were not fighting for political and economic power for its own sake; their aggressive political campaigns were to benefit the family, church, and nation. Furthermore, the prohibition movement fit with the image of women's politics being the leisure-time activity of middle-class clubwomen. The aggressive political and economic demands of the women's movement, however, upset gender role stereotypes. To study this movement meant studying its demands for improving women's situations. It also meant recognizing that women can be full-fledged participants in the political world. Thus, it was easier for sociologists to ignore these movements than to question their own preconceptions about women and politics.

Sociology of Organizations

Despite the large numbers of women who participate in modern organizations, they have had little sociological visibility. The variable of sex has been given little attention as a determinant of organizational behavior or in the distribution of positions and other scarce resources in organizations. "The ways in which women have been connected to organizations and have operated within them, and whether these ways differ from those of men, have been underinvestigated in social research . . . there has been little attention paid to the patterned relationships between women and men in organizations." [46]

Powerful positions in modern organizations have been dominated almost entirely by men. Sociologists, like other people, are attracted to powerful figures. Hence, organizational sociology has focused on leadership, formal power, and the formal structures of power. Informal sources of power and influence receive much less attention. Yet women, as "administrative assistants," secretaries, or wives are more likely to exercise what influence they have through such informal networks.

Male domination of managerial positions has led sociologists to assume that masculine values of aggressiveness, competitiveness, domination, and emotional insensitivity are necessary to the modern managerial role. And, as Kanter asserts, this has functioned to justify the absence of women from such positions. Questions concerning the causes and effects of the sex hierarchy and gender roles in organizations have not been asked. "We need to know the barriers to women in organizational leadership and also what difference their presence makes: how culture and behavior are shaped by the sex distribution of managers." [47] We cannot simply assume that it is natural for women to be the secretaries of the higher ranking male managers.

Medical Sociology

In medical sociology women have been invisible as high status practitioners, but their sociological visibility has been high as patients. According to Lorber, medical sociologists have until recently excluded female professionals from their research on the medical profession because of their small numbers. Yet the differences between the experiences of men and women might provide interesting comparisons and highlight previously unrecognized dimensions of the professional's role. Lorber suggests that they are ignored because they would expose the advantages given to white Protestant males from upper-middle-class backgrounds in the protégé system of the medical profession. "Treating the medical profession in America as if it were homogeneous (all-white, all-male, all-Protestant) has exaggerated the notion of the universalism of medical practice; its particularistic qualities have been merely deplored as problems, not analyzed as systematic biases." [48]

Sexist views of females have colored the treatment of the female patient. Much of this stems from the medical profession itself. But rather than examine these aspects of medical ideology, medical sociologists have allowed such biases to affect their own work. For example, Lorber and Bart both point out that women's reproductive functions have been treated as diseases in need of professional care rather than as natural functions which may or may not develop complications that require medical care.[49]

Our society's emphasis on "mothering" instead of "fathering" or "parenting" has affected the medical profession's and the medical sociologists' views of women. Lorber charges that mothers have been blamed for many of the illnesses their children and husbands suffer. "Much more research is needed on how, as agents of social control, not only psychiatrists but doctors of physical medicine as well, stereotype and respond differently to members of different social groups."[50]

Deviance

Gender-role stereotypes have also affected the sociology of deviance. Oakley points out that male deviance has been simplistically interpreted in relation to the male's role as provider and breadwinner, while female deviance has been viewed in relation to the female's relations with men. Therefore, emphasis has been placed on criminal behavior in men and sexual deviance in women.[51] The incidence of female deviance and criminality is lower than that of males, but it has not received a proportional treatment in the literature.[52] According to Millman, male sociologists find male deviants easier to study and male deviance more interesting and exciting as research topics. Hence females are excluded even from discussions of types of deviance almost as widespread among women as among men, such as alcoholism and drug addiction. Males do, however, find prostitution to be an interesting type of female deviance and most treatments of female deviance concentrate heavily on the prostitute. But even here the sociologist has been more likely to interview the pimp than the prostitute.[53] Furthermore, the different patterns of crime and deviance for women and men have not been fully researched or explained. Juvenile delinquency studies have concentrated almost exclusively on male delinquents and studies of juvenile gangs rarely include female gangs.

Millman also found a sexist bias in the different motives attributed to male and female deviance. Male deviants are seen as protesting the inequities they suffer in life. Female deviance is seen as secondary: instead of having real economic or political motives of her own, the female deviant "does it all for love." She is often seen as led astray by the male deviant she loves and admires. Oakley found that the major way women are represented in the deviance literature is in the theory of "feminine identification" which blames crime, deviance and juvenile delinquency on mother-headed families.[54]

Marriage and the Family

Women may be invisible in the other areas of sociology, but in the sociology of marriage and the family, their sociological presence far outstrips their social presence. This has been considered an appropriate specialty for female sociologists. Since this field studies women and has more female specialists than other areas, it has been a low prestige specialty.[55] Sociology departments have often resisted offering courses on the family, leaving them to home economics, child development, or social work departments if possible. This has been true even though marriage and family draw more students than other sociology courses.

The overrepresentation of women in this field as practitioners and as subjects reflects sexism just as clearly as does the underrepresentation of women in the other areas. Our gender role stereotypes have placed women in the home and so has sociology. Carol Ehrlich's content analysis of marriage and family textbooks documents the biases in this field. She characterizes the treatment of women as "primarily collections of folklore and social stereotype . . . . The female as viewed by the American male sociologist of the family belongs at home, ministering to her husband and children and forswearing all other interests." [56]

Functionalist theory, as exemplified in the work of Talcott Parsons, promoted the view of women as expressive nurturers who provide an emotional haven for their children and husbands. Men, on the other hand, play the instrumental roles of provider, decision maker, and disciplinarian.[57] It was long accepted that this division of gender roles actually exists and allows for the harmonious operation of society and family life. Such gender roles were viewed by functionalists as beneficial for both males and females and for society as a whole. Cynthia Epstein challenges this Parsonian division of sex roles into expressive versus instrumental roles. This polarization serves to maintain our gender role stereotypes, but it does not help us understand our gender roles and sexual division of labor. It obscures the instrumental or pragmatic dimensions of the female role and the expressive or emotional dimensions of the male role.

"One could pose a counter-model to Parsons'," Epstein states, "one using the family as the instrumental institution in which the business of educating and training youth to participate in the culture is carried out and where the distribution of goods and services is assigned. Politics . . . might easily be seen as the expressive institution where typically people posture and manipulate each other in what can easily be defined as games . . . . The assumption that men, but not women, are rational and instrumental is clearly political in its effects: to provide a theoretical rationalization for a perpetuation of male domination." [58] Both males and females are expressive and rational. Roles in the workplace and roles in the home require both expressiveness and instrumentality. Adults cannot be so easily categorized.

The feminist perspective in sociology is challenging the discipline's adherence to such gender role stereotypes, exposing the ideological basis of much gender role-related research and publications, and insisting on a fuller, more objective treatment of the role of women in society. Similar challenges are also being made in other fields of social science.

The Male Gender Role

Another important effect of feminism on social science, especially sociology and psychology, has been the development of scholarly interest in the male gender role. The male role has been perhaps even more taken for granted and ignored than the female role. Since males have been the dominant gender, few people have considered the implications, in particular the negative implications of this status for men. Although empirical research is still very limited in this area, several works have appeared recently that address themselves to these theoretical and research hiatuses.[59]

VIEWS OF WOMEN IN OTHER SOCIAL SCIENCES

Anthropology

Anthropology is often defined as "the study of man" and until quite recently it has indeed been the study of men with only brief attention to women. Like the other social sciences, anthropology has been and still is predominantly a male profession. Approximately 20 percent of the Ph.D.s in anthropology are earned by women, but women's representation in college and university faculties, research institutes, journal editorships, and research grant awards is even lower.[60] A few women, such as Margaret Mead and Ruth Benedict, have risen to prestigious positions in the discipline. But they are the exceptions rather than the rule.

Reiter points out that not only are most anthropologists male but also that the females in the discipline are trained by males and the selection process has operated to reward those males and females who agree with the existing male biases in the field as to what the important questions are and how they should be answered. This has even been reflected in the field research methods:

It is often claimed that men in other cultures are more accessible to outsiders (especially male outsiders) for questioning . . . we think that men control the significant information in other cultures, as we are taught to believe they do in ours. We search them out and tend to pay little attention to the women. Believing that men are easier to talk to, more involved in the crucial cultural spheres, we fulfill our prophecies in finding them to be better informants.[61]

Thus, much of the anthropological data available on women has actually been collected from men talking about the women of their society. The male view of the society has often been the only view presented. Furthermore, Western preconceptions about gender roles have influenced what anthropologists have seen and how they have reported it.

> What women do is perceived as household work and what they talk about is called gossip, while men's work is viewed as the economic base of society and their information is seen as important social communication. Kinship studies are usually centered on males, marriage systems are analyzed in terms of the exchanges men make using women to weave their networks, evolutionary models explain the origin and development of human society by giving enormous weight to the male role of hunting without much consideration of female gathering. These are all instances of deeply rooted male orientation which makes the anthropological discourse suspect.[62]

Similarly, Eleanor Leacock argues that male bias creeps into the interpretation of field observations. She gives as examples the mystique of the hunt as compared to childbirth and menstruation. Anthropologists have tended to stress the importance of the hunt as a source of excitement and a focus of ritual and religion. However, childbirth and menstruation are likely to be more important sources of mystery and foci of ritual and awe among primitive peoples. Yet because modern people consider childbirth and menstruation as routine occurrences but find the hunt exciting, anthropology as a science has been dominated by considerations of the importance of hunting. Leacock also notes the revealing semantic twists that occur in anthropological writings dealing with female activities: "Women are spoken of as 'isolated' in 'menstrual huts' so that the men will not be contaminated. Where men's houses exist, however, they are written about respectfully; here the exclusion of women betokens men's high status."[63] In both cases one sex is segregating itself from members of the other sex. The differential interpretation sometimes given this segregation by the people under study may be the result of the influence of Western missionaries, traders, and even anthropologists.

Thus the standards for the interpretation of data often differ depending upon how the data fit with gender role preconceptions. Ruby Rohrlich-Leavitt, Barbara Sykes, and Elizabeth Weatherford note that this has been especially true in the continuing debate over the existence of matriarchal civilizations. For example, ". . . although it is generally accepted that religious practices reflect the secular life, when the archaeological record reveals the prevalence of goddesses, the corresponding secular dominance of women is denied, despite the acceptance of masculine secular supremacy when male gods are found to predominate. And scientists who provide proof of the existence of matriarchies are stigmatized as non-scholarly.[64] Similarly, the political leadership of women is either denied or ignored even when the evidence indicates that it exists. Western ideas concerning women's roles are projected onto non-Western societies and then used as proof that these roles are universal.[65]

Thus the ethnographic data are often distorted by researchers' androcentric (male centered) preconceptions. Rohrlich-Leavitt states that a basic assumption of ethnographers is the universality of male supremacy. Since they assume male dominance will be found in all societies, it is not surprising that they find it. However, now that women, particularly feminists who attempt to avoid the androcentric biases of their field, are studying the roles and statuses of women in different cultures, dramatically different findings are emerging. Where men have found women to be the oppressed slaves of men, female anthropologists have found a high degree of egalitarianism, female independence and mutual respect between the sexes. For example, Jane Goodale's *Tiwi Wives* presents almost a mirror image of what male anthropologists had written on the same peoples.[66] Furthermore, the masculine orientations of anthropological language, theory and methods have come under critical review. This does not mean, however, that all anthropologists are now consciously trying to rid their discipline of androcentrism and sexism. Brjra and Barker both assert that research related to women's studies is often treated with contempt by male anthropologists and those who specialize in women's studies are often treated with condescension.[67] But at least the work is being done.

Psychology

Contemporary psychology is still somewhat influenced by Freudian psychoanalytic theory and still incorporates aspects of the Freudian view of gender roles and the female psyche. This encourages a view of women as the opposite of men and incorporates a denigrating terminology for describing the female.[68] Prior to the current feminist attack on sexist social science, there were few forces to support the development of a less sexist psychology. As Phyllis Chesler points out, the professions of psychology and psychiatry in America are dominated by men.[69] Men far outnumber women in all of the therapy professions except for social work and men predominate in the higher ranks of social work. Women earned only 19.3 percent of the Ph.D.s awarded in psychology between 1930 and 1969.[70] Men in particular numerically dominate the most powerful and prestigious field of psychotherapy: psychiatry. Furthermore, female psychologists have been trained in and have to operate within the male-dominated milieu of their profession. Therefore, it is not surprising that they often incorporate the same sexist perspectives into their own work.

Broverman, et al., have documented the sexist perspectives and adherence to a double standard of mental health among clinical psychologists.[71] Samples of clinicians were asked to describe the characteristics of a healthy adult, a healthy adult male and a healthy adult female. The ratings for the healthy adult and the healthy adult male were essentially the same. However, the healthy adult female was characterized by traits which would have been considered sick in the non-sex specific adult or the adult male. Broverman, et al., found a powerful negative assessment, which incorporates traditional gender role stereotypes of women, among both male and female clinicians. They found that clinicians believe that

> healthy adult women differ from healthy men by being more submissive, less independent, less adventurous, less objective, more easily influenced, less aggressive, less competitive, more excitable in minor crises, more emotional, more conceited about their appearance, and having their feelings more easily hurt.[72]

Research on the psychiatric referral process for children also documents the effects of gender role stereotypes in judgments of mental health. John Feinblatt and Alice Gold examined the records of an outpatient child-guidance clinic and found that children who exhibited gender role inappropriate behavioral characteristics were more likely to be referred for psychiatric help than children with behavior problems which did not involve gender role inappropriate characteristics. They found, for example, that "more boys than girls were referred for being emotional or passive and more girls than boys were referred for being defiant and verbally aggressive."[73] They also had graduate students in clinical and educational psychology rate the problems of children in hypothetical case studies. Identical cases were labeled as female for half the sample and as male for the other half of the sample. The judgments concerning the severity of the child's problems were related to the sex of the child. A child described as very emotional and withdrawn was judged more severely disturbed and in need of treatment if the child were a boy than if the child were a girl. Similarly a child described as aggressive and defiant in the case study was viewed as more severely disturbed by the sample which was told the child was female.

In addition to the gender role biases which are part of the behavior therapy professions, gender role stereotypes have been found to affect psychological research itself. Chesler notes that females have often been excluded from psychological experiments, especially if the experiments deal with stereotypically male traits such as achievement motivation, or aggression.[74] Earl and Rae Carlson for example, found an overwhelming use of males as compared with female subjects in personality research.[75]

Recently, however, feminist influences and pressures have begun to affect research in psychology. As Lois Hoffman points out, the recent research on women has forced the expansion and revision of existing psychological theories. Feminism has affected the topics of research as well: for example, issues related to the causes and effects of psychological androgyny, achievement motivation and fear of success in women, the nature of masculinity and femininity (including the rejection of masculinity and femininity as discrete, polar concepts), the documentation of gender role stereotyping and gender role socialization, and the effects of gender roles on personality structure and mental health. Hoffman notes also that psychologists have begun to re-evaluate certain important but vague concepts. "For example, a common generalization is that women are more passive and dependent than men and less aggressive. But the questions are now being asked—passive in what situations? Dependent in what sense? Are women less verbally aggressive or only less physically aggressive?" [76]

Human Sexuality

An area of research and therapy which has both influenced and been influenced by feminism is the study of human sexuality. Therapists, biologists, physicians, and social scientists have until recent years assumed that males are more highly sexed than females. The image of the passive, almost asexual female has dominated the scientific and therapy literature on female sexuality. Freud, as discussed above, held that the vaginal orgasm was the mature response in adult females while the clitoral orgasm represented immature psychosexual development. Masters and Johnson, however, in their research on human sexual response found that the clitoris is the only physiological source of orgasmic response in human females.[77] The vaginal orgasm is a myth. However, for years women who admitted that they did not have vaginal orgasms were labeled as frigid and therapists often advised them that this was the result of not having properly adjusted to their female role.[78]

As we have seen, early anthropologists, sociologists, and psychologists believed that the human female's lack of sexual drive along with the intense sexual needs of the human male account for the development of human society, civilization, gender roles, and the family. Masters and Johnson's documentation of the greater orgasmic potential of the female as compared with the male disputes a basic assumption of such theories. The male domination of science has allowed the actual experiences of females to be ignored in writings on female sexuality. Gender role stereotypes and ideology have blinded scientists to the reality of their subject matter and kept them from investigating it objectively. Furthermore, data which contradicted accepted beliefs were ignored. For example, Kinsey disputed the vaginal orgasm in 1953, and although his work received a great deal of attention, that particular finding went unmentioned in the discussions that followed his publications.[79]

Diana Scully and Pauline Bart's examination of gynecology textbooks found that Freudian ideas of female narcissism, masochism, and passivity still dominate their considerations of female sexuality. Kinsey's research made no impact on the books published between 1953 and 1962 and Masters and Johnson's research is ignored in most of those published between 1963 and 1972. The textbooks continue to present the male sex drive as stronger and the vaginal orgasm as "mature" for females. In addition they exhibit a greater concern for the patient's husband than for the patient herself.[80] Similarly, Michael Gordon and Penelope Shankweiler found that marriage manuals persisted in the view of female sexuality as less intense, more problematic, and slower to develop than male sexuality.[81] Although these manuals claimed to be based on sceintific fact, the impact of ideology is stronger than the impact of scientific data. Masters and Johnson's work had not been incorporated into most marriage manuals in the late 1960s. Sexuality remained a highly ideologized topic.

Sociobiology

Partially as a backlash to feminist demands and successes, there is currently a growing interest in and revival of the old "biology is destiny" theories of gender roles. Contributors to these positions come from a number of fields but the general debate has been subsumed under the label "sociobiology of gender roles." The attempt again seems to be to find scientific justification for the Western sexual stratification system. Sociologists Stephen Goldberg and Pierre van den Berghe, anthropologists Lionel Tiger, Robin Fox, and Desmond Morris, biologist Edward Wilson, ethologist Konrad Lorenz, and popular writers such as Midge Decter, George Gilder, and Robert Ardrey have all attempted to develop theories of the biological necessity of male dominance and female subordination.[82]

Such theorists tend to draw heavily upon animal research and often use inappropriate or at least highly questionable analogies between animal behavior and human behavior. The major difficulty lies perhaps in the selectivity they use in choosing the animal research to "prove" their points. For example, a great deal of attention is given to the gender role related behaviors of the Hamadryas baboon. In this species males are highly aggressive and exhibit the extreme of male dominance. The dominant males forcibly keep the females in harems. As Wilson himself states this is the most sexist of the primate species,[83] yet it is often taken as the model of "natural" gender roles. The animal world exhibits tremendous diversity of gender roles: some are highly male dominant, others female dominant, others egalitarian, along with innumerable combinations depending on the type of dominance being measured. There is certainly no clear-cut pattern of animal gender roles analogous to Western gender roles and sexual stratification. Furthermore, even the diversity we find in the animal world does not tell us the limits of what is possible for human beings. Naomi Weisstein points out that on the basis of the logic that human gender roles have the same natural limits as primate gender roles, we could conclude "that it is quite useless to teach human infants to speak, since it has been tried with chimpanzees and does not work." [84]

The effort to locate innate biological mechanisms which trigger our gender role related behavior patterns has been similarly biased. Goldberg, for example, puts forth a hormonal determinism theory of male dominance and patriarchy. He argues that the male hormone testosterone gives males an "aggressivity advantage" which results in males defeating females in competition for any high-status nonmaternal position in society. The data he cites in support of this hormonal aggression advantage are often misused. Animal researchers have found a link between testosterone injections and senseless, unprovoked vicious attacks on other members of the same species. This type of aggression is, however, quite different from the "need to win" in human beings. Furthermore, there is no evidence to support the implicit assumption that those who are successful in human society have higher testosterone levels or even higher aggressivity. Perhaps the aggressive individuals are the failures—the prison inmates, the violent criminals, the psychiatric patients.

The current sociobiology debate has, however, arisen in a different context than the "biology is destiny" theories of the past. Today, although women are underrepresented in the fields of science and higher education, there are still significant numbers of female and male feminists in the scientific world who are willing and able to challenge the scientific bases of such theorizing.[85]

Even feminist scientists, however, have been influenced by sociobiology. Alice Rossi, for example, argues that cultural determinism has gone too far. Instead she calls for a biosocial perspective linking culture, society, and our biological heritage, acknowledging that sex differences have some evolutionary, genetic basis.[86] Rossi maintains that hormonal differences between the sexes affect the ease with which males and females learn certain behaviors. Females, for example, find it easier than males to master nurturant mothering behaviors. Furthermore, Rossi argues that females have many built-in, unlearned positive responses to infants which she attributes to evolutionary selection. Men can learn to be good nurturant fathers but it is more difficult for them than women to learn these behaviors. Rossi does not argue that biology renders women inferior to men. She supports equality between the sexes but holds that such equality must be based on a recognition of the inherent differences between the sexes.

History

Interest in women's history has been directly tied to the influence of women's movements. Many books were published on women's subjects between 1850 and 1920 as a result of the first wave of feminism.[87] But interest lagged again until the second wave of feminism in the 1960s. History's tie to feminism is also evident in another respect. What work that has been done on women's history focuses almost exclusively on organized feminism and its leaders. This is true despite an abundance of material on women in different social contexts.[88] This, of course, reflects the male biases and male domination of the discipline: It is only when women are behaving in ways usually regarded as masculine—that is, politically and collectively—that they merit historical discussion.[89]

Even in their treatments of feminism, however, historians display biases. The full range of feminist leaders, activities, ideologies, and organizations is rarely covered. Instead, the woman's suffrage movement and the more respectable leaders receive the bulk of attention. Furthermore, feminism is often treated as illogical, irrational, or frivolous. The married lives and children of feminist leaders are emphasized.[90] Rossi's study of biographical writings on women finds a heavy-handed use of psychoanalytic interpretations of feminist behavior: "One reads . . . about latent homosexuality, penis envy, Oedipal complexes, lack of identification with the mother, and the neuroticism of the spinster—all rooted in the quality and particularity of early family relations.[91] In addition, they are often described as manhaters despite evidence of close emotional ties to men. Rossi notes that this use of psychoanalytic concepts in the treatment of feminism and feminist leaders constitutes a form of social control. It serves to label such people and their ideas as deviant or sick. It denies the importance of their ideas, demands, and struggles. It ignores the social conditions which gave rise to feminism. On the basis of an analysis of major current works in feminist movements, Gordon, et al. conclude that "Nowhere in these books do we find a sustained investigation of the real social conditions which are the source of women's problems and rebellion." [92] An extensive content analysis of 27 leading college level American history survey textbooks found that discussions of women constituted from .05 percent to 2 percent of the material in these works. Moreover, when women were mentioned it often entailed insulting language such as "the petticoat vote" or "the softer sex." [93]

Aside from discussion of organized feminism, women have been almost invisible in historical writing. History is a highly androcentric discipline. As is true of the other scholarly disciplines considered here, its members are predominantly male. Women constitute about one-third of the history professors in women's colleges, but only 5.5 percent of those in coeducational liberal arts colleges, and 1.5 percent of the faculties of the top ten graduate departments of history in the United States.[94]

The traditional subject matter of history is probably even more androcentric than the sex distribution of the practitioners of history. History has focused on events in the political and economic institutions of society, those likely to be dominated by males, and has ignored the social institutions in which women participate—marriage, the family, and social relationships. History has been interested in those who receive rewards and recognition. Thus, the discrimination which women experience in the wider society is translated into their insignificance to historians. Because they are rarely involved in the big "marker" events such as wars and the creation of new political policies, women are viewed as timeless, ahistorical creatures. Sheila Ryan Johansson characterizes this as using the concept of "Woman" instead of studying "women." She states:

> Most often it has been those hostile to women who have written of "Woman" and her true unchanging essence. Descriptions and analyses of the eternal feminine have usually been put forth by those anxious to justify the continuance of various forms of social and legal restrictions which confine women to one or two highly circumscribed roles and which condemn rebellious women to the category of genetic sports, nature's mistakes, or exceptions that prove the rule.[95]

This is bad history. Women change just as men do. To ignore this is to violate the canons of good historical scholarship. But it can serve the function of justifying the status quo in gender roles by affecting our perception of what is possible. If women are portrayed as having always been "this way," then we are likely to assume that women will always remain "this way."

Although it has still not been granted full legitimacy as a historical speciality,[96] women's history is currently receiving attention. The lives of women, in particular definite groups of women and not "Woman," are being studied in relationship to the wider social contexts. The goal is to integrate women's experiences into the mainstream of history and to reject the traditional approach of treating women as a special category of only secondary concern.[97]

Political Science and Economics

Like history, political science and economics have traditionally focused on institutions dominated by men. Yet the subject matter itself does not excuse the neglect of women. Women do participate in political and economic institutions even if they do not control them. Yet women's political participation, political attitudes, and party affiliations have until recent years received little analysis by political scientists.[98] And until the issue was forcefully raised by feminists, the barriers to women's fuller participation in political structures went unnoticed and unstudied. Discrimination against women was such a taken-for-granted aspect of political life that no one saw it as in any way remarkable.

The same myopia has affected economics. Sex segration and discrimination in the work world were viewed as natural until feminist demands for change served to focus public attention on issues of economic discrimination against women. Gender role stereotypes of women's place being in the home, not the workplace, and of men being the leaders and appropriate breadwinners so colored the work of economists that they failed to recognize the ways in which our economic institutions force these gender roles on people and help to maintain them in the society.

New research is, however, focusing on sex discrimination, sex segregation, institutional sexism and women's participation and experience in our political and economic institutions. Although we still find the concepts of "political man" and "economic man" in the work of political scientists and economists, "political woman" and "economic woman" are becoming more visible.[99]

TOWARD A THEORY OF GENDER ROLES IN SOCIETY

Although research on gender roles is burgeoning, most of it deals with gender roles and sexual stratification systems only in modern industrial society, or only in preindustrial society, or only in a specific society or time period as a case study. There is no comprehensive work currently available which integrates the theoretical and empirical literature on women and men in society in a comparative and historical perspective. It is not sufficient merely to describe gender roles or to analyze the ways in which they are maintained in a particular society through ideology, cultural imagery, socialization, and discrimination. It is also important to analyze why these phenomena exist at all and why they are maintained in societies. To accomplish this task an interdisciplinary, cross-cultural, and historical approach is necessary. The remainder of this book is devoted to the task of integrating and synthesizing the available literature from the various social sciences in an attempt to understand the origins, maintenance, and evolution of gender roles in different types of societies.

SUMMARY

Examination of the roles of women and men in society must begin with realization of the pervasiveness of scientific sexism. The works of nineteenth-century social theorists such as Auguste Comte and Herbert Spencer in European sociology; the social evolutionists in anthropology; early psychologists dealing with female intellectual inferiority, the variability hypothesis, and maternal instinct; Sigmund Freud and psychoanalysis; the American liberal sociologists Frank Lester Ward and W. I. Thomas are all examples of sexist biases in the social sciences. Frederick Engels was the nineteenth century exception. Engels questioned Victorian assumptions concerning woman's inferiority, the domestic role for women, and the proper family structure.

In addition this history of sexist biases, contemporary perspectives that continue to incorporate separate and unequal gender roles for women must be acknowledged. Sociology and its various subspecialties are not free from such bias, although recent trends toward nonsexist scholarship inspired by the feminist movement should be noted. Contemporary anthropology, psychology, human sexuality research, sociobiology, history, political science, and economics all contain deep-seated biases that have colored their view of human society. More cross-cultural and historical research on women's and men's positions in society is needed. The need for development of a more comprehensive theory of gender roles is urgent.

Notes

1. For example, Pauline Bart's work on depression in middle-aged women received a lukewarm reception from editors and publishers until the feminist movement forced them to pay attention to the growing market for books on women's issues. See Pauline Bart, "Sexism in Social Science" *Journal of Marriage and the Family,* 33 (Nov., 1971), 734-746.
2. Auguste Comte, *System of Positive Polity, Vol. 1,* trans. John Henry Bridges (1851; New York: Burt Franklin, 1968), p. 169.
3. Comte, p. 200.
4. Herbert Schwendinger and Julia Schwendinger, *Sociologists of the Chair* (New York: Basic Books, 1974) p. 310.
5. Herbert Spencer, *Social Statics* (1850; New York: Robert Schalkenbach, 1954), pp. 137-153.

6. Herbert Spencer, *Principles of Sociology, Vol. I* (1897; Westport, Conn.: Greenwood, 1975), pp. 753–758.
7. Spencer, *Principles,* p. 758.
8. Johann Bachofen, *Myth, Religion and Mother Right: Selected Writings of J. J. Bachofen,* trans. Ralph Manhein (Princeton: Princeton U. Press, 1967); John McLennan, *Primitive Man: An Inquiry into the Origin of the Form of Capture in Marriage Ceremonies* (1865; London: Bernard Quaritch, 1876); John Lubbock, *Origins of Civilization and the Primitive Condition of Man: Mental and Social Condition of Savages* (1870; N.Y.: Appleton, 1873); Lewis Henry Morgan, *Systems of Consanguinity and Affinity of the Human Family* (Washington: Smithsonian Institution, 1870); Morgan, *Ancient Society,* ed. Eleanor Leacock (1870; New York: World, 1963).
9. Frederick Engels, *The Origin of the Family, Private Property and the State* (1884; New York: International Publishers, 1972).
10. Stephanie Shields, "Functionalism, Darwinism, and the Psychology of Women: A Study in Social Myth," *American Psychologist,* 30 (July, 1975), 739–754.
11. Alexander Bain, *Mental Science* (New York: Appleton, 1875); Havelock Ellis, *Man and Woman: A Study of Secondary and Tertiary Sexual Characteristics* (London: Heinemann, 1934); Paul Mobius, "The Physiological Mental Weakness of Woman," *Alienist and Neurologist,* 22 (1901), 624–642; J. B. Walker, "Studies on the Growth of Emotions," in *Psychologies of 1925* (Worcester, Mass.: Clark University, 1926).
12. Havelock Ellis, *Studies in the Psychology of Sex: Vols. I and II* (1905; New York: Random House, 1942); Francis Galton, *Inquiries into the Human Faculty and Its Development* (London: Dent, 1907); Edward Thorndike, *Educational Psychology, Vol. III: Mental Work and Fatigue and Individual Differences and Their Causes* (1914; Westport, Conn.: Greenwood Press, 1970).
13. William McDougall, *An Introduction to Social Psychology* (Boston: Luce, 1921); McDougall, *Outline of Psychology* (New York: Scribners, 1924); Edward Throndike, *Educational Psychology, Vol. III;* Alexander Sutherland, *Perspectives in Social Inquiry* (1898; New York: Arno Press, 1974).
14. Shields, "Functionalism," p. 751.
15. William Masters and Virginia Johnson, *Human Sexual Response* (Boston: Little, Brown, 1966).
16. Lester Frank Ward, *Dynamic Sociology, Or Applied Social Science, Vol. I* (1883; New York: Greenwood Press, 1968); Thomas's essays on sex roles originally appeared as articles in sociology journals. The collection of these essays was published as *Sex and Society: Studies in the Social Psychology of Sex* (Chicago: U. of Chicago Press, 1907).
17. Ward, p. 649.
18. Ward, p. 649.
19. Ward, pp. 649–650.
20. Ward, p. 640.
21. Thomas, p. 18.
22. Thomas, p. 224.
23. Schwendinger and Schwendinger, pp. 287–334.
24. Jessie Bernard, "My Four Revolutions: An Autobiographical History of the ASA," *American Journal of Sociology,* 78 (January, 1973), 777.
25. Bart, p. 736.
26. Arlene Kaplan Daniels, "Feminist Perspectives in Sociological Research," in Marcia Millman and Rosabeth Moss Kanter, *Another Voice* (Garden City, N.Y.: Doubleday Anchor, 1975), p. 347; Gunnar Myrdal, *An American Dilemma* (New York: Harper and Row, 1944); Helen M. Hacker, "Women as a Minority Group," *Social Forces,* 30 (October, 1951), 60–69; Simone de Beauvoir, *The Second Sex* (1949; New York: Bantam, 1968); Betty Friedan, *The Feminine Mystique* (New York: Dell, 1963).

36   Chapter 1

27. Helen MacGill Hughes, ed., *The Status of Women in Sociology: 1960–1972* (Washington, D.C.: The American Sociological Association, 1973).
28. Ann Oakley, *The Sociology of Housework* (New York: Pantheon, 1974).
29. Peter M. Blau and Otis Dudley Duncan, *The American Occupational Structure* (New York: Wiley, 1967). For further discussion of the exclusion of women from the sociology of work, see Martin Meissner, "Industrial Man: Interested Omission in the Study of the Social Relations of Production," paper presented at the Canadian Sociology and Anthropology Association, Fredericton, New Brunswick, 1977.
30. Norval Glen and David Weiner, "Some Trends in the Social Origins of American Sociologists," *American Sociologist,* 5 (November, 1969), 291–302.
31. Bart, p. 739.
32. Oakley, p. 19.
33. Laurence Casler, *Maternal Deprivation: A Critical Review of the Literature* (New York: Child Development Publication, 1961); Michael Rutter, *Maternal Deprivation Reassessed* (Baltimore: Penguin, 1972).
34. Oakley, p. 20.
35. Oakley, p. 19.
36. Pamela Roby, "Sociology and Women in Working-Class Jobs," in Marcia Millman and Rosabeth Moss Kanter, eds., *Another Voice: Feminist Perspectives on Social Life and Social Science* (Garden City, N.Y.: Doubleday, 1975), p. 206.
37. Oakley, *Sociology of Housework* (1974a), and *Woman's Work* (New York: Vintage, 1974b); Helena Lopata, *Occupation: Housewife* (New York: Oxford U. Press, 1971).
38. Louise Kapp Howe, *Pink Collar Workers* (New York: Avon Books, 1977).
39. Sara Lawrence Lightfoot, "Sociology of Education: Perspectives of Women," in Millman and Kanter, p. 133.
40. Joan Acker, "Women and Social Stratification: A Case of Intellectual Sexism," *American Journal of Sociology,* 78 (January, 1973), 937.
41. U.S. Department of Commerce, Bureau of the Census, "A Statistical Portrait of Women in the U.S.," Current Population Reports, Special Studies, Series P23, No. 58 (April, 1976), pp. 15–17.
42. Dorothy E. Smith, "Some Implications of a Sociology for Women," in Nona Glazer and Helen Youngelson, eds., *Woman in a Man-Made World* (2nd Ed., Chicago: Rand McNally, 1977), p. 21.
43. Randall Collins, *Conflict Sociology* (New York: Academic Press, 1975); Lucille Duberman, *Social Inequality: Class and Caste in America* (Philadelphia: Lippincott, 1976); Rae Lesser Blumberg, *Stratification: Socioeconomic and Sexual Inequality* (Dubuque, Iowa: William C. Brown, 1978).
44. Thelma McCormack, "Toward a Nonsexist Perspective in Social and Political Change," in Millman and Kanter, p. 12.
45. McCormack, p. 24.
46. Rosabeth Moss Kanter, "Women and the Structure of Organizations: Explorations in Theory and Behavior," in Millman and Kanter, 1975, pp. 34–35. Recent work filling these gaps include Rosabeth Moss Kanter, *Men and Women of the Corporation* (New York: Basic Books, 1977); and Margaret Henning and Anne Jardin, *Managerial Woman* (Garden City, N.Y.: Doubleday, 1977).
47. Kanter, 1975, p. 38.
48. Judith Lorber, "Women in Medical Sociology: Invisible Professionals and Ubiquitous Patients," in Millman and Kanter, p. 97.
49. Lorber, p. 98; Bart, 1971.
50. Lorber, p. 98.
51. Oakley, 1974a, pp. 5, 229.

52. Recent exceptions to this are Freda Adler, *Sisters in Crime* (New York: McGraw-Hill, 1975); Adler and Rita James Simon, *The Criminology of Deviant Women* (Boston: Houghton Mifflin, 1979); Simon, *Women and Crime* (Lexington, Mass.: D.C. Heath, 1975).

53. Marcia Millman, "She Did It All For Love: A Feminist View of the Sociology of Deviance," in Millman and Kanter, p. 258.

54. Oakley, 1974a, p. 8.

55. Cynthia Fuchs Epstein, "A Different Angle of Vision: Notes on the Selective Eye of Sociology," *Social Science Quarterly,* 55 (December, 1974), 656.

56. Carol Ehrlich, "The Male Sociologist's Burden: The Place of Women in Marriage and Family Texts," *Journal of Marriage and the Family,* 33 (August, 1971), 430.

57. Talcott Parsons, "Age and Sex in the Social Structure of the United States," in *Essays in Sociological Theory* (1942; New York: Free Press, 1954), pp. 89–103.

58. Epstein, p. 656.

59. See, for example, Deborah S. David and Robert Brannon, eds., *The Forty-Nine Percent Majority: The Male Sex Role* (Reading, Mass.: Addison-Wesley, 1976); Warren Farrell, *The Liberated Man—Beyond Masculinity: Freeing Men and Their Relationships With Women* (New York: Bantam, 1975); Marc Feigen Fasteau, *The Male Machine* (New York: McGraw-Hill, 1974); Herb Goldberg, *The Hazards of Being Male: Surviving the Myth of Masculine Privilege* (New York: New American Library, 1976); Michael Korda, *Male Chauvinism! How It Works* (New York: Random House, 1973); Jack Nichols, *Men's Liberation: A New Definition of Masculinity* (Baltimore: Penguin, 1975); John Petras, ed., *Sex: Male Gender: Masculine* (Port Washington, N.Y.: Alfred Publishing Co., 1975); Joseph Pleck and Jack Sawyer, eds., *Men and Masculinity* (Englewood Cliffs, N.J.: Prentice Hall, 1974); Joseph Pleck and Robert Brannon, eds., *Male Roles and Male Experience,* special issue of the *Journal of Social Issues* 34:1 (Winter, 1978); Doris Wilkinson and Ronald Taylor, *The Black Male in America: Perspectives on His Status in Contemporary Society* (Chicago: Nelson-Hall, 1977).

60. Ann Fischer and Peggy Golde, "The Position of Women in Anthropology," *American Anthropologist,* 70 (1968), 337–343; Committee on the Status of Women in Anthropology, "Statistical Data on Occupational Status of Women in Anthropology Departments," *American Anthropological Newsletter* (November 1973), 10–11; Diana Barker, "Women in the Anthropology Profession—1," in Ruby Rohrlich-Leavitt, ed., *Women Cross-Culturally: Change and Challenge* (The Hague: Mouton, 1976), pp. 537–546; Pat Caplan, "Women in the Anthropology Profession—2," in Rohrlich-Leavitt, pp. 547–550.

61. Rayna Reiter, "Introduction," in *Toward An Anthropology of Women* (New York: Monthly Review Press, 1975) p. 14.

62. Reiter, p. 12.

63. Eleanor Leacock, "Introduction" in Frederick Engels, *The Origin of the Family, Private Property and the State* (New York: International Publishers, 1972); p. 40.

64. Ruby Rohrlich-Leavitt, Barbara Sykes, and Elizabeth Weatherford, "Aboriginal Women: Male and Female Anthropological Perspectives," in Rohrlich-Leavitt, pp. 567–580.

65. Rohrlich-Leavitt, Sykes, and Weatherford, pp. 567–579.

66. Norma Diamond, "Toward and Anthropology of Women," in Dorothy McGuigan, ed., *New Research on Women* (Ann Arbor: University of Michigan Center for the Continuing Education of Women, 1974); pp. 4–6; Jane Goodale, *Tiwi Wives* (Seattle: U. of Washington Press, 1971); Rohrlich-Leavitt, Sykes, and Weatherford; Constance Sutton, et al., "Women, Knowledge, and Power," in Rohrlich-Leavitt, pp. 581–600; Ruby Rohrlich-Leavitt, "Conclusions," in Rohrlich-Leavitt, pp. 619–641.

67. Janet Brjra, "Women and Fieldwork," in Rorhlich-Leavitt, pp. 551–557; Barker, pp. 537–546.

68. Joy K. Rice and David G. Rice, "Implications of the Women's Liberation Movement for Psychotherapy," *American Journal of Psychiatry*, 130 (February, 1973), 191–196; David C. McClelland, "Wanted: A New Self-Image for Women," in Robert J. Lifton, ed., *The Woman in America* (Boston: Beacon, 1964), pp. 173–192.

69. Phyllis Chesler, *Women and Madness* (New York: Avon, 1972), pp. 62–63. For an example of the biases still existing in psychiatry, see the formal statement by the profession in Group for the Advancement of Psychiatry, Committee on the College Student, *The Educated Woman: Prospects and Problems* (New York: Scribner's, 1975).

70. V. Kistiakowsk, "Women in Engineering, Medicine and Science," revised version of paper presented at the Conference on Women in Science and Engineering, National Research Council, June 1973; Ronald G. Walton, *Women in Social Work* (Boston: Routledge and Kegan Paul, 1975).

71. Inge K. Broverman, et al., "Sex Role Stereotypes: A Current Appraisal," *Journal of Social Issues*, 28 (1972), 59–78.

72. Broverman, et al., p. 78.

73. John Feinblatt and Alice Gold, "Sex Roles and the Psychiatric Referral Process," *Sex Roles*, 2 (1976), 109.

74. Chesler, p. 65.

75. Earl R. Carlson and Rae Carlson, "Male and Female Subjects in Personality Research," *Journal of Abnormal and Social Psychology*, 61 (1960), 482–483.

76. Lois W. Hoffman, "Psychology Looks at the Female," in Dorothy McGuigan, ed., *New Research on Women* (Ann Arbor: University of Michigan Center for the Continuing Education of Women, 1974), pp. 17–18.

77. Masters and Johnson, 1966.

78. Anne Koedt, "The Myth of the Vaginal Orgasm," in Anne Koedt, Ellen Levine, and Anita Rapone, ed., *Radical Feminism* (New York: Quadrangle, 1973), pp. 198–207.

79. Alfred C. Kinsey, *Sexual Behavior in the Human Female* (New York: Pocketbooks, 1953).

80. Diana Scully and Pauline Bart, "A Funny Thing Happened on the Way to the Orifice: Women in Gynecology Textbooks," *American Journal of Sociology*, 78 (January, 1973), 1045–1050.

81. Michael Gordon and Penelope Shankweiler, "Different Equals Less: Female Sexuality in Recent Marriage Manuals," *Journal of Marriage and the Family*, 33 (August 1971), 459–466.

82. Steven Goldberg, *The Inevitability of Patriarchy* (New York: Morrow, 1974), Pierre van den Berghe, *Age and Sex in Human Society: A Biosocial Perspective* (Belmont, Cal.: Wadsworth, 1973), and "Bringing Beasts Back In," *American Sociological Review*, 39 (December, 1974), 777–788; Lionel Tiger, *Men in Groups* (New York: Vintage, 1970); Tiger and Robin Fox, *The Imperial Animal* (New York: Holt, Rinehart and Winston, 1971); Edward Wilson, "Human Decency is Animal," *New York Times Magazine*, October 12, 1975, 38–50, and *Sociobiology* (Cambridge, Mass.: Harvard U. Press, 1975); Konrad Lorenz, *On Aggression* (New York: Oxford, 1966); Desmond Morris, *The Human Zoo* (New York: McGraw Hill, 1969); Midge Decter, *The New Chastity and Other Arguments Against Women's Liberation* (New York: Ben Hey Medallion, 1972); George Gilder, *Sexual Suicide* (New York: Quadrangle, 1973), and *The Naked Nomads* (New York: Quadrangle, 1973); Robert Ardrey, *African Genesis* (London: Collins, 1966).

83. Wilson, *Sociobiology*, p. 534.

84. Naomi Weisstein, *Psychology Constructs the Female* (Andover, Mass.: Warner Modular Publication 752, 1971), p. 5.

85. See, for example Ann Arbor Science for the People Collective, *Biology As A Weapon*

(Minneapolis: Burges, 1977); Gina Kolata, "Primate Behavior: Sex and the Dominant Male," *Science,* 191 (1976), 55–56; Charlotte O'Kelly, "Is Patriarchy Inevitable? A Critique of Goldberg's Hormonal Theory of Sex Roles," paper presented at the annual meeting of the Society for the Study of Social Problems, Chicago, August 1977; Marshall Sahlins, *The Use and Abuse of Biology: An Anthropological Critique of Sociobiology* (Ann Arbor: U. of Michigan, 1976); Ruth Bleier, "Myths of the Biological Inferiority of Women: An Exploration of the 'Sociology of Biological Research,' " University of Michigan *Papers in Women's Studies,* 2 (1976), 39–63.

86. Alice Rossi, "A Biosocial Perspective on Parenting," *Daedalus, 106* (1977), 1–31; and "The Biosocial Side of Parenthood," *Human Nature, 1* (June 1978), 72–79.

87. Hilda Smith, "Feminism and the Methodology of Women's History," in Bernice Carroll, *Liberating Women's History* (Urbana Ill.: U. of Illinois, 1976), pp. 368–384.

88. Ann Gordon, Mari Jo Buhle, and Nancy Schrom, "Women in American Society: An Historical Contribution" (Andover, Mass.: Warner Modular Publication 94), 1973.

89. Ann Gordon, Mari Jo Buhle, and Nancy Schrom, "The Problem of Women's History," in Carroll, p. 77.

90. Linda Gordon, et al., "Historical Phallacies: Sexism in American Historical Writing," in Carroll, pp. 55–74.

91. Alice Rossi, "Feminist History in Perspective: Sociological Contributions to Biographical Analysis," in Dorothy McGuigan, ed., *A Sampler of Women's Studies* (Ann Arbor: U. of Michigan Center for the Continuing Education of Women, 1973), p. 86.

92. Gordon, et al., p. 70.

93. Dolores Schmidt and Earl Schmidt, "The Invisible Woman: The Historian as Professional Magician," in Carroll, pp. 42–54.

94. Schmidt and Schmidt, p. 42.

95. Sheila Ryan Johansson, " 'Her Story' as History: A New Field or Another Fad?" in Carroll, p. 403.

96. Bernice Carroll, "Introduction," in Carroll, pp. ix–xiv.

97. See, for example, Mary Hartman and Lois Banner, ed., *Clio's Consciousness Raised: New Perspectives on the History of Women* (New York: Harper 1974); Elsie Boulding, *The Underside of History: A View of Women Through Time* (Boulder, Col.: Westview 1976).

98. An important exception is Maurice Duverger, *The Political Role of Women* (Paris: UNESCO, 1955).

99. See, for example, Susan Tolchin and Martin Tolchin, *Clout: Womanpower and Politics* (New York: Putnam, 1974); Jo Freeman, *The Politics of Women's Liberation* (New York: McKay, 1975); Marianne Githens and Jewel Prestage, ed., *A Portrait of Marginality: The Political Behavior of the American Woman* (New York: McKay, 1977); Linda Fidell and John Delamater ed., *Women in the Professions: What's All the Fuss About?* (Beverly Hills: Sage, 1971); Robert Smuts, *Women and Work in America* (New York: Schocken, 1971); W. Elliot Brownlee and Mary M. Brownlee, *Women in the American Economy: A Documentary History, 1675 to 1929* (New Haven: Yale, 1976); Ann Stromberg and Shirley Harkess ed., *Women Working: Theories and Facts in Perspective* (Palo Alto, Cal.: Mayfield, 1978).

2

Theoretical Perspectives

Since the domestic and social spheres of life are not really independent . . . it is difficult to conceive of a completely egalitarian domestic relationship when only the male partner is regarded as fully adult beyond the bounds of the household.

Karen Sacks, ''Engels Revisited''

In the preceding chapter we considered how social science has either ignored women and gender roles or given the subject biased treatment. In the remainder of the book we attempt to counter these gaps in social science through a careful consideration of the different roles and statuses of women and men in various socioeconomic and historical contexts. Although gender roles and sexual stratification systems vary widely from one time and place to another, they do not vary randomly. The positions of women and men in different societies are to a large degree conditioned by the nature of the society in general and by its economy in particular.

This theoretical position emphasizing the causal influence of economic arrangements on gender roles and sexual stratification originated in the work of Frederick Engels.[1] In this chapter, we shall examine Engels' theory in more detail and then turn to the more recent attempts to expand, revise, and refine Engels' formulations.

ENGELS' THEORY

On the basis of Karl Marx's work and previous collaboration of Engels with Marx on the subject of the family and woman's oppression, Engels constructed a theory of the subjugation of women. Engels' theory was *evolutionary* (dealing with changes from one type of society to a significantly different type of society) and *materialistic* (focusing on the economic institutions as shapers of non-economic institutions). He argues that primitive, noncapitalistic hunting and gathering societies without private property are sexually egalitarian. But as these societies developed capitalistic institutions of private property, power became concentrated in the hands of a minority of men who then used their power to subordinate women and non-property owning men (slaves and workers), and to create political institutions designed to maintain their power (the state). Engels entitled his work *The Origin of the Family, Private Property and the State* to show the common origin of these institutions. He further argued that to free society from the subordination and exploitation of women, society must again forego private property and other capitalistic institutions. Engels believed that socialism was the only solution to the "woman problem."

A major precept of Marxian social theory is that the *mode of production,* that is, the tools, technology, and organization of work, is of primary importance in determining the nature of other aspects of a society, such as its religion, ideology, class structure, family structure, and child rearing practices. Therefore, on the basis of this principle we would expect to find, for example, that different pre-industrial agricultural societies (which use similar modes of production) would be significantly similar in such areas as religion and family life and significantly different from industrialized capitalist nations or simple hunting and gathering peoples (who would be using different technologies and work organization). In his consideration of women's and men's positions in society, Engels expands this principle of the causal influence of the forces of production to include also the *reproduction of the species* (childbearing and childrearing):

> According to the materialist conception, the determining factor in history is . . . on the one side, the production of the means of existence, of food, clothing, and shelter and the tools necessary for that production; on the other side, the production of human beings themselves, the propagation of the species. The social organization under which the people of a particular historical epoch and a particular country live is determined by both kinds of production: by the stage of development of labor on the one hand and of the family on the other.[2]

Engels maintains that to understand the basis of the subjugation of women in society, we need to understand the development of the family and the evolution of women's position in the family. The type of family found in a particular historical epoch and a particular society is related to the mode of production (the economic institutions) of that society. And the type of family, in turn, largely determines the positions of the sexes in that society. Engels proceeds to develop a history of the family to explain the origins of women's subjugation.

Unlike many other theorists of his day (see Chapter 1), Engels did not believe that women were naturally inferior to or subordinate to men. Nor did he believe that the subjugation of women characterized all societies. Instead he saw women's subordination in the industrial societies of nineteenth-century Europe as the product of certain important economic and political developments. Furthermore, he predicted that as these economic and political conditions changed, the positions of men and women in society would change.

Drawing upon Morgan's stage theory of the family (see Chapter 1), Engels posited that the earliest humans were essentially promiscuous with no marriage or family systems to limit their sexual freedom. But the forces of natural selection operated to favor groups that limited inbreeding by imposing taboos on sexual intercourse with blood relatives. The first of these restrictions applied only to having sex across generational lines and resulted in the first stage of the development of the family: the *consanguine family* with *group marriage*. Under this form, which Engels states is long extinct, sex is prohibited between parents and children, but all males and females on the same generational level, including brothers and sisters and close cousins, had legitimate sexual access to one another. The second form of the family, the *Punaluan family,* continued group marriage but extended the incest taboo to actual brothers and sisters.

One of the inevitable results Engels sees arising from group marriage practices is *matrilineal descent,* a system of establishing kinship relations using only female generational links; that is, reckoning descent through the mother's but not the father's line. Engels argues that matrilineal descent would prevail because:

> In all forms of group marriage, it is uncertain who is the father of a child; but it is certain who its mother is. Though she calls *all* the children of the whole family her children and has a mother's duties toward them, she nevertheless knows her own children from the others. It is therefore clear that in so far as group marriage prevails, descent can only be proved on the *mother's* side and that . . . only the *female* line is recognized. And this is in fact the case among all peoples in the period of savagery or in the lower stage of barbarism.[3]

Engels' terms "savagery," "barbarism," and "civilization" were the accepted anthropological terms of his day to refer to hunting and gathering, simple horticultural, settled agricultural, and, later, to industrialized peoples. The terms have been dropped from scholarly usage because of their pejorative connotations and implied invidious comparisons. However, the stages of economic or technological development implied in their usage are still important bases of categorizing different peoples, although the bases for differentiating the stages are not exactly the same as Morgan or Engels used. "Savagery," now called hunting and gathering or foraging society, is characterized by people who gain their subsistence through foraging for wild vegetable and animal food. They do not domesticate plants or animals. "Barbarism," now called horticultural society, is characterized by domestication of plants and animals and simple crop planting and animal herding done in a shifting, nomadic manner. People in such a society exhaust the soil and plant life in one area and then move on to another, often leaving the exhausted area fallow for many years to recover its fertility. Engels and Morgan used the term "civilization" to refer to settled agricultural societies which have improved farming methods to allow for permanent settlements and the almost continuous use of the same land for crops and grazing.

Group marriage continued to dominate through the stage of "barbarism," according to Engels, but a transitional form of marriage arose which Engels refers to as the *pairing family.* Loose temporary pairings of individual men and women occurred in the consanguine and Punaluan family forms, but these pairings eventually became more stable. This was brought about, according to Engels, by the extension of the incest taboo to more and more blood relatives. The increasing extensiveness and complexity of the incest taboo made it more and more difficult to define the marriage groups necessary for the continuance of group marriage. Out of this situation the pairing family developed.

In this stage, one man lives with one woman, but the relationship is such that polygamy and occasional infidelity remain the right of the men, even though for economic reasons polygamy is rare, while from the woman the strictest fidelity is generally demanded throughout the time she lives with the man and adultery on her part is cruelly punished. The marriage tie can, however, be easily dissolved by either partner; after separation the children still belong as before to the mother alone.[4]

Although the pairing family involved the semipermanent cohabitation of one man and one woman, Engels argues that it was still too unstable a unit to be the basis of the household. Households were therefore constituted on the basis of the matrilineage, which he calls the *gens*. The matrilineage is based on a kinship group whose members are related through their mothers. These matrilineal communal households, according to Engels, gave women important control in primitive society and resulted in a high status for women:

> Communistic housekeeping . . . means the supremacy of women in the house, just as the exclusive recognition of the female parent, owing to the impossibility of recognizing the male parent with certainty, means that the women—the mothers—are held in high respect . . . . the position of women is not only free, but honorable.[5]

In addition, Engels argues that women were recognized as important contributors to the primitive economy and accorded respect for that as well. The high position of women in primitive society is not contradicted by the fact that they were also overburdened with work:

> The division of labor between the two sexes is determined by quite other causes than by the position of women in society. Among peoples where the women have to work far harder than we think suitable, there is often much more respect for women than among our Europeans. The lady of civilization, surrounded by false homage and estranged from all real work, has an infinitely lower social postion than the hard-working woman of barbarism . . . . [6]

Despite his rejection of many of the contemporary Victorian views of women and woman's place, Engels had not completely freed himself from the prevailing ideas. This is particularly apparent in his treatment of sexuality. He continued to believe that males were much more highly sexed than females and that females find promiscuous sexual relations at least uninviting if not abhorrent. The female approach to sex coupled with the breakdown of the matrilineage and communal housekeeping arrangements, according to Engels, led women to desire the pairing marriages. "This advance could not in many cases have originated with the men if only because it has never occurred to them, even to this day, to renounce the pleasures of actual group marriage." [7] Women had introduced pairing marriage, but the males took advantage of it. They demanded strict fidelity from women but allowed the sexual double standard of license for men. Thus monogamy from its inception has, in Engels' view, required chastity of women, but not men.

Males gained power and were able to enforce monogamy and female subordination because they controlled the new private property. The domestication of animals created a new form of wealth which Engels argued was owned by males because males had customarily owned the instruments of labor necessary for food production. Females traditionally owned household goods. Before the domestication of animals, this division of property had not been significant. Neither household goods nor tools were of great value in "savagery" or early "barbarism." In these stages of low productivity there were no sources of important wealth.

At this stage production was for *use value*, not *exchange value*. That is, people produced food, clothing, shelter, tools, and ornaments because they themselves needed to use these items. They did not produce objects in order to sell or barter them (exchange value).* Markets are undeveloped in the primitive economy. No one has any surplus with which to buy the product of someone else's labor. And people do not produce enough to have a surplus beyond their subsistence needs to sell. However, according to Engels the accumulation of herds of livestock allowed for the amassing of wealth, development of the market, and growth in the importance of production for exchange value. People owned large herds not because they needed that much milk or meat or animal labor power, but because the animals were valuable objects for exchange. They could be sold for a profit. This represented the development of a new economic order.

Engels maintained that because custom placed this new form of wealth in the hands of males, males gained the power advantage over females. Furthermore, the new wealth disrupted and eventually destroyed the matrilineal communal family structure. The development of the pairing family had already added the new element of paternity to the family: "By the side of the natural mother of the child it placed its natural and attested father with a . . . warrant of paternity . . . . [8] However, with matrilineal descent, inheritance proceeded through the female line rather than the

---

* The same product or labor can have either use value or exchange value. For example, a parent preparing a meal for his or her family is usually not paid for labor or for the food s/he serves. S/he prepares the meal because s/he and the family need to eat a meal—s/he prepares it because of its *use value*. A cook in a restaurant, however, may prepare the same food but s/he is paid for the work and the product of the labor—the food—is sold to customers. The customers buy it because they need to eat, but the product is produced not so much for its use value as for its *exchange value*, the price it can command in the marketplace.

male line. Hence, the attested father could not pass his property to his own children. They inherited from their maternal uncles (the mother's brothers). The father's property went to his sisters' children, not his own. This created an unstable situation as males accumulated more important property and could know who their own children were.

> Thus, on the one hand, in proportion as wealth increased it made the man's position in the family more important than the woman's and on the other hand created an impulse to exploit this strengthened position in order to overthrow, in favor of his children, the traditional order of inheritance. This, however, was impossible as long as descent was reckoned according to mother right. Mother right, therefore, had to be overthrown, and overthrown it was . . . . the male line of descent and the paternal law of inheritance were substituted for them.
>
> The overthrow of mother right was the *world historical defeat of the female sex*. The man took command in the home also; the woman was degraded and reduced to servitude; she became the slave of his lust and a mere instrument for the production of children. This degraded position of the woman . . . has gradually been palliated and glossed over, and sometimes clothed in a milder form; in no sense has it been abolished.[9]

Because of the new importance attached to property and inheritance, the paternity of children becomes a paramount concern of the males. The *patriarchal family* form arises in response to the new conditions. The wife becomes the property of the husband who can use whatever means necessary to guarantee her sexual fidelity and, thereby, the paternity of his children. The marriage tie is strengthened. It is no longer the temporary pairing of one man and one woman. Divorce is forbidden to women, but the husband can still dissolve the marriage if he wishes. The sexual double standard comes to prevail. Thus, the sexual advantage of group marriage still accrues to the male, but the freedom and status which group marriage afforded to women are lost, replaced by the subjugation of women within the patriarchal family and monogamy.

Problems with Engels' Theory

The major problem with Engels' theory is the inaccurate anthropological data he employed. Evidence does not support his contention of an original state of promiscuity nor of the stages based on widening the incest taboo. He placed far too much importance on natural selection and the prohibition of incest. He also placed too much emphasis on livestock as the first important form of exchangeable private property. Furthermore, he did not adequately explain why individual males would have been the sole owners of this form of private property.

Engels was also ethnocentric in his views of original primitive society. He assumed incorrectly that women would have been primarily house-wives and mothers and that men would have been the breadwinners. Women are important breadwinners among almost all known primitive peoples. He also assumed incorrectly that primitive females would have disliked sex and opposed polygamy and sexual permissiveness in general.

The Matrilineality Debate

Despite its limitations and perhaps because of them, Engels' theory has given rise to several important debates in the area of sexual stratification. Engels' insights into the relationship between political economy and women's position have been the basis for several attempts to construct a more historically and anthropologically accurate theory of women's place than Engels was able to do with the limited and often inaccurate cross-cultural data available in the late nineteenth century. One area of contention has focused on matrilineality and the status of women. Engels asserted, as we have seen, that matrilineality is associated with a relatively high status, respect, and personal autonomy for women. Cross-cultural research has not, however, found this to be true. The relationship of matrilineality to men's and women's positions in society will be discussed in detail in Chapter 4. Briefly, however, the type of descent system or systems found in a particular society does not appear to correlate highly with women's roles. Simple hunting and gathering societies are the most highly egalitarian of the world's societies, but they are predominantly patrilineal in their reckoning of descent. They do not, however, have patriarchal family structures. There are also matrilineal societies that degrade and abuse women rather than treat them with respect and afford them high status.

Household Composition

The type of descent system may not be as important a variable as Engels suggested, but communal housekeeping arrangements, in particular communal households organized around a core of agnatically related (related by blood) women does seem to provide certain advantages to women. If a group of mothers and daughters, sisters, or close female cousins who have been reared together with close ties and feelings of reciprocity share housekeeping and childcare tasks, their close ties provide an important basis for alliances against males and other outsiders. The support system created by these female networks can be important in muting the power of the husbands, brothers, or fathers over the females. Such female-focused households are more common in societies with matrilineal descent systems than in those with patrilineal systems, thus giving some basis for a correlation between matrilinealtiy and higher status for women.

On the other hand, when the communal housekeeping arrangements are focused on the male core of fathers and sons, brothers, and close male cousins, the females are the unrelated outsiders with few bases for close ties or alliances. The women often compete with each other for male attention and favor. And since the males have been reared together and have developed close ties and common interests, they have the strong bases for alliances against the females. This type of household arrangement is more likely to occur in societies with patrilineal descent and patriarchal family structures.

Women also appear to be at a disadvantage to men when they are cut off from close kinspeople in the *isolated nuclear family* (husband, wife, and dependent children). When the woman lives alone with her husband and small children, she has no other adults in the household to call upon for help if disputes arise with the husband. Thus, if the male has the economic advantage by virtue of a higher paying job and better job opportunities and the physical advantages of strength and socialization for aggression, the wife is in a vulnerable position should the husband choose to abuse his powers over her. We shall treat the issues of household composition and its effects on woman's position in society in relation to different types of societies in chapters 3 through 10.

Women's Work

Another focus of scholarly attention has been the issue of women's economic contributions and their relationship to women's position in society. Engels implies that where women make a significant contribution to the economic production of a society their status is high. In light of more recent cross-cultural research, this does not appear to be completely true. Women do important work in all the world's societies, although some classes of both women and men may be exempt from most work in some societies. However, the relative status of women and men varies widely. It is true that in some societies women work very hard, provide important input into the economic production of the society, and have a relatively high social position. However, in other societies women work very hard, provide important economic input, and have very low positions. The factor of women's work alone does not seem to determine the sexual stratification system of a society. However, the nature of women's and men's work and the source of control over the work process and the product does seem to be important. This will also be examined in hunting and gathering, horticultural, pastoral, agricultural, and industrial contexts in the remainder of the book.

Capitalism and Woman's Place

Engels' work has also resulted in scholarly and feminist social movement debates as to whether or not capitalism is the ultimate cause of women's subordination in modern society. Socialists have long argued that problems associated with sexual stratification will disappear under socialism. In the years just after the Bolshevik Revolution in the Soviet Union feminist agitation was silenced by invoking the principle that once socialism was achieved, their demands would almost automatically be met. Some factions of the current feminist movement argue that socialism is at least a necessary first step towards women's liberation. But the examples provided by existing socialist countries make it difficult to argue convincingly that socialism will automatically liberate women.

Another side of this debate has led to the further examination of the development of capitalism and its impact on the position of women in different countries and in different social classes. The rise of capitalist institutions has certainly had an important influence on women's and men's roles and statuses in society. It has not, however, been a simple situation of all loss for women and all gain for men. Pre-industrial agricultural societies generally accord women a low position and very little power or personal autonomy. These societies are in the stage Engels called "civilization." And it does indeed appear that compared to hunting and gathering societies, women have suffered a loss in status and an increase in subordination.

However, capitalism developed out of these agricultural societies and in many ways improved the lot of women, even if it did not produce sexual equality. Furthermore, the context and nature of women's subordination changed dramatically with the rise of capitalism. Although sexual stratification continued, it took on significantly different forms. For example, women continue to suffer discrimination in job and educational opportunities and in political positions and power, but they are not kept veiled and isolated in women's quarters. It is also less likely that virginity and chastity will be enforced on pain of death. And husbands and fathers no longer have life and death powers over their wives and daughters. Engels may refer to this as merely glossing over the subordinate status of women. But it is a glossing of important consequences for females who would probably prefer that the males in their lives not have the right to kill them. These debates and issues will be examined in depth in chapters 7 through 10.

Comparative and Historical Analysis

Another important impact of Engels' work has been its generation of interest in comparative and historical analyses of sexual stratification systems. His evolutionary perspective did not have to be absolutely accurate to stimulate interest in the relationships between the evolution of society and the evolution of gender roles and sexual stratification. If one studies gender roles and women's and men's positions only in one's own society or only in contemporary societies, it is difficult to gain an understanding of why such roles and statuses exist at all. We need also to recognize whence we have come and the nature of the weight of history upon us. Furthermore, comparing and contrasting sexual stratification in different types of societies and attempting to isolate causal variables related to gender roles and hierarchies can also help us determine the bases of sexual stratification systems and the institutions that maintain such systems. Recognizing the variability and diversity of roles of men and women cross-culturally and historically helps to undermine the belief that gender roles are somehow innate or predetermined by nature. Examining how and under what conditions these roles and statuses have changed can help us to evaluate the potential effectiveness of different proposals for social change in the area of gender roles.

RANDALL COLLINS' CONFLICT THEORY OF SEXUAL STRATIFICATION

Drawing upon the theories of Max Weber and Sigmund Freud, Randall Collins[10] has constructed a conflict theory of sexual stratification which emphasizes *sexual aggression* as well as the *market relationships* emphasized by Engels. From Freud he takes the proposition that humans have strong sexual and aggressive drives. He does not, however, argue that males have stronger drives than females. Instead, Collins maintains that because males are generally bigger and stronger than females and because females are made more vulnerable by childbearing and childcare, males are more successful at sexual aggression than females. Therefore, they are more apt to use sexual aggression. Females generally take a defensive posture to the potential threat of coercion in male–female relations.

Collins goes on to argue that the institution of *sexual property* is the fundamental feature of sexual stratification systems. Sexual property is:

the relatively permanent claim to excusive sexual rights over a particular person. With male dominance, the principal form of sexual property is male ownership of females; bilateral sexual property is a modern variant which arises with an independent bargaining position of women.[11]

Collins views marriage and kinship systems as institutions for enforcing sexual property rights. He asserts also that once women have been acquired as sexual property, they can also be used as subservient laborers inside or outside the home. According to Collins, sexual stratification is probably the most primitive or earliest form of stratification. It is found even in the lowest-technology hunting and gathering societies. He further argues that is likely that women were the first slaves and that slavery was later extended to include men.

Although all societies have exhibited male sexual property in women and sexual stratification due to the physical strength of males and the greater vulnerability of women, Collins recognizes that important variations have existed historically and cross-culturally. He states that the variations result from two related factors: patterns of *social organization* that distribute the use of *force and violence,* and patterns of social organization that affect the *bargaining power* or market positions of men and women:

> Where force operates freely, the distribution of power among males determines the nature of sexual stratification quite straightforwardly, and women have no bargaining power of their own. In such a context, any market of sexual exchange operates only as part of the system of bargaining among heads of families and is based on family resources, not on the personal resources of individual men and women. A market for personal sexual qualities and other personal resources can only emerge where the private use of force is limited by the state. Thus the emergence of a personal sexual market, like that of an economic market, depends fundamentally on the emergence of a particular form of the organization of power. Hence, social structures determining the distribution of force and those producing individual resources for use on a sexual market must be treated together, as interrelated structural complexes.[12]

Like Engels, Collins devises an evolutionary scheme of the transition of gender roles and sexual stratification systems from one type of society to another. Collins emphasizes, however, the bargaining resources available to each sex and the freedom or limits on the use of force found in the society. The emphasis on force and violence is not part of Engels' theory, but the variable of the bargaining power of the sexes is related to Engels' consideration of the power of women in pre-class society and their subordination in class society due to male control of private property. Like Engels, Collins divides societies into different types or stages, but his consideration of sexual stratification differentiates between different types of class society and deals with the important variations in sexual stratification within class societies.

Like Engels, Collins argues that there is a minimum of sexual stratification in the more primitive *low-technology tribal societies.* Because these societies produce little or no surplus beyond subsistence requirements, there is little basis for any kind of stratification system. Males and females have fairly equal bargaining resources. Male force is superior to female force, however, and gives males the advantage. But since worker productivity is so low, this force advantage cannot be used to force females to support males, although women do seem to work longer than men.

> Since there is little surplus and little economic and political stratification, which intermarriages occur makes little difference to the affected families; where the economic system does not permit substantial bride-prices and dowries and no families are powerful enough to be highly preferred for political alliances, there is little reason for daughters to be strongly controlled, since they are not used as property in a bargaining system. Thus it is in low-technology tribal societies that most known norms favoring premarital sexual permissiveness are found.[13]

Thus Collins like Engels treats the low productivity and lack of important wealth-producing private property in low-technology tribal society as the important causal variable in producing the low level of sexual stratification found in such societies. Collins goes on to assert that male control over daughters increases as the economic productivity of women's share of the labor of these societies increases. Again we see the factor of private property translated into male control over females.

The second type of society Collins considered is the pre-industrial agricultural society such as was found in medieval Europe or what he calls *fortified households in stratified society*. These societies would be included in the stage Engels termed "civilization." They are settled agricultural societies with class inequality, but the state has not yet developed strong centralized power. The legitimate use of force and violence remains in the hands of the powerful warrior class of nobles who head the local estates or *fortified households*. These households contain not only the lord's own family members but also a large number of servants and other workers.

There is marked sexual stratification in this type of society, according to Collins, and male sexual property rights in women are strongly enforced. Virginity is strictly enforced in unmarried women by their fathers and brothers in order to maintain male honor and preserve the women's value as objects of exchange. The purpose of marriage is to forge alliances between fortified households. Chastity is strongly enforced on wives by their husbands, again to maintain male honor. The honored male is the one who controls the most property in the form of land, servants, workers, consumption goods, and women. Women have a very low status in such a society and are often viewed as innately immoral, inferior, and unclean. Because control over the forces of coercion and over bargaining resources is concentrated in the hands of an elite class of males, the power of these males in the sexual and class stratification systems is maximized. Women have few or no bargaining resources in this type of society:

> The concentration of force and of economic resources in the hands of household heads gives them virtually unopposable control. Where sharp inequality among households permits, an upper class may practice polygamy or concubinage, monopolizing more than their fair share of females. Correspondingly, men of the servant and laborer classes are sexually deprived, and may never be permitted to marry. Women are most exploited in such societies; they are likely to make up a considerable proportion of the slave class if there is one . . . . Wives and daughters as well do most of the menial work, while men concentrate on military pursuits or leisure.[14]

With the growth of the centralized state, however, force and arms and the legitimate use of violence are gradually removed from the hands of heads of households and instead become the prerogative of the central government. The great household or estate declines in importance as does the power of its head. Capitalist business flourishes in small shops and crafts and later in large factories separate from the household. Also, larger and larger numbers of people work for the expanding state bureaucracy. All of this business and governmental activity serves to separate the workplace from the home.

> The result is that households become smaller and more private, consisting more exclusively of a single family. With the expansion of a market economy, more persons can afford households of their own; a private family-oriented middle class appears.[15]

Collins calls this type of society *private households in market economy*. Individual males lose control over the instruments of force, but retain control of the economic resources. Men monopolized the better jobs in new businesses and government bureaucracy.

Family wealth and power are still sometimes of importance in making marriages. But as the government and outside economy take over more and more of the functions of the household and kinship groups, interfamily alliances through marriage ties become less and less important. This also helps free women to negotiate their own marriages instead of relying on marriages arranged for the benefit of the wider kinship group. Women's positions are somewhat improved by these changes in social organization:

> Women become at least potentially free to negotiate their own sexual relationships, but since their main resource is their sexuality, the emerging free marriage market is organized around male trades of economic and status resources for possession of a woman.[16]

Collins maintains that this type of marriage market gives rise to the ideology of *romantic love* and to strong *sexual repression*. Both of these developments serve to strengthen the female's bargaining position in relation to that of males in the marriage market:

> The most favorable female strategy, in a situation where men control the economic world, is to maximize her bargaining power by appearing both as attractive and as inaccessible as possible. Thus develops the ideal of femininity, in which sexuality is idealized and only indirectly hinted at as an ultimate source of attraction, since sexuality must be reserved as a bargaining resource for the male wealth and income that can only be stably acquired through a marriage contract. An element of sexual repression is thus built into the situation in which men and women bargain with unequal goods.[17]

Since sexual repression serves to raise women's bargaining position, it is more strongly defended by women than by men. Unlike the fortified household society in which males enforced female chastity, women are the chief enforcers in private household society. A remnant of male honor remains but women now condemn women who trade their sexual favors for immediate rewards instead of holding out for the long term economic support within marriage. Keeping the amount of sex available outside of marriage low is advantageous for women who combine sexual repression and sexual attraction in bargaining with men.

As servants move out of the middle class household into the industrial labor force, women take over their work. As the household becomes smaller and more isolated, women become more important for companionship and emotional support. Hence, according to Collins, women trade their sexuality and ability to produce heirs, their household labor, companionship, and emotional support for the long term economic support of the male in marriage. This constitutes an improved bargaining position for women over the fortified household type of society.

Collins argues also that women use their increased bargaining power to extend chastity to husbands and to limit the sexual double standard. Men continue to be freer than women to participate in extramarital sex because they have less to lose in violating the marriage contract. But adultery is socially taboo. The institution of sexual property is extended to husbands as well as to wives. Therefore, men must be more discreet about their alliances. The husband is supposed to love and honor the wife as much as she loves and honors him:

> The romantic love ideal is thus a key weapon in the attempt of women to raise their subordinate position by taking advantage of a free-market structure. Used in courtship, it creates male deference; after marriage, it expresses and reinforces

women's attempt to control the sexual aggressiveness of their husbands both toward themselves and toward other men. The idealized view of the marriage bond as a tie of mutal fidelity and devotion calls for absolute restriction of sexuality to marriage, thereby reinforcing the sexual bargaining power of the wife, since she is the only available sex object. Idealization further has the effect of reducing female subordination within marriage by sublimating aggressive male drives into mutual tenderness.[18]

Collins points out, however, that this strategy for improving the female's position in society has inherent limits. It can never result in equality for women because it requires a degree of segregation of the sexes that leaves males in control of the political and economic structure. It requires the idealization of women and a view of women as the weaker sex in need of male protection from the harsh realities of the real world. Such idealized females cannot be permitted into the hard worlds of politics or economics. Male dominance in these areas remains unchallenged.

However, modern industrial society has undermined this ideal of femininity and romantic love which arose in the early stages of capitalism and industrialization. In the *advanced market economy,* Collins maintains, large numbers of women are needed in the labor force. Increased employment and educational opportunities open new economic resources to women and again changes their bargaining position relative to men. The ability to support herself helps free a woman from the control both of her parents and potential husbands. An independent means of support allows a woman to reject marriage if she chooses, and her earning power within marriage increases her power in the marital relationship:

The freedom of women from economic dependence on men means that sexual bargains can be less concerned with marriage; dating can go on as a form of short-run bargaining, in which both men and women trade on their own attractiveness or capacity to entertain in return for sexual favors and/or being entertained. Where women bring economic resources of their own, they may concentrate on bargaining for sexual attractiveness on the part of men. The result is the rise, especially in youth culture, of the ideal of male sexual attractiveness.[19]

The "playing hard-to-get" strategy of the private household stage is no longer necessary for women. The rejection of the ideal of femininity and romantic love frees women to reject their segregation from the worlds of power, money and sex. Feminist movements demanding an end to discrimination against women in top economic and political positions are likely to arise. Women do not have to accept the limits imposed by the idealization of feminine weakness and dependence. Males are still physically stronger, however, and the use of violence in the form of battered wives and increased incidence of rape may represent male attempts to maintain male dominance under social conditions which have undermined that dominance.

Implications of Collins' Theory

Collins' theory has certain interesting implications. For example, the transition from one stage to another may render the generations incomprehensible to one another. The woman reared under the social organization and market conditions of the private household in market economy understands the "importance" of a young woman maintaining a "good reputation" and playing "hard-to-get." She understands the economic consequences of being "loose." Making a good marriage, which means finding a husband who can support her well, is a woman's road to success. To do this she should take care of her looks (but not look "cheap," meaning too overtly sexual), learn the skills of a good housewife, accept her destiny as devoted mother to her husband's heirs, and learn to be a good companion and provide essential emotional support to her husband. So girls are taught to be good listeners to their boyfriends, to be non-assertive and compliant to all but their sexual demands, to exhibit the appropriate inferiority and weakness by losing at games of skill and not outshining males in course work and grades.

A woman reared in such a manner is prepared to make the most of her secondary position in society. But she is not prepared in personality or skills to compete with men in the worlds of work and politics. She cannot, therefore, understand the outlook of a young woman, her own daughter perhaps, who grows up in an advanced market economy in which women expect to receive a higher education and to have careers (even though the economic return from this education and career may not be as high as that of a similarly trained male). The daughter does not have to lose at games or hide her intellectual skills to succeed in attracting the most desirable husband. She can reject males who attempt to demand this of her. She can insist that the men in her life provide her with companionship, emotional support and sexual fulfillment and share in household upkeep.

Women reared in the private household society do not have the resources necessary to reject male dominance. They are often fearful of social movements and social politics which would facilitate more egalitarian sex roles. Having invested their resources in the old system, they do not feel adequate to participate in the new. These women may provide the backbone of antifeminist movements.

Collins' theory combines the ideas of Engels on the importance of control of the means of production (economic resources), the insights of Freud on sexual aggressiveness and sexual repression, and Weber's analyses of pre-industrial agrarian civilizations and the rise of capitalism. His theory is perhaps weakest in analyzing low technology tribal society. As will be seen in chapters 3 and 4, this very broad classification obscures important variations in women's and men's positions. But Collins improves upon Engels' classification scheme by refining the category of "civilization" into the categories of fortified households, private households, and advanced market economy, and in pointing out the bases of the variations in sexual stratification among these different types of "civilized" societies.

KAREN SACKS' "REVISITATION" OF ENGELS

Anthropologist Karen Sacks has developed a refinement of Engels that takes into account his inadequate and at some points inaccurate treatment of the simpler hunting and gathering and horticultural societies, and revises his theory of the basis of female subjugation in "civilization" or class society.[20]

Sacks tests Engels' theory of the simultaneous deterioration of woman's status and development of male property, production for exchange, and class society. Her method is a comparison of ethnographic data from four African societies. The Mbuti pygmies of Zaire are a simple band level hunting and gathering society. Both males and females participate in economic production of use values. The productive resources are communally owned. Class inequality does not exist. The Lovedu of South Africa are hoe agriculturalists who are also geared to production for use value with both sexes involved in the social production, but the land is owned by the patrilineal extended family. The Pondo of South Africa are involved in some production of domestic livestock for exchange value. The Pondo males perform the labor in the exchange economy, but both sexes participate in the production of use values. The productive resources are again owned by the patrilineal extended family. The Ganda of Uganda are more deeply involved in production of exchange values and a market economy. They are a class society. Men own the productive resources and women work within the household. In these four societies, women have the lowest social position among the Ganda.

The degree of discrimination against women in the social sphere increases steadily as we move from the Mbuti, through the Lovedu and the Pondo to the Ganda. In areas such as giving and receiving food and mutual aid, having the right to represent oneself in disputes, opportunity for socializing, extramarital sex, access to divorce, holding political offices, disposing of wealth, mediation of extra-domestic disputes, and mediation with the supernatural, Sacks concludes there is no discrimination against women among the Mbuti or the Lovedu. There is some active discrimination among the Pondo. And there is active discrimination against women in all of these areas among the Ganda.

Sacks found a somewhat different situation in the areas related to the marital relationship. Among the Mbuti there is no discrimination against women in the domestic sphere. However, the Lovedu, who accord women full adult status in the social sphere, discriminate against women in the inheritance of the family property, in the wife's authority over domestic affairs, and in adultery compensation. The Lovedu impose some menstrual and pregnancy restrictions. The Pondo and the Ganda actively discriminate against women in these domestic areas as well as in the social sphere.

Sacks thus argues that women's positions as social adults varies somewhat independently of their positions in the marital relationship.

> What determines how, or whether, women are regarded as adults is not the same thing as what determines their positions vis-á-vis their husbands. Basically, women are social adults where they work collectively as part of a productive group larger than or separate from their domestic establishment. The meaning and status of "wife" though, depend on the nature of the family in much the way Engels suggests. Where the estate is familial, and the wife works for it but does not share in its ownership, she is in much the same relationship to her husband and his kin as is a worker to his boss. Where there are no private estates, or perhaps where the family estate is jointly owned, the *domestic* relationship is a more egalitarian one. [However], since the domestic and social spheres of life are not really independent . . . it is difficult to conceive of a completely egalitarian domestic relationship when only the male partner is regarded as fully adult beyond the bounds of the household.[21]

Thus Sacks agrees with Engels that male control over family property results in the domestic subordination of females. However, she disagrees with his proposition that male property ownership is the basis of male dominance in class societies. Many females own property in class society and yet are subordinated to males. And many males own no property and yet enjoy male supremacy over women. Instead, Sacks argues that class societies have given rise to a separation of the domestic and public spheres of life. Power in the domestic context cannot usually be translated into public power or position. Women have been denied full adult social status in class societies because they have been limited to the domestic sphere.

Sacks maintains that this split originated in the pre-capitalistic, pre-industrial agricultural class societies in which the ruling classes obtained much of the surplus production necessary to maintain their power through the forced social production of others. Taxation of domestic production alone provided insufficient wealth for the ruling classes. To increase productivity, workers were required to work in public projects as well. This form of social production took the worker and the productive process out of the domestic sphere. These agricultural ruling classes did not use women in their social production projects. Sacks holds that women were not exploited by the ruling classes in this way because men were more efficient sources of such labor. Men do not have to bear and nurse children. Women thus continued in the production of use values in class societies, while men, even non-property-owning men, were drawn into social exchange production. This, according to Sacks, provided the basis for the sexual divide-and-rule policy of the ruling classes.

> Whether such policies are conscious or not . . . the effect of state legal systems and other aspects of ideology developed mainly by ruling classes has been to convert differences between men and women in terms of their roles in production into a system of differential worth. Through their labor men are social adults; women are domestic wards.[22]

To ease the burden of their exploitation, males are rewarded with power over women. Women's productive activity in the household is dependent on male earnings from work in the public economy. Domestic labor, though important for survival, is devalued because it does not produce exchange values in a society organized around exchange production.

Sacks holds that this dichotomization of men's and women's work began under the agrarian class societies but has been maintained under capitalism and industrialization. Women are still responsible for housework and childcare, and this disadvantages them in the public labor force. When women enter the public labor force they accept two roles: domestic worker as well as public worker. Thus domestic work continues to weigh them down and limit their ability to achieve full social adulthood through public labor. Sacks concludes that

> For full social equality, men's and women's work must be of the same kind: the production of social use values. For this to happen, family and society cannot remain *separate economic* spheres of life. Production, consumption, childrearing, and economic decision making all need to take place in a single social sphere . . . what is now private family work must become public work for women to become full social adults.[23]

MARGARET BENSTON AND WOMEN'S WORK IN ADVANCED INDUSTRIAL SOCIETY

A similar position is found in the work of Margaret Benston, who also applies a Marxist perspective to the analysis of sexual stratification in modern society.[24] She argues that women's domestic labor in the modern industrial world remains pre-industrial. That is, it is small-scale, reduplicative, and kin-based production of use values. Work outside the household has, however, been industrialized. It is large-scale and non-reduplicative. (One large factory produces masses of clothes rather than large numbers of separate households each producing its own clothing.) Industrialized work is not organized on the basis of kinship ties and it is performed for a salary or profit rather than for simple use value.

In a society organized around market relationships as advanced industrial society is, especially capitalist societies, work is evaluated on the basis of its exchange value. A doctor is seen as being "worth more" than a garbage collector because s/he earns much more. Work that does not earn exchange value is, therefore, "worthless" under this system of valuation. Benston points out that women's domestic labor falls into this category of non-paid and therefore worthless work. Thus, when the full-time housewife is asked "Do you work?" she replies, "No, I'm just a housewife." This indicates that she does not see her work as real work.

Like Sacks, Benston proposes that modern society industrialize housework as a step toward ending sexual stratification. This would include a tremendous expansion of twenty-four-hour child care facilities and a change in domestic architecture and organization to facilitate professionalized food processing, household maintenance, and laundry. In short, she argues that it is necessary to remove the bulk of household work and childcare from the family or household setting just as we have removed most of our food, clothing, furniture and tool production, educational and religious instruction, and recreation from the household. She believes, however, that this is not likely to occur in capitalist societies because it is more profitable to keep women doing these tasks in the household without direct compensation. Women's ties to domestic work also make them an easily exploitable reserve labor force for the business community to call out in times of labor shortage and return to the home without cost in times of labor surplus. Benston argues that a socialist setting would be more conducive to creating the institutional changes she describes. But she does not believe that socialism will automatically result in these changes.

MICHELLE ROSALDO AND THE DOMESTIC/PUBLIC SPLIT

The emphasis on the domestic/public dichotomy and its causal importance in woman's subordination has also been analyzed by Michelle Rosaldo.[25] She maintains that in all known societies male activities are more highly valued than female activities. For example, in hunting and gathering societies, female gathering provides 60 to 80 percent of the daily food intake measured either by calories or by weight. However, the meat provided by males is the preferred food and the giving of meat confers more prestige on the provider than the giving of vegetable products. Similarly, an activity such as shelter building may be done by females in some societies and by males in others. Where it is done by males it is likely to carry more prestige than where it is done by females. The medical profession is disproportionately male in the United States and is highly paid and highly regarded. In the Soviet Union, where most physicians are female, the profession is not highly paid and does not carry high prestige.

Rosaldo argues that these asymmetries in the cultural evaluations of the sexes derive from the division of labor between the domestic and the public spheres of society. She defines *domestic orientations* as "those minimal institutions and modes of activity that are organized immediately around one or more mothers and their children." *Public,* on the other hand, refers to "activities, institutions, and forms of association that link, rank, organize, or subsume particular mother-child groups." [26]

Rosaldo argues that the focus of women's lives on the domestic sphere results largely from their ability to give birth and nurse children. These roles limit women's participation in non-domestic activities. Hence, males have more freedom to participate in and control the public sphere. Rosaldo argues that because men can separate themselves from the domestic sphere, they can develop and maintain an image of sacredness, authority, integrity, and worth. Intimacy breaks down such image manipulation. Keepers of the domestic scene cannot avoid intimacy and involvement and cannot maintain the distance necessary for image control. This gives men another advantage in controlling the public sphere.

In societies in which the domestic and public spheres are firmly separated, Rosaldo points out that *extra-domestic ties* with other women are an important resource for women in their bargaining power with men. Solidarity among women can be used as a power base against abuse or demands from males. Rosaldo maintains further that some of the variation in sexual stratification and the degree of female subordination in societies is attributable to the degree to which the domestic and public spheres are differentiated and the availability of female solidarity.

Women's status will be lowest in those societies where there is a firm differentiation between domestic and public spheres of activity and where women are isolated from one another and placed under a single man's authority, in the home. Their position is raised when they can challenge those claims to authority, either by taking on men's roles or by establishing social ties, by creating a sense of rank, order, and value in a world in which women prevail. One possibility for women, then, is to enter the men's world or to create a public world of their own. But perhaps the most egalitarian societies are those in which public and domestic spheres are only weakly differentiated, where neither sex claims much authority and the focus of social life itself is the home.[27]

Rosaldo explains the high level of egalitarianism in hunting and gathering societies by the lack of differentiation between the domestic and public spheres. As production, politics, religion, cultural development, and so on are removed from the household context, women lose status and power in society. According to Collins' emphasis on the control of resources, this would constitute a shift of resources out of the household and a weakening of those who remain tied to the increasingly irrelevant domestic sphere.

Rosaldo agrees with Collins' discussion of women's strategies to increase their position in what he called "private households." These isolated private households are firmly differentiated from the public sphere. Rosaldo states:

In those societies where domestic and public spheres are firmly differentiated, women may win power and value by stressing their differences from men. By accepting and elaborating upon the symbols and expectations associated with their cultural definition, they may goad men into compliance or establish a society unto themselves. Thus, for instance, the traditional American woman can gain power covertly, by playing up to her husband's vanity (privately directing his public life). Or in everything from charities to baking contests, she may forge a public world of her own. Elsewhere, women may form trading societies, church clubs, or even political organizations, through which they force thoughtless men into line.[28]

Thus women can take advantage of the cultural barriers separating men from women. But success in this strategy either in emphasizing women's better qualities (more virtuous, humane, etc.) as a way of influencing men or by establishing a separate women's world with its own ladders to success cannot be converted into power in the male public world. Many women find out from direct personal experience that their years spent in volunteer work directing charitable organizations and running women's clubs are not considered to be useful or relevant experience when applying for jobs requiring the same skills in the male world of work.

Rosaldo, therefore, like Sacks, concludes that continued segregation of the sexes and the creation of female public spheres in addition to the male public spheres is probably not the best road for women's liberation. Instead she holds that it is necessary both to bring men more into the domestic sphere and women into the public sphere to end the subordination that is based on women's unequal ties to the household.

JUDITH BROWN AND THE DIVISION OF LABOR BY SEX

Judith Brown has attempted to explain one important aspect of women's and men's position in society—the *sexual division of labor*.[29] She focuses on the limitations women's reproductive and child care roles have on their productive roles. Childbearing and child care help tie women to the domestic sphere and hinder their participation in the public sphere. Brown notes that in primitive societies women are often assigned the dull, monotonous, repetitive work that is not particularly hazardous and does not require sudden spurts of energy. Men, on the other hand, are more often assigned the more dangerous tasks taking them longer distances from camp.

Brown dismisses physiological and psychological differences between the sexes as inadequate explanations of the sexual division of labor. Instead, she begins with the observation that no society assigns primary responsibility for child care to men. All known societies place the bulk of this burden on females. These child care responsibilities then determine the degree to which women can participate in other aspects of social life, in particular, the subsistence activities. Women tend to participate in those tasks that are compatible with child care and to be excluded from those which are incompatible such as hunting dangerous prey, deep-sea fishing, herding large animals, and plow agriculture. Brown notes that many women could do these things as well as many men.

> However, it is easy to see that all these activities are incompatible with simultaneous child watching. They require rapt concentration, cannot be interrupted and resumed, are potentially dangerous, and require that the participant range far from home.[30]

But gathering, hoe agriculture, and a wide range of domestic tasks are compatible with child care. For women to participate more widely in the subsistence activities of a society, they must be freed from the responsibility of child care. Many societies, of course, have institutional arrangements that free women at least part of the time. This is clear in modern institutions such as schools, child care centers and baby sitters, and modern methods of birth control and abortion which can free women from motherhood itself. Other such arrangements include the sharing of child care among a number of adults, the institution of the *child nurse* (assigning a slightly older child, usually a girl, to care for the infants and toddlers), and the use of the elderly as child watchers. Although Brown points out a potentially important limitation on women's full participation in society, it is not an inevitable limitation even in primitive contexts. But where women are burdened with full-time child care with few alternatives to free them from its responsibilities, we can expect this to be a severe hindrance to their full social participation.

MARVIN HARRIS AND THE IMPACT OF WARFARE

A quite different theory of male dominance and female subordination has been developed by Marvin Harris.[31] He explains the origins and variability of male supremacy in pre-state level band and village peoples (societies without centralized political institutions) as a result of the need to limit population growth. In brief, he argues that reproductive pressure leads to primitive warfare and primitive warfare results in the male supremacy complex.

Primitive societies lack safe and effective birth control and abortion techniques. Yet unrestrained population growth would in most cases expand their numbers beyond the capacity of their ecological system. The one effective population control technique available to them is *infanticide,* in particular female infanticide. Female infanticide is far more effective than male infanticide in limiting population growth, because, as Harris puts it, males are "reproductively superfluous." One male can keep dozens of females pregnant. The fertility of a group is determined by the number of women, not the number of men. Killing males then has no long-term effect on population growth, but killing females does.

However, Harris points out that it would require a powerful force to motivate people to kill their daughters or to allow them to die. Women make important contributions in primitive societies and daughters are important as a labor force and as sex objects. Yet the often drastically imbalanced sex ratios in primitive societies with severe population pressure, defense, and warfare problems indicates that female infanticide is widely practiced among these peoples.

It is the *warfare complex* that motivates parents to kill their daughters. Under primitive conditions males make the best warriors, not because they are innately aggressive, but because they are, in general, taller, heavier, stronger, and better runners than females. Females could be socialized to be fierce warriors, but societies using male warriors would have the advantage and would probably overrun the female war parties. But Harris adds that this does not explain why the strongest, fastest females are not trained as warriors instead of the weaker male members. Why not have mixed-sex war parties comprised of the strongest regardless of sex? Harris replies that this does not occur because of the need to motivate humans to become fierce warriors willing to withstand pain and to risk their lives in battle. Like Collins, Harris attributes importance to the male control of force and violence. But Harris provides a more adequate theory of why males use force and violence and its relationship to sexual stratification.

Two kinds of rewards are possible to induce people to be fierce. One kind of reward is to allow them access to more and better food and other creature comforts. However, the corollary to this would be to deprive the less brave and less successful warriors of food and comforts. This would weaken the overall strength of the fighting force and would be counterproductive to the goal of maximizing fighting strength. Hence this form of reward and punishment is not a primary one among primitive warriors. Rather, they rely on the second kind of motivator. Successful warriors are rewarded with the services and subordination of women. Women are turned into the sexual and menial servants of men as part of a system to motivate men to be brave warriors. Poor warriors are not given access to women, and this deprivation does not weaken them for battle as food deprivation would.

Harris acknowledges that it would be equally possible to train women to be warriors and to motivate them with males' services as the reward. There is nothing inherent in the nature of either sex to make one the natural warrior sex and the other the natural subordinate. And in fact the female control over young children deriving from women's ability to give birth and nurse children would make it especially easy for women to render males the subordinate sex. Boys could be selectively allowed to die in favor of girls. Boys could be punished for displays of aggression and rewarded for passivity and carefully trained as servants for their mothers, sisters, and wives. Yet this does not happen because the female fighting force would be less effective than a male fighting force.

If all societies used female warriors, there would be no disadvantage in rearing males to be subordinate and passive. But as long as one group uses male warriors, other groups must protect themselves by using male warriors as well. Since the motivation system requires one sex to be the rewards of the warrior sex, this subordinate sex is always the females. Even the potentially effective females are denied access to training for warfare because the inclusion of females in the fighting force would upset the sexual hierarchy and ruin the motivation system and ideology necessary to make anyone want to be a warrior. Warfare, therefore, leads to female subordination.

Thus Harris notes a strong correlation between population pressure and warfare and the following other phenomena: patrilineality (kinship traced through the father's line), patrilocality (residence with the husband's kin), bride-price, male control of political institutions, cultural imagery of women as unclean, including pregnancy and menstrual taboos, and female assignment to the tedious, menial, drudgework in the division of labor:

> My argument is that all of these sexually asymmetric institutions originated as a by-product of warfare and the male monopoly over military weaponry. Warfare required the organization of communities around a resident core of fathers, brothers and their sons. This led to the control over resources by paternal-fraternal interest groups and the exchange of sisters and daughters between such groups (patrilineality, patrilocality and bride-price) to the allotment of women as a reward for male aggressiveness and hence to polygyny. The assignment of drudge work to women and their ritual subordination and devaluation follows from the need to reward males at the expense of females and to provide super-natural justifications for the whole male supremacist complex.[32]

It is, furthermore, adaptively advantageous for primitive peoples to practice warfare because this provides the motivation necessary for female infanticide. The group that maximizes its male muscle power is the group that is likely to prevail in the constant feuding and fighting. Therefore, given the fact of limited resources to rear children, male children are given preference in survival. Women need the male warriors for defense against other groups' males as much as the men do. These warfare-generated problems serve as the motivation to kill off daughters. This then limits population because it also eliminates all the children the daughters would have had if they had been allowed to live. (Male deaths in warfare do serve to limit the population in the short run but are not important in limiting over-all population increase.)

A vicious cycle comes into operation with the warfare complex. Female infanticide aids in maximizing the fighting strength of a group in its competition with other groups for scarce resources in land and game. But female infanticide also increases the need to fight. The shortages of women induced by female infanticide and by the monopolization of numbers of women by the most successful warriors increase the motivation of the males without women to raid other groups for women. Hence, disputes over women provide an important basis for going to war. Having to fight in wars in turn induces the groups involved to keep killing off their daughters, which makes the female shortage problem chronic. As Harris notes, once a population is involved in the warfare complex, it is very difficult to break out of the cycles it creates.

Harris cautions us to remember that it is not war as such that causes female subordination, but the population pressure that gives rise to war in the primitive (but not the modern) context. When game or land become scarce due to population growth and over-exploitation of the environment, people are likely to fight over these resources. Warfare serves to distribute them more widely and sometimes to leave disputed areas fallow which allows them to regain their fertility. But most important for purposes of population control, it results in female infanticide.

Thus Harris argues that female subordination is likely to be greatest among primitive peoples with population pressure problems and the resulting warfare complex. However, not all warrior groups follow this pattern. It is necessary to distinguish between *internal* and *external warfare*. The pattern of warfare leading to male supremacy is associated with internal warfare in which geographically close and culturally similar peoples are involved in chronic intermittent warfare over local resources.

External warfare creates a different pattern of female status. In fact, external warfare often results in an improved social position for women instead of degradation and subordination. The Iroquois Indians of upstate New York are often cited as a near *matriarchy* (a society ruled by women) because of their matrilineal descent system (tracing kinship through the mother) and the important political and economic power their women held. Yet Harris points out that they were an extremely vicious warlike people. However, their wars were fought against distant, culturally different peoples and involved the consolidation of local groups into large federations. Furthermore, this type of war is not the result of local population pressure and does not involve disputes over women. Males of the local groups are not encouraged to feud with each other. This type of warfare takes the men away from the home base, often for long periods of time. Women are left in charge of the family economic holdings and exercise a great deal of control over decision-making and a high degree of personal autonomy. Absent males cannot exert much control over their women. Thus *male absence* for long-distance war and for other purposes such as for work or trade allows for higher female status and power.

What appears to be external war among *nomadic pastoral peoples* (people who make their living by herding livestock from one grazing area to another) results in the same high degree of female subordination as the pattern associated with internal war. Harris notes, however, that although these nomadic herding peoples move great distances in their war and attack culturally dissimilar peoples, it is really a form of internal war because they have no permanent home base. Their wide-ranging warfare does not require them to leave their property, women, and children behind. "Home" is taken with them as they attempt to conquer new grazing lands and water holes. It is another variation on the population pressure, warfare, male supremacy complex with the element of wide-ranging nomadism added.

Harris states that hunting and gathering peoples may develop analogous situations. Hunters and gatherers such as the Eskimos usually do not get involved in the warfare and male supremacy complexes and in general exhibit highly egalitarian gender roles. The Eskimos are, however, the most inegalitarian of hunters and gatherers and they practice female infanticide. But maximizing male muscle power and motivating males for the difficult and hazardous arctic hunt is similar to the need for male muscles and motivation in the warfare complex. The Eskimos do not have a problem of overpopulation and the consequent danger of "eating up" the environment. They simply have to find enough to eat to sustain themselves. Furthermore, female gathering is practically nonexistent in the arctic environment because of lack of vegetation. Male hunting and deep-sea fishing are the almost exclusive sources of food. This makes sons more valuable than daughters and motivates female infanticide and the devaluation of women in the absence of war.

The impact of internal warfare and of dangerous hunting in a scarce environment on sexual stratification and gender roles holds only for pre-industrial band and village level peoples. Harris maintains that male dominance has a different basis in *industrial societies*. Male muscle power is of little importance under industrialization. Neither the females' weaker musculature nor their physiological processes associated with childbirth, lactation, and menstruation can explain male dominance in modern societies. None of the aspects of *sexual dimorphism* (physical differences between the sexes) have much causal influence on the division of labor, sexual hierarchies, or gender roles. Harris holds that male dominance continues because males control the key institutions. He believes that industrialization makes sexual equality possible but not inevitable:

The fact that warfare and sexism have played and continue to play such prominent roles in human affairs does not mean that they must continue to do so for all future time. War and sexism will cease to be practiced when their productive, reproductive, and ecological functions are fulfilled by less costly alternatives. Such alternatives now lie within our grasp for the first time in history. If we fail to make use of them, it will be the fault not of our natures but of our intelligence and will.[33]

PEGGY SANDAY AND WOMEN IN THE PUBLIC DOMAIN

Peggy Sanday's model of women's and men's positions in society draws together many of the variables emphasized by Engels, Collins, Sacks, Benston, Rosaldo, Brown, and Harris.[34] Sanday acknowledges the importance of differentiating respect, power, and authority within the *domestic sphere* from respect, power, and authority in the *public sphere*.

She also notes the difference between the recognized legitimate power of *authority* and the ability to get one's decisions obeyed that comes from de facto *power* whether that power is considered legitimate or not. Sanday states that "although female authority *may* imply power . . . , female power does not necessarily imply authority." [35]

Thus in one society females may exercise important power indirectly through their influence on their husbands or sons but have no recognized authority to make decisions. This would constitute a different female status from a situation where females had a legitimate right to make decisions and could expect to have those decisions obeyed. Sanday bases her evaluations of *female status* on the following variables:

1. female authority in the domestic domain
2. female power in the domestic domain
3. female authority in the public domain
4. female power in the public domain
5. deferential treatment of females in the domestic domain
6. respect accorded females in the domestic domain
7. deferential treatment of females in the public domain
8. respect accorded females in the public domain

Although all eight variables are important for a complete understanding of female status, Sanday does not attempt to develop an analytical framework for each one. She chooses to deal only with *female power and authority in the public domain.* She separates this into four dimensions:

1. *female control over material objects* outside the domestic realm such as land and produce
2. *the demand for female produce* or the exchange value of goods and services produced by females.
3. *female political participation*
4. *female solidarity groups* for protecting female political or economic interests

Research on a number of societies indicates that female *economic power* must precede female *political power* and *authority.* Female control over material objects and high demand for female produce gives women economic power in a society. This economic power then gives women a basis for political participation and increases the likelihood that female solidarity groups will develop to protect and enhance female political and economic interests. Economic power is of primary importance in raising female status in the public domain.

In analyzing the relationships among economic power, political power, and female status, Sanday begins with the proposition that humans have survived as a species by devoting themselves to *reproduction, de-*

fense, and *subsistence activities.* These activities have been differentially allocated on the basis of sex, and the nature of this division of labor has differed in different times and places. But since reproductive activity always falls disproportionately on females, this limits the total amount of female energy available for defense and subsistence. Because these activities are most important in gaining experience and control of the public domain, this division of labor is responsible for female powerlessness in relation to males in the public domain. Furthermore, according to Sanday, variations in the division of labor in these three major areas of activity account for much of the variation in female status. She argues that

> initially female energy is concentrated in the reproductive and child-rearing sphere, whereas male energy is concentrated in the subsistence sphere. Over time, the presence of human predators causes men to move out of the subsistence sphere and into the defense sphere. Depending on the nature of the warfare, its prolongation, and its interference with male subsistence activities, females move into the subsistence sphere to replace the displaced male energy. Females remain in the subsistence sphere according to whether males continue in warfare activities or become involved in other activities resulting in prolonged male absence. Even if men move back into the subsistence sphere, some women may remain. Over time their numbers may grow as men periodically flow in and out of the subsistence sphere . . . . This process may in time give rise to a condition of balanced division of labor, i.e., both sexes contribute to subsistence activities. *

ike Harris, Sanday focuses on the effects of *male absence* and *warfare* on female status in the public sphere. However, her argument has some problems. Although it is useful to distinguish among the divisions of labor in reproductive, defense, and subsistence activities, there is little reason to assume that among early humans females concentrated almost exclusively on reproductive tasks. Among the simplest existing human groups, females are important subsistence workers. Furthermore, the balanced division of labor associated with more egalitarian gender roles, which Sanday sees as a possible end result of war taking men out of subsistence labor, is found among the hunters and gatherers who practice little or no warfare and are probably more like our primitive ancestors than any other contemporary peoples. Moreover, involvement in reproductive activities does not explain why females not burdened with motherhood would not have involved themselves in defense or subsistence activities.

Although this model may not be useful in understanding the origins of sexual stratification among early humans, it is useful for analyzing variations in sexual stratification among different societies. It does appear that where women have little economic power their power and authority in other public spheres is limited. However, it is not necessarily true that where women make important economic contributions they have public power. Sanday finds that women have a low status in the public domain in societies in which they make little economic contribution as well as in societies where they make a very high economic contribution. High female status is found where there is a balanced division of labor.

An important factor which Sanday emphasizes is women's *economic control* rather than their *economic contribution*. A woman may produce a great deal, but if her father, husband, brothers, employer, or owner has the power to dispose of this product, she loses much of the potential power this economic productivity might have provided her. As we have seen in Harris's model, local warfare creates defense needs that may render women powerless even though they are important economic contributors. If females cannot defend their economic products, they lose much of the power economic productivity might have afforded them. We need Harris's model, however, to explain why females have not been used in defense activities.

Sanday goes on to consider the possible importance of male supremacy in *magico-religious beliefs* as a causal variable in explaining low female status in the public domain. She discounts its causal importance, however, and offers instead the theory that the belief system changes to justify and legitimize whatever dominance system comes to prevail in a society. Where women gain status, she posits that a belief system focusing on maternity, fertility, and female deities may develop to legitimize this higher status. Where women have little power, authority, or status in the public domain, the belief system of the society is likely to support male dominance and female subordination.

SUMMARY

This chapter considered several attempts to build theories of sexual stratification. These various theoretical perspectives on the positions of women and men in society are not mutually exclusive and are not as contradictory as might appear at first glance. A problem so large and as multifaceted as sexual stratification is not likely to have one simple cause. Furthermore, the many variations in sexual stratification systems found around the world can be caused or influenced by a multitude of different factors. Thus, the remainder of this study will draw upon these different social scientists' works in an attempt to understand the bases of the different gender roles and sexual hierarchies in different societies.

Engels sensitizes us to look at the type of economic institutions, the role of markets and exchange production, descent systems and family structure, and household arrangements. Collins tells us to examine the role of force, violence, and sexual aggression in addition to type of society, control over economic resources, and family structures. He also demonstrates how differential access to resources can result in ideologies of gender roles such as idealized femininity and romantic love. Sacks suggests we look at women's position in the wider social structure separately from their position in the marital relationship. Along with Benston and Rosaldo, she also emphasizes the importance of the domestic/public dichotomy and the degree to which women are isolated in the domestic context versus the bases available for extradomestic ties with other women or close kin. In addition, Benston points out the significance of the nature of women's work in relation to the wider society. Harris underlines the importance of population pressure, warfare, and male absence on the sexual stratification systems of pre-industrial peoples. Brown notes the possible impact of full-time child care responsibilities on women's participation in society. And Sanday focuses our attention on female economic control, political participation, and solidarity groups along with the division of labor among reproductive, subsistence, and defense tasks as determinants of female status.

Consideration of the possible impact of all these variables helps to guide us in our attempt to sort out why a particular society has the gender roles and sexual stratification system that it does. It can also help us understand the forces facilitating or inhibiting change in the social positions of women and men in specific societies.

Notes

1. Frederick Engels, *The Origins of the Family, Private Property and the State*. (1884; New York: International Publishers, 1972).
2. Engels, pp. 71–72.
3. Engels, p. 106.
4. Engels, p. 110.
5. Engels, p. 113.
6. Engels, pp. 113–114.
7. Engels, p. 117.
8. Engels, p. 119.
9. Engels, pp. 119–120.
10. Randall Collins, "A Conflict Theory of Sexual Stratification," in Hans Peter Dreitzel, ed., *Family, Marriage, and the Struggle of the Sexes* (New York: Macmillan, 1972); and *Conflict Sociology*, (New York: Academic Press, 1975).
11. Collins, 1972, p. 59.
12. Collins, 1972, p. 61.
13. Collins, 1972, p. 62.
14. Collins, 1972, p. 64.
15. Collins, 1972, p. 66.

16. Collins, 1972, p. 67.
17. Collins, 1972, p. 67.
18. Collins, 1972, p. 68.
19. Collins, 1972, p. 72.
20. Karen Sacks, "Engels Revisited: Women, the Organization of Production, and Private Property," in Michelle Zimbalist Rosaldo and Louise Lamphere, eds., *Women, Culture, and Society* (Stanford: Stanford U. Press, 1974), pp. 207–222.
21. Sacks, p. 219.
22. Sacks, p. 221.
23. Sacks, p. 222.
24. Margaret Benston, "The Political Economy of Women's Liberation," *Monthly Review*, 21 (Sept., 1969), 13–27.
25. Michelle Zimbalist Rosaldo, "Women, Culture and Society: A Theoretical Overview," in Rosaldo and Louise Lamphere, ed., *Woman, Culture and Society* (Stanford: Stanford U. Press, 1974), pp. 17–42.
26. Rosaldo, p. 23.
27. Rosaldo, p. 36.
28. Rosaldo, p. 37.
29. Judith Brown, "A Note on the Division of Labor by Sex," *American Anthropologist*, Vol. 72, No. 5, (Sept.–Oct., 1970), 1073–1078.
30. Brown, p. 1076.
31. Marvin Harris, *Cows, Pigs, Wars and Witches* (New York: Vintage,1974), pp. 35–110; *Culture, People, and Nature* (New York; Thomas Y. Crowell, 1975), pp. 258–280; *Cannibals and Kings* (New York: Random House, 1977a) pp. 31–66; "Why Men Dominate Women," *New York Times Magazine*, November 13, 1977b, pp. 46, 115–123.
32. Harris, 1977a, p. 60.
33. Harris,1977a, p.66.
34. Peggy Sanday, "Female Status in the Public Domain," in Rosaldo and Lamphere, pp. 189–206.
35. Sanday, pp. 190–191.
36. Sanday, pp. 193–194.
37. See Elise Boulding, *The Underside of History* (Boulder, Col.: Westview Press, 1976), chapters 3 to 5 for a discussion of the contributions of women to earliest human society.

3

Hunting and Gathering Societies

Although there is a recognized division of labor by sex, it is far from rigid at any age level. Boys, and even men occasionally sweep the house and cook. Girls and their mothers go on fishing or bird-hunting trips. Members of each sex can usually assume the responsibilities of the other when the need arises . . . . .

Norman Chance, *The Eskimo of North Alaska*

The previous chapter concluded that one of the most important variables for understanding the different positions that women and men occupy in various societies is the type of economic system found in the society. Certain important patterns in the data on gender roles and sexual stratification systems become apparent once we compare societies and gender roles on the basis of type of economy.

When dealing with small-scale societies with pre-modern technologies and relatively simple divisions of labor, this type of economic analysis usually takes the form of *ecological analysis*. Such analysis deals with the interaction between social and cultural behavior and environmental phenomena. Andrew P. Vayda notes that such analyses usually take one of two forms:

> either showing that items of cultural behavior function as parts of systems that also include environmental phenomena or else showing that the environmental phenomena are responsible in some manner for the origin or development of the cultural behavior under investigation.[1]

Occasionally one finds a social or cultural practice that does not appear to be adaptive to the existing environment. However, closer examination may reveal that such a practice evolved under conditions that no longer exist, or that the practice does fulfill functions which are not easily discernible. An example is Marvin Harris's analysis of the warfare complex (discussed in Chapter 2): its functional relationship to population pressure was not readily apparent.

Ecological analysis is more useful for low-technology societies than for advanced technology societies because the advanced technology can be used to reduce the impact of environmental phenomena on social and cultural behavior. But the economic systems associated with advanced technological societies exert an important impact on the social and cultural patterns of these societies. In this chapter we shall use ecological analysis in a consideration of societies with the simplest technology: *hunting and gathering* or *foraging societies*.

ECONOMY AND TECHNOLOGY

As the term hunting and gathering suggests, these people support themselves by hunting game, fishing, and gathering wild plant foods. Their technology is simple but effective. They have various types of bows, arrows, spears, knives, poisons, nets, axes, and clubs for bringing down game and a variety of digging sticks, knives, axes, and containers for gathering and transporting wild berries, grains, and roots. They are of necessity *nomadic*, moving their camps regularly in response to fluctuating supplies of game, edible vegetation, and potable water.

Foragers produce only at the *subsistence level*. Foragers usually have an adequate diet, simple shelters, and clothing appropriate to the climate, but they have little in the way of material possessions beyond the necessities. Hence, little private property exists in these societies. Even though they could produce more goods, they could not keep them. The demands of their nomadic life force them to travel light. Any urges to build bigger and better homes or to accumulate more goods are checked by the regular need to abandon or transport these goods on foot to new areas.

Production is geared almost exclusively to *use values*,* that is, food is gathered for people to eat it, not because it can be sold or exchanged for some other product. Foragers do not have a *market economy*. What little production for *exchange value* they do is with other peoples and typically does not constitute a significant part of their economy. Pygmies, for example, establish trade partnerships with neighboring Bantu horticulturists and exchange meat for bananas and metal arrowheads.[2]

Exchange within foraging groups does not involve market relationships as we know them or even the formality of trade partnerships. Sharing or *reciprocity* is the norm among hunters and gatherers. Richard Lee describes the Bushmen returning to camp after a day of foraging. They share all they have found even with those who have done little or no work that day. Each family's evening meal is made up of contributions from the other family groups. "There is a constant flow of nuts, berries, roots and melons from one family fireplace to another until each person resident has received an equitable portion. The following morning a different combination of foragers moves out of camp and when they return late in the day, the distribution of foodstuffs is repeated."[3]

Food Sharing

Food sharing is highly adaptive for foragers. It serves as a form of insurance. The product of foraging can be unpredictable. If you give generously when you are successful, you can expect others to provide for you during those times when you do not forage or when you are unsuccessful. In these societies giving also confers prestige and the recipient incurs a debt although it is never stated as such. No one says, "I'll share with you this time if you'll share with me next time." It is simply accepted that the recipient of food feels obliged to reciprocate some time in the future. This serves to encourage those who owe gifts to work harder to even the balance or to tip it in their own favor and gain prestige them-

*See Chapter 2 for a detailed explanation of use values and exchange values.

selves. Reciprocity thus encourages subsistence level productivity without the use of coercive mechanisms to force people to work.

Aspects of foraging technology are often physically demanding. Gatherers may walk many miles carrying heavy loads of roots, nuts, and berries, and hunters may run for hours without a rest through thick jungle undergrowth in pursuit of game. However, the Westerners' image of primitive peoples and particularly of primitive women as overworked, undernourished, and always living on the edge of starvation is inaccurate. Hunters and gatherers have a great deal of leisure time. They rarely work a forty-hour week: an average work day of two or three hours is usually sufficient. Famine is not a recurring problem among most foragers. Their knowledge of nature's resources combined with their nomadism usually can see them through times of shortage. In fact, more advanced agricultural peoples who live near foragers often turn to the foragers for help during droughts and other times of crop failure. The diets of foragers are also usually more varied and often more nutritious than the diets of farming peoples.

SOCIAL ORGANIZATION AND LEADERSHIP

Camp Size and Composition

Foraging technology requires that the communities be small and flexible. The camps of foragers living and working together range in size from twenty-five to two hundred people. Membership in the camps is flexible and based on a wide network of *kinship ties*. People can change from one camp to another quite readily. There is a continuous process of new kin arriving, others departing, and of visiting relatives in other camps for varying periods of time. Furthermore, the camps themselves periodically break up into smaller units to fan out over a larger foraging territory. They then regroup later when it is no longer advantageous or necessary to disperse.

Leadership

There is little inequality of any kind in these societies. Since there is little private property there are no social classes; no one is rich and no one is poor. There are no rulers and there is no specialized institutional form of government. Leadership is gained through the force of one's personality, skill, and intelligence. A leader, furthermore, has no powers of coercion. He or she can only persuade, cajole, or shame people into obeying. The leader, furthermore, usually has to set the best example by working the hardest and sharing the most. Leadership does not confer privilege among foragers. Decision-making is dispersed in these societies. Even recognized leaders cannot make decisions alone or enforce decisions on anyone who does not agree with the decision.

In general, the person who engages in a particular activity, male or female, is the one who makes the decisions concerning it. When group decisions are required, however, those who have demonstrated skills necessary to the topic being discussed (such as skilled hunters when the decision is when and where to have a collective hunt), will be more likely to have their opinions deferred to than those who do not excel in the relevant task. But even the respected skilled hunter or gatherer will usually not impose his or her opinions on others. Cooperativeness and non-assertiveness are highly valued traits. Eskimos, for example, often find it excruciatingly embarassing to express a direct opinion on a debated issue. Sensitivity to other people's desires and willingness to compromise are norms for participation in the decision-making processes. Aggression and dominance are usually frowned on in these societies. Foragers tend to be peaceful, non-violent peoples.

Aggression and Territoriality

Although many popular writers have argued that human beings are innately aggressive, hierarchical, and territorial because of the evolutionary impact of the hunting technology on our ancestors, current hunting and gathering societies do not confirm this view.[4] Use of hunting technology has not rendered these peoples aggressive, hierarchical, or territorial. Aggression and dominance are not encouraged and are rarely displayed in these societies. Furthermore, partly because of their geographic mobility, they are not highly territorial. The common response to encroachments or threats by other peoples is to withdraw to an undisputed area. Violence and warfare are relatively rare among hunters and gatherers.[5]

Family and Kinship

Kinship is extremely important among foragers. Almost all of their social, economic, and political relationships are embedded in kinship relations. Collective work is organized, food is shared, camps are organized, and disputes are settled through the use of kinship ties. Because of the importance of reciprocity and the open flexibility of camp organization, it is adaptive for hunters and gatherers to recognize as wide a range of kin as possible.[6] Foragers, therefore, tend to have *bilateral descent systems;* that is, they recognize kinship ties on both the mother's side and the father's side. One of the characteristics of bilateral descent systems is that they have no logical stopping points. One can theoretically establish ties to second, third, and fourth cousins. For foragers this is again a form of insurance. In time of need or difficulty a wide kinship network means there is a large number of people one can turn to for help. If a third cousin is an excellent hunter, for example, it can be advantageous to recognize that kinship tie and move in with his camp.

Foragers also tend to be at least serially *monogamous* (to have only one spouse at a time) and to live in *nuclear family* structures of mother, father, and dependent children. Although they tend to be monogamous in practice, there are usually no rules prohibiting multiple marriages and *polygyny* (a man having more than one wife) is not uncommon. *Polyandry* (a woman having more than one husband) is, however, almost unheard-of among foragers. In the hunting and gathering context, there is little motivation for polygamy of any type. Productivity is usually not high enough for one worker to produce in excess of his or her own subsistence needs consistently.

Taking multiple wives, then, does not free a man from productive labor or provide him with greater wealth (common motivations for polygyny). But he does have to deal with the problems associated with polygyny—jealousy and disputes among co-wives. Collin Turnbull describes one polygynous family group among the Pygmies he studied.[7] The man did not receive prestige from having multiple wives. He did not have greater leisure time: in fact, he probably had to work harder than other husbands in order to provide as much for each of his three wives as most Pygmy husbands provide for their one wife. Furthermore, the internal disputes among his wives made him the object of ridicule and gossip.

The nuclear family form is widespread among foragers because it is well-suited to their highly mobile way of life, their flexibility of camp membership and organization, and their sexual division of labor. Harris describes the changes typical in camp membership and their relationship to the nuclear family structure.

On a daily basis, smaller task groups leave the camp to carry out specialized subsistence activities such as collecting fruits or berries, grubbing, or hunting of large game. Sometimes task groups split off for longer periods—weeks or months—in which case they will usually consist of several genealogically related nuclear families. From time to time—days or weeks—depending on the regional ecology, the local band will break camp and move as a group to another site within a range generally comprising about fifty to seventy-five square miles. Before, during, and after such moves, genealogically linked nuclear families may migrate independently from one band to another. During periods of environmental stress, the bands may break up entirely into several groups of nuclear families. Under extreme duress, the band may even break up further into single nuclear families. Such families, however, will not survive long on their own. Wherever food and water are sufficiently abundant, nuclear families reaggregate into local bands. Similarly, several local bands, related by a criss-cross of marriage and descent, tend to aggregate into larger camps whenever local conditions permit.[8]

This continual shifting or nomadism is also related to the fact that foragers tend to be *bilocal* in residence patterns. That is, the married couple sometimes lives with the wife's relatives and at other times with the husband's kin, depending on such factors as abundance of food in one camp's area, friendship patterns among kin, and even whim. Again, however, it reflects the importance of having widespread kinship ties as a means of knitting these shifting, often amorphous groups of people together without any real governmental apparatus.

Family Size.   Family size is small among foragers. The women of hunting and gathering societies typically space their children about four years apart. They achieve this without modern contraceptive technology, although most groups have knowledge of various abortion techniques. The low birthrate is achieved partially through placing a taboo on having sexual intercourse with a lactating female. (Women usually breast-feed their children for four years.) But such sexual taboos are difficult to enforce, so physical causes of the low birthrate have been sought. There appears to be a causal relationship between lactation, body fat, and the cessation of ovulation. Research indicates that for every woman there is a critical body weight below which the woman ceases to menstruate or to ovulate and is, therefore, infertile until her weight increases. Although they often have a nutritious diet, hunters and gatherers typically have a low-fat diet which results in low body fat. Lactation burns up approximately 1000 calories per day. Hence, for most forager women, lactation pushes them below their critical weight and renders them temporarily infertile.[9]

This mechanism is highly adaptive for the hunting and gathering way of life. It serves to control population growth and it keeps pregnancy and child rearing from interfering with the female's essential role in production. A woman can continue most of her food-producing activities throughout pregnancy. Although gathering is demanding work, it does not require spurts of great energy expenditure which would endanger the pregnant woman. The woman can also return to productive labor soon after the birth of her child. She can usually manage to carry one child with her on her foraging expeditions and breast-feed it without unduly disrupting her work. However, she could not manage her productive tasks with two or more infants or toddlers. By the time a child is four years old, he or she can be weaned and easily be left in camp under the supervision of others whenever the mother must leave camp, or the child can sometimes accompany the mother without being carried. Thus pregnancy and child rearing with wide childbirth spacing do not render women the economic dependents of men. The vision of the woman weighted down by the burdens of childbearing and child rearing, awaiting a food supply from the unhampered male breadwinner, does not seem to be the case for existing hunters and gatherers.

GENDER ROLES AND SEXUAL STRATIFICATION

Writers who argue that hunting gave rise to human aggression, territoriality, and hierarchical social organization often argue that the hunting technology gave rise to *male dominance* and *female subordination* as well. However, current hunting and gathering societies tend to be very low on male dominance and sexual stratification is minimal. Hunting does not necessarily confer greater power and prestige on males. Tasks are not ranked in most foraging societies. For example, hunting is not usually considered more important than gathering, nor is gathering more prestigious than food processing. All work is considered important. However, individuals are ranked according to their skills in performing different tasks. So one may be known as an excellent hunter or as a particularly skilled gatherer. Respect is given to those individuals, male or female, who acquire exceptional skills.

Sexual Division of Labor

The demands of different aspects of foraging technology do usually result in an important sexual division of labor. Hunting, in particular the hunting of large game and dangerous deep sea fishing, are male specialties; while gathering, hunting small game, some fishing, and the bulk of child care, home building, and cooking are done by women.

It appears that pregnancy and child care can be combined with the gathering technology, but it is difficult to combine pregnancy, child care, or gathering with the hunting technology. Hunting under primitive technological conditions often requires arduous long-distance tracking of animals both before and after they are wounded. It also sometimes requires a great deal of physical strength. These activities could be especially difficult for a pregnant woman or for someone carrying a nursing child. Great skill and precision are often required in spearing animals, reptiles, and fish or bringing down birds and animals by means of a throwing stick. Such precision is difficult to maintain for a person carrying a burden. Pregnancy and lactation both burden women with limitations on their speed and endurance in tracking and the chase and inhibit their precision in spearing and throwing.

Furthermore, the presence of an infant or young child is likely to be a disruptive factor in the hunt, both because a child is likely to be noisy and thus frighten away the prey, and because of the problem of protecting the child from the potential dangers of the hunting situation. Since females in hunting and gathering societies spend most of their late adolescent and adult lives either pregnant or nursing, they do not constitute a potentially valuable labor force for hunting. It would therefore be a waste of resources in most instances to expend time and energy training females to hunt. In addition, gathering and hunting both require specialized skills and the skills involved usually cannot be combined on the same expedition. Carrying large quantities of vegetable foods limits one's ability to pursue large game, just as pregnancy and child care interfere with the practice of the hunting technology. It is therefore functional to practice a division of labor that allows some adults to concentrate on gathering and others on hunting. Given the need for women to involve themselves in pregnancy and lactation, it is probably functional to assign females primarily to gathering and leave most of the hunting of large game to males.[10]

However, while a clear division of labor by sex exists in hunting and gathering societies, it is not rigid. Foragers are pragmatic about their division of labor. It is not considered demeaning to do the tasks usually performed by the other sex. So men are often involved in gathering and child care, and women sometimes participate in hunting. George Silberbauer, for example, states that the G/Wi Bushmen place little emphasis on masculinity and femininity and have few strongly contrasted gender roles:

> Among subsistence activities, the only generally valid distinction is that women do not hunt or work with bows, arrows, or spears. Most gathering and preparation of plant foods for household consumption is done by women, but men collect their own plant food while out hunting and also help in providing for the household in early summer. In most households women build the shelters and huts at each new campsite, but many husbands habitually help their wives without there being any regularity in the range of tasks of each partner. Similarly, the allocation of the chores of collecting firewood and setting pit-oven fires is a matter settled by each couple.[11]

Food Sharing and Sexual Inequality

As noted earlier, foragers regularly share food among camp residents. This food sharing has a differential impact on the sexes. The products of gathering expeditions are typically more reliable sources of food than the wild game from the hunt. Furthermore, game cannot be stored and often comes in sizes too large for an individual or one small family to consume immediately. Thus meat is likely to be shared more widely than are vegetable foods. Even when they have the technology for drying and preserving meat, foragers do not necessarily do so. If a family went to the trouble of preserving their kill for future use they would have to eat it in full view of other camp members. This would create jealousies and disrupt camp cooperativeness and harmony. Moreover, it would undermine the "insurance system" built into reciprocity and generosity. In addition, since hunters and gatherers typically prefer meat to vegetables (perhaps because of its more unpredictable and scarce nature in most environments), it would be more disruptive not to share meat than it would be to withhold the less desirable vegetables.

Since women primarily contribute vegetables, they are less likely to be involved in the intricate networks of reciprocity ties which arise from food sharing. Men are usually required, often on the basis of elaborate rules concerning how much to give to whom and in what order, to share the product of their hunt. The sharing of meat thus forges important links between men of different households. In the hunting and gathering context, these links do not result in large power differentials between men and women. But they provide an organizational basis for the exercise of power in case a surplus is ever produced or if the society turns to planting instead of foraging. And even in the foraging context, meat-sharing networks can provide the basis for greater prestige and influence for the male hunters than for the female gatherers.

Ernestine Friedl argues that the sharing of meat is the basis for whatever sexual inequality exists in hunting and gathering societies, and that there is a direct relationship between the extent of male dominance and the proportion of meat supplied by men.

> The opinions of hunters play an important part in decisions to move the village; good hunters attract the most desirable women; people in other groups join camps with good hunters; and hunters, because they already participate in an internal system of exchange, control exchange with other groups for flint, salt, and steel axes. The male monopoly on hunting unites men in a system of exchange and gives them power; gathering vegetable food does not give women equal power even among foragers who live in the tropics, where the food collected by women provides more than half the hunter–gatherer diet.[12]

Patterns in the Sexual Division of Labor

Friedl notes that the nature of the division of labor in hunting and gathering societies, and in particular the extent of the male monopoly over the supply of animal protein, has important consequences for the positions of men and women.[13] Although all hunting and gathering societies are highly egalitarian in gender roles compared to other types of societies, there are important differences among foraging societies. Some foragers are less egalitarian than others. Friedl points out four distinct patterns of sexual division of labor among foragers.

Men and Women Gather, Men Hunt.   In pattern one both men and women gather, largely individually, and men do a little hunting, but the contribution to food supply from hunting is not great. In this situation, each individual has ready access to food resources and can support himself or herself independently of others. The *Hadza* of Tanzania provide an example of this pattern.[14] Although the land occupied by the Hadza appears to Western eyes to be barren, it is actually rich in wild foods and abundant in game. An abundant supply of edible vegetation is probably a prerequisite for this pattern. The desert dwelling G/Wi Bushmen, for example, must make maximum use of all the available food resources and cannot so often afford to pass up opportunities to hunt.[15] The Hadza can afford the luxury of individual independence in food-gathering. Furthermore, this example may indicate that hunting, in particular collective hunting, may be an adaptation to a poor natural habitat. Scarcity may necessitate the concerted efforts of several hunters. Hence, collective hunts may not have developed until fairly late in the evolution of human species.[16]

Among the Hadza, women and children leave camp every day in groups for the leisurely task of food gathering. Most of what they gather is eaten on the spot to satisfy their immediate hunger. Some is brought back to camp to be eaten later by the women and children and some is shared with the men in camp. However, men do not rely on the foods the women gather. The men for the most part do their own gathering individually. Unlike the women they do not bring vegetable foods back to camp to share. They do share meat whenever they are successful in hunting, after they have cooked and eaten their fill at the scene of the kill. However, this is rare. Meat and the honey gathered primarily by men constitute only 20 percent of the diet of the Hadza. The men are not avid hunters despite their love of meat, the abundance of game, and their self image as hunters. Woodburn notes that

> although vegetable foods form the bulk of their diet, the Hadza attach very little value to them. They think of themselves and describe themselves as hunters. From informants' assertions, one would gather that little but meat is eaten. In addition to being the preferred food, meat is also intimately connected with rituals to which Hadza men attach great importance.[17]

Subsistence activities do not consume a great deal of the Hadza's time or energy. Woodburn estimates that they average less than two hours per day obtaining food.

The sexes are highly independent of each other for food among the Hadza, but women still depend upon men for whatever meat they eat. Women also depend on men for items obtained through trade with other peoples. The Hadza do not depend on trade except for luxuries such as tobacco, but males control this trade network through their control over the key item of trade—honey. However, to obtain and keep wives, men must supply their wives and mothers-in-law with meat, tobacco, beads, and cloth. These obligations create interdependencies of the sexes. Within the Hadza economic system, males and females are independent of each other in gathered foods and males control meat and trade goods. Friedl concludes that the Hadza represent a situation of minimal sexual stratification which is possible because of the economic independence of the sexes.[18]

Males and Females in Communal Hunting and Gathering.   Pattern two is characterized by male and female participation in collective hunting, fishing, and gathering expeditions. The Pygmies of the Zaire rain forest are examples of this pattern. Like pattern one, this division of labor gives rise to highly egalitarian gender roles. The collective nature of the division of labor creates an important interdependency of the sexes in subsistence activities.

The *Mbuti Pygmies* inhabit the dense Ituri rain forest. They live in an environment of relative abundance in wild vegetation and game. But unlike pattern one societies, instead of individuals hunting and gathering alone, the Pygmies organize their subsistence tasks, as well as most other work, communally. This cooperative interdependence is associated with highly egalitarian gender roles. As Turnbull describes it:

The woman is not discriminated against in BaMbuti society . . . . She has a full and important role to play. There is relatively little specialization according to sex. Even the hunt is a joint effort. A man is not ashamed to pick mushrooms and nuts if he finds them, or to wash and clean a baby. A woman is free to take part in the discussions of men if she has something relevant to say.[19]

The woman is an essential partner in the economy. Without a wife a man cannot hunt, he has no hearth, he has nobody to build his house, gather fruits and vegetables, and cook for him.[20]

Hunting among the Pygmies requires the organization of several family groups and the cooperation of the sexes. The men arrange their nets in a large semicircle and wait with their spears for the women to beat the game toward the nets. The animals caught in the nets are speared by the men and then carried away by the women. The animal "belongs" to the man in whose net it was caught. However, the meat is always shared according to rules and past obligations. Women do most of the cooking and food processing, but an unmarried male does not find it demeaning to cook for himself and other bachelors. "Between men and women there was . . . a certain degree of specialization, but little that could be called exclusive." [21] Friedl argues that pattern two results in minimal sexual stratification and sexual inequalities because of the economic interdependence of the sexes. [22]

Males Hunt, Females Gather.   In pattern three men hunt and women gather. There is a complementary division of labor but the greater value foragers attach to meat gives males an advantage (although not a major one) over women. The *Washo Indians* of the Great Basin in California and Nevada are perhaps intermediate between pattern two and pattern three. Friedl classifies the Washo as pattern two primarily on the basis of the participation of men, women, and children in fishing during the spring runs and the pine nut harvest in the fall. However, these are not the only sources of subsistence for the Washo. Furthermore, these were the most predictable, but least skilled of their subsistence activities.

The other two equally important sources of food were more firmly divided according to sex—males hunted and females gathered. Gathering for immediate consumption was done individually, primarily by women. In the summer, "while the men fished the lake and streams, the women spent more and more of their days wandering in the mountain meadows in the foothills gathering plant food." [23] And "except for the pine nuts and those foods taken in small amounts and eaten on the spot, all gathering was done by the women." [24] Furthermore, women did most of the food processing and wove the baskets necessary for gathering and as cooking utensils. Moreover, although gathering required great skill it was not a focus of ritual and magical powers as hunting was. "All in all, gathering was a much more mundane and rational activity than either hunting or fishing." [25]

In the fall, men continued to hunt as women began the very important pine nut gathering. Pine nuts were the basic staple of the Washo diet throughout the barren winter months. Without an adequate supply of pine nuts, they would starve before the spring fish runs and vegetation appeared. Men cooperated with women in the pine nut harvests. Husbands and wives and their households worked furiously to gather as many as possible during the short harvest season. The heavy loads of pine nuts were then transported by the men and women to their winter camp.

Hunting was the exclusive activity of males and was taboo to women except under exceptional circumstances. Men were expected to hunt throughout their lives. Hunting required great skill in stalking as well as accuracy with the bow and arrow. The hunter had to know in detail the hunting grounds and the habits of his various prey. But even a skilled, knowledgeable hunter could not be certain of success. Therefore, he turned to magic and ritual. "In addition to physical and weapon-using skills and a knowledge of animal lore, a hunter had to learn the ritual and magic that were part of hunting. It was a long apprenticeship and a demanding one that was not complete until a youth was a young man."[26] A man was eligible for marriage when he killed a deer with antlers large enough for him to crawl through when set on their points.

To socialize the apprentice hunter into the importance of sharing the catch, he was never allowed to eat any animal he killed. "Usually he gave the game away to neighbors or relatives, displaying at once the Washo virtue of generosity and learning the important lesson of mutual dependence and . . . building up a number of small debts which he might someday call in if he needed food or assistance."[27] Thus hunting allowed males to create important food-sharing networks and reciprocity arrangements from which females were excluded by virtue of the sexual division of labor.

Unlike the Hadza, a great deal of pressure was put on the Washo male to hunt. In the environment of scarcity, the Washo could not afford to waste hunting opportunities. "Hunting virtually dominated the Washo's image of himself. Even today to suggest that a man had no taste for hunting and preferred to remain in camp with the women is an oblique way of attacking his entire character. The ritual of hunting, preserving the usefulness of his weapons, the respect shown to the hunted animal all combined in a pattern of behavior which influenced most of the day-to-day routine of a Washo man."[28] Thus hunting created important cultural, life-style, and perhaps personality difference between men and women.

The Washo as well as the Pygmies (pattern two) differ from the Hadza in their high degree of economic interdependence between the sexes. Survival requires a partnership between a man and a woman among the Washo and the Pygmies. Marriage is desirable among the Hadza, but the relative economic independence of the sexes does not elevate it to an issue of survival.

The Washo differ from the other hunters and gatherers considered here in that they had greater problems with scarcity, they were more territorial or property oriented, and they had more severe defense problems. The Washo probably worked much harder in their subsistence activities than the Hadza or Pygmies. They had to be much more diligent in their food gathering activities in order to store enough surplus from warm months to see them through the winter. Such surpluses are not necessary for Pygmy or Hadza survival. Furthermore, the Washo subsistence techniques did not require the group efforts characteristic of the Pygmies. The Washo work group was the *household* consisting of a husband and wife, their children, and sometimes young unmarried relatives or elderly relatives. This work group was large enough for the communal fishing and pine nut gathering and large enough for the sexual division of labor between gathering and hunting. These household groups had firm property rights over specific winter camp sites, fishing areas, and pine nut groves. Downs notes that "if a man found a stranger trespassing on his pine nut plot, he seized his equipment, broke it and confiscated the nuts." And "men might come to blows over the use of a fishing platform, but here again custom established who had prior rights . . . ." [29]

Friedl argues that food sharing outside the household was not significant among the Washo and therefore that "only a limited difference in opportunities for distribution were (available) to each sex." [30] But food-sharing networks did exist among the Washo and sharing meat from the hunt was probably more important than other types of food sharing, again because of the unpredictability of the hunt.

The defense problems of the Washo were also different from those of the Hadza and the Pygmies. Washo territory was bounded by that of other Indian groups who often encroached upon Washo food sources. Downs describes the Washo as essentially peaceful, but they could not afford to lose any of their food supplies. They would attack only those trespassers who took valuable foodstuffs. Washo warfare was primarily defensive in nature, but even *defensive warfare* creates another male specialty in primitive society. Furthermore, households travelling outside the center of Washo territory had to be vigilant against attack, thus limiting the women's freedom to gather alone over a wide area. It was important for the males to be available to defend their households under such circumstances.

A clearer example of the pattern three sexual division of labor is found in the various groups of Bushmen who live in the Kalihari Desert of southern Africa. The *G/Wi* and the *!Kung Bushmen* do not suffer the seasonal scarcity problems of the Washo despite the fact that they live in a harsh desert environment. They follow fluctuating supplies of water, but food is always available. Hence there is no attempt among the Bushmen to build up a surplus. During the harsh dry season they merely turn to less desirable edible vegetation. Thus the Bushmen are not characterized by periods of intense subsistence activity like the Washo during their fish runs and pine nut harvests. They lead a much more leisurely life and like the Hadza and Pygmies devote only an average of few hours a day to subsistence work.*

Like the Washo, Bushmen males specialize in hunting, but they do some gathering to satisfy their own immediate hunger while away from camp. They also gather some vegetable foods to bring back to camp if they

*Recent policies of the South African government confining these peoples on reservations have severely disrupted their way of life. The patterns described here would not be found unchanged under such severe conditions.

are unsuccessful on a hunting expedition. Women specialize in gathering and typically do not take part in the hunt. Game is scarce in the Kalihari and the Pygmy style of collective hunting using game beaters would not be effective here. Both hunting and gathering take the Bushmen many miles from camp, and the hunter typically ranges farther than the gatherer.

Vegetable foods again constitute the bulk of the diet (60 to 70 percent), but meat is preferred. The successful hunter gains prestige, builds up obligations from others, and attracts kinsmen to his camp. However, among the Bushmen the vegetable foods are also shared throughout the camp and the skilled gatherer can also gain prestige and incur obligations. But these are probably less significant than "meat debts" because the gathering is predictable once one has learned the necessary skills.

As with the Pygmies and the Washo, among the Bushmen men and women are economically interdependent. The hunting and gathering is more sex-segregated than among the other two groups, but it is *complementary*. In general, these first three patterns in the sexual division of labor result in situations of separate but fairly equal gender roles. In the fourth pattern, however, males are almost the sole providers of the group's food supply, and this appears to result in less egalitarian gender roles.

Men Hunt, Women Process the Catch.   In pattern four men hunt large game and do dangerous deep-sea fishing while women process the product from these male activities. Gathering is an insignificant source of food. The various *Eskimo* societies use this pattern. The frozen tundra provides little in the way of edible vegetation, and game, sea animals, and fish are the staple foods. This pattern carries with it the least egalitarian gender roles of any other type of hunting and gathering societies. Women are economically dependent on men in a sense that does not occur in the other patterns. This results in a power advantage for males and more subordinate roles for females in other areas of the society and culture. For example, at meals men and boys are served first, then the girls, and the mother last.[31] There is an important degree of sex segregation in village life, and even in her own home the woman remains passive in predominantly male gatherings.[32] Moreover, the most influential individuals are the male *hunting-group leaders,* who are important community leaders, and the *shamans* (religious specialists). Many hunting-group leaders increase their influence through practicing shamanism themselves. The group leaders earn their influence through the power of their personality, hunting skill, and possession of sufficient wealth to outfit and support a boat crew. The hunting boat leader "owns" the largest share of the kill which he distributes to gain prestige and obligations from others or sells for profit. Only males participate in trade with non-Eskimos. Females cannot obtain this kind of prestige, leadership, or control of resources. However, women can become shamans if they demonstrate the appropriate skills of spirit possession. Leadership within the extended family is another source of influence in Eskimo society. It usually goes to the eldest male; younger men, but not females, could gain influence through hunting skills, physical strength and good judgment.

Despite a greater degree of inequality than is characteristic of other hunting and gathering societies, Eskimo gender roles and sexual division of labor remain quite flexible. "In theory there are domains which are predominantly male such as sea mammal and caribou hunting, running boats, and doing the heaviest household chores; female domains include doing indoor housework, caring for children, butchering meat, and sewing skins. Nevertheless, members of each sex know the other's skills and can perform these roles when necessary." [33] It is not uncommon, for example, for fathers or husbands to teach females to hunt. In particular, women with few child care responsibilities may take up hunting.

Eskimo women are more housebound than women in other hunting and gathering societies. Since there is little or no gathering for them to do, they usually remain in camp to do their work—processing the skins and meat from the male hunt. The severity of the arctic winters also requires great vigilance in attending to children to prevent their wandering out into the cold unprotected. In conjunction with the frequent need to break up into small units that sometimes consist of only one nuclear family, this means that women are often tied down with the sole care of small children and have little freedom of movement. But in the village setting the mother does share responsibility for infant care with older children and other female relatives. Fathers have traditionally been the dominant, more distant parent, leaving most child care activities to the females.[34] Thus there is a greater domestic/public split among Eskimos than is found among other foragers.

There is a complementarity in the tasks of males and females in Eskimo societies, but there is little food sharing between the sexes. Males provide almost all the food and reap the prestige, benefits, and debts from food sharing. Hunting dominates the Eskimo male's image of himself. Courage and daring are highly valued traits in males. There is a large body of traditional magical practices and taboos associated with hunting, especially the difficult and dangerous whale hunt.[35]

Both men and women view the male life as more glamorous and exciting than the female life. The hunter role is seen as more important. But males and females both recognize that women's skills are also indispensable to survival. Eskimo men do not denigrate women.[36] Furthermore, according to Norman Chance, a woman has the personal autonomy "to make many decisions such as whether or not she will accompany her husband on a long hunting trip or visit relatives in another village." [37] Individualism is culturally valued for females as well as for males. However, Jean Briggs argues that among the Eskimos she studied, a wife must ask her husband's permission to accompany him or to visit relatives. According to Briggs, decision-making is male dominated, although wives may be able to influence or manipulate the husband's decision. She notes that among the Utku Eskimos, "men also direct domestic affairs . . . . In general, an Utku woman decides for herself how she is going to spend the day. . . . However, her husband may veto her plan if he sees fit, whereas the reverse is not true . . . . Moreover, an Utku wife tends to serve her husband in small ways more than he serves her." [38]

Friedl notes that there is more sexual aggression against women among Eskimos than among hunters and gatherers of the first three patterns. Rape of unmarried girls is often an acceptable practice. "Physical and verbal aggression among men is frowned on, but sexual aggression against women in the form of abduction or sexual violence is common." [39] Friedl also goes so far as to describe Eskimo women as "objects to be used, abused, and traded by men." [40] But anthropologists who have studied Eskimo peoples extensively, such as Briggs and Leacock, disagree with such a characterization and emphasize the egalitarian aspects of Eskimo gender roles as compared with more technologically advanced societies.[41]

Women Hunt and Gather, Men Hunt and Fish.   In addition to the four patterns outlined by Friedl, there is perhaps a fifth pattern in which men fish and hunt some animal species and women hunt other animals and gather. The *Tiwi* of the Melville and Bathurst Islands off the coast of Australia exemplify this division of labor. Their division is not on the basis of hunting versus gathering, but rather females are responsible for land resources which include vegetable foods and land animals, while males are responsible for food resources in the water and air, which include birds and aquatic reptiles and mammals. Friedl places the Tiwi in pattern two, but they differ significantly from the division of labor of the Pygmies and the Washo. Of particular importance is the way many men are freed from subsistence activities.

The Tiwi woman hunts with the aid of her highly trained dog which is considered as important as a family member. The female hunter uses a stone ax which she makes and maintains herself. Men use different tools and techniques in hunting birds, reptiles, and turtles. Females also collect plants and shellfish. This division of labor is probably related to the differences in strength required and the danger involved in hunting the different types of prey. The land animals on the islands are not as likely to be large and dangerous as the crocodiles and other reptiles pursued by the men. Males do usually hunt the few large game animals available such as the wallaby. Jane Goodale concludes:

> The outstanding characteristic of Tiwi hunting is related both to the abundance and to the nature of the fauna of the islands. There is no land animal, with the possible exception of the wallaby, that cannot be killed with a minimum of physical strength, skill and equipment. Thus, the women not only could but did provide the major daily supply of a variety of foods to members of their camp. Children too could learn the necessary techniques at an early age, and since strength and energy were minor requirements, they began early to contribute to the larder. Men's hunting required considerable skill and strength, but the birds, bats, fish, crocodiles, dugongs, and turtles they contributed to the household were luxury items rather than staples.[42]

Single males and husbands with only one or two wives participate in the daily hunting parties, but a man with many wives can depend on them to provide food for him and his small children. As with the other foragers considered here, the Tiwi's sexual division of labor seems sharply defined. In reality, however, it is flexible and at many points deviates from the model. Goodale points out that men sometimes hunt "female" game and collect vegetables and women sometimes accompany the males on turtle or goose hunts. The Tiwi do not consider these deviations to be "wrong" and do not believe that bad luck or any other evil result from such cross-sex behaviors.[43]

Both males and females participate in elaborate food sharing networks. Among the females the hunter relinquishes her catch to the "cook" (also female). The cook receives her share of the catch. The cook and the hunter then further share their portions among their kin in a set order of priority. In the case of a large catch, portions will be shared with all those present in the camp. Males first distribute the product of a turtle or crocodile hunt according to their positions in the canoe. Then each man's share is distributed along the same kinship priorities and camp residents as the women's distribution.[44]

Although monogamy is the primary form of marriage in most hunting and gathering societies, among the Tiwi polygyny is the rule for males and *serial marriage* is the rule for females.* This is probably related to the high productivity of Tiwi females in the collection of both vegetable and meat foods. Polygyny in this situation does not require a man to work harder to keep two or more wives in meat as would be the case among the Eskimos, Bushmen, Washo, Pygmies, and Hadza. Rather, the extra wives free the

---

* *Serial Marriage:* having several different spouses in one's lifetime, but never more than one at a time.

husband to stay in camp. This is especially important since a man with several wives is likely to be advanced in age and therefore in need of food from others.

The Tiwi marriage system is incredibly complex and has been the subject of considerable scholarly debate. Some writers have viewed their marriage structure as clear evidence of sexism and sexual inegalitarianism. C. W. Hart and Arnold Pilling, for example, characterize women as little more than currency in a male system of competition and exchange.[45] Goodale's research on the same people has served to balance this point of view with a female perspective on the marriage structure.

Among the Tiwi, females are always married. They are betrothed by their fathers before their birth in a system of reciprocity among males. Males gain prestige through the number of marriage contracts they make. Marriage contracts are highly valued, even if the wife is not yet born or not yet old enough to join the husband's household. Since the husband has to be at least a young adult before the infant girl can be married to him, a female's first husband is much older than she. For this reason, she is likely to be widowed at an early age. Her father (or her brothers if her father is dead) then has the right to make a new marriage contract for her upon the death of her husband. Given the male prestige system based on marriage contracts, all women are valuable as wives, even the aged. There is no such thing as an unmarried female among the Tiwi.

The young girl joins her husband's household before puberty and is gradually initiated into sexual activity by her older husband. She works in his household along with her co-wives and is under the authority of her older co-wives and her husband. But her husband is required to keep his household in the same camp as the young wife's mother, so she continues to be under the protection of her own kin, who have the right to intervene if she is mistreated.

Since her husband is elderly, the young wife is likely to engage in extramarital affairs with the young unmarried men of the tribe. The wife's full adult status is achieved with the birth of her first child. And unlike highly patriarchal societies, female children are preferred. Female babies enable the father to provide wives for other males in exchange for marriage contracts from these prospective husbands. They also, of course, represent important productive labor.

An important aspect of the Tiwi marriage system is that women are not simply passive objects of exchange. They are active participants in the system. The marriage contracts do not simply represent exchange relationships between the father and husband. They also involve an important exchange relationship between the mother-in-law and the son-in-law—the *ambruina relationship*. When the young wife has her first female child, she becomes the ambruina to the child's husband, her son-in-law. The son-in-law is obligated to supply the mother-in-law with all that she demands in food and trade goods. As Goodale describes it, "It would seem that although in the marriage 'game' men thought of women as so much capital wealth to manipulate as they wished, in reality, it was through the relationship that women gained a balance of power over a male. A man might lose his temper at his mother-in-law's husband but he usually maintained his control with his mother-in-law, no matter how hard-pressed he might be to fulfill her demands."[46] This relationship lasts until death.

Polygyny, although a source of power and prestige for males, also serves as an avenue of power and prestige for females. The eldest co-wife, the *taramaguti,* is an important figure among the Tiwi. Like her husband, she does not have to go out on the daily foraging parties; she can direct the activities of her household and remain relaxing in camp. Thus the system allows the elderly of both sexes to withdraw from subsistence activities. The taramaguti directs the education of the young wives and gives respected advice on the rearing of the other wives' children. She is influential over her own and her co-wives' adult children. However, the taramaguti's position is never as elevated as that of some of the elder males. "Women are not considered to be 'big bosses' or leaders in a funeral ceremony— this is a man's role—but the men do consult members of the patrilineage that is in charge of the ceremony and the women voice their opinions freely. The nominal male leaders consider these opinions to be important." [47]

While it is true that women can gain the position of taramaguti only in old age, it is also true that males can become "big men" only in old age. Becoming a "big man" requires the acquisition of many marital contracts and this is impossible to accomplish at a young age. Most young men are unmarried. It is particularly difficult to obtain an infant bride because fathers prefer to give them to men who have daughters to give in return. So young men often take an elderly widow as their first wife, again resulting in a large age difference between the spouses.

This system of polygyny for men also carries with it multiple husbands for women. But instead of having several husbands simultaneously, the Tiwi woman has a series of husbands over her lifetime, usually beginning with a husband much older than herself and often ending with one much younger. Moreover, Frederick Rose asserts that women want to be part of these polygynous units because they ease the burdens of childrearing and household tasks.[48]

The contribution by Tiwi women of meat as well as vegetable foods does not result in a female status equal to that of the male in Tiwi society or to that of the hunter in other hunting and gathering societies. Males still have more avenues for prestige and influence, but Tiwi women are not highly subordinated to men. In general this pattern seems to result in a high degree of sexual egalitarianism with the scales tipped somewhat in favor of the males.

MARRIAGE IN HUNTING AND GATHERING SOCIETIES

Almost everyone marries in hunting and gathering societies because the complementarity of the sexual division of labor makes it difficult for single adults to take care of all their needs for food, shelter, and clothing. Marriage usually entails little ceremony. The couple may merely begin living together and come to regard themselves and be regarded by others as married. Marriage alliances between different families are important in general for establishing and maintaining ties within and among the different camps. But usually no particular marriage alliances are important for linking two specific families together to enhance their power or wealth as there is little power or wealth to exchange among foragers. Since there is no economic surplus, there are no wealthy families and no powerful families. There is little reason for parents to favor a marriage alliance with one family over another.

Therefore, marriages are usually made on the basis of the mutual attraction of the two people involved. Where child betrothal is practiced, first marriages are often unstable. Any one person may go through several unsuccessful marriages before settling into a stable union. In Friedl's first two patterns, where division of labor is minimal and where men and women hunt together collectively, lack of male control over food supplies may be reflected in lack of male control over women.[49] Marriages are freely made by the couples involved without elaborate exchanges of property in the form of bride-price or dowries. Marriages end whenever either spouse decides to separate. There is little or no sexual double standard in these societies.

In pattern three where men hunt and women gather, a skilled hunter makes a more desirable husband than an unskilled hunter. Friedl notes that with this type of division of labor, meat can be exchanged for women. This is clearly reflected in customs requiring that the husband perform *groom service* in the form of hunting for the bride's parents often for a period of several years in exchange for the right to marry the woman. However, the skilled hunter may have a marriage advantage even in pattern one. Woodburn notes that among the Hadza, there is little pressure put on men by other men to hunt and a few do not hunt at all. Although poor hunters or nonhunters do not suffer a loss of status among males, they do have difficulty obtaining and keeping wives, who generally prefer marriage to good hunters.[50] However, since gathering is likely to produce a more predictable product, a particularly skilled gatherer is not as advantaged in the marriage market.

In pattern four, where men hunt and gathering is insignificant, the skilled hunter is definitely a desirable husband. In pattern five, among the Tiwi, men desire any female as a wife. With the practice of infant betrothal, females have no choice in marriage partners, but they do have a choice of lovers. Because marriage contracts are a source of prestige for males, the mutual attraction of the partners is not an important consideration. However, the fathers betrothing their daughters prefer more prestigious and influential sons-in-law and therefore are likely to give preference to skilled hunters in deciding upon whom to confer their daughters. Moreover, women can exert considerable influence over the choice of their subsequent husbands and are likely to prefer a man who can provide them with the luxury of crocodiles and turtles.

Divorce is easy in all but pattern five. A marriage ends whenever the couple stops living together. Women as well as men can initiate the separation. Children usually remain with their mother, but there is little or no other property to divide. This reflects the general pattern of a high degree of personal autonomy and individualism in hunting and gathering societies.

Relations between the Sexes

The relations between the sexes are highly egalitarian in hunting and gathering societies. But this does not preclude the possibility of arguments and physical fights between males and females, especially between spouses. Fighting is generally disapproved of in foraging societies, but this does not altogether prevent it. However, other camp members usually interrupt the battle and force the participants to quiet down before they become dangerous. The lack of privacy in these camps allows for public control over private disputes.

Wife beating is uncommon in most hunting and gathering societies, but Turnbull notes that he witnessed physical attacks by women on men as well as by men on women among the Pygmies.[51] However, wife beating is not an uncommon method of controlling wives among the Eskimos,[52] reflecting again the greater sexual inequality among Eskimos than among other foragers. Friedl also notes that the chief cleavage among the Hadza is between the sexes.[53] Females ridicule husbands who cannot keep them supplied with meat or desirable trade goods. However, despite these disputes, hunters and gatherers exhibit more relaxed, easygoing relations between males and females than are found in many horticultural, agricultural, or industrial societies.

Sexuality

Foraging societies tend to be sexually permissive. However, foragers with patrilineal descent systems and patrilocal residence place greater importance on premarital virginity and exert greater control over the young girl's sexual behavior than do foragers with bilateral or matrilineal descent systems.[54] Adultery is not strongly tabooed among most hunters and gatherers whatever their descent systems. Among the Tiwi, for example, extramarital affairs are fairly common, although the husband and sometimes the wife's kin express disapproval: The husband cannot physically abuse his wife for infidelity, but he is allowed to attack her lover.[55]

Extramarital sexuality is a source of great jealousy among the Eskimo and both wives and husbands are quick to suspect their spouses. However, this jealousy exists alongside the practice of sharing or swapping spouses which requires the mutual approval of all participating parties and serves to establish close kinship-like ties among the non-kin involved. As Leacock points out, it is highly ethnocentric to view this as evidence of a low status for women in Eskimo society. Such a view "presumes that a woman does not (since she should not) enjoy sex play with any but her 'real' husband and . . . refuses to recognize that variety in sex relations is entertaining to women (where not circumscribed by all manner of taboos) as well as to men.[56]

Sexual permissiveness is also usually extended to children and adolescents. Among the !Kung Bushmen, for example, sexual awareness begins at a very early age. The lack of privacy in hunting and gathering society often means that children are exposed to adult sexual behavior throughout childhood. Marjorie Shostak found that childhood sex play is common and even includes sexual intercourse. "Parents say they do not approve of this among young and adolescent children . . . . But the parents played this way when they were children and, although they usually deny it, they know their children are playing the same way. As long as it is done away from adults, children are not prevented from participating in experimental sexual play." [57]

Child Rearing

Child rearing practices among hunting and gathering peoples reflect the egalitarian social structure of these societies. Children are reared to be cooperative, generous, peaceful and unassuming, but independent and self-reliant adults. The noncoercive, nonauthoritarian social structure is supported by noncoercive, nonauthoritarian adult–child relations. Adults seem to have infinite patience in dealing with the children of the camp.

Patricia Draper describes one example of this patience among the !Kung Bushmen:

> One afternoon I watched for 2 hours while a father hammered and shaped the metal for several arrow points. During this period his son and grandson (both under 4 years old) jostled him, sat on his legs, and attempted to pull the arrowheads from under the hammer. When the boys' fingers came close to the point of impact, he merely waited until the small hands were a little farther away before he resumed hammering. Although the man remonstrated with the boys (about once every 3 minutes), he did not become cross or chase the boys off; and they did not heed his warnings to quit interfering. Eventually, perhaps 50 minutes later, the boys moved off a few steps to join some teenagers lying in the shade.[58]

Eskimos are well known for their indulgence of children: "I have seen children being allowed to leave and enter a snowhouse four or five times in the course of an hour even though closing and opening the door has a considerable cooling effect in the house. The mother patiently dresses and undresses the child as often as he wishes in these cases.[59]

Obedience is not stressed by forager parents and physical punishments are not used in most foraging societies. Westerners are often shocked by the lack of respect shown parents and other adults by these children. Self-reliance, rather than obedience to authority, is stressed for both girls and boys. The independence allowed even young children is almost unimaginable to Westerners. Shostak concludes from her study of childhood among the !Kung Bushmen that children learn early to assert themselves against the authority of their parents and other adults: "Individualism is encouraged and strict obedience of parental authority is considered neither necessary nor desirable." [60]

Goodale's description of childhood among the Tiwi is vivid on the issue of child independence. Goodale observed two- and three-year-old girls building fires without eliciting any parental concern. Parents do not even tell the children to be careful. The basic principle informing their childrearing practices is that experience is the best teacher. Children's activities are interrupted by adults only if they endanger a younger child who cannot protect itself. Goodale relates the following incident as illustrative of parental acceptance of childhood independence: While a group of Tiwi adults were playing cards, two young girls, Althea and Dennis, and Dennis' younger brother, played around the adults.

> They repeatedly got into fights, but only when the wrangle became serious were they separated. The children received no words of reproach, nor was a hand laid on them, even when they eventually became "cheeky" and rolled about on their mother's laps, kicking sand in the cardplayers' faces and grabbing cards. Then

Dennis "borrowed" a large hunting knife and began swinging it around jabbing at her much younger brother. One of the men took the knife away, whereupon Dennis went into a minor tantrum and the knife was given back to her. She then began to hit herself on the head with the knife and went into a long verbal tirade that sent the adults into roars of laughter. After quite some time the knife was again taken from her and thrown into some dense bushes where she was unable to find it.[61]

The techniques most often employed by hunting and gathering parents to deal with dangerous aggressive behavior in their children is to interrupt the behavior and divert the child's attention elsewhere.

Goodale also describes the remarkable skills as well as independence of two seven- or eight-year-old girls who built a large paperbark raft from bark they cut from trees themselves. Goodale and the two girls spent the day cruising the swamp near the camp. The girls dove into the swamp for plant foods, eggs, and flowers. "Many days later someone mentioned that large crocodiles are quite apt to sleep in [that swamp] . . . and I marveled at the extent of the parents' belief in experience being the best teacher. I asked the girls if they had known about the crocodiles. 'Oh yes,' they said, 'that's why we get on canoe. When no more sun, can't see crocodiles.' "[62]

Along with independence, generosity is another important value stressed in foragers' child-rearing practices. "!Kung children are encouraged to share things from infancy, because exchanging food and possessions is so basic to adult social interactions. Among the first words a child learns is 'na' ('give it to me') and 'i' ('here, take this'). This type of socialization is hard for children, especially when they are expected to share with someone they resent or dislike."[63]

Males as well as females care for children even if the stereotypic ideal of the society is that females care for the children. Leacock notes that among Naskapi Eskimos child care is considered woman's work but their practices are actually flexible.

For the greater part of one day a man sat patiently, lovingly crooning over his sickly and fretful infant of but a few weeks old. His wife was busy. Though worried for the baby's health, he appeared in no way inept or harassed by his responsibility, nor did he call on another woman around the camp for help . . . . This was his task while his wife tanned a caribou skin, a skilled and arduous job that demanded her complete attention. The men knew how to cook and tend the babies when called upon to do so, but did not really know how to tan leather.[64]

Silberbauer also found that among the G/Wi Bushmen both males and females aid in infant and child care and that "men and boys show the same fondness for babies as do women and girls."[65] Whoever is left in camp, male or female, cares for the children. The entire G/Wi camp shares the economic and socialization responsibilities for the children. Any adult is expected to instruct children in toilet training if the occasion arises and to correct them if they misbehave.

Infants receive a great deal of attention and physical contact among the !Kung Bushmen. Not only do !Kung mothers spend significantly more time in physical contact with their infants than do English or American mothers, but !Kung infants also have more social contact with other people.[66] Among hunters and gatherers, infants are nursed on demand and are rarely allowed to cry unattended.

Forager children spend little time with children their own age. Since camps are always small, it is unlikely that there will be many children of the same age in camp. Play groups, therefore, are made up of children of varying ages. Draper notes that this limits the possibility for competitive games and team sports: "The players are at such different levels of motor skill, motivation, and cognitive development that it is difficult and unrewarding to play a game involving intense competition, rules, and fairly complex strategy."[67] The games hunting and gathering children play therefore do not encourage aggressive competition, but rather they encourage individual development and the acceptance of individual differences in skill and motivation.

Not only are children not age-segregated among themselves, but they are not segregated from adults either. Among the !Kung

> the relationship between children and adults is easygoing and unselfconscious. Adults do not believe that children should keep to themselves . . . . The organization of work, leisure, and living space is such that there is no reason for confining children or excluding them from certain activities. Everyone lives on the flat surface of the ground; hence there is no need to protect children from falls or from becoming entrapped behind doors. With the exception of spears and poisoned arrows, adult tools do not constitute a hazard to children. Those weapons are simply kept hanging in trees or wedged on top of a hut, safely out of reach.[68]

!Kung children observe adult work activities but they do not actively participate in them. Girls do not begin regular food-gathering activities until they are about fourteen years old and boys do not begin serious hunting until they are about sixteen. Draper maintains that because the !Kung can feed themselves easily without child labor, they do not train or expect their children to be economically self-sufficient.[69]

Gender Role Distinctions. Although there is little sex segregation among hunting and gathering children, gender role distinctions are recognized and encouraged. Although a great many unisex activities take place in childhood, girls do come to excel in the society's "female activities" and boys focus more of their attention on mastering "male activities." Chance indicates that among the Eskimos

> Regardless of sex, it is important for a child to know how to perform a wide variety of tasks and give help when needed. Both sexes collect and chop wood, get water, help carry meat and other supplies, oversee younger siblings, run errands for adults, feed the dogs, and burn trash.
>
> As a child grows older, more specific responsibilities are allocated to him, according to his sex. Boys as young as seven may be given an opportunity to shoot a .22 rifle and at least a few boys in every village have killed their first caribou by the time they are ten.[70]

Chance further emphasizes the flexibility of Eskimo gender role socialization into sexual division of labor:

> Although there is a recognized division of labor by sex, it is far from rigid at any age level. Boys, and even men occasionally sweep the house and cook. Girls and their mothers go on fishing or bird-hunting trips. Members of each sex can usually assume the responsibilities of the other when the need arises, albeit in an auxiliary capacity.[71]

Among the Bushmen, girls learn the skills of gathering by accompanying their mothers on foraging expeditions and further their socialization into adult womanhood by listening to the uninhibited gossip of the women in the foraging group. Boys learn hunting skills largely through games and listening to the hunters talk of the day's activities. Since youngsters are more likely to be disruptive of a hunt than a foraging party, boys are usually older than girls before they can begin taking part in the adult food getting activities.[72]

Friedl argues that childrearing patterns tend to vary according to the work women perform in a particular social group.[73] Instead of viewing the problem from the standpoint that women's work is adjusted to the requirements of child care as Judith Brown does,[74] Friedl argues that child care requirements are adjusted to the work women do. From Friedl's perspective, then, foraging activities of women in most hunting and gathering societies require such institutions as multiple-child-caretakers and campwide sharing of some child-care responsibilities.

RELIGION AND RITUAL

Most foragers have rituals associated with maleness and femaleness. Females usually undergo some type of ceremony at menarche (onset of menstruation), and males generally undergo a rite of passage into adulthood often associated with their first kill. However, the ceremonial and ritual life of foragers does not typically emphasize male dominance and female subordination as occurs in many horticultural and agricultural societies.

Males and females participate fairly equally in the religious and ritual aspects of their cultures. There is some separation of the sexes, but this entails the exclusion of males from female rites almost as often as the exclusion of females from male rites. Among the Pygmies, for example, females are not supposed to know about the sacred *molimo* (a musical instrument) or any of the songs sung at male ceremonies. But Turnbull found that in mixed-sex ceremonies and female ceremonies the females sang the same lyrics and seemed to understand the *molimo*.[75]

In general, foragers' religions show few similarities with the major religions that developed in patriarchal agricultural societies, such as Judaism, Islam, and Confucianism. Foragers' religions do not denigrate women or exalt the power of fathers or of men in general. They reflect the basic egalitarianism of the hunting and gathering way of life and emphasize the people's relationship to, dependence on, and respect for nature.

FORCES FOR CHANGE

Hunting and gathering societies are remarkably stable. Because of their egalitarian, nonacquisitive, non-property-oriented natures, there are few forces for change within these societies. Their noncoercive mechanisms of conflict resolution (gossip, ridicule, group intervention in private disputes, and simply moving to another camp when disputes arise) prevent the formation of important cleavages and militate against the concentration of power in the hands of any individual or group. Their technology affords the people subsistence without disruption of the environment. Hunters and gatherers generally find their life-style satisfying and are usually unwilling to abandon it permanently unless forced to do so by external circumstances. Turnbull, for example, found that Pygmies regularly move into the Bantu horticulturalists' villages and partake of the luxuries available there. But they soon return to their life in the forest.[76]

The foraging way of life is, however, rapidly disappearing in the contemporary world, not because it is not a viable way of life, but because of the encroachments of more technologically advanced peoples onto the lands occupied by the foragers. National governmental policies in countries containing hunters and gatherers are often aimed at destroying the foraging way of life and at incorporating these peoples into modern society. The results are usually disastrous for the foragers. Their death rates often soar when they are forced into permanent settlements, and the culture and social structure of those who survive cannot be maintained in a sedentary way of life. Unfortunately, one of the consequences of the transition to a settled life is an increase in sexual inequality and the physical abuse of women. Draper's comparison of a traditional nomadic foraging camp of !Kung Bushmen with a group of !Kung living in a permanent village setting is sobering in its implications for !Kung women.[77] She found that a high degree of sexual egalitarianism and personal autonomy for women still prevails among the foraging !Kung. However, in the sedentary context women lost a good deal of their autonomy and their influence over group affairs. Draper found that in the village context a more rigid sexual division of labor developed and that the socialization of boys and girls became more dissimilar. There was a decrease in the mobility of women as compared with men and an increase in male control over important economic resources such as domestic animals. Males, but not females, entered into public politics. Households became more private resulting in a decrease in public control over private disputes which allowed an increase in wife-beating. As Engels suggested, the shift to animal husbandry and crop planting required by life in permanent settlements appears to undermine sexual egalitarianism. As foragers become extinct these examples of male–female relations will probably disappear also.

SUMMARY

Hunting and gathering societies are small-scale, simple, nomadic, kinship-based societies that gain their subsistence through hunting, fishing, and gathering of wild foodstuffs. They produce little or no surplus and have little private property. They are highly egalitarian, having neither social classes nor rulers, and their egalitarianism extends to gender roles. There is a division of labor by sex, but no sexual stratification. Men can, however, gain greater prestige and a limited degree of superiority through their participation in meat-sharing networks. Hunting is usually less predictable than gathering and meat is more scarce than vegetable foods. Thus, to the degree that hunting is a male specialty, it may be used to gain greater power and prestige for males.

Five patterns can be discerned in the sexual division of labor among foragers. Each pattern has different implications for sexual inequality. Where men and women gather and men hunt, the sexes are fairly equal because of the high degree of economic independence of the sexes. There is also a high degree of equality where both men and women participate in communal hunting and gathering. The equality in this situation results from the interdependence of the sexes in subsistence pursuits. Where males hunt and females gather, the sexes are interdependent, but males have a slight edge as providers of the more desirable meat. In societies with little or no gathering, males hunt and females process their catch. Females are more economically dependent in this situation and this results in a higher degree of sexual inequality than is found in the other patterns. Where women hunt and gather and men hunt other species and fish, women are not dependent on men for subsistence and sexual inequality is minimal.

Among foragers marriage is usually contracted by free choice. It is based on mutual attraction and is easily dissolved. Relations between the sexes are highly egalitarian with little wife beating. Foragers are sexually permissive but jealousy is common. Child rearing practices emphasize personal autonomy and independence along with cooperativeness and generosity. Obedience and respect for parents are not encouraged. Gender role differences in socialization are not usually marked. Religion and ritual usually include both sexes and recognize the life experiences of males and females.

Hunting and gathering societies are very stable and provide a satisfying life for their members. However, they are subject to disruption by more technologically advanced societies. Changes toward a more settled, technologically advanced way of life usually entail a loss in personal autonomy and status for women relative to men.

Notes

1. Andrew P. Vayda, "Introduction," in Vayda, ed., *Environment and Cultural Behavior* (Garden City, N. Y.: The Natural History Press, 1969), pp. xi–xvii. For an excellent example of this type of analysis see C. Daryll Fords, *Habitat, Economy, and Society* (New York: Dutton, 1963).
2. Colin Turnbull, *The Forest People* (New York: Simon and Schuster, 1962), p. 23.
3. Richard Lee, "!Kung Bushman Subsistence: An Input-Output Analysis," in Vayda, p. 58.
4. Such popular writers include Robert Ardrey, *African Genesis* (London: Collins, 1966); Konrad Lorenz, *On Aggression* (New York: Oxford, 1966); Lionel Tiger, *Men in Groups* (New York: Vintage, 1970); Lionel Tiger and Robin Fox, *The Imperial Animal* (New York: Holt, Rinehart, Winston, 1971).
5. Marvin Harris, *Culture, People, Nature* (2nd ed., New York: Thomas Y. Crowell, 1975), p. 260.
6. Harris, p. 339.
7. Turnbull, pp. 25–26, 120–126.
8. Marvin Harris, *Culture, Man, Nature* (New York: Thomas Y. Crowell, 1971), p. 300.
9. Paula Weideger, *Menstruation and Menopause* (New York: Delta, 1977), pp. 4–41.
10. Ernestine Friedl, *Women and Men* (New York: Holt, Rinehart and Winston, 1975), pp. 16–18; and "Society and Sex Roles," *Human Nature*, 1:(April, 1978), 68–75.

11. George Silberbauer, "The G/wi Bushmen," in M. G. Bicchieri, ed., *Hunters and Gatherers Today* (New York: Holt, Rinehart and Winston, 1972), p. 304.
12. Friedl, 1978, p. 71.
13. Friedl, 1975, pp. 12–45.
14. James Woodburn, "An Introduction to Hadza Ecology," pp. 49–55, and "Stability and Flexibility in Hadza Residential Groupings," pp. 103–111, in Richard Lee and Irven DeVore, ed., *Man the Hunter* (Chicago: Aldine, 1968).
15. Elizabeth Marshall Thomas, *The Harmless People* (New York: Vintage, 1959).
16. Theorists such as Tiger and Fox who place tremendous evolutionary importance on the development of male/bonding in the collective hunt may have exaggerated its importance among early human beings. They based their observations on current hunters and gatherers' adaptations to life in poor habitats. We can probably assume that paleolithic foragers would have had access to the more fertile areas now under the control of more complex societies who have destroyed their usefulness to foragers.
17. Woodburn, p. 52.
18. Friedl, 1978, p. 73.
19. Turnbull, p. 154.
20. Turnbull, p. 206.
21. Turnbull, p. 110.
22. Friedl, 1978, p. 73.
23. James F. Downs, *The Two Worlds of the Washo* (New York: Holt, Rinehart and Winston, 1966), p. 18.
24. Downs, p. 21.
25. Downs, p. 22.
26. Downs, p. 26.
27. Downs, p. 36.
28. Downs, p. 36.
29. Downs, p. 51.
30. Friedl, 1975, p. 36.
31. Norman Chance, *The Eskimo of North Alaska* (New York: Holt, Rinehart, and Winston, 1966), p. 48.
32. Chance, p. 52.
33. Chance, p. 51.
34. Jean Briggs, "Eskimo Women: Makers of Men," in Carolyn J. Matthiasson, ed., *Many Sisters: Women in Cross-Cultural Perspective* (New York: Free Press, 1974), pp. 262–265.
35. Chance, pp. 37, 40.
36. Briggs, pp. 285–289.
37. Chance, p. 73.
38. Briggs, p. 276.
39. Friedl, 1975, p. 42.
40. Friedl, 1978, p. 74.
41. Briggs, pp. 299–300; Eleanor Leacock, "Introduction," in Frederick Engels, *The Origin of the Family, Private Property and the State* (New York: International Publishers, 1972).
42. Jane Goodale, *Tiwi Wives* (Seattle: University of Washington, 1971), p. 169.
43. Goodale, p. 154.
44. Goodale, pp. 170–171.
45. C. W. Hart and Arnold Pilling, *The Tiwi of North Australia* (New York: Holt, Rinehart and Winston, 1964).
46. Goodale, pp. 126–127.

47. Goodale, pp. 228–229.
48. Frederick G. G. Rose, "Australian Marriage, Land-Owning Groups, and Initiations," in Richard B. Lee and Irven DeVore, ed., *Man the Hunter* (Chicago: Aldine, 1968), p. 206.
49. Friedl, 1975, p. 24.
50. Woodburn, p. 54.
51. Turnbull, pp. 120–125.
52. Peter Freuchen, *Peter Freuchen's Book of the Eskimos* (New York: World Publishing, 1961), p. 171.
53. Friedl, 1975, p. 34.
54. M. Kay Martin and Barbara Voorhies, *Female of the Species* (New York: Columbia U. Press, 1975), p. 188.
55. Goodale, p. 131.
56. Leacock, p. 21.
57. Marjorie Shostak, "A !Kung Woman's Memories of Childhood," in Richard Lee and Irven DeVore, eds., *Kalahari Hunter-Gatherers* (Cambridge, Mass.: Harvard U. Press, 1976), pp. 266–267.
58. Patricia Draper, "Social and Economic Constraints on Child Life among the !Kung," in Lee and DeVore, p. 206.
59. David Damas, "The Copper Eskimo," in Bicchieri, p. 41.
60. Shostak, p. 276.
61. Goodale, p. 36.
62. Goodale, p. 40.
63. Shostak, p. 256.
64. Leacock, p. 39.
65. Silberbauer, p. 314.
66. Melvin Konner, "Maternal Care, Infant Behavior and Development among the !Kung," in Lee and DeVore, 1976, p. 228.
67. Draper, p. 203.
68. Draper, p. 205.
69. Draper, p. 210.
70. Chance, p. 25.
71. Chance, p. 26.
72. Silberbauer, pp. 315–316.
73. Friedl, 1975, p. 8.
74. Judith Brown, "A Note on the Division of Labor by Sex," *American Anthropologist,* 5 (Sept.–Oct., 1970), 1073–1078.
75. Turnbull, pp. 145–160.
76. Turnbull, p. 26.
77. Patricia Draper, "!Kung Women: Contrasts in Sexual Egalitarianism in Foraging and Sedentary Contexts," in Rayna Reiter, ed., *Toward an Anthropology of Women* (New York: Monthly Review, 1975), pp. 77–109.

4

Horticultural Societies

Each sex is a social entity, each has its own internal organization, and each has its sense of solidarity and a consciousness of its own unity and its opposition to the other. The battle of the sexes is not carried on by individual gladiators, as in our society, but by armies.

Yolanda Murphy and Robert Murphy, *Women of the Forest*

Chapter 3 described the positions of women and men in simple hunting and gathering societies. In the evolution of human societies one of the patterns which developed out of the hunting and gathering way of life was *horticulture* or simple digging-stick and hoe agriculture. Early human beings in different parts of the world discovered that plants and animals could be domesticated. That is, they learned to produce their own food instead of depending on nature to provide it to the diligent and skilled forager. These technological advances, although gradual in development and effects, eventually resulted in the evolution of very different types of social structures and cultures. These changes, of course, included significant changes in gender roles and the development of sexual stratification systems.

ECONOMY AND SOCIAL ORGANIZATION

Simple Horticulture.   First and foremost, horticulture requires knowledge of the principles of plant cultivation. Simple horticultural societies practice the *slash-and-burn* or *swidden* method of cultivation. This involves felling the trees, cutting away the underbrush of forest lands, and then burning the dried plant growth. The ashes from the burning process provide necessary fertilizer. The gardens are then planted with the aid of simple wooden digging sticks which do not allow for the soil to be turned to any depth. Depending on the original fertility of the soil, the land can be used for only a few years at most. It is then abandoned for many years, allowing the forest to retake the land and restore its fertility for future slash-and-burn use. Horticulture may be combined with hunting, gathering, fishing, or herding to increase the overall productivity of the group.

In horticultural society, uncleared land is usually available to anyone who wants to clear it and cleared land is usually held communally by extended family groups. Land is a vital resource among horticulturalists, but it usually does not constitute individually owned private property. However, both cleared and uncleared land can represent a scarce resource to be exchanged, stolen, or attacked.

Perhaps the most significant result of horticultural technology as compared with foraging technology is that it allows for the production of a surplus. Horticulturalists have exchangeable forms of wealth in the form of productive garden land, stored food, and domesticated animals. Since they are less mobile than hunters and gatherers, they can also accumulate more and bulkier household goods and personal possessions. Production continues to be primarily for use value. Exchange within kinship groups, villages, and neighborhoods tends to remain *reciprocity based* and not *market oriented.* However, the surplus does allow for the development of trade networks and market relationships between different groups.

Advanced Horticulture. Productivity is often vastly increased in advanced horticultural societies through the knowledge of metallurgy and the development of metal tipped hoes. These permit the farmers to turn the soil to greater depths and thereby increase its productivity and extend its period of fertility. This same technological advance also allows for the production of better weapons and a resulting increase in both the amount and potential effectiveness of warfare. The surpluses in advanced horticultural societies have sometimes been vast, both because of the societies' increased productivity and because of the spoils of war in the form of booty and slave labor.

Community Size and Social Structure

Horticultural technology allows for more permanent, larger, denser populations and for more complex social and political structures than are found among foragers. The production of crops requires a more sedentary life style. Simple horticulturalists may move every several years, more advanced horticulturalists may move only once a generation. Some become productive enough to establish permanent towns and urban settlements. While the median size of communities among hunting and gathering societies is forty persons, it is ninety-five among simple horticulturalists and 280 for advanced horticulturalists.[1]

The society size among hunters and gatherers and simple horticulturalists is the same as their community size because they do not usually have extra-community political organization of any significance. However, advanced horticultural societies often have complex political structures that tie different communities into a wider society network. This gives rise to a median society size of 5,800 persons with some having populations of 20,000 or more.[2]

Leadership and Social Inequality

Simple horticultural societies tend to be highly egalitarian. Their leaders typically have no coercive powers over others. Like headmen among foragers, they can only attempt to cajole, persuade, or embarrass others to do their will. Class inequality does not exist among simple horticulturalists. Access to food, land, and other material resources is egalitarian and the actual distribution of the products of the society is fairly equal. Significant differences in wealth and power do not occur. But in comparison with foraging societies, considerable competition exists and results in vast differences in prestige. Prestige is gained much as it is among hunters and gatherers, through generosity—the ability to give to others and thereby to incur their debt. However, unlike among foragers, boastfulness and overt competition accompany the gift-giving process among horticulturalists. Givers of feasts, for example, openly praise the abundance and quality of the food they offer and denigrate past feasts given by others. The ability to organize kin to produce food for a large feast confers prestige and the status of "big man" on the organizer. This is often a highly coveted status for men. It does not translate into greater consumption rights or differences in economic power for the big man. He gains prestige and influence but not coercive economic or political power. Such a position is also not hereditary; it must be achieved by each individual who aspires to "big man" status.

Advanced horticultural societies often exhibit hereditary class inequality, slavery, and hereditary leadership positions. A noble class of warriors can often exempt itself from productive labor and exact tribute from the commoner (non-noble) and slave classes. Some advanced horticulturalists such as the Incans and Mayans of South and Central America controlled vast empires of conquered peoples. This requires, of course, a large and complex, multilayered political and military structure. These peoples are much less likely to practice village autonomy than simple horticulturalists. Furthermore, those that do develop multicommunity governmental structures tend to develop absolutist monarchies with powerful kings, queens, and court members. Upper class women exercise power over common males by virtue of their class position although they do not have power over males of equal or higher rank.

SEXUAL DIVISION OF LABOR

There are three main patterns in the sexual division of labor among horticulturalists. Among all horticulturalists the task of clearing the land is assigned to men. This is probably due to the strenuous nature of the work involved in felling trees and clearing underbrush, which is highly incompatible with pregnancy and the care of small children. Ernestine Friedl argues, however, that it probably originated in needs for defense and fighting to obtain new land and in the opportunities for hunting provided by the uncleared territory.[3] After garden areas have been cleared, Friedl holds that there are no consistent adaptive advantages to having either males or females perform the planting, weeding, and harvesting tasks. Pregnancy and child tending do not significantly hinder women in this work except (as among the Yanamanö discussed later) where there is danger of attack. This is fairly rare, however, and the pattern of men clearing and cultivating is relatively rare among horticulturalists. Friedl notes that the Hopi as well as the Yanamamö practice this pattern.[4] Hopi cultivation entails an easy clearing process but strenuous irrigation projects. Hopi women tend small vegetable gardens instead of assisting in the production of the staple crops.

Ester Boserup states that predominantly male cultivation patterns are associated with increasing population density and scarcity of land.[5] If a group cannot easily abandon a used garden plot for a new one, the land will require more work to maintain its fertility. The increased labor input necessary may force men to help with cultivation tasks previously left only to women. Increased population density also increases the danger of raiding and makes it more difficult for women to tend the gardens without male protection.

Two other patterns are more common among horticulturalists: men clear and women cultivate, and men clear and both sexes cultivate. The Iroquois Indians practiced the "men clear, women cultivate" pattern and, as will be discussed later, this was associated with high status and important economic control by women. "Men clear and both sexes cultivate" is a very common pattern. Sometimes it involves women cultivating "women's crops" and men cultivating "men's crops." This is particularly true in areas such as highland New Guinea where men raise prestige crops for exchange value while women raise the staple crops for domestic use value. This of course gives men the advantage of participating in reciprocity networks and offers them opportunity of gaining power and prestige through these exchanges. Among other peoples both men and women raise the same crops. In West Africa it is common for both men and women to cultivate both staples for use value and prestige crops for exchange value. Female trading has been an important phenomenon in Africa for raising the status of women and giving them the economic basis to exercise power and personal autonomy.

Female Trading

In advanced horticultural societies in West Africa with well developed market systems, females handle a large share of the trading.[6] Boserup argues that this probably results from female farming systems that gave women control over the products they produce. Thus when markets arose women had products to exchange. She finds that in Africa, in regions of female farming women dominate market trade, while in regions of male farming men dominate trade. She finds that this even overrides the influ-

ence of the Moslem religion which forbids women taking public roles in the
market place as either buyers or sellers. This religious teaching is not
obeyed by Moslem female farmers in countries such as Senegal and the
Sudan.

Women rarely become wealthy or powerful as traders in advanced
horticultural societies, but trading does give them a basis for greater power
in their marital relationship and greater personal autonomy. Since the
husband usually benefits economically from his wife's trading, he is not as
likely to interfere with her use of her profits as he would be with a working
wife's salary. He fears hurting her profits in the long run by interfering in
the short run.[7]

Sidney Mintz also points out that women's trading often allows them
to travel widely, to hire others to care for their children and households,
and even to use their profits to aid their husbands in obtaining a second
wife to assume much of the domestic work load. These women traders are
not isolated in the domestic sphere; they are active participants in the
public economic spheres of their societies. The extent of their commitment
to and participation in their public economic roles was evidenced in the
Women's Riot of 1929–1930 in Nigeria. The colonial government of Britain successfully levied a tax on men in 1926. However, when they attempted to extend the tax to women in 1929, women spread the news
through their market place connections and "rose like an army in massive
protest against this injustice, looting European trading stores and banks,
breaking into prisons to release prisoners, and beating chiefs and court
messengers." [8] The men had not reacted in such an organized political
manner in defense of their interests.

Sex Segregation in Division of Labor

Extreme sex segregation is a striking characteristic of the division of
labor in many horticultural societies and is often reflected in the entire life
of the society. It is not uncommon for women and men to lead almost
separate lives. An example of this is provided by the Mundurucu of Brazil.[9]
Men work continuously in collective groups clearing new land for gardens.
They also hunt in large groups. Women work communally in the gardens
as the primary cultivators, as gatherers, and in the onerous, time-
consuming task of processing the manioc roots into flour. The work and
the worlds of men and women are largely separate. The men live in the
men's house where they eat, sleep, and practice male rituals. Women and
children live in separate houses. Husbands and wives do not sleep together
in this society.

FAMILY AND KINSHIP

Because the technology of horticulture usually requires some collective work effort and often collective defense efforts as well, horticultural societies have tended to develop kinship systems to help them organize to solve these problems. Therefore, horticultural peoples are more likely to have *unilineal descent groups* which jointly hold interests in property and people. As was noted in Chapter 3, foragers are likely to be *bilateral* in their descent reckoning, that is, they recognize kinship ties evenly and symmetrically through both the father's and mother's line. This is functional for hunters and gatherers because it allows them to draw upon the widest possible kin network during times of need. However, it is not a useful system for developing and maintaining corporate ownership of land and other resources. A bilateral system has no logical stopping point and each person has a unique *kindred* or set of kinsmen. For example, a daughter includes all her father's and mother's kindred in her kindred. However, her kindred differs from her mother's which does not include descent lines through the father's kindred (although they are tied by *affinity* or marriage). And it differs from her father's kindred which does not include her mother's descent line. Thus, a bilateral system does not produce a definite, non-egocentered group of people who could live, work, and own property together.[10]

One way a people can define kinship in order to produce a series of such definite, nonoverlapping, corporate kinship groups is to exclude systematically at each generation either the mother's or the father's line. A system which excludes female generational links is called *patrilineal*. Patrilineality involves tracing descent solely through the male line. Systems which exclude male generational lines are called *matrilineal* and trace descent solely through the female line.

The Matrilineality Puzzle

The existence of matrilineal descent systems was considered a puzzle by early Western social scientists. Western kinship systems, although primarily bilateral, exhibit strong strains of patrilineality in naming, inheritance, and in forming one's identity. This seemed only "natural" to early social scientists. They saw no need for explaining *patrilineality,* but they considered the existence of *matrilineality* to be a perplexing question. One of their incorrect assumptions about matrilineality was that it indicated that such societies were also *matriarchies:* that is, they assumed that matrilineal peoples would be ruled by women and practice male subordination. This is not the case, however. Although matrilineality has important consequences for women and can afford them greater power, influence, and personal autonomy than patrilineality, it has not given rise in any known societies to matriarchy. Patrilineality is, however, sometimes associated with patriarchy. Furthermore, from the standpoint of scientific theory both matrilineality and patrilineality need explaining. We cannot assume that one is "natural."

In searching for the causes of these different descent systems, it has been noted that matrilineality is more common among horticulturalists than among any other types of societies. Only 10 percent of hunting and gathering societies practice matrilineality, along with only four percent of agrarian societies and virtually no industrial societies. However, 26 percent of simple horticultural societies and 27 percent of advanced horticultural societies have matrilineal kin groups.[11]

Attempts to explain why some societies, especially horticultural societies, exhibit matrilineality, have often focused on the female economic contribution to the society. There is some connection between this factor and matrilineality, but it does not appear to be the important causal variable. Matrilineality is not likely to develop in societies where males make the primary economic contributions. But where females are the primary producers or at least equal contributors with males both patrilineality and matrilineality are found.[12]

Harris argues convincingly that it is not female economic contribution that is important so much as it is the existence of factors requiring males to be absent from the community for long periods of time such as for long distance trade, work or external warfare. Patrilineality and *patrilocality* (the new couple resides with the husband's father's household) serve to keep men from the same kinship group together and to bring in wives from other patrilineages. These women have not been reared together and are not accustomed to working together in collective enterprises. They often compete with one another for resources from their husbands' patrilineage. They may not develop strong allegiance to the husbands' group. Harris notes that this creates a problem of who will look after the kin group's property and interests while the males are away.

> Matrilocality solves this problem because it structures the domestic unit around a permanent core of resident mothers, daughters and sisters who are trained in cooperative labor patterns from birth and who identify the "minding of the store" with their own material and sentimental interests.[13]

Matrilocality refers to the new couple residing with the wife's mother's household. If male absence encourages matrilocality, in the long run matrilocality is likely to give rise to matrilineality because descent systems usually reflect, legitimate, and regulate actual kinship-related practices.[14]

Furthermore, matrilineality appears to be undermined by *population pressure* and *internal warfare* which give the adaptive advantage to groups which concentrate male fighting strength (see the discussion of the effects of the warfare complex in Chapter 2). Elaborating upon this, M. Kay Martin and Barbara Voorheis point out that

> matrilineal horticultural societies . . . seem to be adaptive in habitats that allow considerable *stability* in human organization . . . . Matriliny is ideally an *open* system, this disperses rather than consolidates its potential sources of power—its men. Such an adaptation seems to arise where resources are equal to or exceed those required to accommodate the needs of extant populations, and where competition between communities in the same niche is absent or infrequent.[15]

Matrilineal societies, therefore, tend to be internally peaceful. If this internal peace is regularly disrupted by defense needs generated by increased local competition over scarce resources, the society is likely eventually to transform its descent system to patrilineality. A transitional form which retains matrilineal descent but concentrates the male power of the matrilineage involves *avunculocal residence.* That is, the new couple moves in not with the wife's mother but with the wife's maternal uncle. The maternal uncle or mother's brother occupies a position similar to that of the father in a patrilineal system.

Effects of Matrilineality on Gender Roles

Apart from their origins or causes, matrilineality and matrilocality are of importance here because of the effects they have on the positions of women and men who practice such *matricentric* (using matrilineality and/or matrilocality) kinship and residence systems. First, since they divide the male fighting force, they promote peace and stability instead of competition and feuding. They are not likely to be associated with the *warfare complex* and the denigration of women that that involves. Second, since they often promote or facilitate female collective work, ownership, and residence patterns, they promote *female solidarity,* which tends to increase female power in a society. With matrilocality, mothers, daughters, and sisters stay together throughout their lives. They can maintain close ties and joint interests and provide support for each other. Husbands enter as strangers and suffer the anxiety, and isolation that a structural position of outsider in a close-knit group entails. This serves to strengthen female power and weaken male power. It does not necessarily mean that women will dominate in such structures, but it does lessen the possibility of harsh, authoritarian dominance of wives by husbands. The wife's close kin are readily available to aid her; the husband may be separated from his kin.

The Iroquois. If matrilineality and matrilocality are also combined with *female economic control,* women may be in a particularly advantageous position for exercising power in the society. The *Iroquois Indians* of upstate New York during the eighteenth and nineteenth centuries provide a fascinating example of such a society.[16] The Iroquois were a matrilineal, matrilocal, simple horticultural people whose women exercised significant legitimate economic and political power. As Judith Brown points out, the high status of women among the Iroquois is evidenced not in deferential, "placed on a pedestal" treatment, but rather can be seen in the real power and personal autonomy accorded women. Males devoted their primary energies to the organization and execution of large-scale external wars involving the federation of different Iroquois villages against far distant non-Iroquois peoples. These wars took the men away from the local communities for long periods, leaving the women in effective control. It was, therefore, adaptive to organize the kinship, residence, and collective work systems around the matrilineal core of mothers, daughters, and sisters.

The longhouse was the symbol of the matrilineage and of the Iroquois people as a whole. Each lineage lived and worked communally as an extended family in its own longhouse. The chief *matron* of the lineage held authority over the longhouse; this authority was not exercised by either her husband or brother. The men of the lineage cleared the land for planting, but groups of women took care of most of the other horticultural production activities. Men also contributed some meat to the food supply through hunting. The crucial factor in explaining the high status and power of Iroquois women is not so much their productive work as the control they exercised over the food supply. Land was cleared by men and owned communally, but use rights were held by women. The food supply and the distribution of food both within and among the households was controlled entirely by women. Even the food from the men's hunt was distributed by the women, not the hunters. Through their control of stored food they could veto the war expeditions by not providing the necessary dried provisions for the long treks. They could also prevent certain meetings of the Council of Elders from being held by withholding the necessary supplies for the accompanying feasts.

Brown maintains that this economic power of women, which originated in their economic control, was institutionalized in their political power. The Council of Elders, which was the highly egalitarian governing body of the village, was all male. But eligibility for office was passed through the female line and members could be nominated only by females. In addition, females could institute impeachment proceedings against office holders who did not perform adequately. The matrons were also consulted on the important decisions made by the Council, including decisions related to the conduct of war and the making of treaties.

Women also participated in the selection of religious leaders and in the ceremonial and ritual life of the tribe. Women's activities were celebrated as well as men's. Marriages were arranged by the mothers. Divorce was easily available to men and women.

Matrilineality does not, however, always confer power and status upon women. Alice Schlegel, for example, has found that under matrilineality women are still usually subject to the authority of males. It may be the brother rather than the husband who dominates, but in 78 percent of the sixty-four matrilineal societies Schlegel examined, females were dominated by males.[17]

The Truk. The Truk of the Caroline Islands in the Western Pacific Ocean provide an example of a matrilineal society with high male dominance.[18] An important difference between the Truk and the Iroquois is that males control the food supply among the Truk while females have control among the Iroquois. The staple food of the Truk is the breadfruit and men control its entire production and distribution. They plant the trees, care for them, harvest the fruit, peel it, and cook it. Access to trees and land may come through the wife's lineage, but the husband has the economic control. He even controls and distributes the fish his wife catches. This food sharing is very important for creating reciprocity ties between the Truk males.

Truk matrilineages live and work together and exercise collective ownership of the land. However, the eldest male of the lineage administers the lineage's resources and organizes and directs the labor of the other members. The Senior Male has power over the entire lineage, but the females are governed more directly by the Senior Woman. The Senior Woman is not the equal of the Senior Man, however, as she must report to and defer to the wishes of the Senior Man. The females must defer to any of the lineage's males past the age of puberty. Husbands dominate their wives and have the support of the wive's lineages in controlling them.

A man has exclusive sexual rights in his wife and has the support of her lineage in punishing any infractions which may be discovered. He expects his wife to treat him with deference, to take care of his clothes, and to fish and cook snacks for him. If she fails in any of these respects he may beat her, and—unless he is entirely unjustified or carries the beatings to extremes—her lineage will not interfere.

Although a man finds it easy to leave in divorce, merely using the pretext of adultery, the wife finds it considerably more difficult to terminate a marriage unless her husband consistently fails in his obligations, when her brother may tell him to leave.[19]

In addition to male economic control, male dominance in this matrilineal, matrilocal society also appears to be encouraged by practices which develop male solidarity but not female solidarity. Females work together under the direction of the Senior Woman, but these communal efforts do not encourage the same degree of interdependence as the collective work of the males. Women depend more on their brothers than they do on the other women of the lineage. Men, however, depend on the other men of their wives' lineages for support in times of need, communal work, and for companionship.

The outsider status of males in matrilocal societies does, however, take its toll of Truk males. Despite their superordinate position in the Truk sexual stratification system, psychological tests indicate that females are more secure while the males are more anxious and insecure. This derives perhaps from the fact that females have stable, secure homes where they are always accepted, whereas males do not. They are secure members of neither their sisters' nor their wives' households. Matrilocality, therefore, appears to cause females few adjustment problems while it may force men to face dislocations as they move from their mothers' households to their wives' homes.

Patrilineality and Patrilocality

Patrilineality is often associated with patrilocality which, of course, places the adjustment burden on females. The wife must leave her natal kin group and move, often as a stranger, into the household and lineage of the husband. Patrilineal societies are also more likely to practice *village exogamy* (marriage partners come from different villages), while matrilineal societies are more likely to practice *village endogamy* (marriage partners come from the same village). Where village exogamy is practiced, the female is separated from her own kin and has little opportunity to call upon them for help. Isolation from her kin thus makes her vulnerable and dependent on her husband and his kin. Thus, while patrilineality is likely to remove the wife from her kin, matrilineality is not likely to isolate the husband from his kin group. In this respect, matrilineality does not disadvantage males as much as patrilineality disadvantages females.

Female solidarity is also inhibited by patrilocality. The women of the household come from different villages. They have little basis for developing close ties. Furthermore, they must often compete with co-wives (where polygyny is practiced) and with the wives of their husband's brothers. Often, each woman is given a separate hut and separate gardens to tend and does her work individually rather than communally. This does not create ties of interdependence and reciprocity among the women. To the degree that women are isolated from one another by competition, jealousy, and individualistic work and consumption patterns, they are not likely to develop the "safety in numbers" associated with strong female solidarity and, therefore, are likely to be more vulnerable and dependent on men.

Competition and Warfare.   Patrilineality is more adaptive to a competitive environment than matrilineality. Where conditions arise requiring the accumulation of greater surpluses, competition is usually necessary to motivate people to expend the extra effort to produce more. And where conditions (such as population pressure) arise that require the group to defend or aggrandize its holdings, patrilocality and patrilineality are adaptive responses because they concentrate the male fighting power of the group. Matrilineality encourages peace, stability, and low competitiveness. Matrilineal cultivation does not, however, produce the same levels of competitive productivity as patrilineal cultivation does:

> Typically, matrilineal groups are concerned with the production of adequate food for their respective lineage and clan members, rather than with the maximization of resources through coercion or increased exploitation.
> Patrilineal subsistence farmers, in contrast, are found in much less favorable habitats, where considerably more effort must be expended to attain similar rewards.[20]

Under conditions of high population pressure and the resulting increased labor requirements and defense needs, peace, stability, and low competitiveness will not help a people survive. The combination of population pressure, warfare, and *patricentric* (using patrilineality and/or patrilocality) kinship and residence patterns is associated with low status for women. The Yanamamö Indians provide a case study of extreme *machismo* and female degradation brought on by the warfare complex in a patrilineal, patrilocal horticultural society.[21]

The Yanamamö.   The Yanamamö Indians practice simple horticulture supplemented by hunting in the tropical forest areas of the Brazil and Venezuela border. They are regarded as one of the most male-dominated societies in the world. The important variables for explaining this extreme of male dominance and brutalization of women appear to be the intensity of the population pressure and protein shortage which results in the warfare complex, patrilineality, patrilocality, male solidarity, and in the male economic control of the productive process and the food supply. (See the discussion of the warfare complex in Chapter 2.) The particular intensity and combination of these variables among many Yanamamö villages produces extremes of situations found to lesser degrees among other peoples.

Marvin Harris and Janet Siskind state that the Yanamamö suffer from a chronic protein shortage. Although they can produce all the vegetable foods they need, they rely on hunted game for protein and game is in short supply. Constant feuding and warring helps keep the villages dispersed over the widest possible hunting area, keeps them from hunting the game to extinction, and helps control population growth through deaths in battle and encouraging female infanticide. Siskind explains that the Yanamamö are involved in intense competition over protein, but this source of competition is masked by the conventionally accepted view among the Yanamamö that they are competing over women as sexual property. If they openly acknowledged the competition over game, this would increase hunting efforts and permanently deplete the area's animal resources. Women serve as the overt goal instead of game for both hunting and fighting. Their economy involves what Siskind describes as the exchange of meat for sex. Siskind further argues that for such an economy of sex to operate effectively, the resource involved—women—must be scarce. The scarcity of women is artificially produced through the practices of female infanticide, polygyny, and strict sexual mores for women. This creates a situation where many men do not have access to women. This encourages them to raid other groups for women and keeps the internal warfare complex operating.

The warfare complex in turn encourages the devaluation and degradation of women and the exaltation of fierce aggression and *machismo* for men. The Yanamamö male's life is devoted to fighting; his body is covered with battle scars and wounds. Men commonly engage in brutal duels which test both strength and endurance. Such duels may involve each man in turn dealing out severe blows with fists, rocks, or clubs to the other man's chest, side, or head. The receiver of a blow will be knocked down, knocked unconscious, deeply bruised, and may suffer broken bones. The point is to prove that "he can take it." For each blow received and endured one can be given in return. Such duels may also erupt into pitched battles between the different groups of males watching the duel. A male must maintain a public image of fierce aggressive bravery.

This aggressiveness is directed toward women as well as men. Yanamamö women are among the most brutalized and victimized women in the world. Their bodies are covered with wounds and scars inflicted on them by their husbands. A man may even stab his wife on the slightest or even no provocation. As Harris puts it, "It help's a man's 'image' if he publicly beats his wife with a club." [22] There are no recognized limits for wife abuse among the Yanamamö. Murder of wives is even acceptable.

The women expect to be beaten, degraded, and humiliated. Adultery on the part of wives is viciously punished.

Marriage is definitely viewed as the exchange of women by men. The Yanamamö words for marriage can be translated as "dragging something away" and divorce translates as "throwing something away." Females are given to their husbands as young children and are expected to serve and obey them and to submit to intercourse as young as the age of eight. Men often exchange sisters, and brothers-in-law are often the closest of friends. This type of male solidarity ends any possibility of the female turning to her kinsmen for protection. Her brother is often more interested in her husband's welfare and interests than in hers.

Wives are also obtained through raiding. The captured women are gang-raped by the successful warriors and then distributed with much haggling to the fiercest, most successful fighters. Polygyny ('having more than one wife) is highly valued as a source of prestige for males. This both maintains an artificial shortage of women and helps motivate men to be brave raiders.

Women are expected to provide menial labor for their husbands, but unlike many horticultural societies, women are not primary economic producers. In addition to the extremely demanding nature of banana and plantain cultivation, the constant threat of attack makes it impractical for the Yanamamö to allocate gardening to women. Men are also the exclusive hunters. This gives the males almost total control over the economy as well as the military might. The combination seems disastrous for the position of women in this society.

Polygyny.   Polygyny is widely practiced among horticulturalists, especially in patrilineal societies. This is related to the productivity of women as well as to the warfare complex. Ester Boserup explains that a man can expand the amount of land under cultivation and the overall productivity of his household by adding more wives.[23] In addition to the increased labor force which multiple wives represent, they also often entitle the husband to land belonging to each of his wives' kin group. In one region of Uganda, for example, there is a direct relationship between number of wives and the amount of land cultivated by men.

Among advanced horticultural societies with class inequality, polygyny may be one of many forms of conspicuous consumption practiced by the noble class. In this case, women are desired as sexual property, for display purposes, and often for their reproductive powers, but not so much for their labor.

Polygyny is less common among matrilocal peoples except for *sororal polygyny* (a man marries two or more sisters). If a man took wives from more than one matrilineage, unless they lived in the same village, it would be very difficult for him to perform his role as husband in each matrilocal household.

Polygyny may facilitate or inhibit *female solidarity.* Where polygyny involves communal work and consumption patterns among the co-wives, it can lead to the development of close ties and mutual support. However, polygyny often involves the separation of women into individual huts with separate gardens. If each wife competes for access to the husband's resources for herself and her children, polygyny does not facilitate female solidarity.

Competitiveness and disunity among women is also encouraged by jealousy. Many societies require the husband of multiple wives to share his time, attentions, and resources equally among wives. But even these rules do not prevent invidious comparisons and hostility among wives.

Bride-price. Marriage among horticulturists usually involves the exchange of large quantities of goods. This is more common among patrilineal groups than matrilineal peoples and usually takes the form of *bride-price* and sometimes *bride-service.* In exchange for rights to the children the woman will bear, the husband must compensate her kin group with goods or services. The payments are often made in stages to be completed at the birth of her first child. If the payments are not made in full, the husband may find that his children belong to his wife's father or brother and not to him or his lineage. Wives represent then significant financial investments for their husbands' lineages and they are expected to produce a return on that investment through their reproductive as well as their productive abilities.

Junior Wives. Junior wives often do not have an enviable status in patrilineal societies whether polygynous or monogamous. In the polygynous situation junior wives are often sought by senior wives to ease the domestic labor burden. The junior wife often functions as little more than a servant in the household. Where the new wife is the man's first wife, she may still be treated as a servant to a harsh and demanding mother-in-law. Her status in the household and her treatment by her mother-in-law often improve considerably with the birth of her first child, especially if it is a boy. This ties the wife more firmly to the patrilineage and also proves she was worthy of the bride-price paid for her.

Sexuality. Among horticulturalists there is a wide range of sexual mores. Some are very permissive for men and women. Among the matrilineal Truk, for example, extramarital affairs are universal. However, husbands, but not wives, may demand a divorce on the basis of adultery. Furthermore, a Truk man may sleep with the wives of any of his brothers-in-law and a woman may sleep with her sisters' husbands. Martin and Voorheis found that in general matrilineal societies are permissive concerning premarital sex for women but that patrilineal societies are more likely to be strict. Among the patrilineal Hagen of New Guinea, for example, virginity is highly valued in brides and chastity in wives. But sex is considered unclean and dangerous for both sexes and males are expected to abstain almost as strictly as females are, although violations are considered less blameworthy in males.[24]

Postmarital sexual freedom for women is allowed in some matrilineal societies and some patrilineal societies and prohibited by others. As Siskind pointed out, however, where competition over women is part of the economy and ecology of a people, as among the Yanamamö, strict control over the sexual activities of wives is an important part of maintaining the necessary shortage of women.

RELATIONS BETWEEN THE SEXES

In general, the social positions of women and men in horticultural societies tend to give rise to a high degree of tension and hostility between the sexes. The hostility may remain below the surface in groups that emphasize internal peace, stability, and harmony. Or it may be openly displayed among internally disruptive, feuding groups. Horticultural societies are not likely to emphasize close, loving, trusting relations between men and women as groups or as individual couples.

Where there is a high degree of sex segregation, conflicting interests on the basis of sex, and solidarity groups of either or both sexes, the relations between the sexes are likely to be particularly hostile rather than close and loving. The Mundurucu exemplify this situation:

Each sex is a social entity, each has its own internal organization, and each has its sense of solidarity and a consciousness of its own unity and its opposition to the other. The battle of the sexes is not carried on by individual gladiators, as in our society, but by armies.[25]

Male dominance is the cultural ideal among the Mundurucu and male informants will assure researchers that men are superior, dominant and in control. Female informants, however, disagree. Mundurucu women do not accept the male standards and evaluations. They openly ridicule men as a group and as individuals. Intersexual hostility and antagonism are openly expressed in words and ritual, yet women do not openly challenge their secondary social position.

They recognize it, and they actively resent it, but they cope with it as a fact of life. One way of coping is through the minor etiquette of female demeanor . . . Women guard their emotions before men, communicate as little as possible of their subjective states, set themselves off with reserve.[26]

Within marriage Mundurucu women and men also remain relatively aloof. Marital partners may develop a degree of affection and intimacy over the years; but the general isolation of the sexes and the creation of solidarity within each sex rather than between individual men and women militates against such closeness. Similarly, Alice Smedley found that among the Udu of Nigeria compatibility between husband and wife is almost irrelevant to domestic and family life. She notes that it is considered good for spouses to be friendly, but that being "in love" in the Western sense can be disruptive of household harmony. As among the Mundurucu, Udu "men and women spend most of their lives in the company of their own sex . . . . Conjugal companionship is generally considered inconsistent with the work conditions of husbands and wives." [27]

Women may also cope with their secondary status through the manipulation of males. Again this does not indicate close, affectionate, trusting relationships between the sexes. Women 's success at manipulating men may also lead them to denigrate men and view them as childlike and foolish. This manipulation, along with the potential threat of withholding domestic duties, sex, or even food, creates a fear of women in men. Friedl maintains that men often develop close trusting relationships only with women who are not sexually available to them, such as their mothers and sisters, while women develop such ties only with males sexually unavailable to them—their sons, fathers, and brothers.[28] Hostilities and tensions are too great for such ties to be forged between husbands and wives and other potential sexual partners.

It is not uncommon for these tensions and hostilities between the sexes to be manifested in cultural beliefs attributing great danger and uncleanliness to sexual intercourse and to women. The Hagen of New Guinea, for example, regard sex and the genitals, especially female genitals and menstruation, as polluting and weakening.[29] The men fear the hidden powers of their supposedly inferior women. They live in almost constant fear that their wives will poison them with menstrual blood. Women, in turn, may use these fears to manipulate and sometimes to coerce males. This fear of women is also manifested in the fear of witchcraft by women.

Control is sometimes exercised over horticultural women through rape and particularly serious offenses by women may be punished by gang rape. Mundurucu women who are flagrantly promiscuous are subjected to painful and humiliating gang rapes. Mundurucu women who leave the village alone, even if it is just to fetch firewood or water, are subject to legitimate rape by any male who encounters them. These practices, of course, increase the hostility and ill-will between the sexes.

The men are thus seen as potentially threatening in a very real, direct, and physical way. They force the women together, make them travel in bands, and actually increase their dependence on each other. The men do enforce the propriety of the women, but they do so at the expense of heightening female antagonism toward them and strengthening female cohesion.[30]

Jealousy between the sexes is also a common problem. Husbands and wives argue often over real or imagined acts of adultery. In polygynous households a husband often has to contend with constant jealousy and bickering over his real or imagined inequitable treatment of co-wives or their children. Wife beating is often legitimized, in horticultural societies, but is less common or less extreme where the wife can rely upon the aid of her kin.

Child Rearing

Child rearing practices among horticulturalists vary in relationship to other aspects of the societies' cultures and social structures. Clear divisions in gender roles are found, however, in the childrearing modes of all these societies. As would be expected, among the Yanamamö fierce aggressiveness is encouraged in young boys while the personality of the passive, submissive, victim is produced in young girls.

When a girl's little brother hits her, she gets punished if she hits back. Little boys, however, are never punished for hitting anybody. Yanamamö fathers howl with delight when their angry four-year-old sons strike them in the face.[31]

The Hopi, on the other hand, do not have pressing defense needs or a warfare complex. They do not, therefore, emphasize aggressive machismo for young boys and men. Instead they socialize both boys and girls to be peaceable, non-competitive, cooperative, and humble.[32] Schlegel notes that females are not expected to control their aggressive impulses as much as males. This is perhaps because male aggression is potentially more harmful and disruptive of the communities' stability and solidarity than female aggression because of the greater potential male fighting strength.

Among the Udu, girls are trained to depend on their brothers for protection while boys are trained to take charge and to play the role of protector of females. Greater emphasis is placed on learning to get along with others for girls than for boys. Udu girls are taught to be submissive, passive, resilient, and flexible. And very importantly, as they learn women's work inside the domestic compound, they are also taught how to manipulate men.[33]

Gender role socialization into the division of labor begins early among horticulturalists, especially for girls. Young girls are often given the job of child-nurse which involves caring for younger siblings or cousins while the mother is busy with other tasks. It is not uncommon to see a small eight-year-old girl carrying a heavy two-year-old for hours. Smedley notes that among the Udu, girls of four and five take care of babies and learn to carry them on their backs.

The sexual division of labor is often quite rigidly enforced by horticultural adults. The Udu rarely strike their children. But the one instance witnessed by Smedley involved a four-year-old boy repeatedly copying the female task of carrying a head pan. Children are clearly impressed with the idea that certain tasks are appropriate only to females, others to males.

Religion and Ritual

The opposition and hostility between the sexes often pervade the religious and ritual life of horticulturalists. Since religion and ritual are largely under the control of males, they usually emphasize the male point of view and legitimate and rationalize male dominance and female submission. Women are not always impressed by such rituals, however. Mundurucu religion, for example, is controlled by males who possess the ritual flutes and keep them hidden from women. The symbolism exalts the power of the penis and portrays women as inferior to men. The Mundurucu myth of origin is similar to myths of origin among other horticulturalists. It postulates a time when females had control of the ritual flutes and dominated males. However, males eventually outwitted the females and stole the flutes and the power they conferred. Such myths probably indicate a real fear of women by men. They are not likely, however, to be remnants of a time in which such matriarchies actually existed.[34]

As discussed above, religion and ritual also often emphasize female uncleaness and attribute dangerous, polluting properties to women and sex. Menstrual taboos and the seclusion of menstruating women and women after childbirth are common. This also probably arises out of situations of real hostility between the sexes and male fears of the imperfectly subordinated female.

Large-scale initiation rites for boys and girls are widespread among horticulturalists and emphasize the differences between their gender roles as they pass into adulthood. Rituals are often associated with different aspects of work, warfare, and fertility for men and women. Religion and ritual are also used to legitimate the positions of "big men" among simple horticulturalists and the powers and privileges of the elite class of men and women among some advanced horticulturalists.

In general, the gender roles and sexual stratification systems of horticultural societies are often symbolized, legitimated, and perpetuated by their religious beliefs and practices. Some horticulturalists, however, have come under the influence of religions developed by more advanced agrarian and urban peoples such as Islam in parts of Africa. This, like other contacts with the external world, may emphasize different and often more subordinate roles for women. However, as pointed out above, where such practices interfere with other aspects of the social structure such as female trading or other female work roles, the religious teachings are likely to be ignored.

FORCES FOR CHANGE

Contact with non-horticultural peoples is probably the most important force for change in these societies. Horticulturalists are often impressed by the goods that can be obtained through trading with or working for more technologically advanced peoples. This sometimes leads to more individualistic practices and the disruption of the traditional corporate kin group patterns. This is also likely to lead to changes in the positions of men and women.

Among the Mundurucu, for example, the rubber trade has led many people to abandon the village life with its collective kinship, work, and residence patterns. The women are particularly desirous of the trade items obtainable through rubber tapping. They pressure their husbands to adopt the new locale and life-style that rubber tapping requires. Paradoxically, however, the new social and economic system typifying rubber tappers undermines the degree of personal autonomy and independence women exercised under the traditional way of life. Both female and male work groups and collective solidarity are terminated by these individualistic economic practices. Each rubber tapper works alone and through his earnings and individual fishing supports his wife and children. Women thus lose their role as primary economic producers. They become firmly tied to the domestic sphere in relatively isolated, individualistic nuclear family units. The separation of the sexes and rigidity of the division of labor characteristic of traditional village life do not continue. Women no longer rely on each other for help in manioc processing, gardening, or child care. Instead, they work alone or turn to their husbands and children for help. The men become the heads of these nuclear family households. The woman's domestic authority is lost and the position of Senior Woman becomes obsolete. The women, however, prefer this pattern. Murphy and Murphy argue that women press for these social changes in response to outside contact and new opportunities more than men do because they see it as narrowing the gap between them and men. The women may not gain, but the men lose. A more objective outsider would probably conclude that both sexes have lost.[35]

Colonial domination has also been an important force for change among some horticultural societies. In some cases this has improved opportunities for women, in other cases it has reduced them. Colonial governments and their settler populations have sometimes created markets for women's produce which allow women to increase their economic independence through trade. In other cases, however, they have undermined female economic activities through the imposition of external standards favoring males as workers, businessmen, or as political leaders. Women may, thereby, be isolated from the new public spheres the colonizers create. In Ghana, for example, British colonial domination undermined woman's status in production, her authority in the family, her political role as queen mother, and her influence on community decision making. The British introduced Victorian ideas of woman's place being in the home, of female chastity, Christian marriage practices, and patriarchy and patrilineality. The Western model of gender roles was imitated by many Ghanians, who extended education primarily to males and recruited only males to fill the new clerical and middle level economic posts. The new cocoa production encouraged male cultivation instead of the traditional female farming. But women did get increased opportunities for small-scale trading and cash cropping which often increased the woman's independence from her husband. With the granting of independence for Ghana, the British influence on woman's position had already been set. Women continue to be excluded from the political system and discriminated against in the educational system and the higher paying sectors of the economy. They also continue to occupy subordinate social positions relative to men. There has been a clear decline in the social positions and status of women since the traditional precolonial period.[36]

The demise of matrilineality and matrilocality has also been a result of the encroachment of the modern world on horticulturalists. Matrilineality is suited to non-competitive, stable environments, but such environments are rare in the modern world. World-wide population increases and the expansion of technologically more advanced peoples have forced the more peaceful matrilineal peoples to change or be conquered. Matrilineality is a way of life which has lost its ecological niche. It is not less "natural" than patrilineality, but it is not as adaptive under conditions of population pressure and competition.

Thus, as with the foragers, the roles and statuses for women and men in horticultural societies may rapidly be disappearing from the face of the earth. Some see the turn to more advanced technologies as progress. But in terms of the position of women in society and sometimes for the majority of men as well, it has often meant deterioration instead.

SUMMARY

Horticultural societies are based on shifting plant cultivation using hoes or simple digging-sticks. They are kinship based. Simple horticultural societies produce little surplus and are usually egalitarian. Advanced horticultural societies are more productive and can support class inequality including a small leisure class of rulers.

The sexual division of labor allocates the more strenuous and dangerous task of clearing the land to males. The patterns in the division of labor include men both clearing the land and cultivating it, men clearing but women cultivating, and men clearing and both sexes cultivating. Where men control the production and distribution of products for exchange in market relationships, this contributes to male dominance. Where females are active traders, male dominance is undermined by female economic independence.

Horticultural societies are sometimes highly sex segregated with males and females living and working in separate groups. Both patrilineality and matrilineality are practiced by different horticultural societies. Matrilineality, female solidarity, female economic control, and male absence in long-distance war or trade all contribute to a high position for women and sexual equality. Patrilineality, male solidarity, male economic control, population pressure, and important local defense needs and the warfare complex lead to the subordination of females. Polygyny is fairly common among horticulturalists, especially where females are economically productive or where female infanticide and the warfare complex turn women into sexual prizes for brave warriors.

Horticulturalists are often sexually permissive, but some practice a sexual double standard and severely control the sexuality of women. Relations between the sexes are often distant and aloof, if not openly hostile. Women in relatively powerless positions often resort to the manipulation of males to gain a degree of power and influence. Female subordination also often leads to male fears of women, as manifested in views of women as unclean or in the fear of witchcraft. Wife beating and rape are common means of controlling females.

Child rearing usually emphasizes gender role differences and in particular encourage females to be submissive. Religion and ritual are primarily controlled by males and reflect male lives and interests: religious beliefs legitimate the sexual stratification system. Colonial domination often disrupts these societies and usually worsens the lot of women. Matrilineality and matrilocality are on the decline because they are not adaptive to competitive environments that increasingly characterize today's world.

Notes

1. Gerhard Lenski and Jean Lenski, *Human Societies* (New York: McGraw-Hill, 1978), p. 97.
2. Lenski and Lenski, pp. 97–173.
3. Ernestine Friedl, *Women and Men* (New York: Holt, Rinehart, and Winston, 1975), p. 53.
4. Friedl, pp. 56–57.
5. Ester Boserup, *Women's Role in Economic Development* (New York: St. Martin's Press, 1970), p. 18.
6. Boserup, pp. 88–99.
7. Sidney Mintz, "Men, Women, and Trade," *Comparative Studies in Society and History,* 13 (1971), 266.
8. Kamene Okonjo, "The Role of Women in the Development of Culture in Nigeria," in Ruby Rohrlich-Leavitt, ed., *Women Cross-Culturally: Change and Challenge* (The Hague: Mouton, 1975), p. 37.
9. Yolanda Murphy and Robert Murphy, *Women of the Forest* (New York: Columbia U. Press, 1974).
10. Marvin Harris, *Culture, People, and Nature* (2nd ed.; New York: Thomas Y. Crowell, 1975), pp. 338–341.
11. Lenski and Lenski, p. 162.
12. Lenski and Lenski, p. 163.
13. Harris, p., 344.
14. George Murdock, *Social Structure* (New York: Macmillan, 1949), pp. 209–210.
15. M. Kay Martin and Barbara Voorheis, *Female of the Species* (New York: Columbia U. Press 1975), p. 222.
16. The following discussion of the Iroquois is based largely on Judith Brown, "Iroquois Women: An Ethnographic Note," in Rayna Reiter, ed., *Toward an Anthropology of Women* (New York: Monthly Review, 1975), pp. 235–251.
17. Alice Shlegel, *Male Dominance and Female Autonomy* (New Haven: HRAF Press, 1972), p. 59.
18. The following discussion is based on David M. Schneider, "The Truk," in David M. Schneider and Kathleen Gough, eds., *Matrilineal Kinship* (Berkeley: U. of California Press, 1962), pp. 202–233.
19. Schneider, p. 229.
20. Martin and Voorheis, p. 234.
21. The following discussion is based on Napoleon Chagnon: "The Culture-Ecology of Shifting (Pioneering) Cultivation among the Yanamamö Indians," in Daniel Gross, ed., *Peoples and Cultures of Native South America* (New York: Doubleday, The Natural History Press, 1973), pp. 126–144 and *Yanamamö: The Fierce People* (New York: Holt, Rinehart, and Winston, 1968); also, Marvin Harris, 1975, pp. 83–110, and *Cannibals and Kings* (New York: Random House, 1977), pp. 31–54; Janet Siskind, "Tropical Forest Hunters and the Economy of Sex," in Gross, pp. 226–240.

22. Harris, 1975, p. 89.
23. Ester Boserup, *Woman's Role in Economic Development* (New York; St. Martin's Press, 1970), pp. 37–52.
24. Marilyn Strathern, *Women in Between* (New York: Seminar Press, 1972), pp. 159–184.
25. Murphy and Murphy, p. 110.
26. Murphy and Murphy, p. 137.
27. Alice Smedley, "Women of Udu: Survival in a Harsh Land," in Carolyn Matthiasson, ed., *Many Sisters: Women in Cross-Cultural Perspective* (New York: Free Press, 1974), p. 218.
28. Friedl, 1975, pp. 68–69.
29. Strathern, pp. 164–175.
30. Murphy and Murphy, p. 136.
31. Harris, 1975, p. 90.
32. Alice Schegel, "The Adolescent Socialization of the Hopi Girl," *Ethnology,* 12 (Oct., 1973), 450–451.
33. Smedley, pp. 213–215.
34. Murphy and Murphy.
35. Murphy and Murphy, pp., 179–232.
36. Audrey Chapman Smock, "Ghana: From Autonomy to Subordination," in Janet Zollinger Giele and Audrey Chapman Smock, ed., *Women: Roles and Status in Eight Countries* (New York: John Wiley, 1977), pp. 173–216.

5

Pastoral Societies

The formal structures . . . are based exclusively upon relations among male kinsman. The only enduring social units
are formed through the male descent line, and women are
exchanged among these units to procreate future generations of males, leaving no enduring marks of their own existence . . . .

Bette Denich, "Sex and Power in the Balkans"

Chapters 3 and 4 described the roles of women and men in hunting and gathering and horticultural societies. *Pastoralists* exhibit important similarities with and differences from each of these types of societies, and these are reflected in similarities and differences in their systems of gender roles and sexual stratification.

ECONOMY AND SOCIAL ORGANIZATION

Pastoralism is defined by its primary reliance on the herding of livestock such as cattle, camels, sheep, and goats. The pastoral life is organized around the needs of the herds, and livestock are of primary importance to pastoralists. Like foragers and simple horticulturists, pastoralists are to some degree *nomadic*. They must move to secure sufficient pasturage and water for their animals. Although pastoralism is usually combined with some cultivation of vegetable foods, these peoples do not have the high levels of productivity necessary to keep their animals fodder-fed in stalls or in small fields. Their low productivity means they have little surplus. However, they do have a form of important exchangeable concentrated wealth in their livestock which is extremely vulnerable to theft and raiding.

Production is primarily for use values, especially within the pastoral communities themselves. Exchange within pastoral societies is almost entirely conducted through kinship ties. The selling and bartering of animals among kinsmen is rare, because the animals change hands frequently but not through market relationships. Pastoralists resist selling their animals to outsiders even when such a market exists. Only old, barren or otherwise useless animals are offered for sale. Maintaining and increasing the size of one's herd is a chief concern of pastoralists. Selling an animal would usually defeat this goal and is therefore done only as a last resort.

The work involved in caring for herds of large animals such as cattle or camels is physically demanding. (The herding of sheep and goats is less strenuous.) In addition to the strength required to handle the larger animals, the herder often has to labor for hours hauling water for them. The livestock also must be continually protected from both human and animal predators. Theft and raiding for livestock are endemic to pastoral peoples.

Despite the importance of herding in their lives and cultures, few pastoralists rely solely on herding for their subsistence. Most do some gardening or foraging as well. Those who combine cultivation with herding are referred to as *facultative pastoralists*, while those who rely almost entirely on herding are *obligative pastoralists*. Martin and Voorhies note that greater reliance on crops limits the nomadism of pastoralists and allows for larger communities and the development of more complex sociopolitical institutions.[1] Obligative pastoralists are generally found in rugged, barren areas that cannot be cultivated. They are highly mobile, live in small camps often with fewer than fifty people, and have uncentralized, tribal-level political structures.

Facultative pastoralists range in population density from small camps for those with less dependence on crops, to villages as large as 1,000 inhabitants among those with a higher (up to 50 percent) dependence on crops. The larger communities of pastoralists have more centralized and powerful political institutions such as chiefdoms and even small states. Some very powerful pastoralists can rely almost entirely on their herds and obtain agricultural products through their control of agricultural communities or through raiding or trade with agricultural peoples.

Like foragers and horticulturists, pastoralists rely on a high degree of *reciprocity* and *collective work organization* in their economic production. However, pastoralists are stricter than foragers in requiring that each person do his or her share of the work. Robert Paine suggests that while hunters and gatherers' values focus on distributing and consuming food and being generous and sociable, the pastoral economy gives rise to values focusing on owning livestock and expanding the size of the herd: "with 'food' all around them in the herd, it is only the size of the herd, not the size of the meal, that really demonstrates merit among pastoralists." [2] Pastoralists are involved in production and are future oriented rather than concerned with gathering for immediate consumption. They have, therefore, a more severe *work ethic* concerning doing one's share of the collective work. They also work longer and harder than most foragers. And, according to Paine, they place a great importance on inheritance, which is uncharacteristic of foragers.

SEXUAL DIVISION OF LABOR

The sexual division of labor within pastoral societies is tipped toward male dominance of the economically productive tasks. Probably because of the strength required to handle and care for large animals, males are the exclusive herders of these animals. Females may, however, herd smaller animals and serve as dairy maids for large and small species. Martin and Voorhies' study of forty-four pastoral societies found that the female contribution to the diet of herders is small. Men do almost all of the herding and women dairy in only about one-third of the societies. Men also do most of the cultivation in half of their sample. However, where cultivation is based on horticultural techniques, women are either the exclusive cultivators or men and women share equally in cultivation. [3]

Martin and Voorhies also found significant correlations between a group's dependence on crops, the sexual division of labor, and the degree of nomadism. Societies which do no cultivation tend to be highly nomadic and men and women share in the care of the herd. Where there is a low dependence on crops (less than 25 percent of the diet), the society tends to be nomadic or seminomadic and men are the primary herders and cultivators. Where there is a moderate dependence on crops (30 to 40 percent of the diet), the group is seminomadic or semisedentary and men are the primary herders while men and women share in the cultivation tasks. Groups with a high dependence on crops (50 percent of the diet) are sedentary. In some cases men are the sole herders, in other groups men and women participate in herding activities. There is also a strong tendency for men and women to share the cultivation work.

Martin and Voorhies suggest that among herders with a high dependence on crops, the variations found in the sexual division of labor may be a result of the influence of the *parent community* out of which the pastoral society developed. Therefore it might be a carryover of institutions and traditions developed in a different socioeconomic context. Those with a horticultural background are perhaps more likely to share tasks and those with an agricultural background more likely to continue to assign primary productive tasks to men.[4]

Other dimensions of these variations in the sexual division of labor can be partially explained by the factor of who goes with the herd and who stays behind. In societies that are completely nomadic, both males and females move with the herd and stay with it throughout the year. There is no period in which women are separated from the herd. Therefore, they can be regularly assigned tasks associated with the herd, such as dairying. This is true also in fully sedentary communities where the herd is usually not moved far from the settled village. However, among groups that practice *sex-segregated nomadism,* where for long periods only the men go with the herd, male dominance of the economic activities results. Women in these societies are usually excluded even from dairying. Similarly, in fully sedentary communities where the women are always in close proximity to the fields, women's participation in cultivation has a status equal to men's. Among sex-segregated, seminomadic peoples, men usually do the cultivation: they plant the crops while on the move with the herds, leave the crops unattended when they move on, and return to the cultivated area with the herd at harvest time.[5]

Elise Boulding also points out the marked sexual division of labor among herders. But she notes that this division of labor does not create a sharp dichotomy between *domestic* and *public spheres.* Women's tasks are more likely to take place in camp than men's tasks, but they do not involve the isolation of women in the household. Much of women's work is done in cooperation with or at least in the close company of other women. Both men and women participate in collective work patterns with other members of the same sex. Camps are typically divided into *women's spaces* and *men's spaces*, but almost all activities are carried out in the open, thus avoiding the development of private domestic spheres for women versus public spheres for men. Women's work may be household work, but it is public household work. Boulding argues that women participate more fully in the total life of these societies than they do in settled agricultural communities.[6] Martin and Voorhies argue, however, that the male dominance of economic production gives rise to male dominance in the wider culture and social structure of pastoral societies.

Economic Control

Ownership and control over the disposition of livestock lies predominantly in male hands, as Engels suggested. However, females are sometimes at least the nominal owners of some livestock through inheritance, dowries or purchase. But even the owners of livestock cannot usually dispose freely of their animals. They are bound by an intricate web of kinship-based exchanges which requires them periodically to give large numbers of animals to close kinsmen, as bride-prices to the bride's family, as dowries to the groom, and as compensation for violation of certain rules, especially in the case of homicide. Furthermore, certain animals in a herd may be held jointly with others or held in the interests of others and are subject to many limitations on use and disposal.

In brief, males who control large herds do not necessarily derive significant economic power from these herds, since they cannot always use them in their own interests. A large herd, however, brings prestige and influence to the man or family who owns it. But ownership of large herds is often a cyclical or temporary phenomenon. Bridewealth and sometimes bloodwealth (fines for homicide) payments regularly deplete one family's herd while vastly increasing the size of another family's herd. Families are unlikely to maintain a large herd consistently. In addition, kinship obligations often require the owner of livestock to share with less fortunate kin. These exchanges militate against the development of *class inequality* among herders and the concentration of power in the hands of individuals or families. Herding societies are *ranked:* some individuals or families at any one time have more wealth, influence, and prestige than other individuals or families. But they are not usually *stratified:* no one family or group of families can maintain unequal shares of wealth and power from one generation to the next.

Females usually have little or no control over the disposition of livestock, especially large livestock. However, they do sometimes have economic control over small animals and sometimes can earn income through the sale of han-icraft items or domestic produce to outsiders. But more important, among herders who assign women the task of dairying, women generally also have control over the disposition of the dairy products. Their control, however, is often limited by customs requiring sharing with certain kin and neighbors. Where males are not allowed to dairy, an economic interdependence is created between the sexes which gives women an advantage they do not have where they are the economic dependents of men.

GENDER ROLES AND SEXUAL STRATIFICATION

Pastoralism creates forces that tend toward both sexual egalitarianism and male dominance. The lack of firm differentiation between the domestic and public spheres is a force toward sexual egalitarianism. Where women have some economic control this is a factor in raising women's status. Male economic control and female economic dependence, however, are forces toward male dominance and sexual stratification. Other factors of primary importance in supporting male dominance are the defense needs and warfare practices of herders and the patricentric kinship systems which internal warfare generates.

Internal Warfare

Livestock are extremely valuable property. Each camel or head of cattle represents a tremendous investment of material resources and human labor. Yet livestock are easily stolen. If one calculates the relative costs involved in stealing livestock versus raising livestock, it is usually clear that it is more efficient to steal than to raise your own. In addition, in areas of high population pressure there is competition over scarce pasturage and waterholes, both between different camps of pastoralists and between pastoralists and agricultural peoples. Thus, pastoralism is often associated with internal warfare. Chapters 2 and 4 discussed Harris' theory of the effects of internal warfare between geographically proximate, culturally similar peoples involving shifting alliances and treachery. Harris argues that these factors lead to the development and maintenance of fierce, aggressive, warlike males and a high degree of sexual inequality. The situation among many pastoralists lends support to Harris' model.

Analyses of the warfare complex within and among pastoral peoples indicates that war can become, as Harris suggests, an integral part of the economic and political structure and serve as a type of functional adaptation to the ecology of herding. Louise Sweet, for example, has studied the practice of camel raiding among North Arabian Bedouins.[7] Camel raiding is a primary concern and activity of Bedouins to the extent that the main occupations of the majority of the men in a Bedouin chiefdom or clan section have to do with keeping and guarding the camels and particularly with prosecuting raiding expeditions. The security of the family, lineage, clan section and chiefdom rests in the possession of adequate numbers and kinds of camels.[8]

Within local groups camels are exchanged through the above-mentioned mechanisms of bridewealth, bloodwealth, fines, gifts, hospitality, and tribute. But between distant groups, raiding is the chief mechanism of distribution. Sweet found that camel raids served to distribute both camels and human populations more evenly and, therefore, in a more ecologically adaptive manner over the desert areas and oases available to Bedouin pastoralists.

Reciprocal camel raiding, as a continuous practice, operating at both long and short distances between tribal breeding areas, maintains a circulation of camels and of camel husbandry over the maximum physical range for camels and the societies which specialize in their breeding and depend upon them. The continued exchange by mutual raids serves thus to recoup local losses owed to failures of pasturage and water, or disease.[9]

The raiding triggers institutional mechanisms which integrate the disparate camps into loosely structured chiefdoms occupying large zones. The threat of raids motivates different camps to enter into truces to limit their number of potential enemies, and the potential spoils of raiding motivate different camps to form alliances for joint raids. Furthermore, a camp suffering from raids often attempts to appeal to the chief to force the guilty group to pay compensation or return the stolen camels. Raiding thus maintains a process of trucemaking and breaking, alliance-making and breaking, and provides a continual basis of integration for the very loosely confederated camps of herders. Confederation is important to maintain, for it is potentially useful in organizing defense against encroachments by non-Bedouins.

Raiding is also practiced against non-Bedouin peoples living in or near the Bedouin zones. Bedouins often obtain goods they do not produce themselves from such non-Bedouins through trade, tribute, and raiding. In this case raiding serves to maintain Bedouin control of the district while simultaneously allowing for the continuation of symbiotic relations between these different peoples.

Sweet states that, in addition to these economic and political functions, camel raiding also serves to support the whole culture and social structure of Bedouin life. Male dominance is one aspect of the culture and social structure of raiding. Raiding encourages the development of fierce, aggressive personalities and skills in Bedouin men. These personalities and skills can be used to dominate Bedouin women as well as other men. Furthermore, if Harris's model of warfare and female subordination is accurate, female submissiveness to males constitutes an important reward or motivation for the males to risk the dangers inherent in raiding and defense against raiding.

Boulding found that the taming of horses by pastoralists in open areas that are conducive to riding great distances at great speeds tended to produce a *warrior aristocracy* and social and sexual inequality. However, in areas less amenable to warfare on horseback, the nomads remained more egalitarian and peaceful. She found, for example, that the more warlike and richer Mongols of the Asian steppes had more pronounced class inequality and were more strictly patriarchal than the somewhat less warlike Bedouin pastoralists. However, given the nature of internal warfare among pastoralists, women as well as men were often trained as aggressive defensive fighters. Although raiding and some more important battles were conducted away from the camps, much of the fighting involved the tent camp itself:

> The distinction was not always clear between the "army" and the total tribe. One of the first things Genghis [Khan] did was organize the wagons as part of the tribal battle formation, with women and children trained to shoot and defend the wagons and babies . . . women were also trained to fight from horseback . . . probably only women of the warrior aristocracy received such training.[10]

Furthermore, the women of these pastoral warrior aristocracies were more influential and more openly involved in political affairs than were the women of agricultural warrior aristocracies, who were not typically trained to fight or directly involved in warfare. Boulding has found several examples of *warrior queens* in the history of warring pastoralists. Among state-level herders such as the Asian Mongols, the Khatun (wife of the Khan or chief ruler) had a court and her own diplomatic corps of princesses and shared the duties of state with her husband. Some of them even led armies into battle. However, contact with settled urban populations often undermined the position of women. Assimilation to urban life changed the texture of pastoral life, and one of the consequences was the increase of male dominance and a loss of personal autonomy and public power on the part of upper class pastoral women.[11]

Although Boulding's examples of warrior queens appear to contradict Harris's theory, it may be that these women's elevated position in the class structure partially neutralized the effect of their sex in regard to learning the skills of mounted warriors. Similarly in our society a wealthy upper class woman is often in a position to give orders to a working class male. This does not undermine the sexual stratification system in our society, because it is recognized that class position takes precedence over sex status in this context.

Further support of Harris's warfare theory in relation to pastoralists is found in data on the relative sexual egalitarianism of the Fulani of Niger in Africa. The Moslem Fulani are pastoralists who must compete for scarce resources. But they have avoided direct involvement in the warfare complex which often accompanies pastoralism in a competitive environment. They accomplish this through a division of labor with closely related Fulani sedentary agriculturalists. The sedentary Fulani act as the fierce, warlike attack force for the more peaceful, accommodating Fulani pastoralists. As the pastoral Fulani migrate into new areas they are accompanied by their sedentary kinsmen. Opposition to the pastoralists is dealt with by their sedentary kinsmen who readily involve themselves in warfare.[12] Because the pastoral Fulani do not have to fight their own battles for expansion, they do not have a culture and social structure emphasizing aggressiveness, male dominance, and hierarchy which usually accompanies local warfare.

KINSHIP SYSTEMS AND WARFARE

Patrilineality, Male Honor, and Female Sexuality

The problem of the warfare complex manifests itself in yet another manner in pastoral society and again has important consequences related to sexual stratification. Pastoralists are overwhelmingly patrilineal and patrilocal. The ecological conditions of pastoralism and the defense problems engendered by population pressure are functionally related to the pastoral preference for patrilineality and patrilocality and to pastoralists' widespread emphasis on male honor, shame, and female chastity.

Jane Schneider has found these connections to be especially characteristic of Mediterranean pastoralists of Europe and North Africa.[13] Population pressure and competition over scarce resources are acute in these societies. Intracommunity conflicts over land, water, and animal theft are common. Such disputes are overlain with an ideology of male honor and shame. Maintaining one's own or one's family's property is a matter of honor. Shame comes to males who cannot defend or increase their property. Furthermore, strong central governments had not, even in the recent past, penetrated these areas sufficiently to maintain law and order and to remove the settlement of disputes from the local areas. Schneider argues that the codes of honor and shame are means of social control adapted to a competitive environment in the absence of state level controls much as Collins described in his ideal type of the "fortified household" (see Chapter 2).

Since pastoralism requires nomadism, the determination of grazing and water rights is likely to be problematical. Permanent ownership, property lines, and fences are not adapted to a migratory life. Schneider maintains that access or temporary property rights is established through the credible threat of force. Maintaining an impressive fighting force is then of key importance to local groups of herders. They achieve this partially through the practice of patrilineality and patrilocality with at least some kin ownership of resources. The kinship and residence system concentrates the power of closely related male kinsmen who are reared together with a strong sense of common identity and common purpose. This maximizes the strength of the collective work group necessary for herding, protection, and aggrandizement.

Bette Denich found that a highly *patricentric* kinship and residence pattern based on an extended household of brothers and male cousins characterizes *Montenegrin pastoralists*.

The formal structures . . . are based exclusively upon relations among male kinsmen. The only enduring social units are formed through the male descent line, and women are exchanged among these units to procreate future generations of males, leaving no enduring marks of their own existence in terms of the formal structure . . . . The exchange of women leads to the formation of male groups, not groups acknowledging the equal participation of both sexes.[14]

The Montenegrins do not even count daughters as children.

The Montenegrin male kinsmen own sheep and goats and rights in pastureland collectively and share in the work of herding and guarding them. As Schneider notes, population pressure and the consequent competition for scarce resources creates chronic defense problems. This

requires that herdsmen band together with allies to ward off actual attacks and discourage potential threats to their means of subsistence. The organizational solution to this problem has followed the pattern developed around the world by populations in analagous circumstances: patrilineally related groupings bonded through the dynamics of fusion against common external enemies . . . the public face of each group vis-à-vis the external world represents its competitive posture toward potential rivals . . . . Since all public arenas have the potentiality for combat, they are designated as male. The household's external environment is exclusively a male domain.[15]

This system is supported and encouraged by the concepts of honor and shame which help to maintain the solidarity of nuclear and extended family groups. Any perceived insult against one member of the group is taken as an affront to the entire group and must be avenged. Feuding among males is endemic. Males are socialized to be quick-tempered, aggressive, courageous warriors. Denich argues like Harris that this aggressiveness is necessary for survival in this context of high population pressure and scarce resources. Furthermore, each domestic unit acts as a fortified household, that is, taking care of its own defense needs and settling disputes through the personal use of violence. As Harris' and Collins' models predict, these are highly male-dominated societies.

The presence of women actually becomes problematical for these peoples. Women are necessary for their labor and procreative abilities, but their loyalty is suspect because they are not members of the patrilineage and because their interests often lie with the nuclear family rather than the extended family. Women are a potentially disruptive and divisive force. Every attempt is made to subordinate women to the authority of the male kinsmen. Females must exhibit deference to the males of the household at all points of contact. Physical punishments are employed to enforce male authority. Denich notes that this deference is shown in public by the wife customarily walking several paces behind the husband, carrying his burdens, and walking while he rides. Within the household, men are served food first and women eat the leftovers later with the children. *Degradation ceremonies* including such rituals as washing the feet of the men are common. The wife's name also reflects male dominance. Among the Montenegrins, after her marriage, the wife is referred to only by the possessive of her husband's first name. Thus, a wife might become simply "John's."

The ideology of male honor and shame deflects many of the conflicts between men over land, water, and animals onto women through its corollary emphasis on females as *sexual property*. Schneider notes this treatment of women as another form of male property:

> In a sense, they are contested resources much like pastures and water, so much so that kidnappings, abductions, elopements, and the capture of concubines appear to have been frequent occurrences at least in the past.[16]

Virginity and chastity are required of women on the pain of death. A woman who violates these sexual codes dishonors herself and her male kinsmen. But to seduce another group's women brings honor to the seducer. Women are expected to share in the defensive burden of protecting their sexuality by always acting in a chaste manner. They should appear in public as seldom as possible, and when they do, they must dress conservatively, deemphasize sexual attractiveness as much as possible, and keep their eyes lowered so as not to invite any male advances. Women are socialized to regard themselves and are regarded by men as shameful temptations who are potential traitors to the household.

Controlling the sexuality of their women is a primary concern of males. An unmarried girl's loss of her virginity or adultery on the part of a wife brings tremendous shame to her family. The family's honor must be avenged and this requires the joint efforts of all close male kinsmen to kill the seducer or at least to obtain some compensation for the insult. Schneider states that the concern in maintaining the modesty of women and avenging violations serves to solidify the male kinsmen in the face of divisive pressures:

> Men not only want to control the sexuality of women; women are for them a convenient focus, the most likely symbol around which to organize solidarity groups, in spite of powerful tendencies toward fragmentation.[17]

In addition, Denich explains that this intense concern with controlling female sexuality derives from the need to present a fierce public face to ward off potential attacks on livestock and pastures: "Evidence of lack of control over women would indicate weakness and possibly reveal the men's vulnerability to other external challenges."[18]

Patrilineality, Organizational Flexibility, and Male Dominance

Although patrilineality is functional for the maintenance of a unified male core for collective work and fighting, it is also associated with a high degree of internal competition and divisiveness. The divisiveness is kept under control to a degree by the solidarity generated by common interests and the ideological supports of honor and shame. However, the divisiveness itself can be adaptive when the household and its herds get too large for the available resources to support. Both the processes of *fusion* and *fission* among pastoralists can generate male dominance and female subordination.

Like the nomadic hunters and gatherers, nomadic herders require an organizational flexibility based on kinship ties which allows them to fuse into larger groupings to take advantage of temporarily lush pasturelands, but more important, for defense against external enemies. They also must break up into smaller units, sometimes down to the nuclear family unit, in order to spread over and utilize the largest area possible. The feuding and raiding among camps and villages partially serves the function of dispersing the population over wide areas as defeated groups move on to avoid further losses. However, the fissioning and dispersal processes are regularly required within the patrilineages or extended family households themselves.

When too many brothers, cousins, sons, and grandsons are within the same domestic group, there is an intense pressure to divide. The amount of pasturage and water necessary to maintain a very large household and its herds are difficult to find without breaking into smaller units and migrating in different directions. There is, therefore, a critical point at which a household that is large enough to defend itself and obtain sufficient grazing lands and water becomes too large for the ecologically allowable population density. Fission is regularly necessary, but the group cannot afford to allow the pressures for division to separate it too soon into units too small for the collective work and defense needs of herding. The problem is thus to maintain household solidarity while simultaneously providing a basis for the eventual destruction of that household. Again degradation and subordination of women are used to symbolize these processes and to deflect the competitiveness of the men on to women as the enemy. Thus, conflicts between brothers are often said to be caused by disputes among wives— "the system can deal with dissension from women more easily than it can with disputes among its male members."[19] As a household becomes too large for environmental conditions, the pressures from wives in the interests of their children become the acknowledged reasons for brothers to divide up their patrimony and set up separate households with their sons. This prevents too much hostility among brothers from accompanying the fissioning and therefore allows the brothers to remain close enough to come to one another's defense whenever necessary. Females are used as *scapegoats* to diminish the impact of the actual rivalries between the male kinsmen.

Where male solidarity is of great importance, it is useful to find an ideological mask for the rivalries among males . . . . The many sources of internal opposition are ideologically combined, and they are articulated in the elaboration of the male–female dichotomy, which both expresses the real opposition between males and females and serves as a screen to conceal the underlying oppositions among males themselves.[20]

RELATIONS BETWEEN THE SEXES

Religion

The cultural degradation and structural subordination of women is supported by the religions of most herders. *Islam* is widely accepted among herders of Asia and Africa, while *Christianity* predominates among European and New World pastoralists. Both of these religions support male dominance; Islam specifically requires female subordination and seclusion. However, the impact of these religions' teachings supporting patriarchy appears to depend on the existence of wider socioeconomic forces toward sexual stratification or sexual egalitarianism. That is, where conditions support a high degree of male dominance and patriarchy, the religious practices supporting these structures are more strictly adhered to, such as among the Mediterranean herders. Where conditions do not so strongly support male supremacy, people are more likely to practice these religions indifferently, for example the Fulani and the Tuareg Moslems. The Tuareg are often noted for the high status of their women despite centuries of adherence to Islam. They have many institutions supporting male dominance, but they are still not as patriarchal or male supremacist as one might expect on the basis of their religion alone.

> The Tuareg woman enjoys privileges unknown to her sex in most Moslem societies. She is not kept in seclusion nor is she diffident about expressing her opinions publicly, though positions of formal leadership are in the hands of the men . . . . She places little value upon pre-marital chastity, stoutly defends the institution of monogamy after marriage, maintains the right to continue to see her male friends, and secures a divorce by demanding it—and she is allowed to keep the children.[21]

Marriage

As we have already noted, pastoralists are predominantly patrilineal and marriage often entails the exchange of women between male-dominated patrilineages. Marriages are often arranged by families to cement political and economic alliances. They usually involve the exchange of large numbers of livestock as *bride-prices* and as *dowries* which further serve to stabilize the marriage arrangements and to solidify the interfamily alliances. Among the Nuer of Africa men view their herds in terms of the number of *wives* they can bring.

> Cattle stand for a wife and are therefore the most important thing in a Nuer's life, because a wife means to him his own home and that he becomes a link in the lineage by fathering a son. Nuer do not grudge the loss of a herd to obtain a wife. They lose cattle, but the wife will bear them daughters at whose marriage the cattle will return, and sons who will herd them.[22]

Divorce is common among pastoralists, however. And men generally have more freedom to obtain divorces than women do. This is particularly true among Moslems who allow men to divorce their wives by merely announcing the divorce in the presence of reliable witnesses. Wives, however, have to undertake litigation to obtain a divorce and the grounds are quite limited. The litigation process, furthermore, usually requires extensive support from some influential male, thus maintaining the dependence of the woman on males even if allowing her a chance for freedom from her husband.

Martin and Voorhies found that *polygyny* characterized the majority of their sample of pastoral societies, and they found a high correlation between the incidence of polygyny and the type of cultivation practiced by pastoralists. The *nuclear family* predominated among those using agricultural techniques while polygyny characterized those practicing horticultural cultivation.[23] This is in accord with the hypothesis that polygyny is more likely to be practiced where additional wives lend increased productivity to the domestic unit, as is usually true in horticultural but not in agricultural societies.

Sexuality

Mediterranean and Asian pastoralists often place great emphasis on female virginity and chastity for the reasons discussed above. They also practice a strong sexual double standard. However, some pastoralists, in particular those of the Sudan and sub-Saharan Africa, allow premarital and sometimes extramarital sexuality for women as well as for men.

The Nuer, for example, are sexually permissive and allow girls as much pre-marital freedom as they do boys. Sexual play is an important part of childhood and after initiation at the age of twelve or thirteen girls begin taking lovers and having both serious and casual affairs. Boys are initiated at about 14 to 16 years of age. They are then expected to take on the rights and duties of manhood in work, play, and war. But during this stage courtship, dances, and affairs are of primary importance. Being attractive to girls in personal appearance and the demonstration of strength and bravery is crucial.

Girls have a great deal of personal autonomy in the Nuer courtship system. The girl may reject or accept a boy's advances. She may want to withhold sexual access in order to demand marriage. However, boys often promise marriage with no intention of actually marrying the girl they are attempting to seduce. It is also possible for the girl to propose marriage to the boy.

After marriage, a sexual double standard is applied. Nuer women should not participate in extramarital sex. A man is supposed to settle down, but if he desires an affair, his wife should not object. Furthermore, a husband can claim compensation for adultery but a wife cannot. Adultery is, however, frequent. It is illegal among the Nuer, but it is not considered immoral. Moreover, the Nuer do not attach much importance to physiological paternity. It does not shame a man to raise children he did not beget.

Female Subordination

Women are subordinate to men in most pastoral societies. Wives are expected to obey their husbands and show respect within the home and in public. Close emotional ties are not likely to develop within these marriages. Women maintain close ties with their children and sometimes with kinsmen and kinswomen and co-wives, but not with their husbands.

Husbands usually have the right to mete out physical punishments to their wives whenever they deem it appropriate. Wife beating is common among pastoralists. But the man who exceeds the culturally acceptable standards of wife beating is likely to be the object of ridicule as one who prefers to fight women rather than men.

Given the subordinate nature of her position in marriage, the pastoral woman typically uses three main tactics in defending her own interests against the power of men: "playing men off against each other, seeking alliances and support from other women, and minimizing contact with her husband." [24] The opposition built into marriage among the Marri Baluch Arabs, for example, leads men and women to view each other as enemies. Love is considered antithetical to marriage:

> Marri men see themselves as opposed by women, as fighting a continuous battle against female recalcitrance and laziness. Women . . . see themselves in a conspiracy of opposition against men.[25]

Among the Marri Baluch it is not uncommon for wives to hate their husbands and in extreme cases to poison them. The men, in turn, regard their wives as polluted, as filth. Sexual intercourse is believed to be polluting. A menstruating woman pollutes anything she contacts and a new mother is polluting for forty days after childbirth. Men express strong disgust with women in general and with their wives in particular.

The power of the husband over the wife is typically limited by the continued guardianship of her kinsmen. In general, females cannot defend their own interests or rights but must depend upon some male or males. The female's father and brothers are expected to protect her interests against her husband and to intervene on her behalf whenever the husband exceeds his proper authority. Among some groups the father has the right to take his daughter away from her husband if he feels she is being abused.

Relying upon male kinsmen for protection, of course, exacts its costs in terms of female subordination. Among the Egyptian Awlad 'Ali, for example,

> It is basically through blind obedience to her father or closest kinsmen that the woman secures the protection and backing of her kin—family, which is the major guarantee of her marital rights. And it is mainly through forfeiting her rights of inheritance that she is able to maintain such protection.[26]

Where there is a high degree of economic interdependence between the sexes and where women can obtain a divorce or separation easily, there is greater equality between husband and wife. If losing his wife means losing his household, his cook, his dairymaid, and sometimes his children, as it does among the Nuer, the husband is more careful not to motivate her to leave. The divorced or separated woman may lose the protection of her kinsmen (especially where they have to return the bride-price to the husband) and find herself in an even more vulnerable and desperate situation than she was with an abusive husband.

Not all pastoral women passively accept abuses by their husbands, however. Evans-Pritchard notes that Nuer women often physically attack their husbands during disputes:

> Should she in a quarrel with her husband disfigure him—knock a tooth out, for example—her father must pay compensation. I have myself on two occasions seen a father pay a heifer to his son-in-law to atone for insults hurled at the husband's head by his wife when irritated by accusations of adultery.[27]

Even though pastoral husbands may have the culturally legitimated authority to dominate their wives and homes, they do not necessarily exercise total power over the women or women's activities.

Child Rearing

Pastoralists' emphasis on the use of force and violence is reflected in their child rearing practices. Like foragers, they encourage a high degree of independence and individualism in their children. But unlike foragers, pastoralists also encourage aggressiveness. Evans-Pritchard notes that among the Nuer, for example,

> from their earliest years children are encouraged by their elders to settle all disputes by fighting, and they grow up to regard skill in fighting the most necessary accomplishment and courage the highest virtue.[28]

Children are expected to begin working at an early age in the sex-segregated division of labor. Boys learn herding and fighting skills from their male kinsmen and neighbors, while girls help with the household tasks and learn from female kin. Among pastoralists who emphasize female chastity, young girls are also taught to be extremely modest and to feel great shame about their bodies. Boys often have to undergo a period as warriors before being allowed to marry, again reflecting the important role of warfare and feuding among herders.

Forces for Change

The pastoral way of life is threatened by the increasing penetration of strong national central governments into the pastoralists' previously remote lands. These governments typically attempt to remove the settlement of disputes from local control. They try to suppress internal warfare, feuding, and raiding. This disrupts the culture, social structure, and ecology of many pastoral peoples, making their way of life unviable. This type of change may be of some benefit to women, as a lessening of the warfare complex may allow some lessening of the male dominance complex which so often accompanies it. But other forces may maintain male dominance and aggressiveness against women even when the warfare complex has been suppressed.

Contact with non-pastoralists has long had a disruptive effect on pastoralism. However, it has not usually brought about an improved status for women. Since more often than not it has introduced sedentary life styles and social structures to these peoples, the subordination of women practiced by sedentary peoples has often been part of the assimilation process. Settled agriculture does not liberate women (see chapters 6 and 7). And yet settled agriculture is often the path forced upon pastoralists by strong central governments seeking to apply national economic developments schemes.

Pastoralists can sometimes escape such pressures for change if they live in areas too barren for exploitation even by modern scientific agriculture. Yet the existence of collectively-owned grazing lands is usually an enigma to government bureaucracies, accustomed to dealing with legal property titles. Modern governments strive to keep close track of their citizens and their resources because they want to know whom to tax and what property belongs to which taxpayer. All such outside controls and influences can disrupt the flexibility of pastoral life. Changes in the basic structure and practice of pastoral life will undoubtedly mean changes in these peoples' gender roles and sexual stratification systems. The changes may not, however, benefit women or lessen sexual inequality.

SUMMARY

Pastoral societies rely on the herding of livestock for at least 50 percent of their diet. The herd constitutes an important form of exchangeable wealth, but market relationships are undeveloped. Exchange is primarily kin based and reciprocal. Collective work groups predominate in both men's and women's labor. There is little class inequality.

The sexual division of labor varies according to the type of nomadism practiced and the amount and type of cultivation. With sex-segregated nomadism women are regularly separated from the herd and therefore do not participate in herding or dairying. This leaves them more economically dependent on men and results in a lower social status. Where women stay with the herd, they are often assigned dairying tasks. Dairying, especially if combined with control over the milk products, affords women greater economic control and a higher social status. Men, however, usually control the most important source of wealth and power—the livestock. Women's contribution to cultivation seems to be dependent on the parent community. Pastoralists who turned to herding from horticulture probably assign women more cultivating tasks than those who emerged from agricultural societies. Although there is significant sex segregation in the division of labor, there is little distinction between the domestic and public spheres. Women's work as well as men's takes place within the wider community.

Pastoralism practiced in competitive environments with a high level of internal warfare exhibits greater sexual stratification than that which does not have severe defense needs. Competitive environments also tend to encourage male dominance by giving rise to patrilineality, a strong emphasis on male honor and shame, and control of females as sexual property.

The religions of pastoralists often legitimate male dominance and female subordination. Males have greater power in the marriage and divorce practices. Close relationships between men and women are inhibited by their patriarchal marriage, family, and gender roles. Child-rearing practices prepare boys for the dominant and aggressive male roles and girls for the more subordinate but often manipulative female roles.

Pastoralism as a way of life is threatened by the penetration of centralized governmental institutions. Change does not necessarily decrease sexual inequality.

Notes

1. M. Kay Martin and Barbara Voorhies, *Female of the Species* (New York: Columbia U. Press, 1975), pp. 337–338.
2. Robert Paine, "Animals as Capital: Comparisons Among Northern Nomadic Herders and Hunters," *Anthropological Quarterly*, 44 (July, 1971), 169.
3. Martin and Voorhies, p. 339.
4. Martin and Voorhies, p. 340.
5. Martin and Voorhies, p. 343.
6. Elise Boulding, *The Underside of History* (Boulder, Col.: Westview Press, 1976), pp. 288–289.
7. Louise Sweet, "Camel Raiding of North Arabian Bedouins: A Mechanism of Ecological Adaptation," in Sweet, ed., *Peoples and Cultures of the Middle East: Vol. I:* (Garden City, N.Y.: Natural History Press, 1970), pp. 265–289.
8. Sweet, p. 272.
9. Sweet, p. 287.
10. Boulding, p. 308.

11. Boulding, pp. 303–312.
12. George Murdock, *Africa* (New York: McGraw-Hill, 1959), pp. 413–421.
13. Jane Schneider, "Of Vigilance and Virgins: Honor, Shame and Access to Resources in Mediterranean Societies," *Ethnology,* 10 (January, 1971), 1–24.
14. Bette Denich, "Sex and Power in the Balkans," in Michelle Rosaldo and Louise Lamphere, eds., *Woman, Culture and Society* (Stanford: Stanford U. Press, 1974), p. 246.
15. Denich, p. 248.
16. Schneider, p. 18.
17. Schneider, pp. 21–22.
18. Denich, p. 255.
19. Denich, p. 256.
20. Denich, pp. 259–260.
21. Robert F. Murphy, "Social Distance and the Veil," in Louise Sweet, ed., *Peoples and Cultures of the Middle East, Vol. I* (Garden City: N.Y.: Natural History Press, 1970), pp. 297–298.
22. E. E. Evans-Pritchard, *Kinship and Marriage Among the Nuer* (London: Oxford U. Press, 1951), 90.
23. Martin and Voorhies, p. 347.
24. Robert Pehrson, *The Social Organization of the Marri Baluch* (New York: Wenner Gren Foundation, 1966), p. 59.
25. Pehrson, p. 60.
26. Safia K. Mohsen, "Aspects of the Legal Status of Women among Awlad 'Ali," in Sweet, p. 233.
27. Evans-Pritchard, 1951, p. 104.
28. E. E. Evans-Pritchard, *The Nuer* (New York: Oxford U. Press, 1940), p. 151.

6

Agrarian Societies
Antiquity and the Middle Ages

As family units shrink in size and increase in self-sufficiency, women come to rely upon their husbands for subsistence. In many cases, economic dependence is complete. Female labor becomes focused upon repetitive, monotonous tasks inside the domicile. Their isolation from "outside" activities eliminates access to avenues of political power and the control of property . . . . In sum, the overall status of women in agricultural or peasant society is one of institutionalized dependency, subordination, and political immaturity.

M. Kay Martin and Barbara Voorhies, *Female of the Species*

As the populations of horticultural and pastoral peoples increase beyond the productive capacities of their technologies and environments, people are motivated to search for more productive means of subsistence. In particular, as land becomes more scarce people can no longer maintain the nomadic life of shifting horticulture or herding. Staying in one place means that they must learn to keep the land fertile for continuous use. To deal with this pressure, people developed the technology and social structure of *settled agriculture*. Agriculture vastly increases productivity and thereby makes possible very different patterns of social organization among sedentary agriculturalists. Out of this process arose such great agrarian civilizations as ancient Egypt, Greece, Rome, and China. The agricultural revolution is usually thought of as progress and often hailed as the "dawn of civilization." However, this progress brings with it a loss of status and power for women relative to men and for the majority of the population relative to a tiny ruling elite.

ECONOMY AND SOCIAL ORGANIZATION

Technology

Agriculture involves first and foremost the use of the plow and draft animals and often entails fertilizing and irrigating the soil. These practices increase the productivity of land and allow for denser populations and more complex social organization. But agriculture is much more strenuous and demanding than horticultural or pastoral production. The agricultural laborer works a longer day and longer seasons than workers in other types of economies. Guiding a plow requires great muscular strength and stamina. Breaking the draft animals to take the harness and plow is a demanding and time-consuming task. Oxen and other draft animals are large and can be difficult to handle. Draft animals cannot be allowed to wander as freely as there is less land for them to roam in and greater danger of their ruining crops if left untended. Therefore, they have to be fed and watered. Their manure must also be collected, carried to the fields, and spread as fertilizer. In addition, agriculture often requires a great deal of strenuous work digging and maintaining irrigation ditches.

The work is so much more demanding than horticultural labor that horticulturalists often resist the introduction of agricultural technique, despite the latter's higher productivity. An agriculture-based economy probably first arose in Mesopotamia and Egypt before 3000 B.C. Agriculture then spread throughout Europe, North Africa, and Asia. Much later it was introduced into the New World and sub-Saharan Africa by European colonists.

Agriculture did not spread to many parts of Africa until forced on the local populations by Europeans, because African peoples' horticultural techniques provided them with an adequate living with much less effort expended. Population pressure on the arable land never became great enough to force the people to increase productivity or face mass famine. Such *population pressure* and *scarcity of resources,* especially land, appear to have accompanied the development of agriculture and its increased productivity in other parts of the world. However, the benefits of this increased productivity do not remain in the hands of the producers. The increased production also often leads to the rise of a social stratification system in which an elite few lived luxuriously off the labor of many.

Class Structure

The level of productivity achieved through plow agriculture allows the production of *surpluses* on a scale unimaginable in hunting and gathering, horticultural, or pastoral societies. For the first time, large segments of the population can be freed from primary subsistence production.* This allows for the rise of urban communities, complex governmental institutions, empires, writing, and a high culture for the elite.[1]

Agriculture transforms the vast majority of the population into *peasants*. Unlike horticultural farmers in non-stratified societies, peasants must give up much of their produce to the ruling class in the form of taxes, rent, tithes, unpaid labor, and gifts. This often amounts to as much as one-half and sometimes more of the peasants' harvest. Except in times of labor shortage caused by wars, famine, or plague, there is a surplus of peasant labor and the elite can afford literally to work peasants to death and replace them. The level of class oppression found in agrarian societies is rarely matched in the horticultural or pastoral societies and never found among foragers.

Slavery is also widely practiced in agrarian societies. Slaves are, of course, even more dependent on and under the control of their masters. Slaves are an especially important benefit of military conquest.

The peasants' high birth rate means that many of the children are forced off the land. These landless peasants are often driven by necessity into the cities and towns and become part of the *urban artisan classes*. These people are sometimes even more despised than the peasantry. They produce necessary goods and services but many lived degraded, poverty-

---

* A very few horticultural societies were sufficiently productive to allow for large urban populations, craft specialization, and leisure classes, but these never reached the scale of the great agrarian civilizations.

stricken lives. The artisans, however, do not constitute more than a small percentage of the population of agrarian societies.

Agrarian societies often had *degraded* or *unclean classes* below the artisan class, such as the Untouchables of India and the Ainu of Japan. These people performed the most despised tasks in the societies such as tanning leather and working with animal carcasses.

Overpopulation among the masses also produces a substantial *expendable class* of criminals, beggars, and chronically underemployed itinerants. Although despised and often living on the verge of starvation, these people provide an important reserve labor force which could be drawn upon in times of labor shortage among the peasantry or artisans.

Above these common classes agrarian societies have important urban *merchant classes* who handle the local and regional commercial activities and trade. This is low prestige work, but it sometimes produces significant wealth.

The *retainer class* of lower government officials, professional soldiers, household servants, and personal retainers who serve the rulers and the governing classes constitute a higher-prestige class. These people mediate between the tiny governing elite and the masses. They are often the ones who perform the tasks directly involved with expropriating the surpluses from the merchants, peasants, and artisans in the form of taxes, rent, and forced labor. Along with the merchants, they deflect the hostility of those being exploited away from the elite onto themselves. The retainer class is not, of course, as wealthy as the governing classes, but they use their positions to amass wealth and live comfortably.

The highest classes in agrarian society are the *governing classes* of top governmental bureaucrats or nobles and the *ruler*—the king or emperor. These people are often fabulously wealthy. They benefit the most from the surpluses produced by the merchant, peasant, and artisan classes.

In addition to these classes, agrarian societies contain one more important class—the *priestly class*. The top leaders of organized religion are drawn from the governing class. These people are often very wealthy and powerful. The lesser clergy are drawn from the lower classes and have little wealth or power. The priestly class serves the governing class and ruler by lending legitimacy to their power and privilege and by helping to control the masses. However, they sometimes challenge the power of the rulers and governing class on the basis of their status as the representatives of god or the gods.

As the above description of the class structure indicates, agrarian societies are characterized by marked social inequality. Exploitation is built into the economy and social organization of great agrarian civilizations.

Community Size

The increased productivity of agriculture makes possible much larger and denser populations than had previously been possible. The cities of agrarian societies have as many as one million inhabitants and societies such as mid-nineteenth-century China contained 400 million people.[2] These societies also controlled vast territories containing ethnically, linguistically, and racially diverse peoples.

Agrarian societies are much more complex than societies based on simpler technologies. Although the rural peasantry constitutes the vast majority of the population and provide the productive backbone, the societies exhibit a high degree of occupational specialization, both regional and local. Trade between different areas is an important benefit of expansion and imperial domination. Transportation and communication systems are needed to maintain the complex political and economic systems.

Leadership and Government

Agrarian societies are held together by powerful central governments or by local warlords. Control of governmental machinery can be used effectively for personal aggrandizement. For this reason, there are continual struggles over power and the privileges that accompany it. There is also continual struggle between the ruler and the governing classes. Most of the time an unstable balance is maintained, giving the ruler certain powers and the governing classes other powers. In some societies, however, one or the other group dominates. In Ottoman Turkey, for example, the ruler was so powerful that even the members of the governing class were his personal slaves, while in medieval Europe the kings had little power compared to the noble governing classes.

Political power and military might are in the hands of the few. Advances in agricultural productivity are accompanied by advances in military technology. The new military technology is used to increase the power of the state and the governing classes at the expense of the masses. The political system is tightly integrated with the economic system. Land is the basis for both economic and political power in agrarian societies. The chief rulers, bureaucrats, and nobles are also the chief landlords.

Warfare

Warfare is chronic in most agrarian states. The societies themselves are formed primarily through conquest. The productivity and technology of agrarian economies makes warfare almost inevitable, and the surpluses produced make conquest profitable. The forcible subjugation as peasants or slaves of foreign peoples increases the exploitable labor supply and greatly expands the wealth available to the conquering elite. Historically, inventions such as the wheel and the sail and the domestication of the horse allowed for the rapid transportation of soldiers, weapons, and supplies over long distances and thereby facilitated external war against foreign enemies. Technological improvements in weaponry also increase the efficiency and destructiveness of warfare.

Warfare is often the chief preoccupation of the ruling classes in agrarian states. Control over the means of violence and warfare such as weapons, transportation, and training is the primary distinguishing characteristic of the elite as compared with the masses. The elite classes gain power and status through warfare and skill in fighting. Warfare pervades their life-style, self-concepts, and culture.

Moreover, as mentioned above, warfare is internal as well as external. The gains from political office are so great that they encourage continual struggles among members of the elite and continual jockeying for power among the different elite classes.

Religion

The religions of the agrarian states reflect the wider social and economic situation. The great universalistic religions—Christianity, Islam, Hinduism, Buddhism, and Judaism—spread and became institutionalized within agrarian societies. Unlike the religions of foragers and horticulturalists, these religions do not emphasize local cults and local gods. Rather, the god or gods reign over all people regardless of residence or group membership. This, of course, mirrors the empire-building of these states and the rule of their monarchs.

The religions also support and legitimate the power of the ruling classes. An extreme example of this was found in ancient Egypt where it was believed that the pharaoh was god and ruled because he was divine. Most agrarian states were not, however, such complete theocracies. Instead, the rulers were seen as ruling because of "divine right" given by God, but not because the rulers themselves were gods. Religion was used to enforce the power of the rulers, and it served as a relatively effective non-coercive means of encouraging the peasants both to produce a surplus and to give much of it up to the secular and sacred rulers.

The religious specialists are themselves often members of the governing classes. Many of them are the younger sons of the nobility who cannot inherit the family estate because of the rule of primogeniture (the eldest son inherits the entire estate). They often live a luxurious life at the expense of the peasantry. Furthermore, religious institutions often own large amounts of land, peasants, and slaves just as the governing classes do.

While reflecting and legitmating the stratification of agrarian states as a whole, the religions also legitmate the sexual stratification system, patriarchy, and male dominance. The teachings of Christianity, Islam, Hinduism, Buddhism, and Judaism all prescribe female subordination to greater or lesser degrees.

Family and Kinship

As the state takes over the integrating functions of agrarian societies, family and kinship ties decline in importance. Political and economic functions are performed by non-kinship-based institutions. (An important exception to this was China, which retained an elaborate clan network as the basis of its economic, political, and class structures.) As land ownership and use rights come to be more and more invested in the individual instead of the corporate kinship group, the unilineal kinship groups or clans, which are so important in horticultural and pastoral society, give way to *bilateral kinship systems*. Large extended families and patrilocal residence patterns decline as *neolocal residence* and smaller domestic units become important.* *Polygyny* also declines among the bulk of the population as the economic productivity of wives declines under the male-dominated agricultural production. Polygyny continues to be practiced, however, among some of the elite. In this case polygyny is a form of conspicuous consumption rather than a means of increasing productivity through increasing the family labor force. For the majority of agrarian populations, *monogamy* increases in importance. Neolocality and monogamy are especially prevalent in the cities and towns. Again, China and other wet-rice culture regions continued to practice polygyny widely. This was probably because women continued to contribute substantially to agricultural productivity in this highly labor-intensive form of agriculture. Furthermore, more wives could produce more sons and thereby increase the male labor force.

Kinship ties remained important in politics and in the inheritance of position and wealth. This, of course, affects only the upper classes, but among the common classes family ties remain important in economic matters as well. Businesses are usually family businesses and agricultural land is usually worked by families.

Marriages are made as economic alliances among all but the poorest people and for political alliances as well among the upper classes. It is important to join two plots of farmland together through marriage or to cement a truce by marrying one's sons and daughters appropriately. Love

---

* *Neolocal residence:* the married couple lives separately from either the husband's or the wife's kin.

and attraction are not important considerations in making marriages. Husbands and wives are not expected to develop close emotional bonds.

Child Rearing. Child rearing practices reflect the wider political and social stratification system. Discipline and obedience are emphasized; love and affection are not. Among the common classes children are put to work at an early age. Socialization is highly sex segregated. Girls are taught domestic skills in all classes. Among the elite they are also expected to learn the feminine social graces for pleasing men. Girls are also taught modesty and submissiveness to men and sometimes the skills required to manipulate men. Commoner boys are taught economic skills. Elite boys learn the arts of warfare and politics and sometimes art, literature, and high culture in general.

GENDER ROLES AND SEXUAL STRATIFICATION

Agrarian societies are characterized by marked sexual stratification as well as class stratification. The subordination of women reaches its highest degree in agrarian civilization. One of the important factors in reducing the status of women in agricultural as compared with horticultural societies is the sexual division of labor. As was pointed out earlier, agricultural labor requires great muscular strength, long hours, and often takes the worker far from the home and places him in dangerous work situations. Much of it is therefore not compatible with pregnancy or child care. Women thus lose their roles as primary economic producers under agriculture.

Peasant women do not remain idle, however. They work long hard hours within the home processing the products of men's labor: baking, preserving food, weaving, and sewing. Women undertake a great deal of agricultural labor, but the tasks are of a secondary nature. They usually do not clear the land, plow, or dig the irrigation ditches. They also become intensive breeders of the labor supply. Agricultural women have more children more closely spaced than horticultural women. Peasants react to their poverty by trying to produce large numbers of sons. The birth rate in agrarian societies is higher than in any other type of society and the spacing between children is much shorter. Rae Blumberg notes that peasants have little control over the amount of land or capital at their disposal, but they can attempt to expand their labor supply through having children.[3] In terms of the short run interests of individual peasants or peasant families, large families increase their chances for survival. A large number of children, expecially sons, allows them to increase productivity through increased labor inputs. It also helps ensure that the aging peasant man and woman will have someone to care for them when they can no longer produce for themselves. However, in the long run the high birth rate undermines the position of the peasantry as a whole by keeping the overall labor supply high. Any one peasant is often expendable and easily replaced by other hungry, eager workers.

X   Women also constitute an important reserve labor supply which can be used in periods of peak labor demand such as the planting and harvesting seasons. Blumberg suggests that the chronic labor surpluses of agrarian societies are more important in explaining women's lowered status than is the strenuous nature of the work.[4] Women can perform the agricultural labor, but they are not likely to be as efficient as male laborers. Since these societies usually have an abundance of laborers, males are given first preference as workers. Women are in that sense another group of expendables who can be kept out of the primary production or paid a much smaller share of the crop than men. They can, furthermore, be kept busy at auxiliary tasks and child care and still be available when male labor is insufficient. In highly labor-intensive areas such as China women remained a part of the regular labor supply. No reserve labor was needed because extra labor could almost always be used to increase productivity without expanding the amount of land under cultivation.

This sexual division of labor gives rise to a separation of the sexes in the public/domestic dichotomy emphasized by Rosaldo (see Chapter 2). As women lose their productive roles in agriculture they are more and more isolated into smaller domiciles. Large collective female work groups decline. And the bases of female solidarity decrease:

> As family units shrink in size and increase in self-sufficiency, women come to rely upon their husbands for subsistence. In many cases, economic dependence is complete. Female labor, encapsulated as it is, becomes focused upon repetitive, monotonous tasks inside the domicile. Their isolation from 'outside' activities eliminates access to avenues of political power and the control of property, both real and portable. In sum, the overall status of women in agricultural or peasant society is one of institutionalized dependency, subordination, and political immaturity.[5]

The dependency may not, however, be as extreme as Martin and Voorhies suggest. The sexes are really interdependent. Men need the labor of their wives and women need their husbands. But it is an unequal interdependence because of the male control over primary economic production and the female relegation to secondary tasks.

The low status of women in agrarian societies is probably also related to the militaristic nature of these societies. Warfare, as discussed earlier, is endemic to these societies. This increases the male emphasis on aggressiveness and bravery. As Collins pointed out (see Chapter 2), the concentration of military might in the hands of powerful warlords is likely to lead to females becoming just another form of property to be conquered and ruled. Such control over women is a matter of male honor among many agrarian warlord classes. This is likely to be especially true when warfare is conducted close to home. However, when warfare takes the men away for long periods of time, as Harris suggests, women are often left in control of the family holdings. Enterprising women are sometimes able to turn this opportunity into power, privilege, and personal autonomy for themselves.

Sexuality

The isolation of women in the domestic sphere and the view of women as a form of property for males are accompanied by strict controls on female, but not male, sexuality. Agrarian societies tend to place extreme importance on premarital virginity and chastity for married women. Women are not supposed to do anything that can give the slightest suggestion of sexual activity or interest. Violations of these sexual taboos are often severely punished for females. To help ensure the sexual purity of the family's females, females are subjected to spatial separation and isolation in the home. The less contact with nonkin males, the better. This is difficult to enforce among poorer families who cannot afford separate living quarters, courtyards, high walls, and elaborate veils to protect their women from view. But upper-class women are severely isolated from men. The practice of *purdah* among Moslems is an extreme example of such seclusion. Females of the wealthier classes are expected to live their whole lives without being seen by a non-kinsman. Separate female quarters are maintained in the home. If male guests are present, females retire to their quarters or serve them from behind screens. Errands outside the home are performed by males or lower-class servant women. If the woman has to leave the home, she goes accompanied by servants and covered from head to toe in a veil with only small slits for her eyes. When railroads were introduced into India, special windowless cars were made available for women practicing purdah.

Although some upper-class women in agrarian society have become influential behind-the-scenes manipulators, and many can enjoy the luxurious life-style afforded by great wealth, they are still likely to be isolated and subordinated to the men of their class. Upper-class females are also likely to be used as pawns in male political and economic alliances. Their class status gives them some privileges and some power over lower-class males and females, but it does not necessarily lessen the gap between them and their men.

Ideology and Gender Role Stereotypes

Agrarian societies also develop elaborate religious, moral, and legal justifications for their sexual stratification systems. Thus the religions of agriculturalists emphasize male dominance and female subordination and often female inferiority and uncleanness as well. They legitimate the patriarchal family structure and rationalize women's isolation in the domestic sphere. Martin and Voorhies note that ideologies of agriculturalists come to include gender role stereotypes which emphasize the male's physical, intellectual, and emotional fitness for public roles. Females are viewed as inherently suited for domestic tasks and as incapable of assuming public political and economic roles. Furthermore, stereotypes of females present them as needing male direction, supervision, and protection.

Now that the general characteristics of agrarian societies and the positions of women and men within them have been considered, specific historical examples of agrarian societies are offered, beginning with the maritime society of ancient Crete and the full-fledged agricultural society of ancient Greece. This is followed by examinations of ancient Rome and medieval Europe.

ANCIENT GREECE

A review of the changing positions of women and men in Greek society from the Minoan civilization on the island of Crete to the Hellenistic period in Athens and Sparta provides illustrations of some of the evolutionary changes in sexual stratification that accompany the rise of agrarian society.

Minoan Civilization

Minoan civilization arose and flourished on Crete from about 3000 B.C. until it was destroyed by earthquakes in 1500 B.C.[6] Crete never developed a full-fledged agricultural society, nor did it ever exhibit a truly patriarchal, strongly male-dominant sexual stratification system. The primary source of wealth on Crete was seafaring trade. The fertile land supplied the people with food, but population pressure was never so great as to force them into more intensive agricultural practices or into exploitative compulsory systems of production and exchange. Instead they retained the horticultural pattern of small-scale, independent female gardening, although they used such technological advances as irrigation.

In addition to the lack of serious population pressure, the lack of defense needs also helped keep the independent farmers from being transformed into a heavily taxed peasantry. Minoan civilization was not militaristic or warlike. They increased their wealth through trade, not through internal or external conquest. No large powerful warlords or landlords arose. Their island location protected them from outside attack. Thus there was no need for centralized military leadership and no need to collect taxes or forced labor for weaponry and fortifications. Political power remained decentralized among the merchants with a great deal of struggling between rival houses. But there was no need for males to develop fierce aggressive personalities at the expense of women's autonomy and social position.

In the absence of pressure to increase agricultural productivity and in the absence of war, the development of a wealthy stratified society and high civilization on Crete did not bring about the destruction of female economic participation, nor the destruction of the matrilineal clan structure. Females continued to be the primary food producers and participated with men in the trading and commercial activities which were the backbone of the economy of Crete. Women also hunted and practiced various arts and crafts. Women were not, therefore, transformed into the economic dependents of men nor were they isolated in the domestic sphere away from the public worlds of the economic, political, and social structure. The high status of women is reflected in the religion of Minoan Crete. Goddesses were of great importance, but no powerful king or dominant male god has been found.

Bronze Age Society

Because they could maintain a peaceful society without population pressure or war, Crete followed a very different developmental cycle than that found during the Bronze Age on the mainland of Greece.[7] Mainland Greeks were extremely vulnerable to attack. The warlike Achaeans had subjugated the local peoples and developed urban centers by 1600 B.C. This was a society ruled over by military kings who were seafaring warriors. The local peoples were reduced to peasant status. The peasant surpluses and the booty from conquest were used on weaponry, fortified palaces, and strong walls. Women did not have as high a status among the Achaeans as among the Cretans. However, the women of the dominant warrior classes were not totally stripped of power nor were they secluded, because the distant wars across the seas kept the warrior males away for long periods of time. This left the lady of the household in charge of its management. Although a patriarchal family structure was becoming the established norm, women were still not considered inferior or incompetent.

Thus male absence diluted somewhat the male dominance that accompanies a militaristic society.

But the fierce aggressiveness and competition among males did render females as prizes to be won by the bravest warriors. The women of a conquered people were taken as slaves and concubines of the victorious group. The domination of women accorded prestige to men and an extra measure of prestige accrued to the man who held as slave a wife or daughter of a high-status male opponent. The female slaves were, of course, sexually available to their masters. However, virginity and chastity were required of these same males' daughters and wives. But violation of the sexual code by females was not as severely punished during this period as it came to be later. Bronze Age women were expected to be modest, but they were not as firmly secluded in the household as Greek women came to be in Classical times. The division had already arisen, however, between the domestic sphere for females and the public sphere for males. Free women and slave women worked at the household chores while free men busied themselves with matters of war and politics. The lower classes and slave men and women carried out the menial work of the society.

The kinship system of Greece during the Bronze Age reflects its transition to the agrarian way of life from simpler, nomadic foraging and horticultural practices. Both matrilineality and matrilocality, and patrilineality and patrilocality were practiced, depending on which pattern best suited the interests of families making the marriage alliances. An especially important example of the continuance of matrilineality is seen in the marriage of Helen of Troy and King Menelaus of Sparta. Helen's father had been the previous king of Sparta and Menelaus held his throne by virtue of his marriage to Helen. She may indeed have been beautiful and desirable, but this is rarely sufficient reason for waging a costly war. When Helen ran away with a Trojan prince and took him as her husband, Menelaus had to fight the war with Troy and recover her as his wife in order to retain his legitimate right to the throne. For this same reason he could not punish her for her treachery. She was his link in the matrilineal and matrilocal succession. However, the need for strong male leadership under conditions of a constant threat of war led to the decline of matrilineality and matrilocality as a general practice among Greeks.

The Dark Ages

The Bronze Age ended when aggressive nomadic tribes from the north overran the mainland in the twelfth century B.C. and ended the Mycenaen civilization. Writing disappeared and Greece entered its Dark Age followed by the Archaic Period.[8] These were also periods of great internal strife among local warlords. Gender roles continued to emphasize the male as warrior and the female as producer of warriors. Marriage alliances between powerful warrior families were an important part of the overall political structure. Women were used to solidify agreements between powerful families.

This was also a period of great population pressure. And as we would expect on the basis of Harris's theory, not only was warfare a constant problem, but infanticide was also widely practiced. Female infanticide was more common than male infanticide. And, as Harris's theory predicts, the status of women was low. However, variations did occur among the different city states and between women of different classes.

Athens. In Athens free women were firmly tied to the domestic sphere. Although poor women and slave women were often forced to work in the public sphere, the only respectable public roles for women were centered around religious festivals and funerals. Sarah Pomeroy suggests that women acquired their role as mourners of the dead because of their dependency on males. The death of her kinsmen often meant that the woman had lost her protection and support and would suffer greatly as a consequence. She had a great deal to mourn under such conditions.

Institutionalized frigidity for women was also established in Athens by the Dark Ages. "Good" women were not supposed to show any interest in sex. They were to submit to their husbands because it was their duty to bear sons. This was accompanied by a sexual double standard for men, sexual exploitation of slave women, and a concern for male honor through controlling the sexuality of wives and daughters. As Collins predicts, feudal-type warrior classes came to view women as sexual property and to view male status in terms of control over such property.

Sparta. The position of women in Sparta was quite different from that in Athens. Although they never exercised the same political rights as men and although men did not consider them as equals, free women had a great deal more personal autonomy in Sparta. The Spartans were a highly militaristic society, but they were more involved in long distant war than Athens. Males were thus absent for long periods of time. The men also lived most of their adult lives in the military barracks and visited their wives only briefly at night. Adultery was not condemned for women. The emphasis was on the production of healthy Spartan children and women were encouraged to take lovers in order to increase the chances of conception.

Spartan women were not tied to the household or housework. The huge slave class in Sparta performed the menial labor. Citizen women, like citizen men, were expected to spend their time serving the interests of the city-state. This involved both men and women in maintaining physical fitness. Athenian women by contrast did not exercise or receive the same food allotment as men. Spartan women were treated equally with men in matters of health and nutrition.

The freedom of Spartan women in comparison to Athenian women is also reflected in their dress. Spartan women wore short, loose-fitting dresses which left their legs bare and afforded easy movement. Athenian women wore heavy, voluminous, cumbersome dresses which greatly inhibited their freedom of movement.

The greater equality of Spartan women with their men is also seen in the customary age at marriage. Spartans did not practice child marriage for females. Athenians, however, married their girls at the age of twelve to help ensure their virginity. Child marriage also helps ensure the dependency of the wife. It is very difficult for a child bride to be the physical or intellectual match of an adult husband. The Spartans did not institutionalize this type of male advantage in their marriage practices and male dominance and control over wives was not as significant to Spartans as it was to Athenians.

Male absence seems to be of primary importance in explaining the relative freedom and autonomy of Spartan women. Gortyn, one of Sparta's closely related neighbors, differed in the extent of male absence and accorded its women much less freedom. They were not as deeply involved in distant warfare. Therefore, the men were in residence most of the time, although as in Sparta, they lived with their army group. Gortyn women were not, however, as restricted as Athenian women.

Homosexuality was fairly common among males during this period. The long military campaigns and the separation of the sexes encouraged its practice. It was practiced among women, however, only in certain areas of Greece. The island of Lesbos is perhaps best known in this regard because of the work of its great female poet Sappho. Pomeroy argues that where women were disparaged, degraded, and isolated as in Athens, even women could not love women. On Lesbos the situation was quite the opposite:

Women did not . . . turn to other women in desperation due to men's disparagement of them. Rather, it appears that they could love other women in milieux where the entire society cherished women, educated them comparably to men of their class, and allowed them to carry over into maturity the attachments they had formed in the all-female social and educational context of youth.[9]

As Greek society continued to evolve during the Dark Ages and Archaic Period, the class structure became more rigid. The upper class or aristocracy became more powerful and wealthy. In Sparta the change from the rigorous simplicity of earlier years to more luxurious living and the subsequent decline of Sparta's military power were blamed on women. In

Athens women were also penalized for the excesses of the aristocracy. Solon codified the laws of Athens in the sixth century B.C. To curb the activities of the aristocracy, he institutionalized a great many legal strictures on the already restricted Athenian woman. He wrote into law the distinction between good, pure women and bad, sexually available women. This included reserving the legal right to a male guardian to sell into slavery or prostitution an unmarried girl who lost her virginity, even if it was due to rape. Solon established state-owned brothels in order to make Athens attractive to foreign businessmen. He limited the amount of jewels, clothes, and food and drink that free women could have. He restricted their walks in order to restrain the practice of displaying male wealth through the flaunting of expensively adorned wives and daughters. Solon, himself a homosexual, considered women a source of strife among men and attempted to solve this problem by isolating women from the male public sphere. Citizen women were to serve the family and the state by producing children to perpetuate the lines of descent and the ancestor cults based on them. Citizen men were to serve the state through their political and military roles.

The Classical Period

Solon's restructuring of the Athenian law code ushered in the Athenian democracy and what has come to be known as the Classical Period beginning in the fifth century B.C.[10] Athens was the leading political, economic, and cultural power in Greece despite crippling wars with the Persians and Spartans. The position of women reached its lowest point in this period of democracy. The restriction of the public activities of women evolved into the full-fledged seclusion of women. Respectable women were to remain in the home at all times except for certain festivals and funerals. The home itself was divided into the public rooms for males and women's quarters or *gynaeceum*. The gynaeceum was the most isolated part of the house and no males except close kinsmen could legitimately enter it. Here the citizen woman and her children and slaves carried out the domestic routine. The work of the citizen woman was the same as that of the slaves she directed. The work was important to the Athenian economy but it was not valued by Athenians. "Since the work was despised, so was the worker."[11]

Respectable women were under the perpetual guardianship of males. As daughters they were under the authority of their fathers. Authority passed to the husband at marriage and to the son if a woman were widowed and not remarried. Women were often married several times during their lives because of the large age difference between the girl and her first husband. It was common for a girl of twelve to be married to a man in his thirties. Marriages were, of course, arranged by fathers and it was absolutely imperative that the girl be a virgin. If it were discovered on the wedding night that she was not a virgin, the husband had to renounce her and her family was publicly humiliated.

Similarly, the husband was required by law to divorce a wife caught in adultery. Men were greatly concerned with the possibility of being cuckolded, and it did seem to occur often, despite the severe penalties. The wife became a social outcast and lost her rights as a citizen. The husband had the right to kill the seducer or to demand compensation for the damage done to his "property." The penalties for rape were less severe for the male, who had to pay a fine for compensation. The woman, however, was still "ruined property" and had to be divorced and possibly sold as a slave or prostitute.

Women had few independent economic or political rights. Classical law vested almost all power in the hands of the male head of the household, who was expected to act in the interest of the women, slaves, and children who comprised his household. The law did, however, attempt to provide some economic security for the wife by protecting her dowry. In order to marry, the daughter had to be provided with a dowry commensurate with her family's wealth and social standing. The dowry was passed to the husband who could use it as he saw fit, but he could not sell it. It had to be maintained intact and be returned to the woman's guardian for her support if she were divorced. Divorce was easy to obtain and the futures of women would have been even more insecure if their dowries had not had this protection. In the case of women with substantial dowries, the law served to inhibit men from divorcing their wives in order not to lose control over such important wealth or property.

Classical Marriage.   The marriage relationship was not one of close emotional companionship in Classical Athens. Wives were kept uneducated, isolated, and ignorant. They could not be expected to provide the stimulating companionship of the husband's male friends or the noncitizen female companions of men called *hetairae*. Close relationships between men were encouraged and homosexuality was not uncommon. Marriage was intended to produce heirs for the patrilineage. But because population pressure and the costs of endowing a daughter and supporting a son were so great, small families were desired. Few families reared more than one daughter, and two sons were usually sufficient. Infanticide was practiced in particular to limit the number of daughters. Once the requisite number of sons were born, husbands would sometimes cease having sexual relations with their wives. The relationship between husbands and wives was so distant that citizen men were required by law to sleep with their wives three times a month in an attempt to ensure the continuation of citizen families.

Classical Child Rearing Practices.   Child rearing practices in Greece reflected the wider social structure. Girls and boys were socialized into almost opposite personality traits. Girls were reared to be silent, submissive, and to abstain from men's pleasures such as sex, politics, and learning. They were taught domestic skills and married off at an early age: "While her male contemporary was living in his parents' house and developing mental and physical skills, the adolescent girl was already married and had young children." [12]

Philip Slater develops the controversial argument that the Athenian subordination and seclusion of women in the domestic sphere led to the development of psychologically destructive child rearing practices, especially in the raising of sons. [13] Fathers kept their distance from the household and involved themselves very little in child rearing. Mothers acquired by default a great deal of power over the children. Yet they had no other outlets for the exercise of power in Athenian society. Slater maintains that women "were legal nonentities, excluded from political and intellectual life, uneducated, virtually imprisoned in the home, and . . . regarded with disdain by the principal male spokesmen . . . ." [14]

Women's resentment of their low status was focused on their sons. They simultaneously hated their sons as members of the powerful privileged sex and idealized them and desired to experience success in the public world vicariously through the achievements of their sons. Thus sons were alternately belittled and exalted by their mothers. Furthermore, all this occurred in a misogynistic context. The son was reared in a culture which derogated women yet his first years of life were spent in a female-dominated environment. This all served to produce men who feared women. Such men also developed narcissistic personalities and exhibited great concern with how others viewed them and an intense preoccupation with honor, glory, and competitiveness. These concerns grew out of their anxieties about their manhood. Their early subordination at the hands of their resentful, vindictive mothers left them with deeply embedded doubts about their superiority. Yet both their mothers and the wider society expected them as males to be superior. According to Slater this was one reason why "life in fifth-century Athens seems to have been an unremitting struggle for personal aggrandizement—for fame and honor, or for such goals as could lead to these (wealth, power, and so forth)." [15] It also helps explain the emphasis on fierce aggressiveness and the need to fight and win wars with external enemies. They tried continually to affirm their masculinity.

Male Fear of Women. The effects of these child rearing practices on males also contributed to a vicious cycle in the subordination of women. Because women were subjugated and isolated in the home, they vented their frustrations on their sons. The sons then came to fear women and prefer the company of men. They thus grew into men who avoided the home and all things feminine. They derogated women and kept them from participating in public life in an attempt to prove their own male superiority. This of course left women frustrated in the home to produce another generation of misogynistic males.

Slater argues that the same fear of women at least partially explains the high incidence of homosexuality among Greek males. Adult males preferred anal intercourse with young boys to sexual relationships with either adult males or females. The boys sought these emotional and sexual attachments with adult men in order to free themselves from attachments with their mothers. As they grew older, however, taking the passive, feminine role in homosexual relationships became unacceptable. It was viewed as degrading, as too feminine for men. Adult males were

homosexuals of the black leather variety—compulsively masculine, scornful of womankind, phobic about all things feminine, and very concerned with maintaining a dominant and aggressive self-image. By substituting a young boy for a woman the Greek male could realize all these needs simultaneously—still playing a phallic male role but avoiding the dangerous female.[16]

This same fear of women is also seen in some of the beauty practices of Greek women. For example, it was customary for women to remove their pubic hair. The psychodynamics of male fear of women is often related to a disgust for or fear of the female genitals in general and female pubic hair in particular. Removing the pubic hair makes the mature woman seem to be a less threatening, immature girl. The practice of marrying adolescent girls may have a similar psychodynamic origin.

Slater maintains that the Greek male's phobia of women is also mirrored in Greek mythology and Greek literature. The powerful, often dangerous women of Greek myth and literature indicate not that women were powerful, but that men were afraid that women might be superior to them and therefore dangerous.

Nonstereotypical Female Roles. Although the pattern of secluding women may have produced the results Slater suggests, not all Greek women adhered to the ideal secluded domestic pattern. The secluded life was probably practiced by the minority of relatively well-to-do women whose husbands could afford the household structures and slaves required for seclusion.[17] Poor women and slaves worked at a variety of occupations outside the domestic sphere. Foreign women could move freely through the city, exempt from the laws imposed on citizen women. Some women of very high status also had great freedom because of their social position. Perhaps more important, however, was the large class of women known as hetairae that stood outside the legitimate Greek family and citizenship systems.

Modern scholars have tended to lump all these women together as prostitutes, albeit often noting that they were "high class prostitutes." Many of them were prostitutes, but not all sold their sexual services. Boulding notes that it is more accurate to distinguish three classes of hetairae. Some were scholars who "could attend the Academy and the Lyceum and participate in lectures and discussions on an equal footing with the men," [18] such as Plato's pupils Lasthenia and Axiothea. These women were true contributors to the intellectual and political life and the advancement of knowledge in Greece. A second group of hetairae were poets. The modern emphasis on Sappho makes it appear that she was unique, but Boulding points out that she was one of many female poets. The third group were the true hetairae (or sexual companions of men); some of these women were skilled entertainers, cooks, and nurses. Although men enjoyed the company of these women, their feelings about them were ambivalent, for their accomplishments proved that women were not such lowly creatures as Greek ideology maintained.

Despite the participation of the hetairae in Greek intellectual development, the Greeks developed "scientific" explanations supporting female subordination and inferiority. Among the greatest Greek philosophers and scientists were Plato and Aristotle.[19] Their works display misogyny and sexism, although Plato has been considered somewhat of a feminist by some scholars because of certain passages in the Republic. In developing his image of the ideal society in the Republic, Plato argued for greater liberties for women. He wanted to open public life to women, but only to a degree. For example, he felt that women should be educated but believed women were intellectually inferior to men. He would allow women to compete equally with men but expected them to fail. He still supported the view that woman's main function in society was childbearing. Moreover, in his later work the Laws he reversed many of his quasi-feminist positions and asserted the importance of the patriarchal family and male dominance. Plato also idealized love and companionship between men rather than between men and women.

Plato's pupil Aristotle can be credited with introducing the "scientific" proof of female inferiority into Western thought. According to Aristotle nature had created females the physical, mental, and moral inferiors of men. Such inferiority was built into the female physiology and biology: male dominance was nature's plan. Aristotle argued that this was the case even in reproduction. According to Aristotle the male semen played the active role in creation of new life. The female was merely the field for sowing the male seed. (This belief and analogy clearly reflect the agrarian base of Greek society and culture.) Aristotle concluded from his discussion of reproduction that nature intended the female to be passive. He was horrified by the freedom accorded Spartan women.

The Hellenistic Period

This period of Greek history was brought to an end by the consolidation of the Greek city-states into the Macedonian empire of Alexander the Great, whose father Philip conquered Athens and its allies in 338 B.C. This imperial era is known as the Hellenistic Period of Greece.[20] The Greek city-states lost their independence. The local control of weaponry by citizen males was shifted to the standing armies of the central governments of Alexander. According to Collins (see Chapter 2) the removal of arms from the control of the local patriarch should decrease the power of these males and afford a degree of independence for women. This appears to have been true in Hellenistic Greece. Women were not so firmly suppressed and isolated as they had been in Classical Athens. Education, including physical education, was extended to some of the daughters as well as the sons of the well-to-do. There was a re-emergence of female poets. And as Collins predicts, women were able to raise their positions within marriage and the family setting. The marriage relationship became emotionally closer, love-matches increased in importance, and private family life was idealized.

During the Hellenistic period women gained in economic and legal freedom, except in Athens, which firmly held to the principle of male guardianship. But many of the previously male rights that now extended to women were no longer of great value, since decision making and power now lay with the monarch rather than with the citizens. Women did, however, become less isolated, even in Athens. And in other cities, where women gained legal and economic rights, a few women came into control of substantial fortunes and used their wealth for political office and political rights. But these women were exceptions. Women, in general, continued to be excluded from full citizenship rights and political participation.

One force toward greater freedom and public involvement of women came from the example of the Macedonian queens and princesses. Because of the long absences of their male rulers in the wars creating the empire, royal women were often left in charge of the court. Royal wives and mothers were often ruthless in their quest for power for themselves and their sons. Alexander's mother Olympias presided over the court in his absence; her intrigues included the murder of relatives. She eventually failed in her power-hungry quests and was stoned to death by other royal relatives. The Macedonian princesses could not legitimately rule in their own rights, but they were active forces in the political arena. Their public roles provided the example for nonroyal women of the empire and brought many wealthy women out of seclusion. However, even the wealthy women could not come close to attaining equality with men.

ANCIENT ROME

The history of ancient Rome spans a dozen centuries. The *Archaic Period* began in 753 B.C. with Rome's monarchical and feudal stage as an agricultural society. It ended with the overthrow of the kings and the establishment of the Republic in 509 B.C. Rome was involved in almost constant internal and external warfare. Its success in external wars, in particular the Punic Wars with Carthage in the third century B.C., resulted in the conquest of a great empire. With imperial domination abroad lubricating the trade routes to Rome, business and commerce, an urban way of life, and extensive slavery increased in importance. The period of the *Late Republic* was one of great internal strife and jockeying for power among members of the upper class. It ended with the defeat of Antony and Cleopatra by Octavian in 27 B.C. Octavian then declared himself Emperor, took the name of Augustus, and set about trying to curb the excesses and decadence of the Roman upper classes through his strong centralized rule. The *Empire* continued for five more centuries until internal disruptions and external threats finally led to its dissolution and Europe entered its *Dark Ages.*

The positions of women and men in Rome and the nature of the sexual stratification system underwent important changes as the Roman economy and society evolved.[21] As is typical of an agrarian society, a greater or lesser degree of female subordination characterized all the periods of ancient Rome. The Roman woman was, however, never as subjugated and secluded as was the Athenian woman of antiquity.

The evolution of Roman society during the early period provides an illustration of what Collins called fortified households in stratified society (see Chapter 2). However, after Rome's success in the Punic Wars, Rome developed a more centralized government and relied more heavily on a market economy. During this later period, it took on more of the characteristics of what Collins referred to as private households in market economy.

Rome Before the Punic Wars

In the early or Archaic Period Rome was a strongly patriarchal society. The head of the household, or *paterfamilias,* was the absolute power in the patrilineal, patrilocal extended family. He held absolute sway over the lives and fortunes of his wife, children, servants, and slaves. He could have them put to death or sell them at will. A newborn infant was accepted into the family only if the father allowed it. Otherwise, it was exposed and either died or was picked up by slave traders. Infanticide, and particularly female infanticide, was therefore accepted.

The extended family household and the wider patrilineal clan structure were key institutions in Rome's early history. The household was largely self-sufficient. It produced and processed its own food, clothing, and shelter. Thus, Rome was an agricultural society with production primarily for use value. In conjunction with the wider clan structure, the household solved its own political, economic, religious, educational, defense, and social security problems. It was stratified and not egalitarian because power was concentrated in the heads of the extended families. However, the upper class was not a leisure class: its men and women were heavily involved in productive labor. Males concerned themselves primarily with running and defending the agricultural estates while the women devoted themselves to the domestic sphere of housework and child care.

During this early stage women were under the authority of their fathers first and then of their husbands. Marriages were arranged by the fathers in the interests of the families involved. Romance and personal attraction were not important. A dowry was required for a fully legitimate marriage and it became the unquestioned property of the husband. Virtually everyone married, as the society at this time had no place for unattached adults. Marriages and families were stable and divorce was rare. Monogamy was the rule for men as well as women, but adultery was dealt with much less harshly for men than for women. Virginity was highly valued for unmarried girls. Husbands and fathers had the right to kill unchaste wives and daughters.

This earliest form of marriage, which transferred guardianship to the female's husband, was replaced by the practice of fathers retaining guardianship throughout the daughter's life. This was called marriage without *manus:* without turning over authority to the husband. This gave the father the right to continue to direct the daughter's life after she left his household. He could dissolve her marriage at will and order her back to his home. Sons could eventually gain legal independence, daughters could not.

Although marriage without *manus* affirms the legitimacy of the power of the *paterfamilias,* it probably gave the wife more actual freedom than marriage with *manus*. It gave her some physical separation from those who had authority over her: "she was under the authority of a father or guardian who lived in a different household, while her husband, whose daily surveillance was available, had no formal authority over her."[22]

Even if she were married with *manus*, the woman's father ceased to relinquish total control to her husband. The female's male guardians could still look out for her interests and, in particular, could protect her dowry from her husband's abuses. The dowry was no longer the property of the husband. The wife could also usually return to her father's household if she found life with her husband intolerable. This further weakened the power of the husband over the wife.

However, among the wealthy and powerful, marriages were part of the wider political and economic structure and daughters were used as pawns in the game of alliance-making and alliance-breaking. They could be forced into a marriage which benefitted their family and forced out of a marriage which had ceased to be of benefit. Some women actively participated in the political alliance system by choosing their lovers and even their husbands with an eye to the fortunes of their own families. In this patrilineal society, however, children belonged to the father and remained with him if the mother left. The dowry remained with the wife for her support unless the husband could claim a portion of it for damages.

The female could rarely free herself completely of male control. Upon the father's death guardianship was passed to his sons or to the nearest male relative unless he had designated another male in his will. Females had no independent legal standing and could not openly or freely control their own property without the guardian's assent.

The lack of individual recognition accorded to women is also evident in the Roman practice of not giving daughters personal names. They were merely addressed by the family name with a feminine ending. Thus all daughters in the Julii family would be called Julia. This resulted in confusion when more than one daughter was raised. In that case they were differentiated as "Julia the elder" and "Julia the younger" or as "Julia the first" and "Julia the second." Sons, however, were given individual personal names in addition to the family name. Bullough suggests that

> the whole Roman system was designed to suggest that women were not, or ought not to be, genuine individuals, but only a fraction of a family, specifically anonymous and passive fractions.[23]

Despite being a legal nonentity and not fully recognized as an individual, the Roman woman was not secluded. The upper-class woman directed the household and the slaves and in the early stage she participated in the work also. She could leave the household at will for shopping, the theater or games, visiting, walking, and even to protest at political gatherings. Females were also allowed access to education almost as freely as males.

Rome After the Punic Wars

Again, one of the important factors in granting women greater personal autonomy in Rome was the involvement of Roman men in distant wars that took them away from the city and their homes for long periods of time. In addition, the high male death rate in war freed many women from their male guardians. War thus left women in charge of the management of the family estates and in control of their personal lives. Since some families had all their adult males wiped out in war, many females came to inherit great wealth. And although they were never granted full legal rights to control their wealth, they could usually manipulate the guardianship law by choosing a guardian willing to forego his legitimate right to intervene. Thus by the late Republican Period some women were wielding significant economic power.

The Role of the Roman Upper Class.   Success in wars also led to the concentration of political power in the hands of Rome's important military leaders. The tremendous wealth and vast numbers of slaves that flowed into Rome after the Punic Wars allowed for a more powerful central government to develop, run by representatives of a now exceedingly wealthy aristocratic class. This small upper class came to dominate the economic, political, and social structure of Rome. The large slave class and poor free men and women did the bulk of the menial labor in the society. Since women were barred from political participation, the new wealth freed upper-class women from almost all productive roles in society. Even child rearing was turned over to slaves and tutors. Child-rearing practices also changed from an emphasis on stern discipline to indulgence.

As the upper classes became wealthier they were more and more given to extravagant displays of homes, carriages, clothing, and jewels. Women are often accused of having contributed significantly to the decay of Roman life by their luxurious life-style. However, this luxury was often a means for men to flaunt their wealth and status and was not entirely initiated by women, who were the objects of this conspicuous consumption. Some women were also undoubtedly driven to excessive display and leisure pursuits by the boredom forced upon them by their unproductive lives. The economic power of women could not be openly translated into political power. Some managed to obtain behind-the-scenes manipulative political power through their sons or husbands. But more used their wealth to live a life of dissipation.

The greater economic wealth and independence of Roman women provoked an increase in the already misogynistic Roman value system. Political leaders spoke openly and vehemently against women. As Bullough describes it,

> there was a growing denunciation of women by these male writers who believed that the only true state of existence should be a masculine-dominated one. It seems that the more insecure the male feels vis-à-vis the female, the more power he attributes to her, and in the light of historical reality, he has greatly overestimated the real power of women.[24]

Roman literature was strongly misogynistic. Women served as scapegoats for almost all human failings and problems. Men were repeatedly warned that they were better off without women. Even the love poetry condemned women. The lyric poets who popularized the concept of romantic love "managed to make their love affairs sound full of misery, and paint their women in the long run as unworthy of male affection . . . their conclusion was that love (and women) inevitably brought misery to man." [25]

The Romans repeatedly passed legislation to curb the females' use of their own economic resources. The Oppian Law, for example, was passed in 215 B.C. during the second Punic War to prevent women from using their wealth for gold, clothing, ornaments, and chariots. The women did not passively accept these measures. They demonstrated for the repeal of the Oppian Law in 195 B.C. It was repealed, but other laws were eventually passed which attempted the same ends, limiting inheritance by women, and limiting the display of wealth by women. Pomeroy notes, however, that attention was eventually turned more to attempting to control display of men's wealth rather than women's wealth especially as upper-class women became more independent of their male relatives:

> Wealthy upper-class women were considered less as appendages of men, and their displays of wealth brought them status in the eyes of women. But whatever women did independent of men was futile and, though potentially irritating to men, ultimately of minor importance to the state.
>
> When men participated in status-seeking by means of the clothing of their women, then regulation was required.[26]

Women's lack of political power also resulted in poor women being discriminated against in the distribution of welfare benefits. Beginning in the late Republic several relief programs were instituted by the government and some wealthy individuals. Extensive unemployment and poverty threatened Rome's stability, and these programs were intended to quiet unrest and to maintain support for the rulers. Since women could not vote or openly take an active role in politics, they did not receive the free grain.

And men were not given enough to help a wife or family. Some additional programs were set up to care for children, but since their function was to produce future soldiers, they also discriminated against girls.

Decline of Family Life.   Marriage and family among the upper classes lost the stability which characterized early Roman society. Divorce became common and acceptable grounds became more and more trivial. Divorce was easier for the husband to obtain than for the wife, but wives could initiate divorce through their guardians. The rather strict sexual mores of the early period also became more relaxed. Concubinage was quite common, especially for men who desired partners of lower social status. This practice was not as openly permitted to high-status women. The sexual double standard remained strong. Husbands had legitimate sexual access to slaves and prostitutes, because laws extended protection only to women deemed of high enough social status and morality to be worthy of protection. Laws against adultery continued to exact severe penalties, especially for women, but they failed to control the practice. Some Roman matrons went so far as to register as prostitutes in order to protect their lovers from prosecution under the adultery statutes. This loophole was later closed by forbidding high-status women from registering as legal prostitutes.

During this period the marriage and birth rates steadily dropped. This became a grave concern of the rulers, who feared negative consequences from a decline in the numbers of the citizen population and available military personnel. Laws were passed requiring all adult males and females to marry, but they were rarely enforced on males. Yet some people evaded the law by marrying in name only. One law, of particular importance in increasing the personal autonomy of some women, granted full legal independence from the guardianship law to citizen women who bore at least three children and to non-citizen women who had four or five children. Divorce laws were also tightened, but the overall decline in family life remained a problem among the upper classes.

One of the reasons family life lost ground was that the family lost many of its functions. The central government and the developing market economy took over more and more of the power, authority, and functions which the family had previously controlled. The household and the *paterfamilias* were no longer the center of political, economic, religious, educational, and social life. People could live their lives effectively as individuals independent of wider family or kinship structures. This greatly undermined the control the family could exert over its members.

Women's Role in Roman Religion.   In Roman religions women held high status and could participate actively. The Vestal Virgins were the most prestigious, privileged, and influential of Roman priestesses. The safety of

Roman society was believed to depend on their correct practice of ritual and the protection of their virginity during their terms as priestesses. Occupancy of these positions had important costs as well as benefits. From childhood throughout her thirty-year term the Vestal Virgin's life was severely controlled. She had to remain above suspicion concerning her sexual life and moral conduct. Furthermore, when calamities did strike Rome, the Vestal Virgins were likely to be blamed and accused of violating the requirements of their office. This could bring the death penalty to the priestesses.

Pre-Christian Rome had many other cults and religious groups in addition to the Vestal Virgins. Some of them were exclusively female, others were all male. Many allowed for both males and females to participate equally. Husbands and wives also participated in the family ancestor cults of their households, although these declined in importance in the later period. Rome had important goddesses such as Isis, as well as gods such as the militant Mithras popular among soldiers.

The Rise of Christianity in Rome

Christianity arose and spread within the Roman Empire. Since it developed within a more capitalistic market economy of urban Rome instead of the more agrarian societies of the ancient Hebrews, Muslims, Hindus, Buddhists, and Confucians, it is less misogynistic than these other great universalistic religions. It was probably even less misogynistic in its early years when it appealed to the less powerful segments of Roman society. However, it eventually became the state religion of Rome and was incorporated into the male-dominated Roman power structure. Women were soon excluded from equal participation in the religion. Furthermore, as the Roman Empire declined its political and economic institutions were replaced by the agrarian feudalism of the Middle Ages. Christianity, therefore, continued to develop and evolve within a traditional, agrarian, anti-female context and eventually incorporated aspects of female subordination and male dominance.

The earliest Christian followers broke with traditional gender role divisions, minimized sex differentiation, and advocated celibacy. They were detached from traditional family roles. This new way of life was attractive, first to working class and merchant women, and later to women from well-to-do families. The opposition from non-Christians was fierce. A great many women as well as men were persecuted and put to death.

As the Christian movement grew in numbers the concept of celibacy was questioned. In place of celibacy for everyone, the idea of a *calling* arose. This meant that some people were called to raise families while others had the calling to celibacy and would serve the wider society outside the family. This latter group would not allow sexual interests to interfere with their single-minded service to God. Many celibates chose to live lives of solitude in the desert. However, the large numbers of people who chose to withdraw from the world eventually resulted in the founding of monastic communities for communal living. These communities required celibacy, but they were not usually sex-segregated.

After the Emperor Constantine recognized Christianity as the state religion in 313 A.D., the movement began to adopt Roman administrative practices and soon developed a powerful centralized leadership of males. The monastic movement grew in strength as a reaction against this change in church organization. Boulding notes that women were an important part of the monastic movement because "women would have even more reason to protest that hierarchy than would men, since it was crowding them out more than it was crowding men." [27] As women came to be second-class citizens within the church, one of the few outlets for strong women was the monasteries. As canonesses (leaders) and as members they could work and participate in religious and political activities.

The church itself, however, continued to become more and more hostile to females. They lost their public roles and were more firmly assigned to domestic roles under the authority of their husbands. The Church fathers came to equate women with sex, temptation, and sin. Bullough argues that this is linked to the practice of celibacy: "Since the church fathers were male, and many of them became conscious of the physical desires of their bodies when in the presence of women, misogynism became engrained in Christianity." [28] The antifemale belief system defined marriage as a less worthy state than celibacy. The virgin woman came to be admired and the Virgin Mary increased in importance as a religious figure.

As the Roman empire declined and lost power, a powerful, male-dominated, misogynistic Christian church arose within it. The church survived the fall of Rome and continued to be a powerful and influential force throughout the Dark Ages of Europe. Although it had begun as a religion which liberated women and treated them equally with men, by this time it had become a force for subjugating and derogating women.

MEDIEVAL EUROPE

The Early Middle Ages

Little record remains of life in the early middle ages in Europe.[29] The Roman Empire was overrun by nomadic tribes of herders and horticulturalists. Various tribes conquered different areas of the old empire and introduced their own customs. The Germanic tribal traditions mingled with the old Roman customs. As we could expect on the basis of our previous discussion of horticulturalists and herders (see chapters 4 and 5), these tribal peoples had significantly different gender roles and sexual stratification systems than the Greeks and Romans. Women were the subordinate sex among these war-like nomads, but they had greater freedom in some respects. For example, women were less isolated in the domestic household in these tribes. Consequently, women were less isolated in the early middle ages than they became in later periods.

Under the Germanic tribal customs that were incorporated into Roman areas, women were under the guardianship of males, first the father and then the husband. Females were also discriminated against in the inheritance of land and movable property. This originated under war conditions in which conquered land was given to distinguished warriors who were then expected to hold and defend it and provide military service to the lord. Females were excluded from warrior roles and, therefore, were not considered safe defenders of land nor valuable for military support. This tradition persisted, however, long after military support and defense ceased to be important concerns.

Adultery was punishable by death for both males and females. Virginity was highly valued in females. Virgin girls were valuable property for exchange for high bride-prices. For this reason the fines for killing a virgin were double that for killing a man. High fines were also levied for rape and for looking at the body of a virgin girl. In order to discourage attempts to avoid the high bride-prices by abducting girls, the fine for abduction was nine times that of the normal bride-price. The high bride-prices were the result of the severe shortage of women in the early middle ages. As Harris' theory would lead us to expect, Emily Coleman found that agricultural productivity was fairly low in the early middle ages and land was scarce. Population pressure was therefore a problem and female infanticide was widely practiced.[30]

The shortage of women kept the birth rate down and kept the many men who could not acquire a wife from seeking land of their own. This situation also increased the tendencies toward violence and internal warfare. The shortage made women valuable as sexual property, but it did not afford them high status or power. Husbands had the right to beat their wives. Wives were expected to please their husbands but husbands were under no obligation to please their wives. In fact, the shortage of women was also partly the result of women so often being the victims of the violence rampant in early medieval Europe. Thus, as Harris' and Collins' theories suggest, the high degree of internal warfare probably served to keep the female's status low.

Women's Economic Roles

The domestic/public dichotomy between women and men's economic roles had begun to emerge even in the early medieval period. David Herlihy describes women as working very hard in the domestic economy—baking, brewing, and caring for the barnyard animals and gardens.[31] Men were usually kept busy with the heavy cultivation and fighting. The upper class lady was not, however, isolated. The important affairs of the estate took place in the *donjon,* the center of the castle. In this open space which afforded no privacy the lady as well as the lord participated fully. But when war and emigration took the men from the home, women often assumed management of the family property:

> The precise range of woman's inner economy was flexible, expanding or contracting in relation to whether the man had assumed other functions which might keep him from home for lengthy periods or make him disdainful of agricultural labor . . . the Germanic freemen on the eve of the invasions . . . left even agricultural labor to the women and made their contribution to the family fortunes by raids and wars.[32]

Herlihy's study of the records found women as landowners and managers throughout the early middle ages. Similarly, wives of the married clergy often assumed control of their husbands' estates, freeing their husbands to practice their professions. In fact, the economic roles played by many women were so prominent that Herlihy found it was reflected in the widespread use of matronymic names from the mid-tenth century through the eleventh and twelfth centuries.

Royal women also were often important players in the court politics of the time. Boulding notes that the royal princesses were of special importance in the system of marriage diplomacy. Young girls, often no more than ten or fourteen years old, were expected to play important diplomatic roles. The roles were played, moreover, far from their own homes in foreign countries with foreign tongues. Yet, as Boulding's research indicates, they often served admirably as princess diplomats.[33]

Women of all classes served as an important reserve labor force which could be called upon whenever males desired. The roles they assumed during these periods of male labor shortage could bring them power and personal autonomy while they occupied them. But when the males decided to reassume the roles, most females could not prohibit them from doing so. Use of women as a reserve labor force may look like significant change, but it usually does not result in permanent improvement in the position of the group serving as a reserve labor force.

Emily Putnam's work indicates, furthermore, that the concept of the reserve labor force applies even to women's roles in the development of high culture. In the early middle ages with the men concerned with internal strife and the external wars of the Crusades, upper-class women received more education than males. Women were primarily responsible for the development of culture:

> . . . in places where men have leisure for culture, it is believed to belong more or less exclusively to the male type . . . . The learned or the thoughtful woman is rather ridiculous, and certainly a bore. Probably she neglects her children. On the other hand, when men are as a class engaged in the subjugation of the natural world or in struggles with each other, the arts of peace naturally fall into the hands of non-combatants, and are then believed to belong more or less exclusively to the female type . . . . culture is felt . . . to be unbecoming in man.[34]

In the early middle ages women also had important roles in the church. Monasteries were highly autonomous and were often influential and powerful institutions. They were the agents of civilization among the Germanic tribes. They introduced Christianity to the tribal peoples and maintained what little educational instruction there was during this early era. Women as well as men were drawn to the monastic movement, although because there were fewer women's orders it was more difficult for a woman to become a nun than for a man to become a monk. The convents were populated by the daughters of the nobility who either did not desire to marry or could not for lack of a husband or a dowry. Lower-class women could not take vows, but they could often enter the convent as lay sisters and servants to the aristocratic nuns.

Control of the convent gave the lady abbess in particular a powerful position in medieval feudal society. Convents were often large landowners with many peasants attached to them. The lady abbess was sometimes as powerful as a baron or other important lord. Some of the abbesses even headed double monasteries which had a male order as well as a female one. During this early period nuns were not secluded in the cloister. Great freedom of movement and action were allowed to the religious woman:

> Under the presidency of great ladies . . . the abbeys everywhere before the twelfth century were centers where the daughters of nobles might live a pleasant life and receive such education as the time afforded . . . . [A nun] was not always bound by vows, nor distinguished by her habit, nor even required to live in a particular place. Originally she as often as not remained in the world though dedicated to God. When she was attached to a convent it was difficult to find means to constrain her to stay in it.[35]

But the positions and powers that some upper-class women gained in both sacred and secular worlds during the early middle ages could not be sustained. Male dominance was reasserted in all spheres when external warfare diminished and men remained at home, and as the central political institutions strengthened and gained control over the society.

The Later Middle Ages

Kinship and family ties had been important integrating and organizing principles during the tumultuous centuries of the early period. Women could sometimes share in the wealth and power of their families, especially when there were no strong male members to challenge them. But during the later middle ages after the year 1200, kinship began to give way to governmental control of the society. Where power resided in the domestic sphere, women appear to have had some opportunity to share it. When it was removed to the public sphere, they lost those opportunities and women's status in European society appears to have declined substantially. However, Herlihy notes that women's position improved in at least one respect in the late middle ages: "the curtailment of violence in medieval life aided them . . . . The emergence of effective governments assured them greater personal security and protection against rape, abduction and enslavement." [36]

However, this also meant that the shortage of women characteristic of the early period was transformed into a surplus of women. Coleman points out that increased agricultural productivity allowed more female children to be fed.[37] The practice of female infanticide dwindled. Male losses in war and the celibacy imposed on the priesthood meant that more women than men were available for marriage. Women no longer held a high value in the marriage market. High bride-prices gave way to dowries payable by the bride's family to the groom. Dowryless females could not marry.

In the later middle ages the control of the great estates, the state, and the church came increasingly to reside in the hands of men. In their power struggles with the kings, nobles disinherited their daughters and younger sons in order to maintain the size, wealth and importance of the family. The practice of primogeniture, giving all inheritance rights to the eldest son, replaced the practice of allowing all the children to inherit regardless of sex.

In this period, written laws came to replace unwritten tradition as the important ordering principle of society. Women were not treated equally with men under the new laws. Men received rights; women received restrictions.

As the state governmental machinery and bureaucracy expanded, the positions were opened only to males. Education was necessary to fill such jobs. And education was removed from the convents and monasteries (where women had had access to learning) and placed in the cathedral schools and universities which barred women. Women were excluded from culture as well as politics now that men had the time and interest to pursue both.

The church also moved toward a more male-dominated, highly centralized structure. During the later medieval period every attempt was made to reduce the influence, power, and participation of women in church affairs. The great abbesses and convents were stripped of their power and brought under the direction of the male church hierarchy. Stuard argues that the important turning point for women and the church came with the Gregorian reform of the late eleventh century:

> This reform demolished the double monasteries of the earlier era and quite effectively walled women's houses off from the institutional hierarchy of the church. The great medieval church women . . . all belong to the earlier period. As the influence of church women waned, church writings on women showed a greater tendency to regard women as the "other," the basis for a growing misogyny.[38]

As an outlet for the frustrations deriving from their lower status, loss of public roles, and the difficulties even of finding a husband and thus performing a domestic role, women turned to the new heretical movements. In the twelfth and thirteenth centuries single women enthusiastically embraced the Beguine Movement, a lay religious movement not under the direction of the male-dominated church. Beguines lived and worked in all-female communal households and workshops. These contained women from all classes, but all the members lived simply and worked diligently. Their autonomy frightened the church fathers. Independent women did not fit with the church's teachings.

The Gregorian reforms also imposed strict celibacy on the clergy. Bullough argues that much of the misogynistic, antisex stance on the part of the church was the result of the psychological reactions of the clergy to their difficulties with celibacy. Women reminded them of sex and sex was sin; therefore, women represented sin. Eve, the evil temptress of man, came to dominate the church's view of women.

Paradoxically, the emphasis on Eve was paralleled by a new emphasis on Mary, the virtuous virgin mother. The elevation of the Virgin Mary in the church went hand in hand with the increasing fear of women by the church fathers and misogyny in the church's teachings:

> The elevation of the Virgin could only be accomplished by comparing her with the characteristics of ordinary women, and the more she was exalted, the more ordinary women failed to come anywhere near the ideal and the more they could be condemned for their failures.[39]

Furthermore, the church's witch hunts which swept Europe in the fourteenth through the eighteenth centuries were aimed primarily at women and were especially concerned with female sexuality, and in particular with female sexual relations with the devil.[40]

All of the church's teachings were not harmful to women, however. In the early middle ages the church had increasingly taken control of marriage, divorce, sex, and child rearing from the traditional secular authorities. Divorce, which had been easy for males to obtain in the early period, was forbidden to males as well as females. This aided women in that it gave them some protection against repudiation by their husbands at a time when they were becoming ever more economically dependent on men.

The church was highly anti-sex, but it took a long time to impress this on the people. Bawdy plays, tales, and humor were an accepted part of medieval life. Women, even nuns, were not isolated from this aspect of the culture. Boulding argues that

> this shared sense of humor between women and men had egalitarian aspects to it. When men started to creep away to tell funny stories about sex, it was a sign of something more than emerging puritanism. It was a signal that an important dimension of man–woman relationships had atrophied.[41]

As Collins' model predicts, this double standard of enjoyment of sexual humor emerged as the concepts of romantic love and the idealization of women developed. As explained in Chapter 2, women could only maintain their position on the pedestal and reap its advantages at the expense of segregating themselves from the real world of politics, economics, and sex.

Upper-class women supported the developing concept of romantic love as a means of adding interest to their restricted lives. If she could not enjoy the public world of men, the lady could luxuriate on the pedestal. But even romantic love was a double-edged sword of gender stereotypes: "The growth of a romantic and devotional literature extolling women only strengthened the belief in the moral and social dangers of feminine wantonness." [42]

The marriage relationship was not affected by this new emphasis on love. Love was to occur only outside of marriage. Ideally the knight admired and loved his lady chastely and from a distance. She inspired him for battle. He wrote poetry and music extolling her beauty and charms. But he could not marry her because she was married to another. Marriages among the upper classes continued to be made for political and economic reasons, not for love or companionship.

Despite the restriction of their public roles, women continued to serve as a reserve labor force whenever this met the needs of males. Because there was a relative decrease in the number of foreign wars and because the clergy could no longer marry and have wives as managers, upper-class women were therefore less frequently needed to manage family holdings. When necessary, however, ideological and religious prohibitions against public roles for women were relaxed in favor of preserving male and family interests. For example, Susan Mosher Stuard found that among the noble merchant class of Ragusa, an Adriatic city–state, women were important participants in business.[43] The laws of Ragusa severely restricted women's public roles, but merchants who went on distant trade expeditions preferred to leave their businesses in the hands of their wives while they were away, rather than bring nonaristocratic or foreign families into the businesses. This important source of economic power and control was extended to noble women, not because of a commitment to women's individual freedom or rights, but to preserve the interests of the family business and the wider aristocratic merchant class.

The women of Ragusa were the exception rather than the rule. As JoAnn McNamara and Suzanne Wemple describe it, "in the upper reaches of later medieval society, apart from bearing children and acting as sex objects, companions in social functions, and sources of religious or poetic inspiration, women lost their usefulness." [44]

Peasant women and merchant women led very different lives from those of the nobility. Peasant women worked hard both in the fields during peak labor seasons and in the home. They were an important source of labor to both their families and their feudal lords. According to Sibylle Harksen and Edward Shorter, the peasant woman managed the household but her activities outside the household were severely restricted.[45] The husband had the legal right of control over all their goods and property and the wife was legally allowed to dispose of only small sums of money. The wife was expected to be subservient to her husband in all matters. For example, she served him at mealtimes and stood behind his chair awaiting further orders while he ate. She ate after the men of the household had had their fill. Sexual stratification even superseded economic stratification. The peasant wife did not give orders to her husband's male hired hands. Couples who broke the practices of male dominance and female subordination were subject to public ridicule by the community.

Women of the merchant class also remained active in their family businesses even in the later middle ages when noble women's economic activities were curtailed. Wives of merchants often had control over the household and family business because their husbands were often away on business for long periods of time. Harksen maintains that they were indispensable to the conduct of business.[46] Town women, in general, worked at a variety of occupations and were members of many of the guilds that regulated the crafts and trades. Harksen points out, however, that women's guild memberships did not make them the equals of the male craftsmen and tradesmen. Instead, the guilds operated to control the women and often to forbid their competition with men.[47] During periods of high unemployment, women workers were likely to face even more active discrimination in employment.

Common women were also potential targets for sexual exploitation by powerful upper-class males. Bullough notes that

> it was an honor to be a king's mistress, or a king's whore, and while the honor was somewhat less for being a mistress to lesser nobility, there was still prestige attached to the position. The mother of a royal or noble bastard stood to gain too much to reject the advances of a lord or a prospective lord.[48]

Medieval Child-rearing Practices. Child rearing in the middle ages appears to have been quite different from today's Western practices.[49] Infants and small children were not lavished with love or attention. The death rate was so high, even among the upper classes, that parents could not emotionally afford to become too attached to children. Among the lower classes there was the added distraction of the parents' heavy work loads. Neither mother nor father had much time or energy to devote to child care. Discipline was strict. Obedience was an important virtue and was beaten into the child if necessary. The child learned early to show deference and respect to the father in particular.

Children who survived were treated as miniature adults. Phillippe Aries argues that childhood as a separate stage of development was not discovered in Western Europe until agrarian feudalism declined and capitalism developed. Children were, for example, not isolated from adult sexuality. The lack of privacy in medieval homes gave them sufficient opportunity to observe sexual practices. Early marriage also meant that they became sexually active soon after puberty.

Children were also put to work at early ages, and the tasks they were given reflected the adult sexual division of labor. Girls learned domestic skills and reserved behavior. Boys learned their father's occupations or were apprenticed out to others to learn their trades. Even among the upper classes it was common to send young boys into the homes of other nobles for training. There the boy served as a page, or servant, to an older knight. He learned from him the skills and etiquette of knighthood. In particular, he served the knight in preparation for battle and was taught the skills of warfare and combat.

NON-WESTERN AGRARIAN SOCIETIES

These case studies of Greece, Rome, and Medieval Europe provide a brief description of the agrarian experience as it affected the West. However, these are not necessarily representative of all agrarian societies. For one thing, there was a great intermingling of tribal traditions with agrarianism in the West. Another distinction lies in the fact that none of these societies ever developed the truly despotic, highly centralized stable agrarian regimes which characterized many areas of the East. The positions of women and men in these despotic societies undoubtedly differed from those in the West. It would be especially useful to study the impact of wet rice culture and the continued economic productivity of women on gender roles and sexual stratification, but social scientists have done little work in this area.

FORCES FOR CHANGE

In the Western World agrarian practices lost their position as the dominant form of economic production. Capitalist trade and commerce came to be the chief sources of wealth and power. Industrialization soon followed the rise of capitalism and made manufacturing the primary economic basis of European society. Gender roles and sexual stratification underwent important changes as Western societies evolved from agrarianism to industrialism.

Some parts of the world remain agrarian-based. However, they have tended to come under the domination of the more powerful industrial countries. Large peasant populations still exist in the world today. Their gender roles and sexual stratification systems are not exact duplicates of what was found in past agrarian societies, but they do continue to differ significantly from those of the industrialized world. We shall examine contemporary peasants and the Underdeveloped or Third World in chapter seven.

SUMMARY

Agrarian societies depend on settled agriculture involving the use of the plow, fertilizers, and irrigation. The work is physically demanding. However, population pressure and scarce resources necessitate the increased productivity.

Agrarian societies have highly developed class structures, dense populations, specialized governmental institutions, and chronic warfare problems. The subordination of women reaches its highest degree in these societies. Much agricultural labor is incompatible with simultaneous pregnancy and child care, and women become more important as producers of the labor supply than as primary producers themselves. The domestic/public dichotomy is often extreme. Kinship is usually patrilineal and females are often treated as sexual property by males who enforce chastity and virginity to maintain male honor. The religions of agricultural societies support male dominance and female subordination.

Evidence from ancient Greece and Rome and medieval Europe indicates that women in general had a subordinate role in these agrarian societies. However, factors such as male absence in distant wars sometimes gave women temporary opportunities to advance.

Notes

1. The following discussion of agrarian societies is indebted to Gerhard Lenski and Jean Lenski, *Human Societies* (3rd ed., New York: McGraw-Hill, 1978), pp. 177–230; and Gerhard Lenski, *Power and Privilege* (New York: McGraw-Hill, 1966), pp. 190–296.
2. Lenski and Lenski, p. 192.
3. Rae Lesser Blumberg, *Stratification: Socioeconomic and Sexual Inequality* (Dubuque, Iowa: Wm. C. Brown, 1978), p. 45.
4. Blumberg, p. 51.
5. M. Kay Martin and Barbara Voorhies, *Female of the Species* (New York: Columbia U. Press, 1975), p. 295.
6. The following discussion is based on the work of Ruby Rohrlich-Leavitt, "Women in Transition: Crete and Sumer," in Renate Bridenthal and Claudia Koonz, eds., *Becoming Visible: Women in European History* (Boston: Houghton Mifflin, 1977) pp. 36–59; and Verena Zinserling, *Women in Greece and Rome* (New York: Abner Schram, 1972), pp. 10–13.
7. The following discussion of Greece in the Bronze Age is based on Zinserling, pp. 14–21; Sarah Pomeroy, *Goddesses, Whores, and Slaves: Women in Classical Antiquity* (New York: Schocken, 1975), pp. 16–31.
8. The following discussion of Greece in the Dark Ages and the Archaic Period is based largely on Pomeroy, pp. 32–78.
9. Pomeroy, pp. 55–56.
10. The following discussion of the Classical Period is based on Pomeroy, pp. 57–119; Zinserling, pp. 22–33; and Vern Bullough, *The Subordinate Sex; A History of Attitudes Toward Women* (Baltimore: Penguin Books, 1974), pp. 50–76.
11. Pomeroy, p. 71.
12. Pomeroy, p. 74.
13. Philip Slater, *The Glory of Hera: Greek Mythology and the Greek Family* (Boston: Beacon Press, 1968).
14. Slater, p. 4.
15. Slater, p. 38.
16. Slater, p. 61.

17. Elise Boulding, *The Underside of History* (Boulder, Colorado: Westview Press, 1976), pp. 258–266.
18. Boulding, p. 263.
19. The following discussion of sexism in the works of Plato and Aristotle is based on Bullough, pp. 58–69.
20. The following discussion is based on the works of Boulding, pp. 265–266; Julia O'Faolain and C. Laura Martines, ed., *Not in God's Image: Women in History from the Greeks to the Victorians* (New York: Harper & Row, 1973), pp. 29–32; and Zinserling, pp. 34–37.
21. The following discussion is drawn from the works of J.P.V.D. Balsdon, *Roman Women: Their History and Habits* (Westport, Conn.: Greenwich Press,1962); Boulding, pp. 339–379; Bullough, pp. 77–120; O'Faolain and Martines, Pomeroy, pp. 149–226; Stuart Queen and Robert Habenstein, *The Family in Various Cultures* (4th ed., New York: J. B. Lippincott, 1974), pp. 174–219; Zinserling, pp. 48–73.
22. Pomeroy, p. 155.
23. Bullough, p. 82.
24. Bullough, p. 87.
25. Bullough, p. 94.
26. Pomeroy, p. 182.
27. Boulding, p. 369.
28. Bullough, p. 118.
29. The following discussion of men and women in medievel Europe draws on the works of Boulding; Brenda Boulton, "Mulieres Sanctae," in Susan Mosher Stuard, ed., *Women in Medieval Society* (Philadelphia: U. of Pennsylvania Press, 1976), pp. 141–158; Bullough; Emily Coleman,"Infanticide in the Early Middle Ages," in Stuard, pp. 47–70; Sybylle Harksen, *Women in the Middle Ages* (New York: Abner Schram, 1975); David Herlihy, "Life Expectancies for Women in Medieval Society," in Rosemarie Morewedge, ed., *The Role of Women in the Middle Ages* (Albany, N.Y.: State U. of New York Press, 1975), pp. 1–22; Herlihy, "Land, Family, and Women in Continental Europe, 701–1200," in Stuard, pp. 13–14; Herlihy, "The Natural History of Medieval Women," *Natural History*, March, 1978, pp. 56–67; JoAnn McNamara and Suzanne Wemple, "The Power of Women through the Family in Medieval Europe: 500–1100," in Mary Hartman and Lois Banner, ed., *Clio's Consciousness Raised* (New York: Harper & Row, 1974); McNamara and Wemple, "Sanctity and Power: The Dual Pursuit of Medieval Women," in Renate Bridenthal and Claudia Koonz, ed., *Becoming Visible: Women in European History* (Boston: Houghton Mifflin, 1977); O'Faolain and Martines; Eileen Power, *Medieval Women*, ed. M. M. Potan (London: Cambridge U. Press, 1975); Emily Putnam, *The Lady* (1910; rpt. Chicago: U. of Chicago Press, 1970); Queen and Habenstein; Susan Mosher Stuard, "Introduction," in Stuard, pp. 1–12; Stuard, "Women in Charter and Statute Law: Medieval Ragusa-Dubrovnik," pp. 199–208.
30. Coleman, in Stuard, pp. 47–70.
31. Herlihy, 1975, p. 10.
32. Herlihy, 1976, p. 24.
33. Boulding, pp. 429–439.
34. Putnam, p. 131.
35. Putnam, p. 84.
36. Herlihy, 1975, p. 15.
37. Coleman, pp. 50–51.
38. Stuard, "Introduction," p. 8.
39. Bullough, p. 173.
40. Nancy Van Vuuren, *The Subversion of Women as Practiced by Churches, Witch-Hunters, and Other Sexists* (Philadelphia: Westminster, 1973).

41. Boulding, p. 499.
42. Bullough, p. 171.
43. Susan Mosher Stuard, "Women in Charter and Statute Law," in Stuard pp. 199–208.
44. McNamara and Wemple, 1977, p. 114.
45. Harksen, p. 10; Edward Shorter, *The Making of the Modern Family* (New York: Basic Books, 1977).
46. Harksen, p. 23.
47. Harksen, p. 11.
48. Bullough, p. 169.
49. Phillippe Aries, *Centuries of Childhood* (New York: Vintage, 1960).

7

Underdeveloped Peasant Societies

It is clear that the negative effects of automation and new technology in industry fall mainly on women, who being untrained are replaced by men and machines. . . . Thus, women's illiteracy and low social status work to their disadvantage in modernizing industry.

Doranne Jacobson, "Indian Women in
Processes of Development"

THE UNDERDEVELOPED ECONOMY

Although nonindustrialized agriculture is an ancient system of economic production, it still prevails in much of the world today. It is especially characteristic of the underdeveloped world. Although underdeveloped countries are struggling toward modernization and industrialization, their successes have often been minimal.

The term "underdeveloped" is used here instead of the more optimistic "developing" countries to emphasize the lack of much real progress toward a better life for the masses in these areas. In fact, it is useful to distinguish between, "undeveloped" and "underdeveloped" societies. An *undeveloped* economy is one which exists prior to penetration by more technologically advanced modernized countries. An *underdeveloped* economy is one that has suffered such penetration and is to one degree or another exploited in the interests of the more powerful developed world.

An underdeveloped society is likely to have an important mining or plantation sector which produces raw materials for export to developed areas. The developed countries often pay low wages, little or no taxes, and low prices for raw materials of crucial importance to the developed economies. These economic enterprises, furthermore, bring little economic gain to the host country. They disrupt the local economies and introduce new desires for industrial products without introducing the benefits of industrialization. The overall effect is the creation of dependency of the underdeveloped country on the developed country. Dependency is manifested in chronic balance of payments problems, excessive indebtedness, and high inflation and unemployment rates.[1]

Underdevelopment usually creates a small elite class which becomes wealthy and powerful by serving the interests of foreign investors. This group organizes and controls the society's economic and human resources for the foreign companies. Such an elite is likely to be more interested in maintaining its own source of wealth and power than in improving the conditions of the masses. The little industrialization, modernization, or development that takes place is unequally distributed. The tiny urban elite receives most of the benefits just as it did under premodern agriculture. A larger urban middle class benefits somewhat, but the large percentage of the population benefits only minimally, and for the poorest sectors the situation often deteriorates.

Sexual Stratification and Gender Roles

The effects of underdevelopment on the sexual stratification systems and gender roles of these countries also varies by social class. Since these countries are predominantly agrarian and often have long-standing traditions associated with an agrarian-based civilization, their traditional gender roles and sexual stratification practices show many similarities with those discussed in Chapter 6 in relation to the agrarian societies of the past. Women typically have a low position. Exceptions are found in those underdeveloped countries which used female farming and horticultural practices before outside penetration. Imperialistic domination in this case usually disrupts these systems, introduces male settled agriculture, and brings an end to many aspects of economic independence and the freedom and status often associated with such independence.[2]

For the wealthier sectors of underdeveloped countries, increased prosperity and experience with modernization can have two quite different effects on the positions of women and men. For some groups, especially the middle classes rather than the elite, prosperity allows them to follow traditional gender roles more closely: having idle, isolated wives and daughters becomes a mark of prestige. Hence women in these groups often find themselves more firmly tied to the domestic sphere and segregated from the public world. This may bring them prestige in their cultural setting, but such prestige comes at the price of personal autonomy and prevents women from gaining equality with men or exercising overt power and authority in the society.

More modernized segments of the elite, however, are likely to take as their role models men and women of the developed countries. They are likely to be open to fuller female participation in the public world. However, this does not mean that males participate more fully in the domestic sphere. Whatever household duties women of this class may abandon are taken over by an ample supply of domestic servants drawn from the impoverished masses. Modernized elite women are likely to pursue higher education. They may be sent abroad to study. After completing their educations they may be free to practice their professions and even to enter political life. Traditional gender role ideologies limit their activities somewhat, but their high class status allows them to break with many traditions with little or no prestige loss. The men of these classes are so wealthy and powerful that the achievements of their wives and daughters in the public sphere do not threaten their masculine identities. Male dominance is not challenged by the greater public participation of these few elite women.

For the poorer sectors of underdeveloped countries—and these constitute the bulk of the population—modernization has often meant deterioration in the economic positions of men and women. In particular, it has often widened the gap between men and women. As Ester Boserup points out, foreign agricultural experts focus their educational attempts entirely on men. Only men receive the new training and only men can reap benefits of increased productivity or job opportunities. Modern education is likely to be more available to men than to women. Lack of education then serves to lock women out of competition for jobs in the modern sector at the same time that population pressure and high unemployment drive them out of the countryside. Many end up in near slavery as domestics; others turn to prostitution.[3]

Economic Considerations.   Ann Rubbo has documented the effects of rural proletarianization on peasant women and men. This process lowers the women's positions even more than it does men's.[4] Rubbo compared peasant versus plantation modes of production in Colombia and the patterns of social organization which each form generates. The process of creating plantations usually involves quasi-legal methods of forcing peasants to sell their small holdings to a large landowner, often a foreign company. The landless peasants are then turned into a low-paid wage labor force with few rights or social benefits.

Women are sometimes preferred for the most exploitative work because employers consider them more compliant, less troublesome, and cheaper than men. Compared with traditional peasant life, women in the plantation towns are even more economically insecure and more dependent on men. Not only have they lost their subsistence base in the land without replacing it with incomes adequate for support, but the social atomization engendered by the wage economy of the town deprives them of the supportive network of friends and relatives on which peasants traditionally depend.

Advanced technology often hurts poor women's interests more than it helps. Both Burke and Boserup note that automation often puts women out of work by making their labor unnecessary or by shifting a job from low prestige unmechanized women's work to higher prestige mechanized men's work. For example, women haulers have sometimes been replaced by male truck drivers. The unemployment rate among females, therefore, often rises as undeveloped countries become underdeveloped.

Heleieth Saffioti argues that women constitute a huge reserve labor force in underdeveloped countries.[5] Employers can use gender role stereotypes to justify keeping women in the household as dependents on men until the demand for labor increases and women are needed in the paid labor force. If women and men accept the "feminine mystique," they do not protest against the high unemployment rates of women.

The potential benefits of advanced technology are often not introduced to ease the burden of women's domestic labor. Burke points out that the rural women of Africa, Asia, and Latin America spend a great deal of time grinding foods. Simple grinding machines which could alleviate much of this drudgery have not been supplied at a cost most of these women could afford. In addition, they have been encouraged to switch from the more nutritious, sanitary, and free breast-feeding of infants to bottle formulas. Advertising campaigns have aimed at convincing these women that bottle-feeding is better and more prestigious. However, it drains poor families of needed economic resources, and without proper sanitation and refrigeration facilities it can actually be dangerous. Furthermore, because of their poverty mothers often dilute the formulas with too much water and, thereby, fail to give their babies proper nutrition.

Family Structure

The incidence of matrifocal family structures, in which the mother and her kin form the permanent core of the household while husbands or lovers may come and go, is increased by underdevelopment in some areas of the world. The instability of male–female relationships characteristic of many underdeveloped areas might be an adaptive response to the poverty and insecurity of life among the poorest groups. Susan Brown's analysis of mating patterns among landless peasants and those with insufficient land in the Dominican Republic indicates that the females in the multiple-mate pattern were better off than those in the more desirable single-mate pattern.[6]

The multiple-mate pattern was characterized by free consensual unions, male marginality in the household, and a matrifocal family structure. The ideal single-mate pattern included legal marriage and male-headed nuclear family households. Women in the multiple-mate pattern had more flexibility to make the best use of whatever resources might be available. They did not have to defer to a man's wishes. If the man wasted money on drinking, gambling, or other women, the woman could throw him out. Married, single-mate women, however, had to tolerate whatever their husbands did. The multiple mate woman could take a job locally or migrate to look for work. The single-mate woman was usually forbidden to take outside employment even if the family desperately needed the money: it reflected badly on the husband to have an employed wife. The wife had to make do on the husband's earnings no matter how inadequate they might be.

The multiple-mate woman could maintain close reciprocal ties with her mother and other relatives and share domestic tasks, child care, and economic resources. She could also place her children temporarily in other people's homes to earn their own keep. These practices were unacceptable to the single-mate couples. Thus, the women in the multiple-mate pattern suffered a loss of prestige for not establishing a permanent household with a man. But they gained in economic viability in a situation where a man would not typically be able to provide for a family's needs.

Women of underdeveloped countries may often be exploited, but they do not always passively accept their fate or the exploitation of their men. June Nash documents the active participation of women in protests and strikes among Bolivian tin miners.[7] But despite the importance of the women's contribution to the strikes, the males did not give them credit for their actions. The men did not even support the women's attempts to break the power of the company store over the miners' lives by forming a cooperative to bring supplies into these remote settlements. Instead, they ordered their wives back to the semi-isolation of their homes. And when the company undertook mass firings of women workers, the male workers did not support their efforts to keep their jobs. As Nash explains it, "This reaction expresses the fear that the wage slave has of losing his own slave in the house."[8] With the sexes divided against each other, poor men and women often fail to organize effectively to oppose the dominant classes and to defend their own interests.

Although certain characteristics of gender roles and sexual stratification are common in underdeveloped countries, important variations exist. With this general perspective on underdeveloped countries in mind, women's and men's positions in Mexico, India, and Iraq will now be considered.

LATIN AMERICA: MEXICO

Prior to the conquest by the Spanish and the Portuguese in the fifteenth and sixteenth centuries, the native peoples had not adopted agriculture. The area was dominated by advanced horticultural societies such as the Aztec, Incan, and Mayan civilizations; some areas were simple horticultural and some contained hunting and gathering peoples. Mexico was controlled primarily by the advanced horticultural empires of the Aztecs and Mayans. Women's positions in these societies were subordinate to men's, but women of the upper classes had important powers and privileges.

The Spanish conquest of Mexico in 1525 introduced agrarian technology and civilization. This included much more subordinate and oppressive roles for women. The Spaniards brought their ideology of female inferiority and restriction with them. Their positions as conquerors added a further exploitative element to the roles they assigned to native women.[9] The racist beliefs of the Spaniards concerning non-Europeans led them to treat native males as inferior. Native females were ranked below native men, as European females were ranked below European males.

The Spaniards also imposed the Catholic religion on the defeated Indians. Spanish Catholicism embodied negative views of women and supported male dominance. The church supported the division of women into the good, asexual, devoted mother figure of the Virgin Mary and the bad, seductive, Eve figure. The church has continued to maintain up to the present such gender role images and the ideology of woman's place as in the home. In spite of its role in the subordination of women, Mexican women continue to be very religious and support the church in much larger numbers than men do.

Machismo and Marianismo

One important cultural tradition the *conquistadores* and the Catholic Church introduced into Mexico is the *machismo* and *marianismo* ideals for men and women. *Machismo* has been described as a "cult of virility." It is an "exaggerated aggressiveness and intransigence in male-to-male interpersonal relationships and arrogance and sexual aggression in male-to-female relationships.[10] Males are overly concerned with maintaining their honor and showing no weakness with men or women. The other face of *machismo*, according to Evelyn Stevens, is *marianismo* or the "cult of spiritual superiority for women . . . women are semidivine, morally superior to and spiritually stronger than men."[11] The Virgin Mary is the ideal for this cult. Women are supposed to be self-sacrificing, submissive, self-abnegating, and long-suffering. They suffer whatever their men force upon them. Their children, especially their sons, are expected to revere their mothers as the embodiment of ideal womanhood. However, this leaves the sons free to abuse and degrade other women. Any woman who insists on enjoying herself or being assertive violates the cult of *marianismo* and is, therefore, a "bad woman." Stevens notes that *marianismo* does not have to be forced on women. They not only accept it and support it themselves, but they also help perpetuate it into future generations through the socialization of their children. Women who complain of the poor treatment they receive from their husbands still encourage their sons to develop the same behavior patterns and often take pride in their sons' manifestations of *machismo*.

Nora Scott Kinzer argues that North American writers have exaggerated the importance of *machismo* and *marianismo* in Latin American culture.[12] She points instead to women's active resistance to their husbands, to their hostility to men, and to their participation in extramarital affairs. However, it is possible for conflicting behavior patterns to exist side by side. *Marianismo* and *machismo* may be cultural norms without all or even most of the society's members upholding those norms. Stevens argues that many women devote their lives to living up to the ideal of humility and submissiveness while others deviate from it to a lesser or greater degree.[13] Despite strong pressures to conform, many women reject *marianismo*. This does not mean, however, that the *machismo–marianismo* pattern does not exist or that it is unimportant. It remains a part of the colonial legacy. It seems, however, to have affected the *mestizo* or *ladino* (Europeanized) populations more than the indigenous communities, which remain closer to precolonial traditions.

Twentieth-Century Mexico

Mexico gained independence from Spain in 1810. But between 1810 and 1910 little changed in the racial, class, or sexual stratification systems. The Mexican Revolution overthrew the quasienlightenment dictatorship of Porfirio Diaz in 1910 and its leaders attempted to set up a more equalitarian society. Women had been important participants in the Revolution. Many had served as soldiers and a few were officers and led battles. The new revolutionary government rewarded them with important legal and civil rights. (Women did not receive the vote, however, until 1953. It was feared that most women were so conservative that they would oppose the progressive measures of the new government.) Tradition remained strong, however, and the changes were more apparent that real.

The positions of women and men in Mexico today vary among the different sectors of Mexican society. Rural peasant women and men are in a different position from urban and town women and men. Indians differ from *mestizos*. Lower class women and men differ from those of the middle classes and upper classes. Regional variations also occur. Drawing upon various case studies, the next sections glimpse the lives of Mexican women and men in several of these social and economic circumstances.

Rural Peasants.   Oscar Lewis describes in detail the lives of Indian peasants living in a highland village near Cuernavaca, Mexico.[14] His research on the Martinez family was conducted between 1943 and 1948 and again in 1960.

The daily life of Mexico's peasants is hard. Men rise at 4 or 5 A.M. and often walk for one or two hours to their fields. The labor is extremely taxing and the workday is long. Peasant women arise at 3 A.M. in order to grind corn for the breakfast tortillas. Preparing and grinding corn is tedious and arduous work that requires several hours bent over a grinding stone. The domestic tasks of water carrying, laundry, sewing, and caring for farmyard animals and gardens are also demanding and neverending.

Although agricultural techniques are widely used by better-off peasants and large landowners in Mexico, the poorest peasants with the smallest plots on rugged terrain still rely on horticultural methods of production. Hoe agriculture requires much labor but little capital. The tools are simple and easy to make or acquire. Tractors, chemical fertilizers, and pesticides, which are beyond the economic reach of such poor peasants, are unnecessary. Productivity per acre is, furthermore, often more predictable and higher than in the one-crop field method using plow agriculture.

But these small plots usually do not produce enough to sustain the family throughout the year. To maintain themselves at a subsistence level such peasants often have to supplement their farm production. Men work for wages as day laborers in richer people's fields or in village shops. Some migrate temporarily or permanently to the city looking for work in order to send their earnings home. Lucky men get positions as *braceros* (temporary immigrant laborers) during the harvest season in the United States. Women add to their already burdensome domestic and gardening tasks such income producing work as sewing, embroidery, laundry, fruit and vegetable peddling, and day labor in the fields. Some migrate to the cities as domestics. Few have the skills to find other employment.

The sexual division of labor in the Martinez family and in their village clearly embodied the domestic/public dichotomy. Men worked in the fields and women in the household except for emergency situations. Some of the women's work brought income into the household. But in general, women's work was primarily for use value while men dominated production for exchange value. Women were often in charge of expenditures for household consumption and managed that part of the budget. But the man could withhold the money for food and other necessities whenever he chose.

Rural indigenous families such as the Martinez are patrilineal and patrilocal. The father is an authoritarian power figure. The mother and children must obey him and show him respect or face sometimes harsh physical punishments. The father remains aloof from his wife and children. He shows affection by working hard to provide for their material necessities. Emotional displays would weaken his image of strength and power.

The father's image of complete control over the family is belied, however, by the often greater psychological control exercised by the mother. Mothers encourage emotional attachment and dependence from their children. The mother–child bond is extremely strong and children, particularly sons, often idealize their mothers. Children are given little freedom by either parent as long as they remain in the parental home, even if they marry.

Parents try hard to restrict their daughters' freedom and, in particular, to keep them from meeting men. Virginity is prized in unmarried women as chastity is for married women. Even young girls are not allowed to leave the household compound unescorted. Dating is still rare in the villages. It is assumed that females cannot control themselves sexually. If a girl has been alone with a male, it is assumed that she had sex with him and her reputation is ruined.

Despite the attempted close surveillance of their behavior, daughters do often manage to have affairs. Pedro Martinez' daughter, Conchita, had an affair with a married teacher while she was away at school. Her parents were angry and humiliated. But even a wayward daughter is usually taken back into her family home. Pedro and his wife raised Conchita's illegitimate son and continued to help her complete her education so she could support herself as a teacher. Many parents oppose education for their daughters precisely because they fear the consequences of allowing girls that much freedom.

Although virginity is preferred, women with children by other men often find husbands or are able to establish fairly stable free consensual unions. Conchita eventually married a local peasant and became a typical peasant wife despite her training and experience as a teacher and her sexual involvements.

Unlike daughters, sons are expected to involve themselves in sexual experiences early. Village sons are not given much freedom of movement, but parents do not feel it necessary to keep them away from sexual experimentation. If a woman agrees to have sex with a man, it is her fault and not his. Men are expected to pursue sex whenever the opportunity arises. Not to do so would threaten a man's sense of virility. Sexual exploits, both real and imaginary, are the subject of boasting among these males. If a man impregnates a woman, he may or may not recognize the child as his own. He supports it only to the degree that he chooses.

Men prefer that their wives be frigid and sometimes avoid sexually satisfying them. Frigidity on the part of the wife helps convince the husband that she would not be interested in sexual relations with any other man. Lovemaking techniques are therefore used primarily to seduce and maintain the interest of women other than one's wife. Pedro Martinez described several of his sexual affairs to Lewis. His wife was jealous and angry about his affairs, but she could not even complain too openly without risking a scolding and a beating.

Women are expected to stay in the home except when it is absolutely necessary to go out. Wives should not even have close friendships with other women, because such friends could be used to arrange meetings with lovers.

Females are expected to act modestly at all times. In public they should walk with downcast eyes and pull their shawls over their heads. A woman who held her head high or smiled at people would be considered flirtatious and a "bad woman."

Families are large. Husbands see children as proof of their virility, and they feel more secure about their wives' sexual fidelity if they are pregnant or have an infant to care for.

Women are supposed to be ambitious for their men but not for themselves. However, even these traditional peasant women sometimes violate this norm. Conchita Martinez, for example, actively pursued her education and her career as a teacher, sometimes arguing vigorously with her father to be allowed to continue in school.

Despite their belief in male superiority, the village males fear witchcraft from their wives and other women. However, females do not fear witchcraft from males. Fear of sorcery is, therefore, probably in part a manifestation of underlying male fears that their power over women is not complete and that women may seek revenge on them.

Women's attitudes about men were often contradictory among Lewis' villagers. Women admired the tough, domineering man and agreed that males were superior to them. But they expressed a desire for husbands who were more passive. The women also said that the truly submissive wife was a fool even if that was the ideal for women. In violation of the publicly acknowledged ideal of female subordination, the women of the village told Lewis they were proud of their efforts at self-assertion.

Conflicts between the sexes are common. Lewis notes that the women openly expressed hostility toward the men but often reacted to their subordination and abusive treatment with self-pity and resignation. For example, wife-beating was a legal offense in the village, but wives did not avail themselves of the law's protection. The women were martyrs instead. (Younger women, however, seemed to be taking a more independent attitude by 1960.)

Wives were expected to tolerate mistreatment by their husbands, but many did not. A favorite alternative was to return to the natal family. In the Martinez family both Conchita and Macrina married men who beat them and barely supported them. In addition, Macrina's husband spent their already scarce income on his mistress. Macrina returned to her father's house and did not remarry for many years for fear that a second husband would not treat her or her children well either. She did have an affair, however, which resulted in another child and further angered her family. Eventually she remarried and left her father's house for another part of the village.

In another Mexican Indian village, Doren Slade found that remaining single could increase a woman's public power if she also owned land.[15] The important public office of *mayordomo* was open only to heads of households with sufficient cash and corn to support religious ceremonies and fiestas. For a man to be a head of household he had to be married, and to carry out the tasks of *mayordomo* he needed the support of his wife. A married woman could never be a head of household in this patriarchal family structure, but a single woman with land could be a head of household. And through the use of hired labor she could farm her land and might accumulate sufficient cash and corn for the fiestas. Because of patrilineal inheritance of land, most females never receive land. However, daughters without brothers did inherit. Although rare, it did sometimes occur that a female could assume this public office.

Slade also points out that the concept of submissive wife and dominant husband is the ideal, not the reality. The wife loses her legal status as a full adult upon marriage, but she does not lose her ability to exert influence on her community. The division of labor—males in the fields and women in the kitchen—produces an interdependence between the sexes that prevents husbands from ignoring their wives' advice. Publicly wives are deferential to husbands, but privately they participate in making family decisions about such matters as whether to invest in land or livestock and whether the husband should attempt to assume the *mayordomo* office: ". . . male dominance . . . does not extend to the point where men engage in important activities independent of the approval and cooperation of women." [16]

Despite the harshness of village life, it does not give rise to the rootlessness and alienation of the urban milieu. The villages are often ancient, with the same families residing within them for untold generations. Men and women and boys and girls have a strong feeling of belonging to a stable community. But the villages are subject to outside influences, especially now that radios have become common. Better highways and transportation systems have also allowed villagers to venture into the outside world and for outsiders to enter the villages. Educational facilities which have expanded into Mexico's rural areas have introduced new ideas and practices. Lewis noted some of the effects of outside penetration when he returned to his village in 1960. The village appeared to be moving away from patrilocality to neolocality which seemed to undermine the control of husbands over wives. The new wife could not be watched over and dominated by her mother-in-law while her husband was away at work. Girls had more freedom of movement about the village and could associate more freely with both girls and boys. Parents were more affectionate with their children: Lewis noted that village child rearing methods had become child-oriented. The villagers depended less on agriculture and more on non-agricultural jobs. More women held jobs outside the home. But the lower economic group had become poorer as a result of inflation and a curtailment of some agricultural activities. Modernity had its costs.

Urban Mexicans.   The urban environment offers a greater variety of life-styles and job opportunities to women and men than does the traditional village. But life in the city is not necessarily more satisfying. In Mexico there is a constant flow to the cities from the countryside. Rapid population growth means that the rural areas cannot support the younger generations.

Sometimes individuals migrate, such as the thousands of young girls who go to the cities as domestic workers each year. Sometimes entire families, especially the landless, migrate in search of a better life.

Lewis studied several poor urban families in Mexico City in the 1950s.[17] Economic insecurity was ever present. Although it violates the *machismo* ideal, wives and daughters as well as widows and divorced women were often forced to work. Those with little education worked outside the home in such low-paying jobs as street vendor, waitress, and factory operative. Others worked at home as laundresses, seamstresses, and embroiderers. Educated women might find jobs as secretaries or teachers. Poverty often forced families to take their children out of school, however, and put them to work at an early age.

In this crowded urban milieu females could not be guarded as closely as they were in the country. Girls and women often spent a great deal of time out of the household at school, shopping, or working. More opportunities were therefore available to violate female gender role norms of modesty and sexual purity. Although they were disapproved, premarital sex and early illegitimate pregnancy were common. If the male refused to marry or live in free union with the female, she usually had to depend on her irate family for support. Even if the couple did set up a household together, the chances were high that it would not last long. Lewis' studies of five families in Mexico City are filled with descriptions of abandoned wives, husbands, and children. Husbands who deserted their families might not continue to help in their support. The economic circumstances of such deserted women and their children were often severe. If they were lucky, they had kin to turn to. If not, the mother might be forced into dancehall work or prostitution.

In addition to desertion, husbands often established families with other women and thereby spread what little income they had even more thinly. First wives resented this and often complained vociferously. Jealousy was a constant fact of life for both men and women. But if a woman pushed her husband too far, she might lose what little of his attention and money she still received.

The women tended to take the view that "that's the way men are—a woman has to put up with whatever her man gives her." The women and children were also frequently abused by their men. Beatings were common. The patriarchal family was the ideal and men tried to demand the respect due their position. Any sign of disrespect from any family member might send the father into a rage. A woman with a stable income of her own would be less likely to tolerate severe beatings and humiliations than one who was more dependent economically on her man. Girls were, however, socialized by their mothers to accept even abusive treatment by their husbands. As one woman put it, "He had a right to hit me. He was my man.[18] In fact, women often respected these violent, "macho" men more than the husbands who were gentle and generous with their families.

In the families studied by Lewis, men appeared to use their economic resources consciously to control their women. Wives would be forced to beg for money for household expenses. Men preferred that their wives not work so that their economic dependence could be maintained. As one man with a working wife complained, "If I hadn't let her go out selling I would still be giving orders. But now, well she doesn't pay attention to me."[19] In addition to being the economic backbone of the family, this particular woman also lived close to a network of kin who could be counted on for support in disputes with her husband. More economically dependent and isolated women were much more vulnerable to domination and abuse.

Wives accepted it as "bad luck" if their husbands did not support them. One of Lewis' respondents complained that her man wasted his money on other women and only rarely stayed with her and their children, but she accepted his behavior and continued to love him and need him. She did, however, refuse to marry this man legally for fear that he would then use his legal position to take her children away if he wanted to hurt her.

Lower class urban women are exploited both at home and in the workplace. Their domestic tasks are burdensome. A woman who does not engage in paid labor still works very hard all day cooking and cleaning under adverse, overcrowded, and unsanitary conditions. Those who work as maids are given living quarters in the employer's home. Their hours are long and employers often disturb their sleep for a midnight snack or some errand. Maids are paid low wages and treated with little dignity or respect. The little time off they get is sometimes closely supervised by the employer, who thinks she should act as the guardian of the maid's virtue in place of the girl's parents or brothers. Young female domestics, especially those fresh from the country, do often get pregnant, sometimes by their employer or his sons, other times by their boyfriends. This often costs them their jobs. If they do not return to their families in shame, they often end up in prostitution.

Virve Piho described the plight of the female factory worker in Mexico City.[20] These women also work long hours for low pay. Many of them were the major economic supports of their families and often of nonkinspeople as well. Husbands had either disappeared or suffered chronic unemployment or underemployment. In addition to the demanding nature of their factory work and their domestic tasks, some of these women moonlighted as well. Piho found that in line with the *marianismo* ideal, the women tended to accept their situations with passivity, resignation, and self-abnegation. At work the woman worker did not protest the company's demands for fear of losing her job; at home she "never protested the demands of the persons she loved, but saw helping them as a sacred duty even if she had to do additional work that taxed her to the limits of her physical and psychological endurance. . . ." [21]

Industrialization in Mexico has not greatly altered the sexual division of labor. Occupations are highly sex segregated, and women who work are still responsible for the home. Furthermore, the jobs available to women are often extensions of their domestic roles: maid, waitress, cook, textile worker, teacher, and nurse.[22] Lower-class men also suffer exploitation in the labor force. However, a man's position in the sexual stratification system allows him to vent his frustration on his wife and children and to demand respect, obedience, and service from them.

In the urban middle classes, women are less likely to work.[23] The husband's income, although often inadequate to maintain an acceptable middle-class life-style, is usually sufficient to support the family. It is a matter of male honor and *machismo* that the wife not work: she is to devote herself fully to her husband and children. Large families are preferred and the birthrate is high. The wife's domestic burdens are lightened by domestic help, but usually she is still firmly tied to the domestic sphere. Husbands prefer that their wives go out as little as possible to guard against possible sexual encounters with other men and against gossip.

Virginity and chastity are more firmly enforced on middle-class than on lower-class women. Families can afford to be restrictive of the female's freedom of movement, since they are not dependent on female incomes. Extramarital affairs are viewed as signs of virility for men, however. And middle- and upper-class wives complain but put up with male infidelity just as lower-class women do.

The upper-class women have more freedom from domestic tasks than middle-class women. They are more likely to receive university educations and to enter professional careers. However, their roles as wife and mother are supposed to take precedence over career goals and, therefore, career advancement is likely to be more difficult for them than for men. In addition, the professional woman usually must have a supportive husband who does not hold strongly to the traditional ideal of the woman's place being in the home. This does not mean, however, that the husband will share domestic chores. The wealth and class position of the upper-class woman allows her to free herself from the domestic sphere by passing the burden on to lower-class domestics.

Women continue to be discriminated against in Mexican society, even in its more modernized sectors. Politics, for example, is considered a male sphere. Women who venture into this arena usually emphasize their adherence to female roles in other spheres. They must prove they are exemplary wives and mothers and that their political concerns are merely extensions of these typical feminine humanitarian interests. They take a *supermadre* role in politics which does not threaten the male-dominated sexual stratification system or gender role ideology.

INDIA: HINDU WOMEN AND MEN

Historical Background. Settled agriculture in India grew out of a nomadic past.[24] Centuries of warfare led eventually to social and political centralization and the development of an agrarian civilization with marked class inequality in the form of the rigid caste system. As in other agrarian societies, women lost power and status as agricultural life replaced horticultural and pastoral patterns. Hindu law, in particular, became more restrictive of women.[25] Hindu law was first codified by Manu in the second century B.C. Under his reforms women lost much of their freedom and personal autonomy. Child marriage became the ideal. Virginity and chastity were strictly required of females but not of males. Females were placed under the perpetual guardianship of males, first the father or elder brother, then the husband. They lost property rights, inheritance rights, divorce rights, rights over their children, and rights to participate in public life. They were forbidden to read the sacred scriptures and deprived of access to the more prestigious aspects of religious life and salvation. Widow remarriage was forbidden and some areas adopted the practice of *suttee,* which required widows to commit suicide by throwing themselves into the flames of their husbands' funeral pyres. With Moslem domination in the twelfth century, *purdah,* or the rigid seclusion and veiling of women, was introduced into Hindu society. Ideologically females came to be regarded as inferior, insignificant, and unclean. The role of women was to bear children and serve men.

The British came to dominate India in the nineteenth century. They opposed many of the Hindu and Moslem customs related to women, but they were cautious in their attempts to reform Indian society. The British did not want to disrupt Indian society and thereby threaten their own domination or profits. The few laws the British did enact (to abolish child marriage, for example), went largely unenforced. They did provide some facilities for education for girls but few people took advantage of them.

Independence from Britain in 1947 brought a wave of enthusiasm for both modernization and preservation of Indian tradition. Women had been encouraged by Mahatma Gandhi to come out of seclusion and participate openly in the independence movement. Many women did protest and many were jailed. The new Indian government recognized the female participants by granting women legal rights, heretofore unimaginable under Hindu tradition.

Twentieth-Century Rights for Women. India has done a great deal toward eliminating sex discrimination in the law. But such progressive social legislation relating to gender roles and women's position in society are virtually unenforceable. The vast numbers of poor illiterate rural and urban women do not even realize what their rights are; if they do, they do not have the resources necessary to demand their recognition. Furthermore, even educated women who know the laws do not necessarily accept them or desire their implementation. For example, laws pertaining to inheritance now give daughters equal rights with sons and another statute outlaws the dowry system. Traditionally, only sons inherit property, because in India's patrilineal family system only sons continue to belong to the joint family after marriage. Daughters therefore receive as large a dowry as possible at marriage, most of which goes to the groom's family. But they have no claims on the rest of the family estate. Most families ignore the laws that attempt to change this system. Daughters do not actively oppose the dowry system for fear they will not be able to marry, and they do not claim inheritance rights out of respect for tradition and to protect the economic interests and viability of their natal families.

The dowry system has, in fact, gotten worse and has made raising a daughter more financially taxing. An educated higher-caste male can often demand as much as $10,000 in dowry from a prospective bride's family. His family views his wife's dowry as a means of recovering the cost of his education. The bride's family sees it as important to marry her well, but the economic sacrifice can be severe.

Divorce is also now legal. But such a terrible social stigma is attached to divorce that relatively few people are willing to avail themselves of this legal right. The law also provides for the granting of alimony. However, the recipient of alimony must remain chaste or forego the alimony. This applies to males who receive alimony as well as to females, but of course females are more likely to be recipients and have to obey the law. Fathers have automatic custody over the children when divorce occurs.

Many laws still remain that discriminate against women by protecting them especially in regard to employment. Women are not allowed to work in certain dangerous occupations nor are they allowed to work at night. This serves to limit the range of occupational choices available to women. Yet the "protection" is often questionable. Women, for example, do some of the hardest work in the construction industry. They are the rock breakers and haulers of heavy loads such as rocks and earth. As low-paid workers who are often recent migrants from impoverished rural areas, they cannot afford to rent rooms. Therefore, they camp at the edge of the construction sites and their children play nearby as they work.

Technically, the law requires that employers provide maternity benefits and child-care facilities for female employees. Employers who do not want to hire women use this law as an excuse: they say it makes women more expensive than male workers. However, employers such as construction firms who desire to use the lower-paid female work force often do so without bothering to provide the benefits required by law.

Indian women have the right to vote and equal rights with men to hold political office. India has even had a female prime minister. However, few women actually participate in politics. Women are not as likely to vote as men, and many who do vote follow their husbands' instructions as to whom to support. Immediately after independence there was a flurry of political activity by women who had participated in the independence movement. Several women have gained high-ranking political office. These women do not, however, always support women's issues or women's rights. Many see themselves as representatives of other social groups rather than as women's representatives. Furthermore, the percentage of female officeholders has declined over the past decade rather than increased.

Politics is still believed to be too rough or too dirty for women, and the example of Prime Minister Indira Gandhi did not affect the wide acceptance of this belief. Gandhi herself was not an active supporter of women's liberation. She has argued that because Indian conditions are different from those in the West, many feminist ideas are inappropriate there. Furthermore, the harshness of her authoritarian rule led many to maintain that she was proof that women should be kept out of politics. Women supposedly cannot be trusted to act honorably.

All women in India have basically the same political and legal rights, although the law does recognize differences in religious practice: for example, Muslim males are allowed multiple wives, but not Hindu males. The actual positions of men and women vary considerably according to their social and economic positions, however. Many religions are practiced in India: Hindu, Moslem, Sikh, Christian, Jain, Parsi, and Jewish. Since the majority of Indians are Hindu and since Hindu culture has had the greatest impact on India, only Hindu males and females are considered here.

The Caste System.   India is characterized by a rigid *caste system*. Caste regulations and observances used to be enforced by law. The castes are no longer legally recognized and government policy aims at eliminating discrimination against lower-caste individuals. However, as with the laws aimed at equality for women, laws supporting caste equality have had negligible effects.

There are thousands of castes in India, but these can be subsumed under five major divisions. The highest caste (in ritual status and prestige, but not necessarily in actual wealth and power) is the Brahmans or priests. The next highest is the Kshatriya caste of kings and warriors, followed by the Vaisya or traders, and then the commoners, the Sudra, or artisans and workers. The lowest in the hierarchy are the Harijan, or untouchables, who perform ritually polluting work such as butchers, launderers, and sweepers. In addition to the castes, there are other low prestige poor peoples known as tribal peoples.

Traditionally, Hindus married and associated only with members of their own caste. Intercaste marriages and relationships are now legal, but they are such a violation of Hindu tradition that they invariably cause a scandal for the families involved and therefore are rare. The positions of women and men vary somewhat according to caste membership.

Another major division within Indian society is between the vast rural sector and the relatively small urban population. Life in the cities differs from life in the rural villages and among these differences are differences in gender roles and sexual stratification. There is also an important dichotomy between the educated, modernized, Westernized elite and the more traditional urban and rural non-Westernized Indians. Important regional variations also affect women's and men's positions. Because it is impossible to describe fully the tremendous diversity that characterizes so large a country as India (one-sixth of the world's women live in India), this discussion will be limited to the major social divisions of socioeconomic status, rural versus urban, and modernized versus traditional sectors.

The traditional norms are more closely adhered to by the upper-strata rural families and the more conservative middle-class and upper-class urban families. Poorer families are more likely to deviate, both out of economic necessity and because they have little ritual honor or status to lose by violating these customs. Members of the educated, liberal urban elite also often reject many of the traditional patterns in favor of Western practices.

Rural Indians

The vast majority of Indians still live in rural agricultural villages. Villagers on the whole tend to be more traditional than city dwellers, but this depends heavily on caste status. Higher-caste, richer villagers are far stricter in their adherence to Hindu customs than are poorer, lower-caste villagers. Among the tribal and lower-caste families in both rural and urban areas, it is usually economically impossible to isolate females in the home or to maintain a rigid sexual division of labor. Women from these groups must work outside the home. Both sexes contribute to the economic support of the family. The man's contribution is likely to be greater, however, because of wage discrimination against women. Women in agricultural labor earn from 10 to 60 percent of what men earn for the same work. But even meager earnings give women a degree of economic independence they would not otherwise have. These working women still have responsibility for household upkeep and child care. Men do not help with domestic duties except in emergencies.

The man has the legitimate authority, but wives often resist it in poorer families. They may even talk back or strike back in a dispute or beating. Wives of these groups are also more likely to abandon abusive husbands and return to their parental households. There is little consideration of prestige loss among these already degraded peoples to keep them from breaking rules against marital separation. For the same reasons, these groups permit their females greater sexual freedom than is common in higher-caste groups.

The more prosperous, but not necessarily wealthy, Indian villagers continue to practice Hindu tradition. They have a patriarchal, patrilineal, patrilocal family structure. Authority and inheritance pass from father to sons. Men control the chief resource, the land, through the patrilineal family and inheritance system. Daughters are only temporary members of the household and will be transferred to their husbands' lineages at an early age. Daughters therefore do not inherit family holdings, but they receive a dowry of jewelry, cash, household goods and clothing which represents an important share of the family's resources. Families therefore prefer to have sons who will serve the family all their lives and will carry on the family line. Moreover, sons bring wealth into the family through their wives' dowries. The birth of a son is therefore a joyous occasion. A daughter is not so celebrated and may be an occasion for sorrow and grief. The midwife is paid more for the delivery of a boy than for a girl, and female infanticide was practiced among some of the warrior castes until about fifty years ago.

Child-rearing Practices.   Despite the difference in initial response to the sex of newborns, infants are usually treated equally. Boys are favored as they grow older, however. Girls are differentiated from boys at a very young age by distinctive clothing and the use of cosmetics. Hindu child-rearing practices clearly differentiate between the sexes, socializing girls toward modesty and domesticity and the boys toward public work and authority. Daughters, for example, are encouraged to care for their younger siblings when they are about six years old.

Sex segregation is imposed on children during early adolescence. Boys and girls have different games and toys. It is unacceptable for girls to participate in boys' games and, usually, vice versa. Girls who attend school at all are often removed at adolescence in order to insure their virginity and reputations. Girls are carefully trained to develop a modest demeanor. They must not act like boys. They must speak in a controlled, low voice and walk with short steps, keeping their arms at their sides and their heads bowed. Boys are not punished for hitting a girl, but a girl is severely punished for striking a boy. However, children of neither sex are encouraged to be independent or individualistic. From infancy onward Hindu socialization aims to build commitment and subservience to the interests of the familial group. The emphasis is on self-control and effacement of the individual will.

Marriage Customs.   Child marriage is still the norm among traditional rural families. Indians believe early marriage works best because it allows the husband and his family to mold the young wife to best fit into their household. Her youth makes her vulnerable and compliant. By the time the girl is fourteen or fifteen years old her parents will have arranged a marriage for her with a somewhat older boy from another village. The couple rarely meet before their wedding day, although members of the groom's family visit the girl to determine her suitability as a wife. She should be of similar caste rank, modest (virginity is essential), submissive, fair-skinned, and have a dowry commensurate with her family's position and wealth. However, in some areas of India it is traditional for the bride's family to have lower rank than the husband's. Thus the bride and her kin must be deferential to the groom's kin. This places the young bride in an even more disadvantaged position in her new household than is usual in areas where brides and grooms come from families of similar rank.

After her marriage, the young bride leaves her natal family and village and goes to reside with her husband in his extended family. The move is a fearful and painful event for the girl. Her introduction into the physical relationship of marriage makes the early stage of married life even more difficult. Sex is considered too embarrassing to discuss even between mother and daughter, so girls are given little or no information about it. Thus the sexual consummation of the marriage is often a traumatic experience, especially since the husband is a virtual stranger.

The young bride's position as daughter-in-law in her husband's household is not an enviable one. She is under the strict authority of a domineering and demanding mother-in-law. The mother-in-law directs the work of her daughters-in-law. The youngest daughter-in-law is given the most time-consuming, arduous, and menial work of the household. She is also kept under close surveillance by the mother-in-law. Her freedom of movement and personal autonomy are severely restricted. She has to show respect and strict obedience to her mother-in-law and her new male kinspeople. If she violates any of the appropriate standards of behavior, she brings shame to her natal family.

In the rural areas women born in a particular village do not have to veil their faces. However, women from outside must be veiled. This means that daughters-in-law must remain veiled and cannot move freely in the village. The daughter-in-law must remain veiled even within the household, especially in the presence of her father-in-law or her husband's elder brothers. She should even veil herself in the presence of her husband and not speak to him or hand him anything if other people are present. As she grows older and has several children, she becomes a more accepted member of the community and suffers fewer restrictions.

Doranne Jacobson argues that veiling and purdah observances of women help maintain harmony in the joint family, albeit at the cost of female status, independence, and freedom:

> It emphasizes the subordinate relationship of the woman to those in authority in the family and deemphasizes her tie to her husband. Veiling and seclusion in her conjugal home constantly remind a woman of her position as a *bahu* [daughter-in-law] who must quietly subjugate her individual wishes to those of the group.[26]

The young bride usually receives little emotional support from her new husband. Husbands and wives are not expected to provide each other with companionship. Companionship comes from participation in the unisex work groups of the family. In traditional families recently married couples are not allowed to see each other during the day. They get to know each other only at night in bed.

Ideally a woman should treat her husband as a god. She should never speak his name or speak to him in public. Indian women should never openly disagree with any man or offer a man information or advice. This shames a man even if he is the woman's husband. The male ego is thought to be easily injured; females are not supposed to have strong egos. Female subservience is also shown by the wife walking several paces behind her husband. A woman should also eat after her husband has eaten. She can eat his leftovers, but her leftovers would defile him.

The purposes of the marriage relationship is to produce children, sons in particular; to perpetuate the family line; and to provide economic security for the couple in their old age. Children are a mark of wealth and prestige in rural areas. Marriage and children are necessary for full social adulthood for both men and women. In addition, women must have children to improve their position in the husband's family. The childless woman is in a pitiable situation. Her husband may even decide to take another wife. Therefore, the young daughter-in-law and her husband's kin anxiously await signs of her first pregnancy. When she does become pregnant, she becomes the center of attention. She thereby proves her usefulness to the household, especially if she has a son.

Despite the importance attached to childbirth, the new mother and her child are considered unclean and ritually polluting and therefore are kept away from other people for forty days. Similarly, a menstruating woman is subject to taboos because she is considered to be polluting to others. For example, she may not cook or enter the kitchen and she must eat separately from other members of the household. She is prohibited from touching other people and must sleep apart from her husband. Women are believed to be especially prone to pollution and difficult to purify, while men are relatively resistant to pollution and easy to purify. Men are strong, women are weak. Therefore, men are allowed much greater freedom of action and movement within Hindu society. Women do not oppose these taboos, however, because they welcome the rest the taboos provide from some of their usual household duties.

Sexual Division of Labor.   A strict sexual division of labor in traditional Indian society is part of the wider system of sex segregation. Males are to do the outside work, to provide for the support of the women and children, and to control and discipline them. Women are in charge of domestic and child-care tasks. But because it robs a man of status for him to undertake women's work, women have a fair degree of autonomy within the domestic confines. The rigidity of the division of labor and the domestic/public dichotomy is made clear in the task of burden carrying. It often shocks Westerners to see a man walking empty-handed while his wife carries a heavy load of wood, clay pots, or cow dung. Men do not carry items intended for household use because that is the woman's domain.

Women work very hard within the household. For example, Indian food processing and cooking are time consuming. Meals are supposed to be as elaborate as family income allows. As Jacobson describes it,

> in villages women clean grain, grind flour and spices, pare vegetables, pickle mangoes, and cook over smokey fires in dark kitchens. They sweep, fetch water from distant wells, mix straw and mud with their feet, and mud-plaster and whitewash their houses. They clean the barns and shape cow dung cakes for cooking fuel. They collect firewood, scrub dishes with mud and ash, and wash clothes, all the while caring for demanding children and waiting upon their husbands. In cities, women spend many hours in the kitchen each day, producing elaborate meals, in addition to scrubbing and ironing clothing for family members who must look neat at school and office. Many village women also work at agricultural tasks, while women of artisan and service castes have their traditional tasks to perform.[27]

Many women work in the fields, but no agricultural tasks are consistently assigned to females. Males do all of the heavy work associated with plowing. Very poor women are often forced to hire themselves out as day laborers. Wealthier village women may do little or no agricultural work except during harvest time. Indian women who bring income into the household are usually more independent than the higher-status women who confine their work to non-income-producing domestic production. But despite the hard work of women, both women and men perceive women's work as less important than men's, and women see themselves as dependents of men. However, in the wet rice culture areas, women have an important role in primary economic production, and they have greater freedom and a higher status in these areas.

Urban Indians

The conservative, traditional upper-strata urban families follow much the same customs and practices as described for the wealthier rural families. In urban areas, however, women do no agricultural work and therefore are even more permanently restricted to the home. Some girls are allowed to attend school. Primary school is usually considered to be sufficient. Secondary school is sometimes acceptable, but college is out of the question. Not only does it allow the female too much freedom from the household, but it is feared that attending college will interfere with the development of an appropriately submissive personality. Furthermore, a college education is a liability in the marriage market. Husbands must have a higher educational and occupational status than their wives in order to uphold the sexual stratification system. A woman with a college degree has a limited field of prospective mates.

Poorer urban families and the small Westernized elite deviate from these traditional patterns. Poorer families do not have the means necessary to observe traditional customs. Their women must work outside the home, often in domestic service or the construction industry. The modern elite, however, favors what are to them the more prestigious Western customs.

According to Dube, the domestic and public spheres are not as firmly separated on the basis of sex in the modernized families. Men have the responsibility to work to support the family, but women may work if they desire to and can find employment. Women of this group are also more likely to participate in voluntary social work outside the home. Women have greater autonomy and a greater share in family decision-making and authority. Indian women active in the professions, politics, and the arts come from this group. But these women continue to shoulder the responsibility for household and child care unless the family can afford servants. Men do not share these tasks.

Even among the Westernized groups, arranged marriages are still the norm. The boy and girl are more likely to have veto rights over the parents' choice than they did in the past. Love marriages sometimes occur, but they are still uncommon.

Increasingly, urban middle- and upper-class women are taking jobs outside the home. Employment appears to have a liberating effect on women. Marjorie Wood found, for example, that "women who seek employment are more likely to make love marriages, have small families, and relate to members of their households in an egalitarian manner than are their unemployed counterparts."[28]

Educated urban women have more career opportunities now than in the past. But these are still largely in sex-segregated, low-prestige, low-paid occupations such as teaching in primary or girls' schools and clerical work. Women have great difficulty obtaining and retaining positions which require them to assert authority over men, especially if the men are of similar caste rank. The range of jobs is expanding, but there is still a high unemployment rate among educated women. Many Indians feel women should not be allowed to compete equally with men for scarce jobs.

It is still unacceptable for a woman to go out alone at night, and single women are a particular anomaly in Hindu society. It is expected that everyone will marry. Yet highly educated career women often find that no suitable mate is available. They cannot date or even develop friendships with men. If their work requires attendance at social gatherings, they cannot go alone or with a date. They usually rely on a brother or other close kinsman to escort them. Work at night severely damages a woman's reputation.

The traditional patterns are also still evident in the treatment of college women, even among the Westernized elite. College women are carefully protected from men in order to retain their reputations. Female colleges have high walls, night watchmen, and strict rules about male visitors. Even in coeducational colleges, male and female students are not allowed to speak or associate with each other. Friendships between males and females are impossible. The assumption is that contact between the sexes always leads to sexual relations.

But education, like employment, seems to weaken the woman's commitment to some traditions. J. Murickan's study of middle-class women's attitudes found that the educated younger generation of women is less accepting of the traditional submissive role for women than is the older generation.[29] The younger generation is also more supportive of free choice in marriage and the sharing of child care and household work with husbands. They were more likely to believe that education is desirable for girls as well as boys and that the curriculum should be the same for the sexes. They feel that women should be allowed to work but should not allow it to interfere with their duties as wife and mother. The young women also felt that women should be allowed to participate in activities outside the home such as politics, hobbies, or volunteer work.

Like other underdeveloped countries, India has a chronically high unemployment rate. This has affected women more than it has men. Despite attempts at modernization, women's participation in the labor market has declined in both rural and urban sectors, despite advances for college educated elite women. Between 1911 and 1971 women's share of the Indian labor market fell from 34.4 percent to 17.3 percent.[30] Paradoxically, industrialization is hailed as the road to progress, but women's participation in industrial employment has declined markedly over the last few decades. This is true despite important gains by women in education.

Jacobson sums up the situation:

> It is clear that the negative effects of automation and new technology in industry fall mainly on women, who being untrained are replaced by men and machines. Management and unions tend to train men in newly necessary skills, while women lose their jobs. Men tend also to have better access to employment information and job training since they are more educated and physically mobile than women. Thus, women's illiteracy and low social status work to their disadvantage in modernizing industry.[31]

THE NEAR EAST: AN IRAQI VILLAGE

Historical Perspectives

Agrarian-based societies have existed in the Near East as far back as the beginning of recorded history. Agriculture was probably first invented in the area of the Tigris and Euphrates river valleys. As one would expect on the basis of theories of women's and men's positions in society, women have had an equally long history of subordination in this area. Ilse Siebert presents evidence indicating that like in India and Mexico the earliest records show freer and more independent positions for women than are found under the later agrarian empires.[32]

According to Siebert, as early as the seventeenth century B.C. Hammurabi's code of laws clearly embodied the firm subordination of women. The code prescribed the patriarchal family structure, allowing men multiple wives, concubines, and easy divorce. Women, however, were denied divorce rights and required by law to remain chaste on pain of death. Women did have influential roles as priestesses and as queens, queen mothers, and princesses, if they had the intelligence, skill, and motivation to develop the power potential of these positions. Other than the queen, queen mother, and princesses, the women of the royal harems throughout the history of the Near East were the pampered prisoners of the king. They devoted their lives to beauty, singing, and play in order to be pleasing to the king who owned them either as wives or as slaves. They were strictly secluded in a separate building from the palace and carefully guarded by eunuchs.

Women were, as Collins suggested, important as sexual property in these societies (see Chapter 2). The more powerful the male was, the larger his harem would be: women served as objects of conspicuous consumption for males. Some particularly powerful kings are reported to have had as many as 12,000 young girls and women. Lesser kings and the lesser nobility had much smaller harems. Controlling the sexuality of large numbers of women was an important badge of male honor and status. Stealing another man's women inflicted the greatest humiliation upon him. For this reason, women were often the objects of capture during warfare. It was especially prestigious for the victor and humiliating for the vanquished to have the royal harem captured by the conqueror.

Moslem Traditions

The Moslem religion when it was first introduced into the Near East by the prophet Mohammed in the seventh century constituted a move toward improving the status of women. Women were important supporters of Mohammed and his new religion. Mohammed preached the equality of all persons, including women. He laid out rules to protect women's rights of inheritance, property, marriage choice, and divorce. These rights were not, however, equal to men's rights. As Islam spread throughout these patriarchal, wartorn, agrarian societies, it was reinterpreted and applied in such a way as to justify the almost total isolation of women in the domestic sphere, away from the public spheres of power. Women did not always accept these subordinate roles and Elise Boulding documents the active underlife in which some women participated, which allowed a few women to become influential in the world of men.[33] These were, however, always positions of influence or power behind the throne. Power through the underlife rarely allows women to exercise legitimate, publicly recognized authority.

The Near East Today

With these thousands of years of tradition weighing upon them, women in the Near East today still find themselves subordinated to men. In modernizing, heavily Western-influenced urban areas, women have been freed from some of the more repressive aspects of the traditional Moslem agrarian civilization. Among the rural peasantry tradition remains strong, however.

In the late 1950s Elizabeth Fernea and her husband Robert lived in an Iraqi peasant village and studied the women's lives in detail.[34] Fernea adhered to the accepted customs of the village. In particular, she obeyed the rules of *purdah*. The village women adhered strongly to the tradition of domestic seclusion and veiling. They never left the women's quarters without wearing the *abayah,* the heavy black cloaklike garment which completely covers the woman from head to toe.

Young girls are allowed to run almost as freely as boys in the village. However, at the age of about eleven years the girl dons the veil and begins her lifetime observance of purdah. She is strictly isolated in the women's quarters and may never associate openly with non-kinsmen again. She must remain above the slightest suspicion. Her reputation is ruined if men even speak about her in the coffee shops.

One of Fernea's experiences dramatically illustrates the seriousness of these requirements. Fernea was invited by a close female friend to go for a ride in a male cousin's car. This of course was of no danger to Fernea because her husband did not require her observance of purdah. She was practicing it only for research purposes. However, she made the mistake of inviting another of her friends, Laila, to go along. Even though Laila understood the seriousness of riding in a car with a non-kinsman, she accepted. They went for the ride covered in their *abayahs* and without speaking at all to the males.

The children of the community reported back to other adults that they had seen Laila enter the car. (Children and other close associates of the women are able to recognize them when they are veiled. They come to discern the slightest variations in dress and demeanor.) Upon realizing Laila's dangerous position, Fernea and the other woman denied she had been in the car. They covered her by saying that another female cousin, not Laila, had accompanied them. These lies protected Laila's reputation and kept her father from having to kill her to save the honor of the other women of the family and the reputation of the family as a whole. Had there been any more definite evidence against her, Laila would have paid for this brief outing with her life.

The segregation of the sexes was almost total in the village. Wives typically saw their husbands only at mealtimes and in the bedroom. At meals they did not usually eat together. The men were served first and the women and children ate the leftovers from the men's dishes. Men lived in the public world of the village, the women in the domestic world. A woman could not speak to her own husband in public. As a result husbands and wives did not provide each other with emotional support or companionship. Close friendships were formed between members of the same sex. The women were allowed to visit one another in the women's quarters and to move about in the obscure alleys between the high-walled houses. They avoided visits, however, which brought them, even though heavily veiled, into the public eye. They would take a circuitous back route in order to avoid going near the public marketplace. (Men in this society took care of all purchases from the market.) It was considered shameful for a family's women to be discussed in any way—even if the mention were so mild as to say the women were seen visiting other women.

Women, formed close ties with one another and produced an active underlife culture and support system. The segregation in the women's quarters provided some basis for the development of female solidarity. Such female solidarity was, however, more likely to be used for emotional support for a woman in distress than for any important or active opposition to male dominance or to specific men.

Most women of the village accepted their seclusion as right and proper. They did not chafe against it or attempt to rebel. Although they knew that some city women had abandoned the *abayah,* they had no desire to do so. Fernea points out that for the Iraqi village woman to leave the woman's quarters without her *abayah* would induce the same sort of shame and humiliation as it would for most Western women to go out in public naked. Most women firmly accepted the customs and traditions.

The gossip of the women formed an important part of the social control system over women in general. The women themselves were intolerant of violations of the feminine role by other women. They denounced the modern unveiled women who associated freely with men as strongly as the men did. Fernea notes, however, that they were not idle in their gossip. They tried to avoid false accusations of any sort because they knew how terrible the consequences of loss of reputation would be to a woman.

It was, of course, essential that a girl maintain her virginity. Marriages were arranged by the parents and the prospective bride and groom's mothers had an important say in the matchmaking. The couple could not meet before their wedding day without violating custom. However, the bride and groom were likely to be cousins because of the preference for marrying within one's patrilineage, and therefore they were likely to have known each other before the girl entered purdah.

On the wedding day the marriage had to be consummated while the mothers and other friends and relatives waited outside the bedroom. Afterwards the mothers had to inspect the sheets for blood from the broken hymen and publicly announce the proof of the bride's virginity. If it was discovered that the bride was not a virgin, her family suffered severe humiliation and she would probably be put to death as a ruined woman.

Virginity, chastity, and monogamy were not required of males. However, for the poorer males, there was little opportunity for extramarital sexual liaisons. Only the wealthy could pay the bride-prices for multiple wives or buy the sexual favors of concubines and prostitutes. In the village Fernea studied, the local sheik had four wives, but the other men rarely took even a second wife. The women themselves actively opposed being a co-wife. First wives whose husbands were considering a second wife often made their husbands' lives so miserable that they relented and ceased negotiations for the second wife. New wives were often subjected to abusive treatment by first wives. Sometimes, however, the first wife welcomed a second wife to help run the household or to supply children if the first wife were barren.

Childlessness in this culture was always blamed on the woman. Barrenness or bearing only daughters resulted in shame, humiliation, and loss of status for the woman and for the husband, who had the right to divorce such a wife. A woman's and man's highest honor came from producing many sons to carry on the patrilineal, patriarchal family. Daughters were not as highly valued, despite the valuable labor they provided for the household.

Marriage was the only respected adult role for the village women. Yet lack of a dowry or an appropriate candidate for husband kept many of them in perpetual dependence in their fathers' or brothers' homes. Poor clan members often could not raise the necessary bride-price for marriage. Families resisted the idea of marrying their daughters to nonkinsmen even if it meant the woman would never marry. The lack of bride-price could sometimes be solved if the prospective groom could arrange to marry his sister to the brother of his prospective bride. In this way the bride-price payments by the two families would be cancelled out. It was not an enviable fate for either a man or a woman to remain unmarried.

Women had no real basis for economic independence in the Iraqi village. Even if they worked at income-producing tasks such as weaving or sewing, the money belonged to their husbands or fathers. A woman's only insurance against economic disaster was whatever gold jewelry her husband could or would give her. The women of the village were amazed by the paltry amount of gold worn by Fernea. Since her husband appeared both to love her and be a man of means, they could not understand why he had not given her the heavy gold bracelets, necklaces, and earrings they coveted so much.

The jewelry also served as a source of wealth the woman could draw on to help her children if the father either could not or would not support them. For example, one well-to-do father opposed his son's intention to attend college in the city. The mother sold her gold to support her son in opposition to her husband. This was within her rights even though it angered her husband. Thus, women were not entirely submissive to their husbands' wishes.

Mothers often developed close and enduring ties with their children. Sons exhibited a familiarity with and love for the mother that was forbidden in their relationships with their father. In the presence of the father, the son was not allowed to speak without being spoken to. Fathers were to be treated with great awe and respect by their wives and children at all times.

Mothers, therefore, supplied the parental warmth that was taboo from the fathers. The mother–daughter relationship was considered so important and enduring that only harsh circumstances would induce a family to marry a daughter to a man in another community. It was felt that daughters should be allowed to remain near their mothers' households all their lives. Again, the village women were chagrined that Fernea's husband had not brought her mother with them to Iraq to comfort Fernea and keep her company.

The women of the village worked hard in their domestic compounds. Household maintenance and meal preparation had to be done without any help from advanced technology. In addition, there were long hours to be devoted to needlework, laundry at the nearby canal, bread baking, food preservation, and water carrying. Tedious hours were spent by the women of each household cleaning rice by hand. The work was usually done in the presence of other females, however, and this added an element of enjoyment to the boring tasks.

The forces of change were evident in this village in the late 1950s. The modernization of gender roles that had affected significant segments of the urban population in Iraq had begun to filter into the village. Some young people were accepting of the new ideas.

The trend toward providing education for girls as well as boys has had a modernizing effect on many of the educated young women's and men's ideas concerning the feminine role and the proper relations between the sexes. The older villagers live in fear that such ideas as breaking purdah will infect their youth. Change in gender roles and sexual stratification is underway but is not likely to be rapid. The forces of tradition are sufficiently strong to keep most of the younger generation committed to the old ways. And the effects of industrialization are so slight among the poor peasant villages that industrialization has not as yet undermined the agrarian-based social structure. Therefore, the social organization which gave rise to their patterns of gender roles and sexual stratification is still largely intact.

SUMMARY

Underdeveloped peasant societies still rely heavily on nonindustrialized agriculture. But they are underdeveloped, not undeveloped. That is, these societies are exploited by the developed industrialized world and are locked into a pattern of economic dependency and massive poverty.

Gender roles in underdeveloped societies show important similarities with those of preindustrial agrarian societies. But the examples of the prestigious industrialized societies and new forms of exploitation cause them to diverge from previous examples of agrarian society. For example, the modernized elite class often accepts the practices of the industrialized world. Women of this group are allowed greater freedom of movement and access to education and careers, but they are still subordinated to men of their class. The lower classes, especially those who leave the rural peasant life for the cities or the plantations, often no longer practice the traditional gender roles. Their cultural patterns are disrupted by new forms of poverty and economic exploitation. The situation of women among these groups is often worsened, because they have lost traditional forms of mutual support without gaining new forms of economic security.

For the middle classes, however, traditional patterns of female subordination and isolation often remain strong. The husband's income is used to support the family without the wife's help. Female economic dependency is prestigious, but it comes at the expense of female autonomy. Traditional agrarian gender roles also remain strong among those who remain peasants.

The case studies of Mexico, India, and Iraq show how the positions of women and men are affected by underdevelopment. Variations exist, but certain patterns are discernible on the basis of social class and rural or urban residence.

Notes

1. See Andre Gunder Frank, *Latin America: Underdevelopment or Revolution* (New York: Monthly Review Press, 1969).
2. See Chapter 4 and Ester Boserup, *Woman's Role in Economic Development* (New York: St. Martin's Press, 1970).
3. Mary P. Burke, "Women: The Missing Piece in the Development Puzzle," *Agenda*, Vol. 1 No. 3 (March, 1978), 1–5.
4. Ann Rubbo, "The Spread of Capitalism in Rural Colombia: Effects on Poor Women," in Rayna Reiter, ed., *Toward an Anthropology of Women* (New York: Monthly Review Press, 1975), pp. 333–357.
5. Heleieth Saffioti, "Female Labor and Capitalism in the United States and Brazil," in Ruby Rohrlich-Leavitt, ed., *Women Cross-Culturally* (The Hague: Mouton, 1975), pp. 59–94. See also Nadia Haggag Youseff, *Women and Work in Developing Societies* (Westport, Conn.: Greenwood Press, 1974).
6. Susan E. Brown, "Lower Economic Sector Female Mating Patterns in the Dominican Republic: A Comparative Analysis," in Rohrlich-Leavitt, pp. 149–162.
7. June Nash, "Resistance as Protest: Women in the Struggle of Bolivian Tin-Mining Communities," in Rohrlich-Leavitt, pp. 261–271.
8. Nash, p. 269.
9. Thomas G. Sanders, "Mexico," *Common Ground* Vol. 2, No. 1 (January, 1976), 45–55.
10. Evelyn P. Stevens,"*Marianismo:* The Other Face of *Machismo,*" in Ann Pescatello, ed., *Female and Male in Latin America* (Pittsburgh: U. of Pittsburgh Press, 1973), p. 90.

11. Stevens, p. 91.
12. Nora Scott Kinzer, "Priests, Machos and Babies: Or, Latin American Women and the Manichaean Heresy," *Journal of Marriage and the Family, 35* (May, 1973), 300–312.
13. Stevens, p. 315.
14. Oscar Lewis, *Pedro Martinez: A Mexican Peasant and His Family* (New York: Vintage Books, 1964).
15. Doren Slade, "Marital Status and Sexual Identity: The Position of Women in a Mexican Peasant Society," in Rohrlich-Leavitt, pp. 129–148.
16. Slade, p. 147.
17. Lewis, *Five Families* (New York: John Wiley, 1959); *The Children of Sanchez* (Baltimore: Penguin, 1961).
18. Lewis, 1959, p. 259.
19. Lewis, 1959, p. 172.
20. Virve Piho, "Life and Labor of the Woman Textile Workers in Mexico City," in Rorhlich-Leavitt, pp. 199–245.
21. Piho, p. 241.
22. Mary Elmendorf, "Mexico: The Many Worlds of Women," in Janet Zollinger Giele and Audrey Chapman Smock, eds., *Women: Roles and Statuses in Eight Countries* (New York: John Wiley, 1977), p. 147.
23. Sanders, p. 49.
24. This section is based largely on the following works: Margaret Cormack, *The Hindu Woman* (1953; Westport, Conn.: Greenwood Press, 1975); S. C. Dube, "Men's and Women's Roles in India: A Sociological Review," in Barbara Ward, ed., *Women in the New Asia* (Paris: UNESCO, 1963), pp. 174–203; Vatsala Narain, "India," in Raphael Patai, ed., *Women in the Modern World* (New York: Free Press, 1967), pp. 21–41; Doranne Jacobson, "The Women of North and Central India: Goddesses and Wives," in Carolyn Matthiasson, ed., *Many Sisters* (New York: Free Press, 1974), pp. 99–176; Jacobson, "Indian Women in Processes of Development," *Journal of International Affairs,* Vol. 30, No. 2 (Fall–Winter, 1976–77), 211–242; Jacobson, "Purdah in India: Life behind the Veil," *National Geographic,* Vol. 152, No. 2 (August 1977), 270–286; Marcus Franda, "India," *Common Ground,* Vol. 2, No. 1 (January, 1976), 17–28.
25. See A. S. Altekar, *The Position of Women in Hindu Civilization: From Prehistoric Times to the Present Day* (1938; Delhi: Motilal Banarsidas, 1973); Narain, "India," and Dube, "Men's and Women's Roles."
26. Jacobson, 1974, p. 142.
27. Jacobson, 1976–77, p. 223.
28. Marjorie Wood, "Employment and Family Change: A Study of Middle-Class Women in Urban Gujarat," in Alfred de Souza, ed., *Women in Contemporary India* (New Delhi: Manohar Book Service, 1975), p. 51.
29. J. Murickan, "Women in Kerala: Changing Socio-Economic Status and Self-Image," in de Souza, pp. 73–95.
30. Murickan, p. 77.
31. Jacobson, 1976–77, p. 230.
32. Ilse Siebert, *Women in the Ancient Near East* (New York; Abner Schram, 1974).
33. Elise Boulding, *The Underside of History* (Boulder, Col.: Westview Press, 1976), pp. 384–391.
34. Elizabeth Fernea, *Guests of the Sheik* (Garden City, N.Y.: Doubleday, 1965).

8

Capitalist Industrialist Societies

England and the United States, 1700-1920

It is not the family that keeps women in an inferior position in the labor force and in society, but the need for women's marginalized role as workers and as the unpaid producers and reproducers of the labor force that is responsible for family organization and its social-psychological concomitants.

Eleanor Burke Leacock, "Introduction" to
Women in Class Society

Capitalist commercial and productive enterprises developed gradually within the medieval agricultural economy. Small-scale merchants, traders, artisans, and craftspeople became more numerous as medieval society became centralized under the rule of powerful kings. These monarchs' central governments stimulated capitalist development through the provision of standardized laws, money, highways, and the physical protection of the merchant and his or her wares. Cities and towns grew dramatically. Agriculture declined in relative importance in the economy and so did the power of the landed aristocracy which depended on agriculture. The capitalist class was in ascendancy.

The capitalists eventually became powerful enough to limit or overthrow the power of the kings themselves. Parliamentary democracies replaced the rule of absolute monarchs in England, Western Europe, and the United States. These parliamentary governments were run by and for the newly powerful male capitalists. While these changes were taking place in the political and class structures, the process of industrialization was transforming the economy, which developed from small-scale cottage industry and shops to large-scale factory production. And as these evolutionary and revolutionary changes in society from medieval agrarianism to modern industrial capitalism were taking place, they had important effects on the gender roles and sexual stratification systems of these societies.

ECONOMY AND CLASS STRUCTURE

The capitalist economy is dominated by commodity production and exchange value. Simple use values continue to be produced within the home as women cook, clean, and care for children without direct monetary compensation. The trend, however, is for the production of use values to be replaced by the production of exchange values. Market relationships come to characterize the society. Productivity is vastly increased under capitalism and industrialization. This allows for high population densities and the consumption of surpluses impossible under previous modes of production. People become dependent on the money economy for their subsistence and luxury needs.

The economy is based on individual ownership of private property, but most people own little or no important private property. A very few, the capitalists, own or control the important income-producing property such as factories and industrial corporations. To run their profit generating enterprises, they depend on the existence of a *free labor force*. "Free" in this sense does not imply a true personal freedom for the individual. Instead it refers to the individual workers not being bound to a particular employer or occupation as serfs, indentured servants, or slaves. The individual is thus free to sell his or her labor at whatever prices he or she can command from an employer. The employer is also free from the traditional obligations of the lord–peasant, master–slave relationship. He or she can dismiss the employees whenever their labor is no longer needed or desired.

This is adaptive for the fluctuating labor requirements as businesses go through "boom" and "bust" periods of expansion and recession. It is also adaptive for the changing needs for different types of workers. Technological change is rapid under industrialization. It often renders some occupations obsolete and increases the demand for others. Workers, therefore, have to adjust to the highly variable needs of a capitalist economy through their "freedom" to be unemployed, to move from areas of low employment to areas of high employment, and to undertake training to obtain skills which are still in demand.

Class Inequality

There is, therefore, marked class stratification and inequality under capitalism. Some people become wealthy and powerful capitalists while others are left with nothing but their labor to sell in the market economy. Some workers can make a better bargain for their labor than others: that is, they receive better salaries, job security, or better working conditions. For example, those with desirable skills can obtain a better contract than unskilled workers. The working class does not, therefore, constitute a class-conscious, unified group. It is divided and weakened by any number of cleavages such as distinctions between skilled and unskilled or white collar and blue collar workers. Two very important bases for dividing the working class against itself are race and sex. White workers are pitted against black workers so that racism keeps them fighting with each other instead of uniting against the power of the upper classes. And men are similarly pitted against women with sexism focusing their discontent on demands or competition by female workers instead of on the powerlessness of workers in general.

Sexual Division of Labor

Work inside and outside the home is characterized by a high degree of sex segregation. As capitalism develops, some jobs come to be defined as "feminine" and others as "masculine." Sometimes the definitions undergo change. For example, teaching began as a male occupation and later came to be dominated by females and redefined as feminine. Similarly, before World War II, the job of librarian had been feminine. After World War II many men used the G.I. Bill to obtain college degrees in library science and gradually took over the administrative and higher level librarian posts.

As capitalism and industrialization develop work is separated from the home. The domestic/public dichotomy is more fully realized under industrial capitalism than it is in any of the societal types previously considered here. Within the domestic sphere the sexual division of labor manifests itself in assigning primary responsibility for the housework and child care to women. This is functionally related to the needs of capitalist business and industry. As Heleieth Saffioti points out, family responsibilities are used to *marginalize* women from the labor force and to turn them into a vast *reserve labor force*.[1] By being assigned the household and child care tasks, women are limited in their ability to compete with men for jobs in the public market economy. Yet they can still be drawn upon as workers whenever the male labor supply is inadequate to meet production needs. A capitalist industrial economy rarely needs all of its potential labor supply. Labor shortages sometimes occur, however, especially in times of mass mobilization for war or during periods of tremendous economic growth. Extra workers are kept available within the family as housewives. When job opportunities draw them out of the home, the women assume the dual role of worker and housewife, thus allowing employers to take advantage of both their paid and unpaid labor. Their role in the family justifies returning them to the home when their labor is no longer needed. And it justifies discriminating against women in favor of male employees and thus provides a basis for dividing the working class against itself.

The domestic role also allows employers to draw upon the unpaid labor of women to make the male employees more efficient workers. As women take care of the male workers' food, clothing, household maintenance, and child care needs, they free the men to concentrate on their public jobs. Women's unpaid labor is also used to produce and socialize future generations of the labor supply. Mothers consciously prepare their children, and especially their sons, to become obedient, diligent, responsible workers. They aid them in obtaining the necessary education and skills to be more productive and valuable employees.

Women and the family situation they maintain also create a buffer against the intense competitiveness and alienation of the work process. This helps to maintain the emotional and psychological fitness of the workers. Eli Zaretsky states that one of the effects of participation in capitalist work structures is an increase in *individualism* and emphasis on *personal life*.[2] That is, people come to value personal self-development and intimate interpersonal relationships to compensate for the depersonalization and alienation they experience in their work. He argues, moreover, that individualism was first extended only to men. Women's role was to make the personal self-development of the male possible. Males have thus been freed to pursue a personal identity and personal life while women have been bound to the needs of the family and expected to sacrifice their personal needs and self-development whenever they clashed with family priorities.

John Kenneth Galbraith points out another function of the domestic role of women for capitalism.[3] The housewife is a main support for *consumerism* and this underlies the continued profitability and growth of capitalist business. Idealizing women's roles as wives and mothers is what Galbraith calls a "convenient social virtue"—convenient for business and industry. It assigns to women the often onerous tasks associated with consumption. Purchasing, maintaining, sorting, and storing consumer goods are often time-consuming and boring jobs. If each person had to assume responsibility for his or her own consumption, it would limit the desire to consume. However, if some of the burdens of consumption can be shifted to someone else, there are few limitations on one's consumption wants. Women are convinced to assume these burdens by defining the tasks as "virtuous." Thus, a "good wife" may take care of purchasing her husband's ties and taking his suits to the cleaner. And the "good mother" shops for the appropriate educational toys for her children. The housewife's assumption of the role of consumer for the family is of course profitable for business which depends on constantly increasing sales.

Although women's role in the family justifies limiting their participation in the public sphere, it should be realized that this family organization and gender roles for women are the result, not the cause, of the industrial capitalist mode of production and sexual division of labor. As Eleanor Burke Leacock states it:

> It is not the family that keeps women in an inferior position in the labor force and in society, but the need for women's marginalized role as workers and as the unpaid producers and reproducers of the labor force that is responsible for family organization and its social-psychological concomitants.[4]

The marginalization of women from the paid labor force and the domestic/public dichotomy also have an important effect on men and serve the interests of business in yet another way. If women and children are turned into the economic dependents of men, then the responsibility for their maintenance devolves solely upon men. Instead of joint familial responsibility for subsistence needs, the husband becomes the sole bread-winner for the family. This is, of course, a great burden for the husband/father, and this responsibility binds him firmly to his job. He usually cannot afford to quit his job without already having found another. He cannot decide to tell the boss off and suffer the deprivations of unemployment because he will not be the only one to suffer. He must always think of the needs of his family as well. Therefore, placing the burden of economic support on the husband is a means of enforcing labor discipline. The married man with children is easier to exploit as an employee than the single man who has only himself to provide for.

Sexual Stratification

Male dominance is thus encouraged by the sexual division of labor and the family structure it promotes. Male workers are exploited and alienated in their role as workers. Their exploitation is softened by their being rewarded with the subservience of their wives. Wives are expected to tend to the physical, emotional, and sexual needs of their husbands. They are to relieve the males of household and child-care responsibilities and provide them with an emotional haven from the wider world. In return, wives are to receive economic support from their husbands. Collins describes this situation as the private household in a market economy. This type of domestic organization and gender roles arose with capitalism and is still characteristic of many families.

However, as capitalism and industrialization have evolved, the features Collins says are embodied in the advanced market economy have emerged among some groups in advanced industrial societies. The needs of the economy have drawn increasing numbers of women out of the private household into the labor force. Even though these women usually retain the dual role, paid employment still has important liberating effects. As Collins suggests, it improves women's bargaining positions in relation to men by giving them a degree of economic independence. It furthermore develops the skills of the public world in women. Their new skills and economic independence often combine to give women the confidence and motivation to demand an end to sexism and sexual stratification in both the domestic and public spheres. Thus feminist movements tend to arise. Women begin to demand that individualism, self-development, and the pursuit of a personal identity be extended to them as well as to men. These may be elusive goals for both men and women under capitalism. The nature of work and social organization may very well make it impossible for either sex to find a truly satisfying personal life without a reorganization of society. However, many women no longer accept the sexual stratification system which puts them at a disadvantage relative to men.

The Interaction of Class Stratification and Sexual Stratification

Just as sexual stratification creates an important cleavage within the working class, so does class stratification create important divisions among women. Women from different socioeconomic classes are likely to view each other with hostility and misunderstanding. The interests of working-class women, for example, do not always coincide with those of middle-class or upper-class women and sometimes they may actually clash. And black women and white women find it difficult to unite in feminist causes.

Class stratification also sometimes obscures the pervasive effects of sexual stratification. The well-to-do upper-class or middle-class woman may be able to direct and exploit the labor of working-class men and women while at the same time remaining subordinate to men of her own class standing. Furthermore, the fact that some upper-class women can obtain higher educations, pursue prestigious careers, run for political office, or own important property may also make it appear that such positions are as open to women as they are to men. However, it is the class positions of these women which make their achievements possible and give them the resources necessary to overcome to a degree the barriers of sexual stratification. Such women do not constitute proof that sexual stratification does not exist, but they can be used to keep people from recognizing the continuance of sexual inequality.

With these theoretical perspectives and generalizations in mind, this study next considers the impact of the development of capitalism and industrialization in England and the United States. These two countries were the first to embrace fully the new patterns of work organization and productive techniques. They were also the first to experience the impact of capitalism and industrialization on family life, gender roles, and sexual stratification. Although the new economy did not always affect the two countries at the same time or in exactly the same manner, their experiences have been quite similar.

THE PREINDUSTRIAL FAMILY ECONOMY

In the seventeenth and early eighteenth centuries agriculture and small-scale capitalist enterprises dominated the economies of both England and the United States. Women, men, and children engaged in both forms of economic activity as family units. Among the peasants and working classes the family was the unit of production and consumption. Family life, women, and children were not cut off from the public world of work. Women pursued a wide variety of occupations both in the home and outside it. In England they were particularly numerous as agricultural workers, domestic servants, spinners (males did the more difficult weaving), and as brewers and bakers. Women were also important as millers, innkeepers, butchers, fish sellers, pawnbrokers, moneylenders, and in a variety of crafts and skilled trades.[5]

Louise Tilly and Joan Scott characterize the mode of production during this period as *the family economy*.[6] Families worked together in the household, on the land, and in the cottage industries and shops. There was a division of labor by sex and age, but no one was idle. If the family did not require the labor of all its sons and daughters, they were placed in other peoples' homes as domestic servants, laborers, or apprentices and their wages were contributed to the family budget.

Gender Roles

The family work unit was ruled over by the father. Women were viewed as naturally subordinate to men. They were believed to be physically, intellectually, and morally weaker than males. They were not, as they came to be later, idealized as pure mothers who upheld the higher principles of civilization. Instead there existed what John Demos refers to as an undercurrent of fear and suspicion of women.[7] They were associated with evil and corruption. Such beliefs were, of course, clearly manifested in the witch hunts which continued into the seventeenth century in the United States.

Despite these negative images and stereotypes of women, women were not segregated from men. Their labor was too important for female isolation to be practical. A man had to have a wife as an economic partner if he were to run his household and farm or business. Males controlled the important basis of wealth and power—the land—but they needed a wife to work it and profit from it. Therefore, the lives of men and women were not separate. They worked together and shared the same experiences. As active participants in the family economy, women had a say in the family decision-making also.

The important economic participation of women did not produce equality in gender roles in practice or in ideology. Edward Shorter's studies of peasants in Western Europe indicate that although women had considerable economic authority within the domestic economy, this did not translate into authority or personal autonomy in other areas. The sexual division of labor did not necessarily affect the sexual division of social roles.

> Doing such jobs as fattening the chickens or carding the wool did not mean that women enjoyed a status like that of the men they worked alongside. Though female contributions to the farm's prosperity were absolutely essential, the sex roles allocated them were all inferior and subordinate.[8]

The wife was supposed to serve her husband even though she had often put in a longer work day. At meals she stood behind her husband's chair and ate standing up or waited until he had finished. She was not supposed to leave the household except for necessary purposes such as marketing eggs. The husband, however, could freely decide to go to a local tavern for a drink with other men. Females were to take a passive role towards the community outside the household; men were to be the active sex. Individuals or couples who violated these gender roles could be subjected to public humiliation and ridicule by the wider community.[9]

This situation of full-time female involvement in the family economy, although associated with a high degree of female subordination, did not give rise to an ideology of femininity. Women might be weaker, but they were not delicate. A society that expects strenuous labor from its females producing food, clothing, crops, livestock, and trade goods cannot afford to view these women as frail creatures in constant need of male protection and support.

Women were also not viewed as asexual creatures and the society was not antisex. Even the Puritans accepted sex as an important human activity. Their goal was to confine it to marriage and to stamp out fornication and adultery.[10] It was considered a dereliction of duty for either a husband or a wife to refuse sexual access to the partner. Furthermore, in colonial America and preindustrial England it was common for brides to go to the altar pregnant. In many communities engagement made it fairly acceptable for the couple to have sexual relations. If the bride became pregnant before the wedding, the male was expected to marry her immediately. He was not allowed to break his promise of marriage. The families of the couple and the wider community forced him to live up to his obligations to the woman. The pregnancy was no disgrace to the couple or their families as long as the marriage did take place.

Childhood and Child Rearing

If women were not delicate, innocent creatures in need of protection from the realities of the world, neither were children. The importance of children's labor kept children from being characterized as weak dependents, just as women's labor participation prevented the development of a stereotype of feminine weakness. There was a division of labor by age, giving the less demanding, less skilled jobs to younger family members, but age segregation was minimal. Children were treated as miniature adults and fully integrated into the adult world.[11] They were not viewed as different from adults. In particular they were not believed to be innocent and malleable. Instead children were viewed as innately evil and in need of harsh discipline. Parents were expected to break the child's will and to enforce moral principles of behavior. Moreover, child rearing was not assigned exclusively or primarily to mothers. Both fathers and mothers bore the burden of correct child rearing, and the community felt it had the right and obligation to intervene if parents were not disciplining their children in an appropriate manner. Family privacy was not idealized or honored.

Child labor was necessary to the family economy, but infant and child mortality rates were high. Therefore, fertility rates were high to ensure an adequate family labor supply. Women were burdened with many pregnancies which threatened their own lives. And parents could not afford to become too attached to their infants. The chance of loss was too high for people to invest a great deal of emotion in babies. The resulting periods of grief would have been too disruptive. Furthermore, the economic demands on the parents' time left them little opportunity for extensive involvement with child care. Infants and small children were therefore often badly cared for. This in turn contributed to the high mortality rate and created a cycle of parental noninvolvement and infant death. Thus, although women were expected to bear many children in order to reproduce the labor supply, they were not expected to devote their lives to motherhood as such.[12]

Women were expected to adjust the demands of their domestic and child-care tasks to their economically productive tasks. Within the family economic unit, women could combine nursing and the care of infants and small children with their farmyard tasks, their household work, and with such cottage industry work as spinning and textiles. Women who worked outside the home, such as street vendors, solved the problem by taking their children with them. For those who could not or would not combine infant care with their other work, there were wet nurses who nursed infants for pay. The death rate, however, for infants sent to wet nurses was very high. These poor farm women often cared for the babies under the most unsanitary conditions and were tempted to take in more than they had milk for. Well-to-do women also used wet nurses to avoid the bother of infant care. The practice, in general, reflected the lack of strong maternal-infant bonds and emphasis on maternal nurturing.

The Family and the Community

The preindustrial nuclear family was not a private isolated enclave and the domestic-public dichotomy was not firmly established. The family and community were closely intertwined. The community was viewed as comprised of families, not of individuals. Heads of households participated in the public sphere. Females, children, and unmarried adults were not accorded full public rights. In colonial America, for example, the term "town fathers" meant just that. The affairs of the town were decided by the fathers, that is, the householders. According to Demos, the head of the family was also the agent of the state.

The family served many important functions which were later taken over by other institutions. In addition to being the primary unit of production and consumption, the family was the center of education for the young and the provider of such social services as care for the sick and the elderly. People who did not live in such household units were viewed with hostility and suspicion. Unattached adults were often refused permission to live in the early New England towns unless they could find a household in which to live and work.

INDUSTRIALIZATION

The preindustrial society and its system of domestic production gave way to the forces of industrialization and capitalist growth. Nancy Cott characterizes the years between 1780 and 1830 in the United States as a period of deep and far-reaching transformation:

> . . . the beginning of rapid intensive economic growth . . . ; the start of sustained urbanization; demographic transition toward modern fertility patterns; marked change toward social stratification by wealth and growing inequality in the distribution of wealth; rapid pragmatic adaptation in the law; shifts from unitary to pluralistic networks in personal association; unprecedented expansion in primary education; democratization in the political process; invention of a new language of political and social thought; and—not least—with respect to family life, the appearance of "domesticity." [13]

The Wealthy Merchant Families

Barbara Easton notes that a new "ideal of femininity" or "cult of domesticity" was developing in America as early as the eighteenth century among the wealthy merchant class in the commercial towns such as Boston, Fall River, Newport, and Providence.[14] The family domestic economy was already being replaced by the isolated, private nuclear family supported by the father as the sole breadwinner. As businesses grew, they needed more space. It became impractical to continue running the enterprise out of the home. And as the merchants became wealthier, they could afford to establish more elaborate houses in residential areas separate from the business districts. Thus for the well-to-do the home and the workplace became separated. These merchants could also afford to support their wives and required little in the way of productive labor from them. With the English upper class as their role models, they came to expect more in the way of social graces and decorative qualities in their women. Being able to maintain a well-dressed, gracious wife and daughters in a nonproductive but beautifully appointed private home became the symbol of success. (They did not, however, adopt the English upper-class disdain for male participation in business and other productive labor.) Easton found that by the end of the eighteenth century literature was being imported from England and some was being published in the United States directing women in the graces of the lady. At this point, however, the duties of motherhood were still not included in the ideal of feminine womanhood among the upper classes.

The Middle Classes

The aristocratic ideal borrowed from England did not retain a firm hold in the United States. The republican spirit engendered by the Revolutionary War led to an overt disavowal of a class-based society. Even as the United States moved toward more marked class inequality, ideologically the emerging class system was denied. Thus a somewhat different model of womanhood placing less importance on "society" and more emphasis on domesticity was adopted, particularly in the middle classes.

Industrialization gradually removed economic productivity from the homes of the middle classes in both England and the United States. Single women left the household for work outside the home, often as domestics in other peoples' homes or as schoolteachers. The change in the location of work had some positive consequences for single women. They no longer had to live as dependents and virtual servants in their parents' homes. Their work and education outside the household gave them greater independence, variety of experiences, and mobility—some undertook careers as writers, religious leaders, and educators. But it also created insecurity. Work, especially work suitable to their class standing, was sometimes difficult to obtain and was always poorly paid. But the single woman did not have to accept the isolation and decreased variety and mobility that increasingly characterized married women's lives." [15]

The Creation of the "Pedestal."   One result of the transformation of the married woman's role due to the separation of economic production from the home was an increased emphasis on the importance of household management and upkeep and on the importance of mothering and nurturing children. From her study of sermons, literature, and personal communications in the period from 1780 to 1835, Cott concludes

> More than ever before in New England history, the care of children appeared to be mother's sole work and the work of mothers alone. The expansion of nonagricultural occupations drew men and grown children away from the household, abbreviating their presence in the family and their roles in child rearing. Mothers and young children were left in the household together just when educational and religious dicta both newly emphasized the malleability of young minds.[16]

Simultaneously, the home came to be viewed as a retreat from the public worlds of men and the family became more private. According to Easton, the supervision of family life that Puritan courts had engaged in was no longer possible. The individualist philosophy that was coming to pervade the towns and cities of nineteenth century New England allowed for no such intrusions into the family, now seen as the private domain of the husband and father.[17]

The family became an enclave protected from the rest of the world. In it the man could escape the pressures of the competitive capitalist economy. His wife was to provide the emotional support necessary to revive him for the struggle. But the wife with her purity and innocence could never be a part of that public competitive world without losing her ability to maintain the haven so necessary to her husband. Women's and men's experiences thus became increasingly dissimilar. Men were integrated into the time-oriented industrial work world. Women remained in the preindustrial, task-oriented domestic world. What Collins refers to as the private household in a market economy emerged in England and the United States as industrialization proceeded.

These changes in the nature of the middle-class, married woman's work led, as Collins suggested, to the development of a new ideology of femininity. Barbara Welter and Barbara Easton both document the rise in the nineteenth century of an extensive literature extolling the virtues of the true woman. Martha Vicinus notes that the ideal of the true woman or perfect lady was most developed among upper-middle-class English and American Victorian women.[18] Among those who could afford to practice it, this new ideal served to isolate women firmly in the domestic sphere.

Welter describes the new cult of womanhood based on four virtues—piety, purity, domesticity, and submissiveness. Women were seen as the virtuous, moral sex, devotedly religious and pure. Purity required virginity of unmarried women and chastity of married women. All manner of flirtatiousness was to be abhorred in women. Young girls were to be kept innocent of the harsher aspects of life. In particular, they were to be denied all knowledge of sexuality and the facts of reproduction. As a result the onset of menstruation was often a terrifying shock to girls. Women were seen as innately asexual. They were to submit to their husbands' sexual advances only out of duty or to have a child, never out of desire. Their only concern with sex was to be for procreation for they were also believed to have a strong maternal instinct that laid the biological basis for domesticity. The female's life was to be focused almost entirely on her husband, children, and home. Motherhood had become the primary purpose of womanhood, although much of the actual work of child care could be left to nannies and governesses if the husband could afford them. All of a woman's domestic duties were to be carried out with submissiveness and self-sacrifice.

Medical Views of True Womanhood.   Middle-class woman's new role "on the pedestal" as a dependent, delicate creature isolated in the household was reflected in nineteenth-century medical opinion and practice.[19] Doctors viewed women as dominated by their uteruses and ovaries. The reproductive role defined woman's body and being, and this was believed to render women particularly weak and subject to illness. Their frailness, in turn, justified isolating women from the public worlds of social activity, work, and politics. Menstruation and pregnancy were believed to require most of the female's store of energy. Women of the wealthier classes were often advised to retire to their beds for the duration of their menstrual periods. Such advice was not, however, deemed appropriate to working-class women. Maids and other working women were given no special consideration for the supposed weaknesses of women.

On the basis of these beliefs about women, physicians advised that women should not take part in education, work, or other outside activities, because these activites might irreparably damage their reproductive organs. Instead, doctors prescribed a domestic routine of housework and child care as the only activity suitable to the female physiology. Furthermore, adolescent girls and young women should avoid an active social life and the expression of strong emotions, especially anger, because such activities might use up the female's scarce energy supplies and cause her reproductive organs to atrophy.

Many women trying to accept the isolated but often demanding role of full-time housewife as well as live up to the ideal of feminine weakness, dependency, and non-assertiveness succumbed to the disease of hysteria. Hysteria might involve uncontrollable fits, paralysis, depression, and any variety of aches and pains. Carol Smith-Rosenberg argues that hysteria constituted a legitimate alternative to role conflicts for nineteenth-century American women.[20] After being socialized into passivity and dependency, women were faced with demanding roles as wives and mothers. A housewife was expected to be a strong, self-reliant, efficient household manager. Many women found themselves inadequate to these demands. Furthermore, economic changes meant that some of these ill-prepared women had to seek outside employment to help their families through economic crises. Being diagnosed as hysterics relieved them of these role discontinuities. They no longer had to take responsibility for home, husband, or children. Instead, they could legitimately demand that the rest of the family cater to their needs. This was therefore an alternative source of power for women, since they could use their illness to dominate their husbands. Smith-Rosenberg describes hysteria as a form of passive aggression and exploitative dependency.

The condemnation of female sexual responsiveness and the idealization of the pure, asexual woman were also embodied in the medical practices of the Victorians. From the 1860s until the early twentieth century, physicians frequently performed clitoridectomies (the surgical removal of the clitoris) to prevent female orgasm during intercourse and female masturbation. Female sexual desire was believed to lead to mental and physical disease. Surgical removal of the ovaries and the uterus were also accepted treatments for a variety of emotional and physical problems in women. G. J. Barker-Benfield argues that such practices were part of the wider pattern of male dominance and reflected unconscious fears of women by men.[21] Sexual intercourse, although avidly sought by men, was viewed as debilitating for men. Females could therefore drain men of their strength and power if their sexuality remained unchecked.

Romantic Love. As Collins' model suggests, the ideology of romantic love accompanied the high degree of sexual repression that arose in the context of the private nuclear family with the economically dependent wife. Collins argues that the ideology of romantic love, sexual repression, and the ideal of femininity were ways for females to exercise some control over males from their economically powerless positions. These ideals could serve to mute the exercise of power and aggression towards women by requiring husbands and suitors to treat the supposedly delicate and asexual females with tenderness and respect. The practice of sexual repression and the belief in the women's lack of sexual interest gave women a basis for refusing the sexual demands of their husbands. And romantic love and idealized marriage bonds could be used to demand sexual fidelity and love from husbands.

Ryan found that, as Collins suggests, these ideas spread in the United States between 1820 and 1860 as women lost their roles as economic producers in the family household economy but became important for their maternal, housewife, and companionship functions in the isolated nuclear family. As women's and men's spheres pulled farther apart, the romantic love ideology helped bridge the gap between the sexes.

> The euphoric leaps to romantic love could transcend the gulf between worldly men and retiring girls. The fragile, over-specialized female, furthermore, was helpless without a man to support her and accept her emotional riches in return. Romantic love conveyed the urgency of her search for a spouse. Intense heterosexual attraction also helped to wrench a young woman away from the maternal home where she had been thoroughly protected and dearly loved. Finally, a glorified and overpowering sentiment like romantic love could disguise the inequitable relationship a bride was about to accept.[22]

Cott also maintains that the development by 1820 of a separate "woman's sphere" emphasizing the woman's domestic role, religious piety, and moral virtue served to raise middle-class women's status in some respects.

> The doctrine of woman's sphere opened to women (reserved for them) the avenues of domestic influence, religious morality, and child nurture. It articulated a social power based on their special qualities rather than on general human rights. For women who previously held no particular avenue of power of their own—no unique defense of their integrity and dignity—this represented an advance. Earlier secular and religious norms had assumed male dominance in home, family, and religious life as well as in the public world.[23]

The new ideology helped to soften male dominance within the domestic and religious contexts. But Cott notes, again in agreement with Collins' model, that this ideology also created barriers for women by emphasizing woman's distinctiveness from man. It was a separate-but-equal strategy which could not be used to achieve true equality for women. The pedestal for women was accompanied by increases in male dominance in many respects. Women lost the limited legal rights they had enjoyed under the Puritans in the United States. They were excluded from the courts and lost their property rights. They were more firmly defined as the legal dependents of men.

Easton argues that the isolation of women into the domestic sphere was not a necessary aspect of industrialization. Things might have happened differently. If industry had drawn middle-class women as well as lower-class women into the paid labor force, different roles, stereotypes, and ideals of woman's place might have developed. But there was little need to utilize middle-class women's labor outside the home. Waves of foreign immigration in the United States and displaced peasants and immigrants in England provided the necessary expansion of the labor force as industrialization proceeded. The ideal of femininity affected even the lower classes who could not really hope to achieve it. Men strove to earn enough to allow their wives to become full-time housewives and mothers. And women who worked looked forward to the time they could leave the labor force for the home. Thus the domestic ideal undermined even working-class women's commitment to the paid work role.

Slavery.   While most working-class and even lower-middle-class men and women could not live up to the domestic ideals, the ideals were not considered applicable to slave women in the United States. The slave woman regularly worked in the fields alongside the men. No consideration of female frailty or delicacy interfered with the slave owner's profitable exploitation of his slaves' labor. Nor was the slave woman viewed as an innately moral, asexual creature in need of male protection. Slave women were subject to sexual exploitation by their masters and white overseers. Although black men and women tried hard to establish and maintain strong family ties, the slave family was also exempt from the idealization of the family. Slave owners felt free to separate husbands and wives and parents and children when it suited their purposes. However, many of the abolitionists used the Victorian ideals as bases for condemning slavery because it violated the ideal of femininity and the family.

The Family Wage Economy of the Working Classes

Transformations in family structure and gender roles similar to those of the middle classes occurred among the working classes, although not at the same time or at the same pace. The family economy with its household mode of production gave way to the working class family wage economy as the productive processes moved from the home to the factory.[24]

Several forces combined to bring an end to cottage industry. First, the logic of capitalist entrepreneurship encouraged businesspersons to bring more and more of the elements of production under their direct control. Under cottage industry, the family work unit owned its own tools and controlled the productive process. They decided when and how much to work and controlled the quality of the product. This meant that if agricultural or domestic tasks needed to be done, the family would cease spinning and weaving. This left the amount of cloth they could produce unpredictable. The factory system attempted to make production more reliable and predictable. The factory took the workers out of the household. Tools were owned by the factory owner, who also controlled the work process. He told the workers how long and how fast to work. He could also continually oversee the quality of the product.

A second factor moving production from the home to the factory is associated with the technological advances of industrialization. Industrialization first occurred in the textile industry. Technological advances in the eighteenth century vastly increased the productivity of the textile workers. At first, these inventions were incorporated into the household setting. The increased productivity from about 1764 to 1775 in England increased women's employment opportunities and wages.[25] But subsequent inventions changed this. These inventions, in particular steam power, required a large investment and a great deal of space. The cottage industry household could provide neither the capital nor the space for steam power and the much larger looms that steam power made possible. To utilize these technological advances, the factory was necessary. So the family textile workers followed their work into the factory.

At first, whole families were hired and fathers could maintain their positions of family authority by directing the family labor within the factory.

Even where whole families were not hired, however, the family continued to allocate the labor of the family members in the interest of the family economy. But instead of the son or daughter working in the family household, he or she was placed in factory or domestic work in order to bring wages into the household economy.

Effects on Married Women. Tilly and Scott point out, however, that mothers found it difficult to continue combining economic productivity with domestic production and child care. The removal of the productive process from the household made it almost impossible to carry out the two types of work simultaneously. Employers would not allow women to nurse or to care for small children in the factory. Employment opportunities for married women therefore shrunk. Married women were increasingly tied to the domestic sphere while men, single women, and children were incorporated into the industrial labor force.

When economic need was severe enough, however, mothers did join the wage labor force. Tilly and Scott argue that mothers constituted a reserve labor force for their families:

> The survival of the family unit [even] took priority over an infant life. And when need was great and jobs available for them, married women worked even at the point in the family cycle when they were most needed at home.[26]

The work of married women under the family wage economy was, however, irregular. Employers preferred the more reliable men and single women who would not be absent during pregnancy or to care for sick children. Married women could usually find only the lowest paying, low security jobs. This of course increased their lack of commitment to the work role and made it easier for them to justify returning to the home when the family could afford it.

Women, whether working outside the home or not, retained important economic roles within the family as household managers. Besides the demanding tasks of household upkeep, child care, and food processing, they also had to stretch the family earnings to cover all the household expenses. As the family produced less of its own subsistence needs, greater importance was attached to shopping and bargaining. The wife typically handled the family income. A "good" husband turned all his earnings over to his wife and received back for his personal expenditures what the wife deemed allowable. A "bad" husband, however, kept what he wanted to spend on drinking and gambling and other personal expenses and gave his wife the remainder. Wives did not necessarily passively accept this, however. Payday in early factory towns was often a day of fierce disputes between spouses. Children were, of course, also expected to turn their pay over to their mothers.

Tilly and Scott point out also that fertility remained high during this period because infant and child mortality remained high in the over-crowded, unsanitary, undernourished working-class industrial households and because child labor was still pervasive. Children added more to the family income than they consumed. To increase the family's chances of survival, a large number of children was desired. Adult children also continued to support their parents. Children were parents' only hope for support if the parents survived to old age or became too infirm to work. Social services for the poor, the unemployed, and the disabled were either nonexistent, degrading, or even life threatening. The poorhouses were to be avoided if at all possible.

The Development of Childhood and Motherhood in the Working Class.   By about 1820 technological improvements rendered child labor less practical and less necessary. Factory machines had become too complex and often too physically demanding for children to operate them efficiently. Social movements to abolish child labor received more favorable attention as the practice lost importance to the factory owners. A series of laws was enacted during the nineteenth century to forbid the employment of children in industry.

Expenses associated with rearing and training an educated labor force were forced on working-class families. Laws forbidding child labor and requiring school attendance deprived poorer families of an important source of income and required them to support the now dependent children. Even among the working classes, emphasis came to be placed on the socialization and education of children. This fit the changing needs of the industrial economy: child labor was no longer necessary, but an educated workforce became more desirable as the need for unskilled labor was replaced by an increased demand for skilled workers. Children were, thus, freed from the labor force in order to better prepare themselves to enter the labor force at a later date.

The new tasks associated with the care and socialization of children fell to the lower-class mothers, just as they had devolved upon middle-class mothers. With the workplace separate from the home, fathers no longer had the opportunity to participate extensively in child care. Moreover, mothers had already been assigned to the domestic context because of the incompatibility of factory work with care of young children and the discrimination against married women by employers. Thus greater emphasis was placed on "mothering" and motherhood became an important part of the working-class married woman's role. The decrease in infant and child mortality brought about by better care, a somewhat higher standard of living, and a reduction of child labor allowed parents to invest more in each child emotionally. Women were thus allowed to invest more in the maternal role at a time when their economic roles were being taken from them.[27]

Single Women. The wage economy increased the independence of single women among the working class just as work made middle-class single women more independent. To obtain jobs they often had to live away from home as domestics or in mill towns. Their employers sometimes supervised them as closely as their families would have. But there was a gradual increase in their freedom of movement and personal autonomy. Those who lived away from home sent most of their wages home just as those living at home turned most of their earnings over to their mothers. This was similar to the labor contributions they had made under the family economy of domestic production. But their contributions were individualized with the coming of wage labor. As Tilly and Scott point out, each family member was no longer bound to a family enterprise. Instead, each person worked separately to contribute an individually earned wage to the family budget. Thus although their wages were usually too low to allow them a truly independent life, their individual wage made daughters and sons feel less dependent on their families. With the small allowances they kept for themselves, single women could indulge in fashionable clothes and entertainment. They could go dancing with young men and lead a social life with what little free time they had.

One result of this increased freedom was a lowering of the age at marriage. Since few working-class families any longer held land or important property, it was no longer necessary for young people to wait to inherit property from their parents before they could begin families of their own. They would live on their own earnings instead. Thus parents lost control over their children's marriages.

This lack of control was also manifested in the increasing probability that the parents of the bride and groom would not know each other. Migration from the country to the town and moves from town to town in search of work destroyed community ties. Sons and daughters who went away to work would meet and fall in love with strangers. Tilly and Scott note that this increase in freedom for young men and women also led to an increase in vulnerability for the females.[28] In the traditional community, if a man promised to marry a woman, the community would force him to honor the promise, especially if the woman became pregnant. In the more anonymous urban settings family and community ties were less important. There was often no one with the power to force a man into a marriage he had previously agreed to. Some men, of course, took advantage of the situation to seduce young women with promises of marriage. Others truly meant to marry their lovers, but the loss of their job or some other setback would make it financially impossible for them to support a wife and family.

The man would then often abandon the women. The lot of these unwed mothers was often one of severe hardship.

Despite their increased vulnerability most of the working girls did marry, and marriage drastically changed their lives. They could no longer indulge in chocolates and clothes. They had to devote themselves to their households and this meant hard work and self-sacrifice. Their own needs and interests were not supposed to interfere with the needs of their husbands or children.

Women's Higher Education

Women's Colleges and Vigorous Femininity.   Among the first groups to challenge openly the prevailing stereotypes, in particular the medical view of women as physically frail and prone to insanity, were educators associated with the first women's colleges. Medical opinion advised more strongly against mental activity for women than against physical activity. Males were the only people who had sufficient energy reserves to accommodate intellectual strain. Female energy was expended entirely on the reproductive organs.

Despite dire warnings from the medical profession, educational reformers established women's colleges in the post-Civil War era in the United States and later in England. Vassar, in 1865, was the first to open its doors. The college designed its curriculum to emphasize a new image of femininity—what Sheila Rothman calls "vigorous womanhood"—in direct opposition to the image of the delicate woman.[29] The students were required to participate in a strenuous physical education program. This was given a great deal of attention by both educational and medical professionals. To the surprise of many experts, it worked. Instead of succumbing to disease or insanity, these young women were the picture of health. This resulted in an important shift in medical opinion. Instead of prescribing complete rest, physicians began to order programs of exercise for ailing women. The colleges had won the battle over vigorous womanhood. But Rothman argues that they lost the war for equality.

The colleges accepted most of the other tenets of Victorian gender role stereotypes. They organized the colleges like large households in order to emphasize domesticity and the proper moral environment for the young women. Dormitories were closely supervised and a regimen of early rising and early retiring was imposed on all students. Faculty were chosen for their feminine graces and moral stature; academic qualifications were of secondary importance. The women's colleges did go on to challenge the belief in the female's intellectual inferiority, however. Students at Vassar, Wellesley, and Smith undertook rigorous academic work. But this again was associated with an acceptance of the view of women as innately more moral and virtuous than men. Peter Filene describes the prevailing attitudes and actions:

> With a decisiveness quite different from coeducational institutions, these colleges rejected the role assigned to the Victorian female. Or, rather, they rejected some of that role. Their graduates would be intellectually equipped to work in the male world as equal partners with men. Equal, but not identical. Indeed, the alumnae—as cultured and chaste as the most orthodox Victorian could ask—would be socially and morally superior to men.[30]

Thus, aspects of the strategy of the ideal of femininity were still being used to raise women's status.

Coeducation in the Midwest.   Higher education for females followed a different pattern in the midwest. Instead of establishing women's colleges, which these frontier states could not afford, females were allowed to enter the previously all-male state colleges and universities. Administrators at institutions such as the University of Michigan approached coeducation with great caution and apprehension, also fearing that it might lead to physical disease, sterility, or insanity in the women. The programs women followed were not the same as men's. They concentrated on subjects related to domestic science and child rearing. Female students gravitated toward the humanities in such numbers that male students all but abandoned them for the more "masculine" sciences.

Thus, women's higher education did not undermine the ideal of femininity, nor did it turn most of students toward feminism. The feminists were more likely to come from the ranks of the volunteer workers and clubwomen than from the "cultured intellectuals" or "bluestockings" of the women's colleges or the "educated domestics" of the coeducational institutions. Higher education did encourage and prepare a large number of women for careers, however. Although opportunities were very limited, many of these women persevered. But the choice to pursue a career usually also entailed the choice to remain single. Women could participate in the public domain or in the domestic, but not in both. In 1920, for example, 75 percent of female professionals were unmarried.[31] The cult of domesticity carried with it too many responsibilities and too much self-sacrifice to be easily combined with the demands of a career. Female education failed to emancipate women.

NEW JOB OPPORTUNITIES

In the post-Civil War era in the United States a great deal of rhetoric emphasized the increasing employment opportunities for young women, but these new opportunities were not as wide as optimistic observers led people to believe. The job market opened up some new fields to women, but they were highly sex-segregated, low-paid, low-security, dead-end jobs. Better positions were very consciously and openly reserved for men.[32]

The jobs for women that did expand greatly were those of typist and stenographer, department store clerk, and teacher. Originally the job of office clerk and stenographer was one of some responsibility which required working closely with the owner, learning the business, and eventually rising to more important positions, and while this was the case this work was considered inappropriate for women. With the invention of the typewriter and the growth of the clerical staff the job became routine and dead-end. Secretarial work was turned over to women at this time. Employers drew upon women instead of lower-class men because the work did require education. Lower-class men did not have the requisite skills of punctuation, grammar, and spelling. Middle-class men were no longer interested in what had become low-level work. This left only the pool of female high school graduates. The women took these jobs because they were the best they could get. It was clean, safe, respectable work and paid as well or better than factory or domestic work.

The same held true for department store clerical work. Salesgirls were not paid as well as the office workers, but the educational requirements were lower and lower-class girls could more easily qualify for these jobs. Again, sales work opened up for women because middle-class men would not take the positions offered by the new department stores. They offered no chance of promotion. The employers refused to hire lower-class men because they believed lower-class women were more honest with money and stock, easier to control, had better manners for dealing with customers, and could be paid even less than lower-class men.

The third area of female employment was that of teaching. The pay was so low that educated men preferred other employment. When they did take teaching posts, they resented it and used the position as a stepping stone to something better. School boards of necessity turned to women who had crowded into the new normal schools to obtain their teaching certificates. Again however the positions held no hope for advancement. Women could be elementary and secondary school teachers, but the principals, superintendents, and school board members were all male. The few men who became teachers were paid much higher salaries and were quickly promoted out of the teaching ranks into the better paying and influential administrative positions.

As capitalism or what Collins called the market economy developed, job opportunities for women increased in some areas, but males monopolized the better paying, more prestigious occupations. Furthermore, women were squeezed out of what had been female specialities, such as medicine and midwifery,as these became professionalized. As the pay and prestige of medicine increased, males entered the occupation and then organized to block females from the new educational requirements necessary to practice. Thus the new economic world was sex segregated. And as Collins' model predicts, the ideology of the pedestal and femininity were used to justify the exclusion of women from the men's world. Men's occupations and activities, even those that had previously been assigned to females, were defined as too rough for the female's delicate nature.

But employment, even in sex-segregated jobs at low wages, still had an emancipating effect on women. The single, white-collar working woman of the 1890s gave rise to the "New Woman" or "Gibson Girl" image. She violated accepted norms of femininity by working until marriage and by wearing a much simpler style of clothing more suited to a work environment. Yards of petticoats and delicate gowns were replaced by more tailored blouses and by skirts that sometimes rose above the ankles. The tightly cinched eighteen-inch waist also gave way to looser corsets to allow more freedom of movement and fewer fainting spells and damaged internal organs. While the traditional fashions for well-to-do women emphasized woman's lack of important productive roles and her status as an object of display for her husband's wealth, the new style emphasized the new woman's greater independence and her new work roles. Such styles also spread to college women and sportswomen as bicycling, tennis, and golf became popular among middle- and upper-class women.

The Home Economics Movement

As the family consumer economy emerged among the middle class, a new ideology legitimating women's new consumer roles gained currency. Susan Strasser maintains that the home economics movement in the late nineteenth century served to link the large-scale capitalist economy that produced vast quantities of consumer goods to the housewife and the private household.[33] Instead of being told to provide a shelter against the forces of the competitive capitalist economy, women were now told to apply the principles of capitalist business to the scientific management of their households. This meant planning and organizing housework, but more important for the wider economy, it meant developing the skills of the good consumer. This role as director of family consumption integrated women into the economy through the private household. It did not destroy the domestic/public dichotomy; it merely changed the nature of the dichotomy. Women were still defined primarily by their domestic role, but they were encouraged to participate in the public economy as consumers for the domestic sphere. This role would greatly expand the market for consumer goods and was extremely profitable for business. It did not, however, serve to raise the status of women relative to that of men.

The Family Consumer Economy in the Working Class

The middle classes became integrated into the family consumer economy early, but the working classes could not afford it until the early twentieth century. Tilly and Scott point out that the working-class family remained a family wage economy with each member contributing wages. But as productivity increased, as more cheap consumer goods became available, and as wages, at least for men, rose, the wage-earning unit was increasingly focused on consumption needs. And as among the middle classes, the burden of the consumer role fell primarily to the wife. This made the housewife role more distinct from the other family members' roles and set these women apart from the wage earners.

The household management and consumer tasks expanded for married women and their opportunities for wage earning declined farther. Families still required the wages of mothers in times of crisis, but it was more difficult for them to find such work. The real increases in men's wages between 1880 and 1914 and the decline in married women's work options and wages combined to keep married women out of the labor force.

> The choice for married women, when their husbands were present and working, was not between home and paid jobs with good wages, but between market work at poor wages and activity in the household in the service of preferred and better-paid workers. Many wives quite reasonably chose the home role.[34]

Although changes were in many ways forcing married women out of the labor force, another set of forces were motivating women to seek employment. The consumer economy created the desire for more and more consumer goods. Wives who did not have to worry about their families' subsistence needs could now worry about the families' life-style needs. They worked to help keep up their families' standard of living.[35] This was still not work for personal self-development or even personal consumption needs. Their work was in accord with at least one tenet of the domestic ideal—it involved self-sacrifice, not selfishness. So whether they worked entirely within the domestic sphere or held outside jobs as well, women's work was still family oriented.

THE FEMINIST MOVEMENT

1830–1860

Some women used the tenets of the ideal of femininity to avoid the isolation of the domestic sphere. In the early 1800s, church work was the one permissible outlet for the lady's time and energy outside the household. Women simply expanded the boundaries of their charitable volunteer activities. They formed women's clubs and benevolent societies all over the United States and to a lesser extent in England. They attacked social problems such as prostitution, alcohol abuse, and slavery. They justified these activities on the basis of the true woman's sense of morality, piety, and justice. Possession of such sensibilities meant that women owed it to society and civilization to exercise their talents in the public arena as well as the domestic. Participation in club work and social reform allowed women to develop important organizational and leadership skills without violating the prescribed feminine role. These skills were powerfully used in the abolitionist movement and in the growing feminist movement.

By the 1830s some women were openly challenging the "women's sphere" and demanding greater political, economic, and social rights for women. A feminist tract had been published in England in 1792—Mary Wollstonecraft's, *Vindication of the Rights of Women*—but it had a limited appeal at that time. In 1838 the first American feminist argument appeared, Sarah Grimke's *Letters on the Equality of the Sexes,* followed by Margaret Fuller's *Woman in the Nineteenth Century.* These had greater popular success. Women who had been actively involved in various social reform activities had begun to chafe at their legal and political restrictions. Their attempts to improve society were often thwarted by their lack of political rights. Male domination of the public arena was no longer acceptable to many of these middle-class activist women. As they accomplished more in the public sphere, they wanted to do more still. This led them to demand greater freedom to participate legitimately in what had been defined as the male domain, especially politics. And the reformist activities of middle-class women eventually led many of them toward feminism.

It is a paradox that the attack on the Victorian conception of woman's place in many ways grew out of the Victorian image of womanhood. By firmly dividing the public from the private, by assigning men the public political roles and yet defining men as innately immoral, Victorian ideology laid the basis for the supposedly moral, domestic, female to demand the opportunity to exercise her moral influence to improve the public arena which had been so sullied by immoral male control. Furthermore, by emphasizing the virtue of women and the immorality of men, the cult of true womanhood made women the only suitable associates of women. This helped to create a female solidarity, to strengthen ties between women, and to give women a consciousness of kind in opposition to men.

Beginning with the Seneca Falls Convention in 1848, American feminists held state and national conventions throughout the 1850s. Although their numbers were small, they worked diligently to improve the female's legal position. They exposed many of the injustices women suffered, but they did not achieve significant gains.

England. The movement proceeded at a similar pace in England. Reform activities and social experimentation were less developed in England and therefore gave less impetus to women's organizational efforts. But the first woman's suffrage group began in 1851. Action was undertaken in support of a Marriage and Divorce Bill which was finally passed in 1857. By 1860 English women were as reform-minded as their American sisters and were in particular involved in efforts to improve women's social position by obtaining the vote.[36]

Feminism and Women's Suffrage after 1860

The Civil War in America drew many more women into public volunteer work in relief agencies and as nurses and a few became spies and soldiers. William O'Neill maintains that women's war efforts enhanced their self-image and expectations and further convinced women that they deserved the vote. It also gave feminists increased confidence that important changes could be achieved: if slavery could be abolished, so could sex discrimination. After the war, feminist activities increased. Women linked their demand for suffrage to the movement for enfranchising black males. They were rejected even by liberals in this, however. They were told not to interfere with the "Negro's hour." The black man's cause had to be fought and won before attention could be turned to the white or black women's cause. A great many feminists rejected this line of reasoning and lost support from most male liberals.

Another setback in public relations came when some spokeswomen, in particular Victoria Woodhull, linked the feminist cause with "free love" and the sexual revolution. The Victorian era was no period to raise issues of freeing human sexual expression and the public and the government reacted vehemently. Although most feminists did not support free love, they were tainted by association and their demands for increased legal rights for married women, especially divorce, were suspect. The hostility to any perceived attack on Victorian sexual mores or on the Victorian idealization of the family was so great that feminists dropped most public discussion of the subjects as a matter of expediency.

In both England and the United States the repressive social climate led feminists to concentrate on political and legal issues, the vote in particular, to the exclusion of other important women's issues. This meant that they ceased to challenge the domestic roles of women and the organization of domestic life in general. The feminist movement became more conservative. Thus they left intact the domestic/public dichotomy, the cult of domesticity, and the ideal of femininity. Their strategy came to concentrate on using these ideals against male dominance: they argued for votes for women on the basis of women's greater virtue and morality.

Many suffragists were participants in more conservative "moral reform" politics as well, such as the Women's Christian Temperance Union (WCTU) and the "social purity" movement in the United States. In addition to its work for the prohibition of alcohol, the WCTU campaigned for stricter moral codes, for rational dress for women, for kindergartens in the public schools, for child labor laws, for police matrons for female prisoners, and for the peace movement before the United States entered World War I. Women's participation in the WCTU was, furthermore, often a first step toward their involvement in feminism and woman's suffrage. As part of the "social purity" movement suffragists along with other men and women campaigned against prostitution and the sexual double standard that underlay it.

While American women were involved with the WCTU and "social purity," English women crusaded against vice under the leadership of Josephine Butler. Victorian ideals of womanhood were, of course, enlisted in their fight against prostitution, venereal disease, and male vice. English women organized on a large scale for political activity in this cause. This experience led them into other reform activities including the effort to gain women's suffrage.

Feminism and the suffrage movement in the United States became more conservative and orthodox as the years passed. In England, partly because of the personalities of the leaders and partly because of the greater resistance the movement met with, feminism became increasingly militant and violent. But it still concentrated its attention on the vote.

Feminism and the Labor Movement.   The feminist movement never forged strong ties with the growing labor movement. Feminism was dominated by middle-class women who had little real appreciation of working-class women's lives. But some middle-class women as well as working-class women were influential in the founding of the Women's Trade Union League in the United States in 1903. Their aim was to improve working conditions for women. In general, however, even working-class women were not involved in the union movement, primarily because they viewed their work as temporary. Young women planned to work only until they married, and married women expected to work only until a family economic crisis had passed. In addition, their work was often seasonal and unstable. Moreover, their domestic duties as both wives and daughters interfered with their commitment to their work roles and to the union cause. Women workers were, however, often actively involved in strikes. From 1900 to 1910 women were especially active in strikes and were part of some of labor history's most violent confrontations. An important barrier to women's greater participation in the labor movement was also the discriminatory practices of the unions themselves. Women workers often received more help from well-to-do women reformers than they did from the male-dominated, if not exclusively male, unions.

In England World War I expanded employment opportunities for women and aided the fledgling union movement among women. America's involvement in the war was so brief that employment opportunities were not greatly increased for women. The union movement among women emerged even weaker after the war than it had been before it. Working women were not strong supporters of suffrage in England or the United States. They were more interested in pragmatic issues such as working conditions and job security and could not afford the leisure middle-class women had to devote to the vote and general political issues. They were also too desirous of what middle-class women had to worry about what might be lacking from such economically secure lives.

Other Issues. Feminism also never linked itself with the socialist movements among the working classes. The feminists rarely recognized the connections between class stratification and sexual stratification even though they had presented analogies between black slavery and women's oppression.

In the United States the division between working-class and middle-class women was further exacerbated by middle class prejudice against immigrants. Working-class women not only were in a different economic situation, but many of them were also foreign-born Catholics who were seen as carrying a culture threatening to the Anglo-Saxon Protestant way of life.

Xenophobic fears of immigrants provided even clearer motivation for such groups as the WCTU in the late nineteenth and early twentieth centuries. These women used the doctrine of female moral superiority to campaign against the sale of liquor. Drinking alcoholic beverages was a tradition among immigrant groups such as the Irish; the bar was an important social institution for Irishmen. But this represented something foreign and evil to Anglo-Saxons. The campaign for prohibition was therefore in many respects a campaign against immigrant cultural practices and perpetuated a view of working-class men as evil brutes who drank away their families' rent and food money and then went home to abuse their wives and children.

The tendency for most feminists to adhere to the Victorian image of womanhood as asexual also led the early feminists to reject the birth control movement. Since they saw no need to free women to have sexual experiences without the threat of pregnancy, they viewed birth control as a means to gratify male lusts. The recognition of the dangers of childbirth and the burden of large families on women was dealt with through the espousal of abstinence. Women should be free to deny sexual access to their husbands.

The birth control movement was severely repressed by governmental authorities. Abortion, which had been legal until the sixth month of pregnancy under English Common Law, was prohibited by the states after 1860. A high birthrate among the working class meant a large labor supply. And a large labor supply was clearly in the interests of the businessmen and industrialists who controlled the government. It allowed them to keep wages low and to resist worker demands because any one group of workers could be replaced from the large pool of unemployed workers eager for work. The dissemination of birth control information was illegal. Activists such as Emma Goldman who persisted in teaching working-class women about birth control were jailed.

The End of the Feminist Movement.   Eventually, after a long and hard struggle that had included massive, sometimes violent protests, the incarceration of many women, and some deaths, the battle for woman's suffrage was won. It passed in the United States in 1920 and in England in 1918 for women over 30 who were householders or wives of householders and in 1928 for all adult women. The vote did not, however, have the wide-ranging impact on women's status that the early feminists had predicted. Because so much attention had been focused on the suffrage issue for so many decades, the movement had lost sight of its original, more comprehensive, goals. The vote had become an end in itself. Furthermore, suffrage was gained in the midst of a conservative political climate. Reformist causes were not popular. Further gains by women in the political, economic, and social spheres were doomed to defeat.

Moreover, since the domestic role for women had not been openly challenged, it retained its hold on most women. Domesticity became even more attractive and popular in the postwar era. For example, the climate of opinion on sexuality had changed considerably by the 1920s. Married women were now allowed, even expected, to find sexual gratification in their marital relationships. In addition, Freudian psychoanalytic theory supported a new ideology of domesticity which declared that healthy adult women found their meaning and satisfaction through the expression of their maternal instincts. Motherhood was again presented as the only "scientifically" valid role for women. Since the vote had not led to emancipation, this new explanation of the maternal role appealed to women who found themselves barred from other avenues of self-expression. The Victorian cult of domesticity was thus replaced by the Freudian cult of domesticity. The United States and England entered the modern world with votes for women but without female equality or an active feminist movement.

SUMMARY

Capitalism and industrialization developed out of agriculture. Market relationships predominate and population densities increase. Private property and a "free labor force" characterize the economy. Class inequality is marked.

The domestic/public dichotomy remains strong and sex segregation characterizes the public labor force. Women are a reserve labor force used in the public economy during labor shortages, isolated in the domestic sphere during labor surpluses. In the domestic sphere women reproduce and socialize the future labor force and create a refuge from the alienating marketplace for the male workers. Women also increase the market for consumer goods by taking responsibility for the work involved in consumerism. The economic dependency of wives and children serves to tie the husband to his job by making those he loves suffer if he quits or is fired.

Male dominance is supported by males' unequal access to jobs, education, political office, and other important resources, but increases in the demand for female labor undermine the male monopoly over income and help equalize the females' bargaining resources in sexual and familial relationships. As women leave the isolation of the domestic sphere, they tend to develop the skills of the public world and come to recognize the disadvantages of their positions in the sexual stratification system. Feminist movements are a recurring response but they usually meet determined opposition.

In England and the United States, the transition from the pre-industrial family economy to the industrial, individualized economy brought with it changes in women's and men's domestic roles and work, family size and family function, motherhood and child rearing practices, medical and educators' views of women, the ideology of love, sexual practices, and women's political participation in movements for social change. It did not, however, fully emancipate women.

Notes

1. Heleieth Saffioti, *Women in Class Society*, trans. Michael Vale (New York: Monthly Review Press, 1978).
2. Eli Zaretsky, *Capitalism, the Family, and Personal Life* (New York: Harper), 1976.
3. John Kenneth Galbraith, *Economics and the Public Purpose* (New York: Houghton Mifflin, 1973), pp. 31–40.
4. Eleanor Burke Leacock, "Introduction," in Saffioti, p. xiii.
5. Ann Oakley, *Woman's Work* (New York: Vintage, 1974), pp. 17–19.
6. Louise A. Tilly and Joan W. Scott, *Women, Work, and Family* (New York: Holt, Rinehart, and Winston, 1978).
7. John Demos, "The American Family in Past Time," in Arlene Skolnick and Jerome Skolnick, ed., *Family in Transition* (2nd ed., Boston: Little, Brown, 1977), pp. 59–77.
8. Edward Shorter, "Women's Work: What Difference Did Capitalism Make?" *Theory and Society*, 3 (1976), 514.
9. Edward Shorter, *The Making of the Modern Family* (New York: Basic Books, 1977).
10. Mary P. Ryan, *Womanhood in America from Colonial Times to the Present* (New York: New Viewpoints, 1975).
11. Phillippe Aries, *Centuries of Childhood* (New York: Vintage, 1962).
12. Shorter, 1977.
13. Nancy F. Cott, *The Bonds of Womanhood* (New Haven: Yale U. Press, 1977), p. 3.
14. Barbara Easton, "Industrialization and Femininity: A Case Study of Nineteenth-Century New England," *Social Problems*, 23 (April, 1976), 389–401.
15. Cott, pp. 55–57.
16. Cott, p. 46.
17. Easton, p. 394.
18. Barbara Welter, "The Cult of True Womanhood: 1820–1860," in Michael Gordon, ed., *The American Family in Social–Historical Perspective*, (2nd ed.; New York: St. Martin's Press, 1978), pp. 313–333; Easton, 1976; Martha Vicinus, "Introduction: The Perfect Victorian Lady," in Martha Vicinus, ed., *Suffer and Be Still* (Bloomington: Indiana U. Press, 1973), pp. vii–xv.
19. Ann Wood, "The Fashionable Diseases: Women's Complaints and Their Treatment in Nineteenth-Century America," in Mary Hartman and Lois Banner, ed., *Clio's Consciousness Raised* (New York: Harper and Row, 1974), pp. 1–22; Carol Smith-Rosenberg, "Puberty to Menopause: The Cycle of Femininity in Nineteenth Century American," in Hartman and Banner, pp. 23–37; Regina Morantz, "The Lady and Her Physician," in Hartman and Banner, pp. 38–53; Linda Gordon, "Voluntary Motherhood: The Beginnings of Feminist Birth Control Ideas in the United States," in Hartman and Banner, pp. 54–71; Elaine Showalter and English Showalter, "Victorian Women and Menstruation," in Vicinus, pp. 38–44.
20. Carol Smith-Rosenberg, "The Hysterical Woman: Sex Roles and Sex Role Conflict in Nineteenth-Century America," *Social Research*, 39 (Winter, 1972), 652–678.
21. G. J. Barker-Benfield, *The Horrors of the Half-Known Life* (New York: Harper and Row, 1976).
22. Ryan, p. 154.
23. Cott, p. 200.
24. Tilly and Scott, 1978.
25. Oakley, p. 35.
26. Tilly and Scott, p. 133.
27. Shorter, 1977.
28. Tilly and Scott, p. 96.
29. Sheila M. Rothman, *Woman's Proper Place* (New York: Basic Books, 1978), pp. 26–42.

30. Peter Filene, *Him/Her/Self* (New York: Harcourt Brace Jovanovich, 1975), p. 26.
31. Ryan, p. 236.
32. Rothman, pp. 42–60.
33. Susan M. Strasser, "The Business of Housekeeping: The Ideology of the Household at the Turn of the Twentieth Century," *Insurgent Sociologist*, 8:2 and 3 (Fall, 1978), 147–163.
34. Tilly and Scott, pp. 198–199.
35. Tilly and Scott, pp. 202–203.
36. William O'Neill, *The Woman Movement* (Chicago: Quadrangle, 1969), pp. 15–23.

9

Advanced Industrial Society

The United States, 1920-1979

A career . . . involved a drastic modification of woman's status and challenged the basic institutions of society. If women took jobs on the same basis as men, they would no longer be able to assume sole responsibility for the home.

William H. Chafe, *The American Woman*

Since 1920 the United States has developed into an affluent, advanced industrial society with high per capita incomes, an educated, largely white-collar labor force, and a consumer-oriented economy. This does not mean, however, that all groups in the society enjoy a high standard of living. The benefits of industrialization have been unequally distributed on such bases as class, race, ethnicity, and sex. The society is still characterized by a high degree of social, economic, and political inequality. In particular, the sexual stratification system persists despite an apparent ideological commitment to equality of opportunity.

Collins' model suggests that as the market economy or capitalist society evolves into advanced affluent industrial society, the character of the labor market changes and this has important effects on the positions of women and men. In particular, the demand for white-collar and service sector employees expands tremendously. To fill these needs the economy draws more and more women out of the home, where the early market economy placed them, into public paid employment. Women are still disadvantaged relative to men, but paid employment does increase women's bargaining resources. Women can then use this improved bargaining position to demand greater equality and to resist pressures toward subordination. Thus, Collins predicts a somewhat improved status for women in the social, economic, and political world and in their intimate relations with men. He further argues that feminist movements are likely results of the increased economic participation of women and their resulting strengthened bargaining position. This chapter considers developments in the United States from 1920 through 1979 in relation to the inhibition or facilitation of the processes outlined by Collins for advanced industrial societies in general.[1]

1920–1940

With the first world war over and woman's suffrage won, women's groups continued their commitment to social reform measures. From 1920 until 1925 they were successful with several Congressional bills. The female vote was still an unknown quantity and the political parties feared it. Women's organizations fed these fears by assuring male politicians that female voters had more humane sensitivities than males and would vote as a bloc to support reform issues.

By 1925, however, it had become clear that the woman's bloc did not exist. Women presented no more unified front in politics than men did. Woman were just as divided by class interests and other social divisions as the general population. In addition, women suffered the effects of generations of exclusion from politics. Most women were accustomed to leaving politics to men. Many continued to believe that women should not vote. It was not surprising, therefore, that women did not vote in as great numbers as men did. Furthermore, those who did vote tended to vote exactly as their husbands and fathers. One historian argues that "for females to vote at all required a substantial break from their conventional role. To ask that they oppose their husbands or fathers in the process entailed a commitment which only the most dedicated could sustain." [2]

Postwar Conservatism

With their fears of a powerful female voting bloc quelled, the political parties ignored the demands of women's groups. The postwar period was a reactionary political period. A fear of radicalism spread throughout the country. Women's reform groups were suspected of Communist leanings. Some women's groups themselves turned right-wing, such as the Daughters of the American Revolution, and added to the hysteria over Bolshevism and anarchism. It was a period of disheartenment for the liberal, reform-minded women who had fought so hard in the woman's movement.

The vestiges of the woman's movement itself split in particular over the issue of the Equal Rights Amendment and protective legislation. The social reformist segment of the woman's suffrage movement reorganized itself as the nonpartisan League of Women Voters to educate voters and support reform measures. They worked hard for protective legislation for women and children. They remained committed to the belief that women were the weaker sex, physically disadvantaged by motherhood, and therefore in need of protection from working conditions that would not harm male workers. Therefore, they supported maximum hours and minimum pay legislation for women even though many employers then used such laws as excuses not to hire women.

The more militant segment of the woman's movement rejected these positions. They saw the vote as only a first step toward the legal equality and emancipation of women and argued that women had to continue to fight for complete equality. The militants rejected working through the existing party system and organized a third-party movement as the National Woman's Party. They undertook a vigorous campaign in support of an Equal Rights Amendment which would grant full legal equality to women and men and strike down legislation which discriminated on the basis of sex in any way. This position never gained a large following. Most other women's groups actively opposed it. In the conservative, antireform political climate of the time, this serious division of ranks contributed substantially to the death of the woman's movement.

Sexual Emancipation

In addition to these factors, the woman's movement had also lost the younger generation. Women no longer had to fight convention to attend college, join women's clubs, or vote. The woman's movement could no longer offer the spirit of adventure it had offered to previous generations. Instead of rebelling against social convention in the political arena, young women in the twenties rebelled in the social arena as flappers. Adventure came through wearing short skirts, rolled hose, makeup, and bobbed hair. It came through smoking, reading sexual novels, and dancing to jazz. And it came through rejecting Victorian prudery concerning sexual behavior for women.

The older generation of feminists could not tolerate this version of emancipation. They clung to Victorian standards of modesty and chastity and found themselves and their political movement rejected by these gay young women caught up in private self-fulfillment and uninterested in political issues. Of course, only a minority of well-to-do or middle-class young women could even approximate the flapper image. But it was an image that caught the imagination of the country, and single working class women often spent what little extra time and money they had trying to be flappers.

William Chafe analyzes the impact of this sexual revolution and concludes that it did not undermine the sexual stratification system:

> Shifts in manners and morals did not interfere with the perpetuation of a sexual division of labor where women assumed responsibility for the home and men went out into the world to earn a livelihood. The nuances of a relationship might change, but the structure remained the same. A career, on the other hand, involved a drastic modification of woman's status and challenged the basic institutions of society. If women took jobs on the same basis as men, they would no longer be able to assume sole responsibility for the home.[3]

These social changes therefore represented a degree of sexual emancipation without women's liberation. Moreover, the double standard of sexuality and morality continued to be reflected in the fact that although males were as involved in this revolution of manners and morals as females, public opinion placed the blame for what was perceived as social upheaval solely on women.

Economic Considerations

The sexually emancipated flapper was, furthermore, an image which supported the growing capitalistic emphasis on consumption. Business was booming. Advertisers encouraged people to buy, buy, buy. Advertising purposefully exploited the new sexuality in sales pitches and product imagery. Woman's economic role as consumer was expanding as the economy expanded.

Economic progress for women was highly touted in the twenties, but it was more apparent than real. Women, especially young single women, did enter the labor force in greater numbers. The increase was, however, due to population increase. Women did not increase the percentage of their representation of the labor force. Moreover, women's job opportunities remained sex-segregated, dead-end, low-paid, temporary, and seasonal. In no way did women approach equality with men in the economic sphere. Female college students did increase in both numbers and proportion to males. Females also increased their representation in the professions. But again the increase came in female professions such as teaching, not in the more lucrative prestigious male professions. In fact, many medical and law schools, hospitals, and bar associations responded to women's entry into higher education by either setting very low quotas for females or barring their entry altogether. But despite discrimination, many educated women attempted to pursue careers. These new career women tried to reject the necessity of remaining single which the older generation of career women had accepted. To facilitate combining career and family some tried to organize day-care centers and establish egalitarian marriages with their husbands.

Unionization. Among the working class, unions focused almost exclusively on male workers and most of them actively discriminated against females. Women in the garment industry organized themselves as early as 1909, but this example of female labor militancy did not encourage the male-dominated unions to organize women in other trades or industries. Not only did unions refuse to organize women workers, they also refused to admit women when they organized themselves. The American Federation of Labor (AFL) was so disdainful of women workers that it refused even to issue separate sex-segregated charters to female workers analogous to the racially segregated charters it had given to black locals.

It is true that women were, in general, harder to organize than men. Their commitment to the feminine domestic role led them to view their work as a temporary interlude before marriage and childbearing. And women worked in the most marginal, temporary jobs which were always hardest to organize because of the high turnover. Although these were sometimes advanced as reasons for the unions' recalcitrance on the issue of women's unionization, the primary reason was the feeling among union leaders and the male rank and file that women belonged in the home and that paid employment, especially the more remunerative jobs, should be reserved for men. The refusal of the unions to take up issues related to the needs of female workers was one reason women workers turned their attention to protective legislation and governmental help.

After 1935 the Congress of Industrial Organizations (CIO) undertook more massive organizing efforts aimed specifically at the harder to unionize sectors of the labor force. They included women in these drives. Although they sought female members, they did not treat them equally. Labor contracts with separate pay scales and separate seniority lists for females were ratified. The unions helped to protect male members from competition from female workers. Female members paid the same dues but did not receive the same protection from their unions. The union movement continued to incorporate and support the traditional sexual stratification system.

The Crisis of Masculinity

Peter Filene argues that the twenties were a difficult period for males. The definition of masculinity in the modern context was unclear. Work was no longer rugged or individualistic. Bureaucratic or assembly line routine was coming to characterize many men's work lives. Filene suggests that the surge in popularity of spectator sports during the twenties reflected the crisis in masculinity. Men were searching for vicarious experiences of masculinity which they no longer experienced in their own lives. This also accounts for the hero worship of Charles Lindbergh after his solo flight across the Atlantic in 1927. Lindbergh embodied the virtues of rugged individualism at a time when few men could aspire to them.

The crisis of masculinity was also manifest in the widespread fear in the twenties that the family was disintegrating because women were supposedly abdicating their domestic role. "The stereotype of a man's home as his castle was competing in the 1920s with the modern image of the family as a partnership."[4] As Collins suggests, women were using their position in the private household to improve their position relative to their husbands by idealizing the marriage bond and extending sexual fidelity and mutual devotion to men. This undermined the traditional patriarchal authority of the husband/father, who was now expected to be friend and companion to his wife and children. Such intimacy made the image of power more difficult to manage, leaving many men fearing for their manliness.

The Depression

But if modern bureaucratic work and more egalitarian family structures threatened and confused men concerning their gender identities, long-term unemployment in the thirties was even more devastating. The breadwinner role was cut from under a great many men and those with jobs could not be sure they would be able to keep them.

The Depression beginning in 1929 reversed many of the economic and social gains women had fought so hard to obtain in previous decades. It was the death knell to the remnants of the woman's movement, the flapper, the sexual revolution, and experimentation with new forms of domestic organization. Massive unemployment put both women's issues and privatized self-fulfillment in the background.

Feminist arguments in favor of economic equality for women were based on the assumption that both men and women would be integrated into the economy. They had not considered the possibility of one-third of the male labor force being unemployed. Women's position as a reserve labor force was made especially clear during these hard times. In this period of tremendous labor surplus, women were the first fired. The federal, state and local governments passed laws forbidding the employment of married women if their husbands had jobs. Thousands of women were dismissed, including many who were without employed spouses or whose husbands soon became unemployed. The fears, anxieties, and hostilities generated by the Depression were focused in part on the woman worker. Traditional gender roles and sexual stratification were clearly reflected in the popular argument that no women should be allowed to hold a job as long as there were men who needed jobs. These arguments were even advanced against women in jobs for which few men had the necessary training or skills, such as stenographers and typists. In times of crisis the powerless are often the scapegoats; women workers served this function during the thirties.

Moreover, hostility against female workers came from women as well as men. Wives of unemployed males could be as vicious as the men in their attacks on working women. The acceptance of the sexual stratification system and its supporting ideology was widespread among both sexes. Attempts to expand women's economic opportunities and rights were halted, as were programs designed to ease the burdens of the woman worker's dual role at home and at work. Many wives did take jobs, however, especially as domestics, after their husbands' long-term unemployment made it impossible to practice the male-as-breadwinner, female-as-dependent gender roles. This role reversal was very hard for men. The support role was too firmly ingrained in their identities for them to accept easily an economically dependent position in the family. Many swallowed their pride and made the best of the inevitable. Others, however, committed suicide, and large numbers deserted their families in humiliation and joined the ranks of the wandering tramps and hoboes.

Paradoxically, this period of economic setback for females relative to male workers was also a period of expansion of women's political participation in high levels of government. Under the advise and guidance of his wife Eleanor, President Franklin Roosevelt actively incorporated women into his administration and into the administrative ranks of his New Deal programs. A woman was appointed to the cabinet, as a foreign minister, and to a federal judgeship, and numerous women served in high-level positions in the Works Projects Administration. The integration of women into high political appointments did not, however, herald significant advances in women's legal rights or overall social, economic, or political position. The female appointees were dependent on Roosevelt for their political power. They did not move to the top on the basis of their own constituencies or because of their support for women's issues. Rather, these women represented the old feminine humanitarian social reform tradition. The New Deal needed people with these kind of beliefs and interests. Thus these appointments represented an advance for social reformist politics, but not for feminism. The New Deal's lack of commitment to women's ues is evidenced in the fact that its National Labor Relations Board allowed for discrimination against women workers in hiring, promotions, and pay.

The New Sexual Repression.   The overall effect of the Depression and the decade of the thirties on gender roles and sexual stratification was retrenchment and retrogression. Women's gains had been dependent on male prosperity. When males' economic roles were threatened, women's demands were considered trivial at best and dangerous or unpatriotic at worst. By the end of the thirties the impact of the twenties could no longer be detected. Women preferred not to work. The majority voiced their preference for the full-time domestic role with husbands in full-time breadwinner roles. Skirts were longer, bobbed hair was replaced by long curls, virginity was expected of all "good girls." There were no more experiments in day-care facilities, communal kitchens, or egalitarian marriage. The woman's movement had been forgotten. The vocabulary associated with it even disappeared from the language.

The discipline of psychology and Freudian psychoanalysis in particular expanded its influence and popularity in the thirties and forties. Freud's followers elaborated on his tentative beginnings to develop a full-fledged psychology of women. These theories placed women in the domestic role and declared that any woman who was not satisfied as a housewife and mother suffered from emotional or mental illness. Psychoanalysis thereby provided a scientific basis for the "feminine mystique." According to its practitioners women should be sexually passive but not frigid. They were to experience orgasm only through the vagina, not the clitoris which is the true physiological base of sexual response in females. They were to fulfill themselves primarily through motherhood. Ryan argues that from the thirties through the fifties Freudian psychoanalysis helped bring us back almost full circle in terms of the female stereotype and gender role. "Women were directed right back to where they were a century earlier, in the captivity of the cult of motherhood." [5] The only real change from the nineteenth-century cult of domesticity was the addition of sexual attractiveness: women were directed to maintain their physical attractiveness to better satisfy their husbands' sexual needs. Thus, some of the sexual repressiveness of the earlier era was avoided, but the recognition of sexual needs was still not extended fully to women. Women were to achieve satisfaction through satisfying their husbands.

The Black Family

During the twenties most black Americans lived in stable families in the rural South. Contrary to Daniel Moynihan's thesis that slavery permanently undermined the black family, created pathological matriarchal family structures, and emasculated black males,[6] the black family was quite strong and followed the accepted pattern of male authority and dominance. Poor black women, like poor white women, were more likely to work than were their better-off counterparts. The rural tenant farming situation required the labor of all family members. This created an interdependence of the sexes which kept women from being the economic dependents of men and therefore undercut male dominance to a degree, but not in an emasculating manner.

Middle-class black women were as involved in charitable volunteer work as their white counterparts. And the postsuffrage era was as disorganizing for black clubwomen as it was for white clubwomen. The new ideal of femininity and domesticity was accepted by blacks as well as whites.

The Depression hit black people harder than whites. Like the female labor force, black workers constituted a reserve labor force and they were among the first to lose their jobs when the crash came in 1929. Furthermore, they were less likely to receive charitable or governmental aid than were unemployed whites. One response to the collapse of the economy was massive migration of black people from the rural south to urban areas in the northeast, midwest, and west.

Urbanization and massive unemployment and poverty had a disrupting effect on the black family. One-parent households grew in number, throwing primary responsibility for the support of the family on the poor black women. The situation hardly created a matriarchy, but it did cause a lessening of male influence within many poor urban black households. Women came to depend more on one another, on their mothers and sisters in particular, for support networks. Men were often viewed with suspicion or as potential drains on an already precarious household budget. Welfare policies when they were instituted, denied aid to women and children with a male living in the household and exacerbated this situation. An unemployed father often felt compelled to desert his family so they would be eligible for welfare. Black women, however, faced even greater discrimination in the economic sphere than black men. They faced the barriers of both sex and race discrimination. This required them to develop strong self-reliant personalities to withstand the powerful forces against them.

1940–1960

World War II

World War II brought the Depression to an end, re-created strong masculine roles for men in the military, and vastly increased employment opportunities for black and white men and women. The reserve labor force was fully called upon. The ideology of woman's place being in the home was temporarily replaced by patriotic appeals to women to enter the labor force and take "man-sized jobs" in support of freedom, democracy, and the American way. Domestic considerations were not to be allowed to prevent women from heeding their country's call. And the domestic role did not keep them home in the face of high labor demand. Women enthusiastically entered all occupational arenas.

Women entered the labor force as never before, young single women were no longer the only female workers. This group was not large enough to meet the needs of the wartime economy. Business and industry, long accustomed to discriminating against married women, resisted hiring married or older women during the first few months of the crisis. But the attack on Pearl Harbor deepened the crisis and more fully involved the United States in the war, taking more men out of the civilian labor force and increasing the level of economic production and the size of the necessary labor force. In the face of these pressures business and government turned to this last remaining reserve labor force. Women who were already working left the low paying "feminine" occupational sector for "masculine" jobs in heavy industry. And women who had never worked before entered the labor force by the thousands. With their entry into male jobs women's pay almost doubled and the unionization of women proceeded quickly. "Rosie the riveter" became a national heroine.

Women also entered the armed forces in noncombatant roles in large numbers. The idea of the female soldier met with ridicule at first, but these women served their country so admirably that the women's auxiliaries became acceptable though not prestigious. It still compromised a woman's reputation to serve in the military, especially if she was not an officer. (Nurses comprised the bulk of the officer ranks.) It was too independent a role, too masculine, too far from the domestic context to be entirely acceptable for women even during a national crisis. And the female soldier was not treated equally with male soldiers. Entry requirements were higher, pay was lower, promotions were more difficult to obtain, training programs were more limited, and benefits were fewer. Furthermore, women soldiers' duties were usually limited to the traditional feminine spheres of office and clerical work, nursing, and menial labor.

Attitudes toward the Woman Worker. Public attitudes appeared to change during the war years. Opinion polls found a widespread acceptance of the woman worker, whereas the majority of the population had rejected her during the thirties. But this tremendous change in the experiences of women, which came with their full-time participation in paid labor and the widespread public acceptance of work for middle-class as well as working-class women, was not associated with any real shift in gender role ideology. The cult of domesticity and the idealization of the family continued to be primary American values. Women could work to serve their country but not to serve individual needs and not because they had any right to a job.

These feelings were manifested in the unwillingness of business and government to provide adequate child care facilities for working mothers. The women's labor was needed, but mothers had to find individual solutions to the problem of care for small children. Most depended on friends and relatives. Some children received grossly inadequate care, chained to mobile homes or locked in cars in factory parking lots. Despite the desperate need for child care services, the idea met strong opposition. Day care violated American ideals of family life even if reality did not match those ideals. If children should be raised in the home, alternative institutions implied an acceptance of real change in woman's role. Thus the federal government undertook only a limited program of day-care centers which never served more than one-tenth of the children who needed them and quickly abandoned the program at the war's end.

The Postwar Years

This continued acceptance of traditional gender roles was also revealed in the emphasis on the male breadwinner role when the war ended. Demobilization brought thousands of soldiers back into civilian life in search of civilian jobs. It also meant the widespread closing of munitions plants and other war-related industries. Rosie the riveter lost her job.

Women who had so quickly moved into man-sized jobs found out what it meant to be a member of a reserve labor force again. Although many of these wartime women workers wanted to keep their jobs, they were quickly removed from them. Female unemployment rose dramatically with demobilization. But it did not remain high. The economy was rapidly transformed from a wartime to a peacetime economy and the production of consumer goods, long delayed by the war, boomed. Women were brought back into the labor force in large numbers, but this did not indicate the coming of equality for the female worker. The massive firings eliminated women from the masculine jobs, and women's work after the war was almost entirely within the feminine sector. A dual labor market reemerged in which males were recruited into the higher-paying, more secure, and more prestigious jobs. Women were left with the positions males rejected.

Despite these increases in the labor force participation of women, there was a clear decline in the overall economic status of women relative to men in the forties and fifties.[7] Except for the feminine occupational sectors such as clerical, sales, and service work female participation declined relative to men's. The absolute numbers of women in the professional and technical fields increased, but these sectors expanded dramatically and men gained much more than women. Furthermore, female professionals were concentrated in the feminine professions of teaching, nursing, and social work which are not comparable in pay or prestige, to the male-dominated professions. Females also did not increase their incomes relative to men. In all occupational spheres females continued to earn a fraction of what comparably educated and employed men earned. Moreover, females declined in educational achievement relative to men. They moved from overall educational attainments higher than men's in 1940 to slightly less than men's in the early sixties. Furthermore, higher education was now often pursued by young women in order to enable them to find better husbands and in order to make them better wives and mothers. Career goals were often absent or secondary as motivations for college. This is reflected in the higher dropout rate for college women as compared with college men.

Furthermore, the justification and motivation for female labor force participation during these years supported traditional gender roles. Women still could not legitimately work for individualistic reasons. They worked for their families. Inflation was a major problem in the postwar years. Middle and working class families could not support themselves under the standards of the increased emphasis on consumerism without a second income. World War II had set the precedent for married women's employment without any feminist justification. The postwar period merely changed the rationale from patriotic to domestic needs. This justification for women's work also allowed for high levels of female economic participation without ideological change or feminist consciousness. The theory that women worked only for "pin money" or luxuries was widely accepted. This denied the reality that many women worked to support themselves, to support families, or because their husbands' incomes were too low to provide for basic necessities. The "pin money" theory obscured the breadwinner role forced upon a significant number of American women.

The New Domesticity.   The cult of domesticity was carried to extremes again in the fifties as it had been during the Victorian era. The postwar baby boom is reflective of this. Couples had more children, more closely spaced than had occurred for over a century. Child rearing theories such as found in Dr. Benjamin Spock's best selling manual [8] directed the mother to devote almost full attention to the care and socialization of her children. This socialization included clear-cut gender role divisions. Little girls were to be directed toward femininity and little boys toward masculinity from the earliest age. Parents were advised to present the appropriate masculine and feminine role models to their children in their own behavior.

In addition to motherhood, the new cult of domesticity also directed women to devote themselves to furthering their husbands' careers. They were to provide the important backup services such as entertaining business associates and joining the right clubs to maintain the right image and the right contacts for his business interests. Women were still provided few legitimate outlets for the development of their interests. They were to live vicariously through the achievements first of their husbands and later of their children, especially their sons.

This revised version of the cult of domesticity had the further effect of placing women in competition with each other in the marriage market. Winning and keeping a mate was a pre-eminent concern for women in the forties and fifties. These years saw the spread of a new stage of human development, devoted to perfecting the arts of heterosexual attraction and couple formation—the teenager. The teenage girl, in particular, was expected to devote herself to the pursuit of heterosexual popularity without giving in to the male's sexual advances. Movie stars were the important role models and the female stars clearly portrayed this new ideal of femininity. These stereotypes and gender roles took firm hold on the youth of the fifties and early sixties.

The Masculine Role.   Filene argues that the postwar cult of domesticity had a double edge.[9] It affected men and masculinity as well as women and femininity. Men were also saddled with the responsibility for family "togetherness." The authoritarian male family role was outdated, especially among the middle class. Father was to be a part of the family team. This coincided with the increased emphasis on teamwork in the bureaucratic work setting. The successful worker was the one who could get along with others. Dale Carnegie's courses on "how to win friends and influence people" were symptomatic of the age. Definitions of masculinity were vague. The middle-class man could not be sure what was expected of him as a man. Strong male roles had been undercut by the cult of domesticity and the cult of teamwork.

Most men tried to judge themselves in terms of economic success. Masculinity came to be measured by the size of the paycheck. But the combined forces of inflation and consumerism meant one could never earn "enough." In addition, the more time they devoted to economic goals, the less time they had for togetherness with the family. Either way their wives were unhappy. Males were in a no-win situation.

1960–1979

Radicalism and the Feminist Revival

By the mid-1960s the apolitical era of the feminine mystique and the cult of domesticity had given rise to a period of rebellion by the nation's youth.[10] The new generation was rejecting the values their parents had striven so hard for: values related to achievement, material success, political conservatism, acceptance of authority, and eventually ideals of family life and woman's place.

The new radicalism began with the sit-in movement conducted by black college students against racial segregation in the south. Many white college students went south to join in this movement and discovered that American democracy as described in their high school civics texts did not exist. After returning to their northern and western campuses, they cast a critical eye on other aspects of their society. In addition to civil rights and racism, they found the issue of the Vietnam War and the imperialistic involvements of what they had previously believed to be a humanitarian and generous United States government. Thousands of middle-class college students, male and female, protested against the society that had given them so much. They were not the underprivileged. They came from the best homes and best schools and had the most promising futures. Yet they were attacking these same homes, schools, and futures and demanding a more just, more egalitarian society which benefited everyone, not just themselves.

Women in the New Left.   The issue of gender roles and sexual stratification was not a part of the early years of the New Left and the youth movement. Females were very active in the movement. Many were beaten and many were arrested, but few found themselves in leadership roles. Their socialization to be submissive and compliant, to defer to male authority, and to work in background roles kept them from competing for the limelight with their self-confident, assertive male counterparts who disdained females in leadership positions. While these young people rejected so much of what their parents' generation held dear, they were following their examples quite clearly in the area of sexual stratification. Males were the leaders who dominated the movement, females made the coffee, typed the pamphlets, and ran the mimeograph machines. Female roles were clearly secondary and subservient.

By 1964, however, movement women were comparing their positions, both in society and in the movement, with the position of blacks in white society. The critical eye was turned on gender roles and the females did not like what they saw. The males, however, refused to acknowledge the legitimacy of their analyses of sexism. Women found little sympathetic support among the New Left males who embraced sexual emancipation for women but rejected liberation for women in other areas. The sexual revolution was a boon for males, giving them sexual access to females without commitment or responsibility. Women's liberation, however, threatened the radical male's privileged position in the sexual hierarchy and the radicals opposed it as vehemently as their more conservative brothers. When the women of the Student Nonviolent Coordinating Committee (SNCC) argued in 1964 for female equality within this activist civil rights organization, their leader Stokely Carmichael replied that the position of women in SNCC was "prone." Women of the Students for a Democratic Society (SDS) met similar hostilities in 1965 when they attempted to present feminist issues and demands at the national conference. By 1967 women were withdrawing from many of the male-dominated radical organizations to organize separate women's liberation groups. In 1968 they held their first national gatherings. Their experiences in the youth movement had led them to disavow formal structure and leadership. Instead they worked through local small groups without any permanent leaders. They had also come to distrust traditional political activity and eschewed working through the system. Therefore, they turned to political education and service projects aimed at building feminist consciousness and self-help networks.

Feminist Tactics.   One of the tactics supported by these radical women were the rap groups with their consciousness-raising sessions. Groups of women would come together to discuss their personal experiences with sexism and discrimination. These sessions were effective in building a feminist consciousness, resocializing women to see themselves and the world differently, and in changing attitudes. But as effective as they were at the psychological level, they were ineffective beyond that. They provided no structure for action. Therefore, many came to an end or degenerated into bitch sessions. By 1971 they were obsolete. Media attention to the movement and publications by feminist writers had turned women's liberation into a household word. Women discussed the issues with each other spontaneously without needing any groups to organize them. Feminism had become a powerful force in the United States again.

Another important tactic used by the young feminists was the exclusion of males from their groups. In the early stages sympathetic males were allowed to participate in the feminist groups, but it soon became apparent that males always dominated the discussions. Gender role socialization was sufficiently effective that the women deferred to males even in these settings. Males were accustomed to filling leadership roles and asserting themselves while females were not. To solve this problem, the feminists followed the example of black liberation groups which excluded whites: they excluded males. They found that the women could be more open with each other and participate more fully when males were not present.

They also refused to be interviewed by any male reporters and most female reporters as well. The policy of excluding reporters grew out of the consistently negative experiences these groups had with the media. Women's liberation was treated with ridicule by radical, liberal, and conservative media. Their attempts to discuss the relevant issues were not reported. Instead supposed incidents such as bra burnings (which never occurred) dominated media coverage. Female reporters were often as unsympathetic and lacking in understanding of the movement as the males. The women therefore refused interviews. This in turn intrigued the reporters. Social movement participants were supposed to seek media attention, not reject it. This led the journalists to begin investigating the movement and studying its issues more thoroughly. One result was better media coverage. Another was the conversion of many female reporters to feminism. Some of them filed suits against their own employers after filing their stories on the movement.

In the fall of 1969 an incredible media blitz occurred. The movement was given extensive coverage by all the major news magazines and networks. This served to introduce the issues to large numbers of men and women who had not previously taken the movement seriously.

The radical groups also utilized the guerrilla theater techniques of the antiwar movement. They often staged bizarre events to dramatize their points. For example, in 1968 and 1969 demonstrations at the Miss America Pageant included throwing (but not burning) bras, girdles, and false eyelashes into trash cans in order to illustrate their rejection of the feminine role of sex object for males and the cult of beauty. They also crowned a sheep Miss America in their alternative pageant.

Radical women's groups have also been important in organizing the women's health movement, aimed at giving women more control over their bodies and helping them to resist authoritarian and sexist practices by physicians. This has involved efforts to teach women about their bodies, reproduction, and contraception.[11] And it has involved teaching women how to examine and care for themselves without the intervention of the medical profession. They have supported the establishment of local abortion clinics, family planning services, women's health collectives, and more sensitive practices in the delivery rooms of hospitals.

Through their local groups, friendship networks, consciousness-raising techniques, and service projects, the radical women of the women's liberation movement created strong grass roots support for feminist issues and ideas. Their lack of formal structure and national organization, however, kept them from effecting change in the wider political and economic arenas. For such change, the new feminist movement had to rely on the more traditional organizations founded by upper middle class career women.

Middle-Class Liberal Women and Feminism

While the young radicals were organizing into small groups such as the Redstockings and Witch, older, more conservative middle-class career women were also turning to feminism. In 1961 President Kennedy appointed the President's Commission on the Status of Women. This brought together politically active women from around the country to gather the facts about women's position in American society. The Commission created an important communications network among receptive women that provided facts documenting the extensive discrimination experienced by American women. This was an important catalyst for developing a woman's movement.

In 1963 Betty Friedan published her best seller *The Feminine Mystique*,[12] which analyzed the quiet desperation of middle-class women living out the cult of domesticity. This touched a responsive chord among many white, well-to-do women. This was followed in 1964 by a further impetus to movement organization. Congress amended Title VII of the 1964 Civil Rights Act to include sex along with race, religion, and national origins in its prohibitions against discrimination in employment. The amendment was presented as a joke by conservative Southern representatives who hoped to ridicule the bill and thereby defeat it. The bill passed, however with "sex" in its text and feminist Congresswomen and other feminists took it seriously. However, the Equal Employment Opportunities Commission (EEOC) which was to enforce the bill refused to pursue cases related to sex discrimination. Betty Friedan and a number of women employed by the federal government were sufficiently incensed that they founded the National Organization for Women (NOW) in 1966 to serve as a pressure group on the EEOC for consideration of women's rights.

Like the old woman's suffrage association, NOW concentrated on political and legal issues. It emphasized the importance of career opportunities for women to free them from the stultifying effects of the housewife role. As Zaretsky argues,[13] within the context of advanced industrial society women come to demand that the pursuit of individualism be extended to them as well as to men. Women were finally demanding the right to work for individualistic instead of familistic reasons. According to Chafe, a historian of the feminist movement, "Ultimately . . . the feminists traced the 'woman's problem' to the fact that females were denied the same opportunity as men to develop an identity of their own." [14]

In pursuing women's right to individual self-development through a career, NOW focused discontent on the EEOC's and the Justice Department's refusal to pursue sex-discrimination cases. They eventually persuaded President Johnson to amend Executive Order 11246 to prohibit sex discrimination in employment by holders of federal contracts. This involved them in battle with the Office of Federal Contract Compliance (OFCC) to get this order enforced. In 1968 two lawyers broke with NOW and established Human Rights for Women as a tax-exempt corporation to research and defend sex-discrimination cases.

NOW demonstrated the potential power of the new woman's movement by calling for a national strike on August 26, 1970, in commemoration of the nineteenth amendment giving women the vote. There were fears that embarrassingly small numbers would participate, but the opposite occurred. The strike was supported by feminist groups of all persuasions all over the country. Thousands of women in cities across the nation came out in support of equal job opportunities for women, abortion on demand, and twenty-four-hour child-care centers. The strike also served to expand NOW's membership. Housewives and middle- and lower-class women outside the professions joined in large numbers. So did an increased number of radical women, resulting in a great deal of overlapping memberships among different feminist groups which greatly facilitated cooperation and coordination of activities.

The Equal Rights Amendment.   NOW also supported the Equal Rights Amendment which had been brought before Congress in 1923 by the National Women's Party, which was still actively lobbying for its passage. The unions opposed the ERA and NOW lost its offices and clerical staff which had been provided by the United Auto Workers (UAW). The UAW and later the AFL-CIO reversed themselves on this issue after Title VII destroyed the basis of the "protective legislation" which had been hindering women's economic participation for many years. The unions no longer had to fear that the ERA would hurt women's special privileges.

The ERA was finally voted out of Congress in 1972 after a long, hard lobbying effort in the Senate. The proposed constitutional amendment reads, "Equality of rights under the law shall not be denied or abridged by the United States or by any State on account of sex." No real opposition existed at first, except for a weak organization of right-wing groups such as the John Birch Society and the National Council of Catholic Women. The ERA was ratified quickly by twenty-eight states. But the tide was halted by 1973 with the organization of a well-financed "Stop ERA" campaign led by Phyllis Schlafly, backed by right-wing organizations and conservative business interests. As of 1979 thirty-five of the necessary thirty-eight states had ratified ERA and some of those have tried to rescind their passage. The original seven-year deadline for ratification set by Congress would have run out in March of 1979, but against strong opposition, Congress voted to extend the deadline. Passage is still problematical. The remaining states are all conservative southern and western states which are resisting pressures such as the boycott of their cities as convention centers.

Other Issues.   NOW's support for abortion on demand lost it the support of its more conservative members, who founded the Women's Equity Action League (WEAL) in 1968 to pursue issues related to legal and economic rights, especially in the areas of education and employment. WEAL itself, however, gradually radicalized and has supported lawsuits on a variety of women's issues, especially those related to higher education. For example, they used the Executive Order for federal contract holders to file class action suits against hundreds of American colleges and universities for discrimination in admissions, granting of financial aid, hiring, and promotions. At first, the Department of Labor moved very slowly on enforcing this executive order, hoping the support for it would die out. But the issue found ready support among female students and faculty across the country, who kept the issue alive. The departments of Labor and of Health, Education and Welfare were forced to act. This resulted in a large number of legal cases and in the requirement that institutions of higher education file Affirmative Action Plans indicating how they plan to remedy the effects of past discrimination against females.

NOW also supported federally financed child-care centers and child-care legislation was passed in 1971. President Nixon vetoed it with a call for support for the traditional family structure and the cult of domesticity. NOW has also researched, documented, and attacked gender role stereotyping in children's books and textbooks and in elementary and secondary education. NOW has attempted to persuade television advertisers and programmers to rid the medium of sexist images and gender role stereotypes. The campaigns have been effective in some cases, but have failed in many others. NOW and WEAL have pushed successfully for reform in credit and banking practices which discriminate against women. They have met with limited success in equalizing women's opportunities to participate in sports. They have also supported divorce reform which in many cases benefits men by removing the gender role assumptions that mothers should automatically receive custody of the children and the father should provide alimony and child support.

By 1970 feminist groups were mushrooming. The National Women's Political Caucus was formed in 1971 to increase the number of women in elective and appointive public office. *Ms.*, a profit-making slick magazine devoted to feminist issues, was founded in 1972 and met with immediate financial success. *Ms.* also created a nonprofit tax-exempt wing, the Women's Action Alliance, to serve as an information clearing house on women's issues and organizations. Professional women, academic women, black women, and labor union women have also organized feminist groups.

Feminist church groups have been founded and one of the important issues of the seventies has been the demand for the ordination of females in the clergy. The Catholic Church hierachy has firmly refused, but the Episcopal Church admitted females into the clergy and has subsequently suffered substantial defections from antifeminists in the Church.

Black Women and Feminism

The response of black women to feminism in the sixties was largely negative.[15] They perceived the problems of racism as being a greater burden than the problems of sexism. Much of the analysis of sexism put forth by middle-class white women did not sound negative at all. Being isolated in the home, economically dependent on a man, and unable to work sounded like progress to poor women who could not afford to stay home, who could not rely on a male for support, and who worked in low-paid menial jobs. Diane Lewis argues that at this time the gap between black women and white women was larger than the gap between black women and black men.[16]

Furthermore, the influential black liberation movement in the sixties emphasized the need to reconstruct the damaged black male psyche and supported values associated with male dominance and patriarchy. Black men have often been particularly hostile to women's liberation.[17] Increased interest in cultural practices from Africa and in the Muslim religion also contributed to the movement's call for women to step back and support their men. Black women accepted this because they perceived their interests as being closer to black men's than to white women's. However, the successes of the black liberation movement changed this. The white male power structure adopted policies that benefited black males more than black females. Consequently, the gap between black males and black females widened while the gap between black females and white females narrowed. This is true in earnings, education, job opportunities, and political participation.[18]

As the feminist ideology gained more adherents in the white community and as it received more public attention, black women were provided with an additional explanation—additional to racism—for their continued difficulties in the public sphere. By 1972 opinion poll data indicated that black women had become more responsive than white women to women's issues and feminist ideas.[19] By 1973 black women were organizing and joining black feminist organizations such as Black Women Organized for Action and the National Black Feminist Organization. Moreover, this interest in women's liberation has cut across class lines. Whereas feminist ideas have had appeal primarily among middle-class white women, both middle-class and working-class black women have responded favorably. Lower-class black women have also been active in the Welfare Mothers Movement, demanding more humane treatment from welfare agencies, more child care facilities, and better job opportunities to help them get off welfare.[20]

The Social Context of the Sixties and Seventies

The social circumstances in the United States in the mid-1960s facilitated the rise and spread of both the liberal and radical wings of the women's liberation movement. As Chafe notes, feminism had historically found its most fertile soil in periods of generalized social reform.[21] And this was an era of concern for social problems and for disadvantaged groups. Secondly, real change that had occurred in the lives of many women made them responsive to feminist ideology. The increased participation of women in the economic sphere had brought them out of the home and freed many from their isolation in the domestic sphere. The domestic/public dichotomy had not been destroyed: private life in the domestic context remains firmly separated from the public sphere, but many women now participate in both spheres. Paid employment in particular provides them with new experiences similar to those of men. The differences have lessened between the lives of men and women. Women have obtained the opportunity to develop the skills of the public sphere, such as leadership, public speaking, and organizational expertise. The work situation also puts many women in day-to-day contact with other women. With a feminist ideology available, they are encouraged to share their experiences with sexism and discrimination. This has facilitated the development of female solidarity which can be the basis for women making greater demands on the male-dominated institutions. If women had remained as firmly tied to the domestic role as many feminists described them, women would not have responded to the feminist call. The most isolated, most subordinated, most oppressed women are the least likely to join a social movement and press for changes in their position. One effect of extreme oppression is to destroy any feeling of personal efficacy in working for change. The increased freedom of women to work, to pursue an education, to move freely through much of the social world, and to meet and organize with other women provide an important, if not essential, base for the women's liberation movement to develop and grow.

The Backlash

This discussion of the growth and spread of feminism in the late sixties and seventies should not be interpreted to mean that women have achieved equality. Despite these massive efforts in attitude change, cultural change, and change in the political, legal, and economic structures of our society, women are still in an inferior position relative to men. And the situation may well deteriorate rather than improve. Historically the progress of disadvantaged groups has been most active in periods of economic expansion and has been halted or reversed in periods of economic decline. The periods of recession, high unemployment, and inflation in the middle and late seventies have fed the conservative backlash against the women's movement.

Gains in the area of abortion rights have met with serious challenges. The Supreme Court struck down anti-abortion laws in 1973. Since then, the Right to Life movement has worked to make state governments pass restrictive legislation and to make Congress and the states refuse Medicaid payments for poor women who receive abortions. The Right to Life movement has a large and powerful following. It has mounted massive campaigns against the reelection of Senators and Congresspersons who support women's right to abortions. Abortion clinics have been driven out of many communities through legal technicalities and some have been bombed or burned. Physicians have been threatened with expensive criminal proceedings, such as the case of Dr. Edelin in Massachusetts who was arrested and tried for criminal manslaughter for performing an abortion.

The backlash is also clear in the Bakke Case against "reverse discrimination." The Supreme Court ruled in 1978 in favor of a white male who was denied admission to a University of California medical school because some slots were held open for minority group members. This throws into question the legality of many of the affirmative action plans undertaken by universities and private industry to upgrade minority group representation, including that of women. But the Supreme Court ruled in 1979 in the Weber case that affirmative action quotas set by private industry to aid minority groups are legal.

The backlash can also be seen in the scientific and academic community. The growth of the field of sociobiology is an example. One of its assumptions is the biological basis of our traditional gender roles and of male dominance. This assumption is used to challenge the feasibility of any programs of change in the sexual stratification system.

The women's movement has also given rise to its opposite—the Total Woman Movement and Fascinating Womanhood. The movements began in 1971 and spread nationwide by 1975, although support or at least media attention later waned. Founders Mirabel Morgan and Helen Andelin [22] support a return to idealized femininity complete with feigning ignorance, being submissive to husbands, and achieving one's goals through the manipulation of men. The Total Woman Movement places emphasis on sexual attractiveness, while Fascinating Womanhood leans toward biblical supports of patriarchy and female subordination and emphasizes woman's moral role in society. Over 400,000 women have paid from $15 to $30 to participate in short courses designed to teach them to be more feminine and more submissive to their husbands.

These "idealized femininity" movements and continued antifeminist sentiment and activity among many women may well be the result of women's subordination in society. Women who have been reared under the limitations of what Collins called the private household in a market economy have not developed the personalities or skills necessary to participate in the "man's world." Some women overcome these limitations, but others do not. They have structured their lifes around expectations of economic support from males. Movements that undermine traditional gender roles can be threatening to these women, who want their husbands to remain morally and legally committed to supporting them and their children. Not only have many women been socialized to accept the traditional feminine role, but for many women their current economic situation provides strong vested interests in maintaining those gender roles and resisting efforts toward change.

CURRENT ISSUES AND PROBLEMS

Cultural Imagery

Although feminist activists and academicians have endeavored to expose and challenge sexist stereotypes and images in areas such as the mass media, advertising, literature, children's literature, music, and the language, little real change has occurred. [23] Movies still focus on male lives and emphasize macho values of violence and the sexual subordination of women. Television has few positive feminist characters. Traditional gender roles still prevail. Advertisers still appeal to the woman as a domestic, selling cleaning agents and floor polishes to women by using male authorities and scientists to attest to their product's superiority. There has, in fact, been some deterioration in the female's image in the mass media and advertising. The increased cultural emphasis on sexuality in the seventies has led to an emphasis on the female-as-sex-object image and this has often included sadomasochism against women in such areas as clothing ads, store window displays, and record album covers.

With the exception of a new genre of feminist literature and non-sexist children's books, traditional gender role imagery prevails. Some publishing companies have introduced textbooks which avoid sexist and racist stereotyping, but most school systems have not adopted them. Music, especially the hard rock, acid rock, and punk rock so popular among youth, has become even more sexist. It has turned from more romantic gender role imagery to outright misogyny and images of violence against women. Suggestions for ridding the language of sexism, such as the use of "Ms." instead of "Miss" and "Mrs." to avoid emphasizing the female's relationship to men, have met with limited success. Similarly, attempts to replace such male-specific words as "mankind," "he" to refer to males and females, and "chairman," "businessman," etc., with non-gender specific forms has been rejected by most people and treated with levity by many. Gender role stereotypes are still firmly engrained in American culture.

Employment

The employment sphere is still characterized by the dual labor market. Women workers continue to increase in numbers and in proportion to male workers in the labor force, but females earn only about 60 percent of what males earn. And advanced training and career commitment do not pay off for women as much as they do for men. For example, women full-time workers with four or more years of college have average earnings less than male high-school dropout.[24] Women still work primarily in the feminine sector: sales, clerical, services, nursing, and teaching. They have the lowest paid, least secure jobs, with the fewest fringe benefits. They are more likely to be found in part-time, temporary, and seasonal jobs which are traditionally the most exploitative.

Affirmative action plans and other federal, state, and local legislation have lowered some of the barriers to women's participation in the work world, but in a sluggish economy it takes more than legal equal opportunity to create equality. The gap between women's pay and men's widened between 1965 and 1980 despite feminist agitation and advances in legislation in support of women's interests. The legislation may have slowed the pace of change by convincing people that the problem of sex discrimination has been solved, or that women now have the advantage over men in the job market. Many people believe that because the laws are on the books, discrimination has ended. This is far from the truth. The enforcement machinery is still inadequate; therefore many employers can continue to discriminate with little fear of suffering any real penalties. The barriers have been lowered, but they have not been removed.[25]

Education

Women have made important advances in educational attainment. In 1977, males and females both had median educational attainments of 12.3 years.[26] Undergraduate college enrollments are now fairly equally balanced between males and females. Males still outnumbered females in overall full-time college enrollment figures in 1977, but among first-year full-time students females pulled ahead of males.[27] However, a bachelor's degree is no longer a passport to a good job with a secure future. Women have gained in this area only as the degree has become a less valuable resource. On the other hand, although their numbers and proportional representation have increased in college enrollments and degrees granted, women continue to be underrepresented in the granting of graduate and professional degrees. For example, in 1970 women received about 42 percent of the bachelors degrees, 40 percent of the masters, and only 13 percent of the doctors of philosophy degrees.[28] Moreover, women continue to be underrepresented even when proportion of degree holders is taken into account on college and university faculties and administrations.

Politics

There are more women in high political office than in the past. This has been important in pushing feminist legislation through federal and state legislatures. But women are still a tiny minority of the male-dominated political power structure in this country.

In 1977 President Jimmy Carter appointed more women to high office than any other President before him. Although most of these women supported women's issues, his appointments were far fewer than his campaign promises had suggested. Furthermore, when a woman such as the outspoken Bella Abzug criticized his policies on women's issues, he fired her. There has also been a growing support for antifeminist politicians as the backlash against feminism developed among conservative males and females. Some of women's gains may be halted if not reversed in the future.

Domestic Organization and Relations between the Sexes

Despite the fact that approximately half of American women now hold jobs, they still retain primary responsibility for the home and child care. Husbands help out with cleaning, shopping, and taking care of children, but they do not take responsibility for these domestic tasks. The egalitarian, shared role pattern characterizes only a small number of modern marriages.[29] The egalitarian marriage receives more attention than it did at any time in the past, but most couples find it very difficult to put it into practice. The weight of tradition undermines the attempts of even the most committed.

First, the wife is likely to be better trained at domestic tasks than the husband because of gender role differences in childhood and adolescent socialization into the sexual division of labor. This makes it "easier" for the wife to do the work. It is frustrating and time consuming for the husband and wife to undergo the retraining necessary to developing cooking and cleaning skills in the husband and home repair skills in the wife. So they tend to fall back into the old patterns. Second, the rest of society continues to place the responsibility for domestic tasks on the wife. She is the one who is made to feel guilty if the house is dirty or the children's faces need washing. People still will not blame the husband for poor housekeeping. Third, employers are less tolerant of family demands that interfere with a male employee's work than with female's. It is more acceptable for a woman to be absent because of a sick child than it is for a man. Yet this type of absenteeism is later used to justify not hiring or promoting the woman to a responsible position. Fourth, the wife's job is likely to pay less and be less prestigious than the husband's. Therefore, if someone's work is to be disrupted, it seems more rational that it be the wife's, which further inhibits the wife's ability to compete successfully in the labor market. It takes an excessive amount of vigilance on the part of a couple not to fall into these traps.[30] Yet if they do resort to the old patterns, the wife is inhibited in her pursuit of a career through her dual role at home and at work. This is exactly where most working mothers still find themselves. Of course, a large percentage, if not the majority of couples, do not even attempt the shared-role pattern. They continue to assume that the wife has primary responsibility for the domestic chores.

Working wives are, however, more independent than full-time housewives and they exercise more power in the marital relationship.[31] There does appear to be a greater acceptance of egalitarian relationships and less emphasis on the more overt manifestations of male dominance and patriarchy. But the situation does not approach equality.

Violence. Violence against women is one result of male dominance which does not seem to be on the wane. The problem of battered wives has received a great deal of public attention in recent years. It is difficult to determine if it is on the rise because wives have not been encouraged to report it until recently. Rape does appear to be on the increase, however, although it is also an underreported crime. This type of violence against women may represent a reaction against the increased freedom and autonomy of women by some men who feel threatened by changes in the traditional sexual hierarchy. The increased incidence of rape indicates a high level of hostility against women by at least a small percentage of the male population. And this in turn operates to decrease women's sense of autonomy. Fear of rape and physical assault can prevent women from taking a job with late hours or in an unsafe location. It can prevent them from going out alone at night. It can force them to live in more expensive neighborhoods than they can afford or would prefer. Women's groups have responded to the problem by lobbying for better rape laws, demanding more humane treatment of rape victims by police and medical authorities, and establishing rape crisis centers to give the victim emotional and psychological support and to help her prosecute the assailant.

Alternative Life-Styles. In the early seventies some people tried to alter the traditional domestic organization and relations between the sexes by experimenting with communal forms of household organization in both urban and rural settings. Despite their rejection of established practices, gender roles quickly reemerged in most of the communes. Rejections of monogamy usually gave rise to serious problems with jealousy. Responsibility for the burdens of pregnancy and child care almost always fell to the female while the male felt free to move on whenever he wished. The communal alternative is less popular today than it was a few years ago, but several communes, such as Twin Oaks in Virginia, are well established and are also continuing the struggle against gender roles and sexual stratification in adult relations and in the socialization of children.[32]

Other forms of experimentation are widespread. A large number of couples, for example, are choosing to live together either temporarily or permanently without legal marriage. This life-style is no guarantee against having a relationship based on traditional gender roles, but some hope it will help them to maintain a sense of individuality and personal autonomy which they feel legal marriage undermines.

Remaining single has also become a more acceptable and more widely practiced alternative than it was in the forties and fifties. Many people find themselves living as singles because of the high divorce rate. The increased availability of employment makes this, as Collins suggested, a more viable alternative for many women. With improved contraceptive technology and greater sexual freedom, singleness does not mean celibacy. Similarly, more couples are remaining childless voluntarily. Both of these alternatives free women from many of the burdens of the domestic roles. But they of course entail certain costs as well. The choice between a career and a family is still more likely to have to be faced by women than by men.

A few couples are attempting to give a higher priority to the woman's career by maintaining separate residences when their career development takes them to different geographical locations. Others have deemphasized careers for both husband and wife by seeking to share one job or alternating working and staying home at different points in the life cycle. However, these experimental forms of domestic organization are confined primarily to the well-educated upper middle class. Couples with fewer educational and economic resources cannot usually afford this type of innovation and may be faced with inflexible employment situations which force them into the traditional molds. The actual extent of changes in domestic organization may be more apparent than real. Media attention goes to the unusual, not the mundane. But even if only a relative few are living according to different patterns, recognition of such alternatives does help to undermine the taken-for-granted nature of traditional arrangements.

Changes in domestic organization are also evidenced in the growing divorce rate. With increased economic independence, many women no longer have to accept and try to maintain unhappy marriages. Similarly, it is easier for a husband to pursue a divorce if the wife can work to support herself. Two incomes give greater personal autonomy to both parties and contribute to the increased emphasis on individualism found in advanced industrial society. Thus, if the marriage relationship is not perceived as a satisfying one, the individuals involved feel freer to end it.

Sexuality. Women have gained more freedom in the realm of sexual behavior. The sexual double standard has not been destroyed, but emphasis on virginity and chastity has been significantly reduced. Contraception and abortion have freed women to participate in sexual relations without fear of unwanted pregnancy. And as Collins argued, the increased economic independence of women does seem to have given rise to female demands for sexual attractiveness and pleasing personalities in men. Women are on more equal bargaining terms with men in the sexual marketplace. Thus we see a greater emphasis on male cosmetics, hair styles, and clothing. We also see an increased emphasis on male sexual performance, since the male is considered responsible for sexually satisfying the female. This is reflected in the immensely popular literature on the techniques of lovemaking.

Support for the woman's control over her own sexuality is also evidenced in the recent movement against sexual harassment on the job. Women are often threatened with loss of job, pay, or promotion if they do not submit to the sexual demands of male superiors or co-workers. Feminist groups have been working to expose this type of exploitation and are giving support to women in legal suits against individuals and companies that practice this type of discrimination and sexual exploitation.

Child Rearing. There has been a move away from sexist and gender role stereotypical modes of child rearing. Dr. Spock revised his best-selling parents' manual in 1976 to rid it of sexist assumptions and to advocate more androgynous socialization for both boys and girls.[33] However, the unisex direction of child rearing is usually merely a deemphasis of traditional feminine traits and a greater acceptance of traditional masculine traits for girls as well as boys. Thus girls now wear t-shirts and pants, but boys do not wear skirts. Girls are encouraged to be aggressive and to involve themselves in sports, but boys are not encouraged to develop tender, emotional traits or to involve themselves with dolls or playing house. This is an implicit acceptance of the sexual hierarchy. Masculine traits are still viewed as superior to feminine traits: the loss of the traditional feminine interests and personality characteristics may be a loss for both sexes instead of a gain. It also appears that young girls are more accepting of feminist ideas than boys are. Young boys and teenagers are still apt to support male dominance and to subscribe to macho values, again because female traits are still devalued in our culture.

Another important change in child rearing has been an increased recognition of the father's role in child development. This may still be limited primarily to better educated, middle- and upper-class couples.

There has also been an increased acceptance of and utilization of day-care centers and nursery schools.[34] In fact, parents are often encouraged to place their children in the group-care situation for the good of the child; that is, to allow the child to develop social skills earlier. The expansion of such facilities, although they are still expensive, has freed many women from some of the more limiting aspects of the maternal role and has thereby allowed them to participate in paid employment and other outside interests and activities.

FUTURE PROSPECTS

In terms of women's and men's positions in the economic, political, and social structure and in the culture, the seventies have seen massive struggles for change. Tremendous strides have been made, but the battle is a difficult one and the results are often disappointing to feminists. The sexual stratification system and traditional gender roles are still firmly entrenched in American society. Yet the continued existence of a dedicated and active feminist social movement may mean that greater changes will be made in the future. On the other hand, severe national or international crises such as a long, deep economic depression could wipe out the gains made in the seventies just as the Great Depression of the thirties reversed many of the effects of the early feminist movement.

SUMMARY

Since 1920 the United States has developed into an advanced industrial society. Changes in the nature of the labor force have brought ever-increasing numbers of women into paid employment. Women's greater economic independence has given them an improved bargaining position in the marriage and sexual relationship markets, but it has not brought an end to the sexual stratification system or gender roles. Sexist beliefs and discrimination can still be found in employment, education, politics, domestic organization and the relations between the sexes, sexuality, and child rearing. Women's new experiences in the public sphere and decreased isolation in the domestic context have furthermore led to the rise of feminist movements dedicated to increasing women's participation in the public world and destroying sexism and male dominance.

In the 1920s feminism was no longer attractive to the nation's youth. Privatized self-fulfillment and the revolution in manners and morals occupied their attention. But even this form of sexual emancipation was brought to an end by the Depression in the thirties. The earlier gains of the women's movement were halted during the thirties and many were reversed. World War II brought large numbers of women back into the labor force to serve their country in time of crisis. This did not, however, result in a revival of feminism. The cult of domesticity firmly grounded in Freudian psychology dominated American values in the forties and fifties despite the continued increases in female employment outside the home.

A revival of feminism finally occurred in the sixties among two quite different groups. Young radical women disillusioned by their treatment in the New Left and youth movements organized small groups devoted to feminist consciousness raising and the development of self-help networks. Simultaneously, politically aware middle-class career women were organizing NOW to force the federal government to enforce new civil rights legislation against sex discrimination. During the early seventies these groups effected important changes in legislation and in people's attitudes.

The new feminism has, however, also given rise to an important opposition in the "Stop ERA" campaign, the Right to Life movement, "reverse discrimination" cases, and movements to revive traditional femininity in women. The bleak economic situation in the late seventies led to an increase in conservatism in general. This could force a halt to further feminist gains and even reverse some of the trends set in motion over the past fifteen years.

Notes

1. This section draws upon the following works: William H. Chafe, *The American Woman: Her Changing Social, Economic, and Political Role, 1920–1970* (New York:Oxford U. Press, 1972); Peter Filene, *Him/Her Self* (New York: Harcourt Brace Jovanovich, 1975); Mary Ryan, *Womanhood in America from Colonial Times to the Present* (New York: New Viewpoints, 1975); William O'Neill, *Everyone Was Brave: A History of Feminism in America* (Chicago: Quadrangle, 1971); Jo Freeman, *The Politics of Women's Liberation: A Case Study of an Emerging Social Movement and Its Relation to the Policy Process.* (New York: David McKay Co., 1975).
2. Chafe, p. 33.
3. Chafe, p. 96.
4. Filene, p. 163.
5. Ryan, p. 285.
6. Daniel Moynihan, *The Negro Family: The Case for National Action* (Washington, D.C.: U.S. Government Printing Office, U.S. Dept. of Labor, 1965).
7. Dean Knudsen, "The Declining Status of Women: Popular Myths and the Failure of Functionalist Thought," *Social Forces*, 48 (1969), 183–193.
8. Benjamin Spock, *The Common Sense Book of Baby and Child Care* (New York: Duell, Sloan and Pearce, 1945).
9. Filene, pp. 179–180.
10. The following discussion of the rise of feminism in sixties and seventies relies on Freeman, 1975.
11. See, for example, Boston Women's Health Book Collective, *Our Bodies, Our Selves* 2nd ed. (New York: Simon and Schuster, 1976); The Diagram Group, *Woman's Body: An Owner's Manual* (New York: Bantam, 1977).

12. Betty Friedan, *The Feminine Mystique* (New York: Dell, 1963).

13. Eli Zaretsky, *Capitalism, The Family and Personal Life* (New York: Harper and Row, 1976).

14. Chafe, p. 229.

15. For discussions of this phenomenon see Diane K. Lewis, "A Response to Inequality: Black Women, Racism, and Sexism," *Signs,* 3 (Winter, 1977), 339–361; Charlayne Hunter, "Many Blacks Wary of Women's Liberation Movement in U.S.," *New York Times,* November 17, 1970, p. 47. For examples of the opposition to feminism see Toni Cade, ed., *The Black Woman* (New York: New American Library, 1970); Jean Cooper, "Women's Liberation and the Black Woman," *Journal of Home Economics,* 63 (Oct. 1971); 521–23; Nathan Hare and Julia Hare, "Black Women 1970," *Transaction,* 8 (Nov.–Dec. 1970), 68, 90; Mae C. King, "The Politics of Sexual Stereotypes," *Black Scholar,* 4 (March–April 1973), 12; Linda J. M. LaRue, "Black Liberation and Women's Lib," *Transaction* 8 (Nov.–Dec. 1970), 59–64; Inez Smith Reid, *"Together" Black Women* (New York: Third Press, 1972).

16. Lewis, pp. 345–346.

17. William A. Blakey, "Everybody Makes the Revolution: Some Thoughts on Racism and Sexism," *Civil Rights Digest,* 6 (Spring, 1974), 19.

18. Lewis, pp. 349–358.

19. Louis Harris and Associates, *The 1972 Virginia Slims American Women's Opinion Poll: A Survey of the Attitudes of Women on their Roles in Politics and the Economy,* pp. 2, 4.

20. Susan H. Hertz, "The Politics of the Welfare Mothers Movement: A Case Study," *Signs,* 2 (Spring, 1977), 600–611.

21. Chafe, p. 232.

22. For a statement of these women's conceptions of woman's place and their recommendations to women see their best selling books: Mirabel Morgan, *The Total Woman* (New York: Pocket Books, 1973); Helen Andelin, *Fascinating Womanhood* (New York: Bantam Books, 1975).

23. See for example Gaye Tuchman, Arlene Kaplan Daniels, and James Benet (eds.), *Hearth and Home: Images of Women in the Mass Media* (New York: Oxford U. Press, 1978); Mary Anne Ferguson, ed. *Images of Women in Literature* (Boston: Houghton Mifflin, 1973); Molly Haskell, *From Reverence to Rape: The Treatment of Women in the Movies* (Baltimore: Penguin, 1974); Joan Mellon, *Women and Their Sexuality in the New Film* (New York: Dell, 1973); Lenore Weitzman, "Sex-Role Socialization in Picture Books for Preschool Children," *American Journal of Sociology,* 77 (May, 1972), 1125–1150; Robin Lakoff, *Language and Woman's Place* (New York: Harper and Row, 1975).

24. Charlotte G. O'Kelly, "The 'Impact' of Equal Employment Legislation on Women's Earnings: Limitations of Legislative Solutions to Economic Sexism," *American Journal of Economics and Sociology, 38* (October, 1979).

25. O'Kelly, 1979.

26. "Educational Attainment in the United States: March 1977 and 1976," *Current Population Reports,* Series P-20, No. 314 (December, 1977), Washington, D.C.: U.S. Dept. of Commerce, Bureau of the Census, p. 7.

27. "School Enrollment—Social and Economic Characteristics of Students: October 1977," *Current Population Reports,* Series P-20, No. 333 (February, 1979), Washington, D.C.: U.S. Dept. of Commerce, Bureau of the Census, p. 7.

28. Betty M. Vetter and Eleanor Babco, *Professional Women and Minorities: A Manpower Resource Service* (Washington, D.C.: Scientific Manpower Commission, 1975), Table G-D-2.

29. Jessie Bernard, *The Future of Marriage* (New York: Bantam Books, 1972), pp. 142–143.

30. For a description of one couple's difficulties and solution to overcoming the traditional sexual division of labor see Susan Edmiston, "How to Write Your Own Marriage Con-

tract", in Francine Klagburn, ed., *The First Ms. Reader,* (New York: Warner Paperbacks, 1973), pp. 91–107.
31. Bernard, p. 143.
32. See the journal *Communities* for continuing up-to-date discussions of communal experimentation.
33. Dr. Benjamin Spock, *Baby and Child Care* (5th ed.; New York: Pocket Books, 1976).
34. "Nursery School and Kindergarten Enrollment of Children and Labor Force Status of Their Mothers: October 1967 to October 1976," *Current Population Reports,* Series P-20. No. 318 (February, 1978), Washington, D.C.: U.S. Dept. of Commerce, Bureau of the Census, p. 1.

10

Socialist Societies

The Soviet Union and the Israeli Kibbutz

The central thrust of Soviet policy has been to superimpose new obligations of work and citizenship on more traditional definitions of femininity and to reshape to some extent the boundaries between public and family responsibilities—in short, to facilitate women's performance of both their roles—rather than to radically redefine both male and female roles.

Gail Lapidus, *Women in Soviet Society*

Some factions within the current feminist movement argue that socialism is the only path to sexual equality.[1] This argument has it roots in the writings of early socialists such as Frederick Engels and August Bebel.[2] Socialist societies themselves have usually given ideological support to sexual equality and included it among their goals. An examination of the realities of life under socialism, however, shows that socialist countries have been far from successful in this realm.[3]

Ideological support and official rhetoric are not sufficient to achieve sexual equality or women's liberation. To overcome the legacy of sexual stratification inherited from the social structures of the past requires a high degree of commitment and a willingness to allocate important and often scarce resources to this end. Contemporary socialist societies have not been willing to undertake such commitment. The following examination of the history of the "woman question" in the Soviet Union and the Israeli kibbutz indicates the problems and pitfalls that befell these societies' attempts to institute sexual equality.

THE SOVIET UNION

Prerevolutionary Russia

In prerevolutionary Russia the majority of women and men were still rural peasants living in rigidly patriarchal family structures with gender roles typical of agrarian societies.[4] Males as well as females were exploited by the landlord class, but women suffered further exploitation on the basis of sex. Females were subordinated to the will of their fathers, and then to their husbands and mothers-in-law. They had few legal or property rights. They were not believed to be fully human, but were viewed as a subhuman category inferior to males. Furthermore, much of Asian Russia was under the domination of the Moslem religion and practiced even more extreme forms of female subordination, veiling, and seclusion. Feminist consciousness and movements for social change do not arise and flourish under such oppressive conditions.

In sixteenth- and seventeenth-century Russia, even Russian women of the urban elite were in positions inferior to that of women in other parts of Europe. They had fewer rights and were more firmly secluded. Peter the Great in the early eighteenth century, however, attempted to introduce Western ideas and practices into Russian social life. He instituted reforms that gave women more property and legal rights and supported marriage by choice instead of arranged marriages. He also introduced mixed-sex social gatherings. The reforms were aimed only at the elite few and did not reach many of them. Russia remained among the most backward of European societies.

Russia was not, however, immune to the changes taking place in the rest of Europe and the United States. By the mid-nineteenth century industrialization was underway in the cities of Russia and the serfs were freed from their legal if not their economic bondage in the countryside. As in the West, both idealized femininity and feminist movements accompanied these wider social changes toward modernization.

Radical Feminism in Nineteenth-Century Russia. Women's movements arose a few decades later than in the West, but by the 1860s they were an important phenomenon among a small group of well-to-do, educated urban women. An important and influential feminist novel, *What Is to Be Done?*, was published in 1863 by Chernyshevski. He attributed female subordination to the general backwardness of Russian society and called for revolutionary change in the social order, including woman's place. The novel also provided a model for young women of the time to adopt in their search for personal liberation and their struggle for social change.

Many young women answered this call and left their homes for the cities in search of education and employment. They entered study groups and lived in communes with like-minded men and women. Some of them contracted fictitious marriages to gain freedom from their fathers' authority and the necessary passport to live on their own. These fictitious marriages were legal but the men agreed in advance not to exercise the rights of husbands, and most of them honored their agreements. The communes were not places of sexual license, although every attempt was made by the public and the authorities to portray feminists as immoral and depraved. The women, however, rejected all aspects of the sex-object role for females. They refused feminine clothes and grooming and preferred a more mannish look, although they were not so daring as to wear trousers. The males of the communes were expected to support sexual equality and respect for women and to practice sexual self-denial. Sex was considered frivolous, a diversion from more important work.

These first steps toward feminism soon led women into broader radical movements that subordinated the woman's question to the wider problems of freeing all oppressed and exploited peoples. Unlike their Western counterparts, the men and women in these movements interacted fairly equally. Gail Lapidus suggests that the backwardness of Russian society contributed to the solidarity between male and female radicals.[5] The radicals constituted such a small, isolated minority that the men needed the female participants. Neither sex held important political or civil rights so the males were as concerned about these issues as the females. The males could also see the analogies between woman's oppressed position in Rus-

sian society and the oppressed positions of the peasantry and the proletariat (working class). Yet, as Lapidus explains, the women came from a
similar class background and were educated sufficiently to speak the same
language and share the same world view as the male radicals.

Liberal Feminist Groups.   There were numerous radical factions active
in the 1870s, but the Marxists did not appear in Russia until the mid-1880s.
Alongside the radical groups, there also developed an important liberal
feminist social movement. Both the radicals and the liberals came from
urban, educated, privileged backgrounds, but the liberal feminists concerned themselves primarily with the problems of privileged women. They
sought greater educational and professional employment opportunities
and greater political rights. They worked through philanthropy and education and did not seek revolutionary change in the political, social, and
economic structures of Russian society. They demanded only that women
be given greater opportunities, not disrupting of class privilege to any
significant extent. After the 1905 revolution (which resulted in the establishment of the Russian parliament, or Duma, with male suffrage), the
liberal feminists pressed hard for woman's suffrage. The fact that suffrage
had finally been given to males, but withheld from females, increased
women's feelings of relative deprivation. This was true for many poorer
women as well as for the urban privileged groups that comprised the
feminist organizations.

Marxist Attitudes toward Feminism.   The Marxist groups, including
the Bolsheviks, supported women's liberation in theory. Drawing upon
Engels' and August Bebel's works, they saw women's oppression as part of
the overall oppressiveness of class societies.[6] Yet at the practical level they
were suspicious of and often hostile to feminism, feminist movements, and
feminist issues. They viewed the woman question as diversionary, as a
bourgeois concern which drew energy and attention away from the more
important issue of class oppression. Therefore the Marxists undertook few
organizing activities among women. This was true even for women industrial workers, despite the Marxist emphasis on the vanguard role of the
industrial proletariat. According to Rose Glickman, "in real situations as
opposed to paper ones, the workers called to action were envisaged as
exclusively male."[7]

    This neglect of the female factory worker occurred despite the fact that
women were drawn into the industrial labor force in large numbers in the
late nineteenth and early twentieth centuries. By 1887 females constituted
38 percent of the textile workers, 27 percent of the chemical workers, and
11 percent of those working in the manufacture of lime, brick, and glass.[8]
Females constituted 15 percent of the industrial labor force as a whole in

1887, and they continued to move into industrial employment whenever occupational categories opened to them. By 1900 women were 26 percent of the industrial labor force; they were up to 32 percent by 1914.[9] World War I vastly increased female employment opportunities as millions of men were mobilized for the war effort while industry continued to expand.

Industrial work was highly sex segregated, and males received much better wages than females. But this followed traditional patterns of the agricultural sector. Women had been engaged in hard physical labor in the rural areas for centuries and generally received about 25 percent of what male workers received for similar work. Their low wages made them preferable to factory owners and helped to increase female representation in industrial labor, especially as the even cheaper child labor was made illegal or difficult to obtain. Employers also believed women workers would be more obedient, less troublesome, and less likely to drink.

The Marxist myopia concerning the women workers was not shared by the movement's few feminist members such as Aleksandra Kollontai and Inessa Armand, who encouraged organizing and educational efforts among working-class women. They pointed out the successes that liberal feminists were achieving among working women in gaining support for woman's suffrage. Kollontai and Armand were largely responsible for the Bolshevik party's development of a stand on the woman question at all. They attempted to unite feminism and socialism, but most of the other female as well as male leaders accepted this only as a tactical expedient and remained hostile to any separate concern for feminist issues.

Like the rest of the Bolsheviks, Kollontai and Armand were adamantly opposed to the liberal feminists. This was especially apparent during World War I when the Russian liberal feminists, like their counterparts in Western Europe and the United States, actively supported the war in the hopes of being rewarded with the vote after it ended. According to Lapidus, the war served to increase both women's economic and political activity. Women were involved in strikes and demonstrations and it was women workers who started the massive strike that ended in the February 1917 revolution and the Provisional Government which did finally grant women the vote. This activity, furthermore, convinced the Bolsheviks that they should establish a department for party work among women if they were to hope for this important source of support in their own bid for power.[10]

The Bolshevik Revolution

The Bolshevik faction of the Marxist groups seized power on November 7, 1917. Under the leadership of Lenin they attempted to establish in practice the visions they supported. Part of their vision included sexual equality, but they had no firm blueprint for its achievement. Instead, most of the new leadership held a vague belief that once the country had been modernized and industrialized with a socialist political structure, the woman question would be solved. This of course meant that nothing specific needed to be done for women: it was sufficient to dismantle the structures of Czarist Russia and build in their stead a socialist republic.

The Bolsheviks' formal commitment to sexual equality and opposition to the old society were expressed in early legislation related to gender roles and the family. Full political and legal rights were extended to women. Legal restrictions on women's freedom of movement, legal supports for female subordination to males, and unequal property and inheritance rights were abolished. Females were given rights to individual rather than household pay and equal pay for equal work was written into law. Abortion and birth control were legalized. De facto marriages were recognized as legal. Divorce was made easily available on the request of either partner. The distinction between legitimate and illegitimate children was abolished. In addition to this support for equal rights, the new laws also supported the protection of motherhood. Aleksandra Kollontai, as the new Minister of Social Welfare, promulgated the view that the state was responsible for the welfare of mothers and children and for state-supported child-care services.

But however important these laws were as symbols, they did little to change or improve the actual position of women in the new Soviet society. Enacting legislation was easy, but putting these laws into effect would prove to be too costly for the new regime. In the midst of the chaos and civil war that followed the Bolshevik seizure of power, matters relating to the creation of egalitarian socialism were subordinated to the political and military requirements of consolidating power. Social engineering was postponed.

The Zhenotdel. In the interests of consolidating power and building a strong constituency for the new government, some programs aimed at increasing women's participation in the new regime were undertaken. In order to mobilize women for political participation, a woman's bureau, the Zhenotdel, was established and the party's female activists were placed in charge.

The Zhenotdel met with opposition among both the highly traditional Russian people and the increasingly antifeminist Communist party membership and hierarchy. Despite the controversy the Zhenotdel achieved important successes. It mobilized women for party membership, created a communications network for dealing with women's problems and raising women's consciousness concerning sexual equality and their new rights, and spread literacy in order to facilitate propagandizing among women and women's political participation. It also gave women the opportunity to participate in a network of female delegates within the party. This allowed women to gain the necessary skills, experience, and self-confidence to compete with men in the political arena.

The Zhenotdel also worked to increase women's economic participation in order to give women the economic independence necessary for equality. To this end they encouraged the party to undertake educational and training programs to upgrade women's skills and to establish communal dining and child-care facilities to free women from their domestic burdens.

The Moslem areas of the Soviet Union provided a special target for the Zhenotdel. The members worked particularly hard to mobilize the Moslem women in order to undermine the traditional repressive social structures in these areas. Tactics included encouraging the women to exercise their new rights and to file for divorce against abusive husbands. They also encouraged the women to join in throwing off their veils as an important symbolic rejection of their past subordinate roles. The males reacted to these actions with rage. In 1927, for example, 250 women were killed in Uzbekistan for unveiling their faces.[11] To undermine male resistance, the party showed particular interest in appointing women to high posts in the Moslem areas and in incorporating these women into all areas of the political and economic structure, thereby forcing the males to take orders from and to work with women.

Consequences of Reformist Action.   The policies pursued by the Zhenotdel and the party were not entirely beneficial to women, whatever their intent. The new freedom of divorce, for example, left many women abandoned by their husbands without the necessary skills or experience to support themselves or their children. Furthermore, the high unemployment that characterized the years following the revolution meant that real economic gains for women were minimal. What the party preached for women often could not be put into practice. The impact of reform was more limited in the rural areas than in the cities. Peasants remained committed to traditional values, family structures, and gender roles. Self-assertion for women was difficult to bring about here.

The Zhenotdel itself represented a contradiction in the Communist party position on the woman question. On the one hand, strong women ran the department in the interest of women's greater integration into the new political, economic, and social structure. On the other hand, the department served to segregate these strong female leaders from the rest of the party hierarchy. It also served to perpetuate traditional gender role divisions by assigning these women to "social housekeeping" functions (social, health, and cultural issues) and women's issues. The problem of sex segregation was further exacerbated by the fact that the Zhenotdel staff was not treated equally with staff of other departments. Women were often excluded from general policy meetings and called upon to participate only when women's issues were directly involved.

The problem of the second-class status of the Zhenotdel was further increased as the Communist party widened its base among the male population. As the revolutionary vanguard was joined by new male recruits, the new recruits brought with them a much stronger commitment to traditional gender roles. This increased the party's general hostility toward feminism. Ardent feminists such as Kollontai were subject to attacks and smear campaigns. Hostility toward Kollontai focused special attention on her advocacy of sexual freedom. This was used to turn women as well as men against her and her policies. The end result was the abolition of the Zhenotdel in 1930.

Lenin had at least given ideological support to feminist issues. He recognized the limiting effects of the domestic/public dichotomy on women's full social participation and advocated the industrialization of housework to free women from its stultifying effects. Lenin was, however, unable to put these ideas into practice because of the military problems of consolidating power and because of the extremely limited resources of the early days of Communist rule. Priority was given to the development of heavy industry and capital investment in productive resources rather than to the expansion of the service sector necessary to free women from their domestic burdens.

Stalin

When Stalin came to power in the mid-1920s, the emphasis on heavy industry continued, but the earlier recognition of women's unique needs as an especially oppressed segment of the population was lost. The five-year plans, designed to promote rapid industrialization, brought women into the industrial labor force in vastly increased numbers. But this did not stem from a commitment to feminist ideals: it was expedient to draw upon the widest labor supply possible and to allow no resource to go untapped. Stalin himself held particularly negative views of women, seeing them as ignorant, backward, and having a responsibility to society to overcome these limitations. He emphasized the need for solidarity between women and men and condemned feminism as "bourgeois deviationism."

Stalin reversed the party's earlier stand on the need to free people from the repressive traditionalism of the family. Earlier policy had aimed at removing the functions of the family to the wider social order and at freeing people by making marriage and family ties dependent only on love and mutual attraction. These family policies were used as the scapegoat for the disruption and social disorganization that occurred in the aftermath of the revolution and the civil war. The declining birthrate was of particular concern to party officials who wanted population growth to strengthen the new country. Stalin reaffirmed the family as a cornerstone of the new socialist society and introduced legislation to promote its stability. Abortions were banned again in 1936. The law did not appreciably affect the number of abortions performed, but it served to drive women to unsafe illegal abortionists as in prerevolutionary Russia. Large families were also encouraged by material incentives such as state allowances. Sexual deviance was attacked as a crime and campaigns against prostitution and homosexuality were undertaken.

The Soviet Union entered a period of idealized family life and femininity and sexual repression. Housework was redefined as socially useful rather than stultifying. Women were praised for feminine graces such as exhibiting an interest in beautifying the home. Motherhood and child rearing were proclaimed woman's highest calling. However, these redefinitions of woman's role did not preclude paid employment for women. Women were to work full time in the wider economy while simultaneously devoting themselves to their homes and families, and the dual burden was not eased by any increase in the service sector. Stalin's policy was to discourage production in services and consumer goods in favor of heavy industry. The household was forced to provide for itself and suffered a standard of living much lower than that found in other industrialized societies of the period.

In 1944 Stalin issued a Family Edict aimed at further strengthening the family. Divorce was restricted. Unregistered marriages were denied legal recognition. Unmarried mothers were prohibited from filing paternity suits or support suits against the fathers of their children. The state would, however, provide an allowance for the illegitimate child's maintenance. Legitimacy and illegitimacy were written back into law and illegitimate children were marked for life by their birth certificates. The law absolved men of all responsibility toward their lovers and children and encouraged a frivolous attitude toward women. The purpose of these laws was most likely to encourage a higher birthrate among unmarried women by removing the fear of economic responsibility from men, and simultaneously shore up the family by making legitimacy important. This was a period of severe demographic imbalance between the sexes. Massive numbers of men had died in the civil war, World War II, and in Stalin's purges. Millions of women of childbearing age could not marry for lack of enough males, and Stalin did not want these women to remain childless. Women were to be childbearing machines in the service of the state.

As in the United States during the forties, in the thirties and forties in the USSR the demands of the economy drew women into the labor force in ever-increasing numbers and in a wide range of jobs. But this occurred in the absence of a feminist consciousness or an organized woman's movement and therefore could be combined with a Russian version of the "cult of domesticity" and very limited female participation in the political structure or the more powerful sectors of the economy. Women were made to suffer a double exploitation in the public and domestic sectors in the service of the state, and the appropriate "convenient social virtues" were upheld to convince women they wanted to sacrifice themselves. Cultural images of women emphasized submissive heroines who devoted themselves to motherhood and domestic work while simultaneously shouldering a job. The independent, politically active heroines of the past who refused to let family responsibilities compete with political duties largely disappeared.

An organized woman's movement no longer existed under Stalin both because of Stalin's and the party's opposition to independent feminism and because the Soviet Union was affected by the worldwide decline of feminism in the thirties and forties. No international movement existed to prod Soviet women or the Soviet government to recognize women's needs and interests.

The Contemporary USSR

After Stalin's death in 1953 the USSR underwent a change of direction. It repudiated many of his policies, including many of those directed at women and the family. There was, for example, a stepped-up recruitment of women into party membership, which is a prerequisite for political power in the Soviet Union. Increased attention was also given to lightening women's domestic burdens by improving housing and the service sector. The sacrifice of consumer needs to industrial needs had chiefly burdened women by making households responsible for their own services. The 1944 Family Code came under attack and was finally revised to make divorce and abortion more readily available. Despite impressive achievements, however, women's position in contemporary Soviet society is still subordinate to men's.

The Economic Sphere. Women's representation in the economic sphere is far higher than in the non-Communist world. Women constitute 51 percent of the civilian labor force and women are found in large numbers in occupational categories such as professional employment for (example, medical doctors and engineers), which are dominated by males in the West.[12] Women's work is facilitated by a widespread, though still inadequate, network of nurseries, day-care centers, and after-school programs for older children. Women receive generous maternity leaves, maternity benefits, and pension plans. There is also a large body of protective legislation limiting the type of work women can do and barring women from many of the more strenuous jobs. Legislation forbids discrimination against women workers and requires equal pay for equal work.

But the work world in the Soviet Union is as sex segregated as it is in the West and the sex segregation produces similar consequences. There are women's jobs and women's industries and men's jobs and men's industries. And just as in the West, the women's sector of this dual labor market is paid substantially less than the men's sector. The average female worker earns 75 percent of the average male worker's salary.[13] The Soviet emphasis on heavy industry includes the policy of better pay for workers in this area in order to attract more personnel to these occupations. These are the occupations in which men predominate and from which women are sometimes barred by protective legislation.

Even in occupations in which men and women both participate, fewer and fewer women are found as one moves up the scale of power, pay, and prestige. For example, it is a much publicized fact that women constitute 69 percent of the physicians in the Soviet Union. Yet the more prestigious positions and the administrative positions are disproportionately male. Over 90 percent of the pediatricians are female, yet the more prestigious field of surgery has only 6 percent females. The sexual stratification within medicine is further evidenced by the fact that almost all nurses are female. Moreover, current policies are aimed at reducing the overrepresentation of females among medical doctors and the percentage of females in the field is dropping. Male applicants to medical schools are being given preferential treatment over female applicants. Thus this avenue of professional advancement for women may be closing somewhat while other avenues are not opening at a comparable rate.[14]

It is also true that Soviet policies have forced women into paid employment. Wages of both males and females have been kept low enough that most families cannot live on one income. To meet their basic subsistence needs Soviet couples must rely on the wife's income. Furthermore, extra money cannot be earned through part-time work for wives. Political leaders have purposely not allowed the creation of part-time employment in order to force wives and mothers into full-time jobs. This policy is currently being questioned by many women and some members of the political leadership. If the political elite feels the economy can afford to lose part of the female labor supply, part-time work may ease some of women's dual burden in the future. As the experience of women in the United States indicates, however, it is not a path to sexual equality.

The Political Sphere.   Soviet women may have made important strides in the economic sphere compared with women in other countries, but their representation in the political sphere is as low as in the West. Women hold some lower-level political offices, but the higher one goes the fewer women one finds. Women have been virtually absent at the apex of the Soviet power structure—the Central Committee of the Communist Party and the Politburo. Only 3.3 percent of the Central Committee were female in 1976 and only one woman has ever served on the Politburo.[15] Women who are appointed to high political office are usually there for symbolic purposes. They do not achieve important political positions because they have built up political power in their own right: they are tokens. Furthermore, as with the Zhenotdel in the early years of the Soviet Union, female politicians are still primarily found in areas of "social housekeeping": they tend to participate in issues related to health, cultural affairs, public welfare, education, and marriage and family law. They do not take part in issues related to planning, the budget, or foreign policy. Females participate primarily at the local, not the national level.

Women are also underrepresented in the membership of the Communist party. They constituted only 24.7 percent of the membership in 1977.[16] Party membership is an essential prerequisite to political advancement and for many high-level economic positions as well. The party has increased recruitment efforts among women in the last decade and membership did increase a few percentage points, but there have been no corresponding attempts to increase women's representation in the party leadership.

Women's marginal position in the political power structure is of primary importance in explaining the lack of attention given to women's needs by the Soviet leadership. Since the early feminist sector of the Communist party either was silenced or died out, there has been no powerful voice within the political elite to support women's interests. Thus policies have been aimed at using women as a resource but not at serving women or promoting women's causes.

The Domestic Sphere.   The absence or underrepresentation of women in the higher reaches of the economic and political spheres can be partially attributed to the continued existence of the domestic/public dichotomy. Women are not isolated in the domestic sphere and cut off from participation in the public sphere, but they still retain the burdens of the household and child care. The domestic sphere is still women's responsibility. Soviet men do not share domestic tasks with their wives on anything approaching an equal basis. Women provide the necessary backup services to allow their husbands to pursue education or training to improve their occupational status or participate in political work to improve their position in the party or government bureaucracy. Husbands do not take care of domestic tasks to free women for this type of after-work economic and political advancement. Women often prefer the less demanding, less responsible jobs with lower prestige, power, and pay because such jobs are less likely to interfere with family responsibilities. Sufficient services have been provided to allow women to work full-time in the interests of the economy, but not enough services are provided to allow them the time to compete equally with men.

Outright discrimination continues to exist as well. Employers, politicians, and educators prefer not to hire or admit women. They believe women to be less reliable because of their domestic duties, especially pregnancy and child care. Because of this discrimination, women perceive the limits on their opportunities and invest less time, energy, and commitment to their jobs, politics, and educations. Since men have a better chance for advancement, women are willing to support their husbands' careers rather than their own. This in turn reinforces administrators' prejudices against women.

Women have been integrated into middle and lower levels of the economic sphere and into the lower levels of the political spheres, but at no time in Soviet history have men been integrated into the domestic sphere of housework and child care. This has been particularly burdensome because of the inadequate service sector. Shopping, for example, is a much more frustrating and time-consuming process in the Soviet Union than in the West. Shortages, long lines, discourteous clerks, and the necessity of going to several specialty shops instead of supermarkets have characterized Soviet shopping for decades.

Housing is also crowded and often substandard by Western standards. This makes upkeep more difficult. Few labor-saving devices have been available until recently, and now that appliances are available the better off and better educated are the people who purchase them. Among poorer, less educated couples, the husband usually judges it more important to spend the family's savings on a television than on a refrigerator or washing machine.

Women have responded to their double burden by having fewer children. There is little they can do to alleviate the burden of the household upkeep, but they can limit the amount of child care and the increased housework that comes from having many children. The one-child family is much too common in the Soviet Union to please authorities. Abortions outnumber live births in some areas. Most women indicate that they would prefer to have two or three children but do not because of the money and time necessary to care for them. The low birthrate is the primary motivating force behind recent political concern with upgrading the service sector and child-care facilities, and perhaps providing part-time employment opportunities for mothers. Policies aimed at supporting the "convenient social virtue" of motherhood, such as the awarding of medals to mothers of large families, have not worked well.

Child rearing and children's education still embody traditional conceptions of gender roles. Girls are socialized toward "feminine" interests and occupations and boys toward "masculine" activities. In Soviet schools, girls but not boys are given home economics training. Traditional gender roles predominate in Soviet children's literature.[17] The effects of this gender role socialization show up very early in the occupational aspirations of boys and girls, and there is little reason to expect change in the near future. Soviet authorities and the public continue to believe that anatomy is destiny and that gender roles are embedded in the different biological natures of women and men. They see no reason to attempt to socialize girls and boys away from gender roles and traditional femininity and masculinity.

Lapidus concludes:

> The central thrust of Soviet policy has been to superimpose new obligations of work and citizenship on more traditional definitions of femininity and to reshape to some extent the boundaries between public and family responsibilities—in short, to facilitate women's performance of both their roles—rather than to radically redefine both male and female roles.[18]

This results in a changed status for women and in many ways an improved status for women in comparison to their lot in the traditional agrarian society of prerevolutionary Russia. But it does not constitute equality or liberation for women. Furthermore, trends do not indicate that this is likely to change in the near future. There may be, in fact, a tendency to differentiate male and female roles further, with an increasing emphasis on family life, motherhood, and domesticity for women, an increased sex segregation in the labor force as the service sector expands and absorbs more women workers, and no real increase in political power or economic control for women.

THE ISRAELI KIBBUTZ

An alternative to the patterns of social organization and development found in most modern industrial societies can be found in the planned communities of the Israeli kibbutzim.[19] The founders of the kibbutzim consciously rejected the class and sexual stratification systems as they knew them in their home countries.

Aims and Development of the Kibbutzim

The first kibbutz was founded in 1909, but most kibbutzim were established in the twenties or later. They experienced an important surge of growth in the forties as Jewish people fled the horrors of Europe before and after World War II. The first generation of settlers came primarily from Eastern Europe where anti-Semitism and pogroms (attacks on the Jewish communities) were common. They were radical young men and a few radical young women who refused to follow their parents traditional life style. They were no longer willing to submit to the tyranny of the Christian majority group. They rejected the culture and life of the urban ghetto and the rural *shtetl* (area of Jewish villages). They were imbued with the vision of a classless society based on socialist principles. Many of them were ardent admirers of the Russian Bolsheviks until it became clear that the Soviet revolution had failed to achieve many of its ideals. Although these young radicals were dedicated to founding a Jewish homeland, they were not religious. The saw Judaism as an ethnic identity and for the most part rejected it as a religion, and they did not want to found their new society on the hierarchical mode of organization embodied in the sacred Jewish writings. The founding generation spurned, in particular, the traditional patriarchal Jewish family structure. They wanted equality between the sexes, even if this meant abolishing the family altogether.

These young socialist radicals were also devotees of the German youth movement which idealized nature and of Tolstoy's reverence for agricultural labor. They repudiated the urban life of European Jewry and the urban occupations of their fathers. Agricultural work was considered ennobling; it was believed that the rural life would bring out the best in human nature. Imbued with these principles, the pioneer generation settled in the inhospitible swamps and mountains of Palestine to found egalitarian communal societies, the kibbutzim.

To avoid the development of social classes, the settlers abolished private property. All property would be owned communally, and each person would contribute according to his or her skills and abilities and would receive according to his or her needs and the community's ability to provide. For the early pioneers the austerity of the life meant that everyone lived simply and worked very hard. The communities were too poor and the life was too harsh to support the very young, the elderly, or the physically unfit.

Modern Kibbutzim

The communities took hold and prospered. The farmlands and more recently the industries began to produce abundantly. The kibbutzim now have pleasant living quarters, good meals, better clothing, recreational facilities, medical centers, and educational facilities. They can afford to provide members with vacations and spending money for personal luxuries. They also send some of the young people to the universities for advanced training. But with this prosperity they have remained committed

to their socialist ideals. Property and income are still owned by the kibbutz
as a collective. Members who work outside the kibbutz contribute their
salaries to the kibbutz treasury. Decisions concerning allocations are made
through "town meeting" style deliberations and through elected committees. Each person's remuneration is unconnected to his or her work role,
political office, or social status. No one is economically dependent on any
other person. The kibbutz as a whole provides for the needs of the unproductive members such as the children, the elderly, and the infirm. Thus
children are not dependent on their parents and wives are not dependent
on their husbands. This principle was important both in avoiding the development of inherited wealth and privilege and breaking the power of the
patriarchal father over his family.

In addition to economic equality, the kibbutz has continued to pursue
political equality. Every kibbutz member has an equal right to participate in
the decision-making process. Most decisions are made in the "town meeting" through group discussion, debate, and voting. Limited powers are
vested in certain elected managerial offices, but to avoid the development
of an entrenched bureaucracy that may accumulate power through its
experience in organizing and overseeing activities, managerial positions are
rotated. No one can serve a long term in office and leaders, although
temporarily vested with more power than other members have, do not
benefit materially from their positions. No special privileges and no deference practices are associated with office-holding. The leader serves the
community just as the agricultural laborer or the teacher serves it.

Child Care and Socialization. To pursue further the goals of equality
and the development of meaningful community ties and commitment, the
kibbutzim also established a highly controversial system of communal education. This aimed at impeding development of the patriarchal nuclear
family, freeing women from the limitations of child rearing, freeing children
from dependence on their families, and socializing children into the
socialist or communal way of life. The communal child-rearing practices
involve placing the infant, only a few days after its birth, in an infants'
house to be cared for by a professional staff. Mothers are encouraged to
spend a great deal of time with the newborn and to breast-feed them. They
are therefore given time off from their jobs for the first few weeks of the
infant's life. But infants do not live with their parents. They sleep in the
infants' house at night, although parents are called if there is any problem.
After a feeding schedule has been established, the mother returns to her
usual job with time off to breast-feed. Fathers are expected to take a great
interest in their children, but they are not given time off during the day to
spend with them.

As children grow older they are moved from the infants' house to other age-graded houses where they live with other children under the care of trained nurses. The work of child care, such as cleaning, feeding, and disciplining, is carried out by professionals. Parents, however, develop close emotional and affectional ties with their children. They spend several hours each evening in uninterrupted play with the children, and mothers often visit the children's residences during the day as well. Parents are a source of constant love and indulgence.

The other domestic chores of the kibbutz are executed communally. Communal kitchens, dining halls, laundries, sewing and mending centers, and maintenance services take care of the usual housekeeping chores. These jobs are filled either by trained permanent workers or by rotation for jobs considered onerous or boring. The family is not important as a consumption or production unit or even as a private child-care unit. These usual family functions are removed from the household to the community.

The "Woman Problem"

The kibbutz presents a clear example of what Margaret Benston advocates as the "industrialization of housework" (see Chapter 2). But however important this may be as a necessary first step for sexual equality, it has not proved to be sufficient to liberate women. The kibbutzim have been successful in achieving their ideals, except in the area of sexual equality. The kubbutzim have been plagued for years by what they call the "woman problem." Men are more satisfied as kibbutz members than women are, and women are more likely than men to want to leave the kibbutz. When couples do leave, it is usually at the insistence of the wife. Women are also more likely than men to violate kibbutz principles regarding the family structure. In recent years women have agitated for more "feminine prerogatives," in particular, for the right to keep their children in their rooms overnight.

When it has succeeded in solving other difficult problems related to establishing an egalitarian society, why has the kibbutz movement failed to implement its ideology in the area of sexual equality? To answer this question, one must look at the development of the kibbutz and at what the movement did *not* do to change "woman's place" as well as what it did do. In brief, the kibbutzim, like the Soviet Union, never integrated men into domestic tasks: they industrialized or collectivized this work, but they assigned it to women. They also never attacked the prestige differential betweeen men's work and women's work. Thus they reestablished a sex-segregated division of labor which placed women in the more monotonous, low prestige, non-economically productive service sectors. This resulted in less political influence and participation and a greater dissatisfaction with kibbutz life for women. It left women with the feeling that if they could not obtain satisfaction from their work or their contribution to the kibbutz community, they should at least be allowed to receive satisfaction from their maternal role. Paradoxically, since the kibbutzim did not avoid gender role stereotyping, sexual division of labor, and sexual inequality, women are demanding a closer adherence to gender roles. A brief look at the history of the kibbutz will show how sexual inequality emerged despite an original ideological opposition to sexual stratification.

Gender Roles in the Pioneer Stage.   For the pioneers life was hard. Having grown up in urban environments, they knew little about farming. But they persevered, they lived in tents and ate the most meager of food. Most of the pioneers were males, but the few females among them were treated as equals and as comrades. Traditional gender roles were rejected. The females worked alongside the males in heavy physical labor draining the swamps, clearing the land, and planting crops. There was no domestic/public dichotomy. But this was primarily because there was no real domestic sector. Their tent homes required little cleaning and no decorating. Meals came from a simple common pot. Life was too insecure for the communities to consider having children and rearing a second generation. But even during this pioneer stage there is evidence that women contributed more to the few domestic tasks than men did.

The Second Stage of Institutionalization.   Rae Lesser Blumberg suggests that the kibbutzim lost much of their revolutionary zeal as they succeeded in taming the land and establishing themselves as viable communities and economic enterprises.[20] They became dedicated to goals of efficiency. Efficiency led to discrimination against women in the agricultural sphere, because although women could do the same work as men, they could not always do it as quickly.

It was at this stage that the kibbutz could afford a second generation. Women in advanced stages of pregnancy were more inefficient than other women and often had to be replaced in the fields by other laborers. Also, Freudian psychoanalytic theory had made an imporant impact on kibbutz child-rearing ideology. In particular, psychoanalysis led to an emphasis on breast-feeding. New mothers were expected to breast-feed and to devote several hours a day to their infants. The paternal–child bond did not receive attention analogous to the maternal–child bond. This interfered even further with women's agricultural contribution relative to men's. The fields are usually located some distance from the residential community, thus requiring mothers to walk many miles through the hot sun in order to attend to both their children and to agricultural work. Most mothers responded to these difficulties of combining field labor with child care by transferring into occupations located closer to the children's houses.[21]

The demand for labor continued to be high in the kibbutz. The need for their labor kept women in the fields during the pioneer stage. But in the second stage an important new source of labor was available through immigration. The immigrants were predominantly young childless males who were attracted to the kibbutz ideology and the ideal of an agricultural commune. They did not come to the kibbutz to care for children or to cook, clean, or to do dishes; they came to labor in the fields. Blumberg argues that it was so important to attract and maintain the commitment of these young men that kibbutz seniority rules were violated in order to place them in the "glamour sector" of agriculture.[22] The dedication of the pioneer mothers was strong enough that they could be assigned the domestic chores with little fear of their defection.

This was also the period of rapid expansion in the service industries. Children's houses were established, residences were built and enlarged, and kitchens and laundries were built. All of this required a staff which was drawn almost exclusively from females. Thus the sex-segregated division of labor between the domestic sphere and the public sphere was never broken. As soon as domestic tasks were necessary on a large scale, they were assigned to women.

Even though the service sector expanded in importance in the life of the community, its importance was not recognized in the ideology or the prestige system. Agricultural work continued to be idealized. The kibbutz bookkeeping methods reflected this ideology and reinforced the prestige and importance of agricultural work. Blumberg points out that the kibbutz members, as subscribers to Marx's labor theory of value, considered labor hours as the only valid measure of productivity and efficiency. The only cost they considered in computing the relative efficiency of different sectors was the number of labor hours expended versus the return. They did not include the cost of capital investment or land in their calculations. This made agricultural production appear much more productive than other areas of production, because the large costs of capital investment and land were not considered. By contrast, the more labor-intensive horticultural gardens worked by the women near the settlements looked inefficient. They required a great many labor hours but little capital or land. On the basis of their labor theory of value bookkeeping, the kibbutz decided to abandon the horticultural mode of farming.

The service sector, the dairy, and the poultry sectors staffed primarily by women were also judged to be less important than agriculture. The dairy and chicken farms used up more work hours relative to profit than field cultivation. The service sector of course produced no profit at all. Workers in these areas were judged less important and the kibbutz was less willing to allocate money for improvements in these areas. Capital was channeled into advanced technology for agriculture while the women labored under primitive conditions in the kitchens and laundries. The lack of prestige combined with poor working conditions further decreased women's satisfaction with and commitment to the kibbutz. The men reaped most of the benefits of kibbutz life.

The prestige differential between the male-dominated agricultural sector and the female-dominated service sector also served to undermine political equality. The kibbutz still accords equal rights to all members, and each member has an equal right to take part in political discussion and debate. But the general feeling is that those who actively participate in and have expertise in a particular area are the appropriate discussants. Thus matters concerning new investments in agriculture are debated almost exclusively among the male agricultural workers. Policy regarding the children's houses or kitchens is debated by women. Yet the most serious decisions, especially with regard to economic allocations, are likely to involve agriculture rather than services. Thus these norms effectively exclude women from political participation in the most important decisions. Furthermore, a great deal of decision-making authority is vested in the economic committees which organize and run each sector. Again, the most important committee is the one for the agricultural sector and women rarely hold office in it. The prestige of this committee and of agriculture in general gives its workers an edge in running for other kibbutz offices. The general management of the kibbutz is predominantly male.

A further factor contributing to the failure of sexual egalitarianism in the kibbutz is the wider social, political, and cultural environment in Israel and the international setting. As noted above, Freudian psychoanalysis with its traditional subordinate role for women influenced the kibbutz for several decades. The decline and almost total disappearance of feminism around the world from the twenties through the sixties undermined kibbutz support for feminist goals. The founding of the state of Israel in 1948 brought a great many traditional, conservative Jews to the area. Middle Eastern Jews and Orthodox Jews from Eastern Europe brought with them patriarchal family structures and a firm commitment to male dominance and female subordination.

These groups had an impact on the Israeli nation. The state was based on the Jewish religion and rabbinical law which the kibbutz movement had rejected. The kibbutz members now found themselves bound to a legal structure which often incorporated rabbinical law into secular law. For example, Israel recognizes only religious marriage ceremonies and restricts the legal rights of illegitimate children. The kibbutz had rejected religious marriage and divorce in favor of free consensual unions entered into whenever a couple decided to move into shared quarters and dissolved when they decided to separate. Traditional marriage was believed to demean women and to embody female subordination. Under Israeli law, however, kibbutzniks must undergo the religious marriage ceremony to protect the rights of their children. This serves to emphasize the couple and the family as a unit instead of the individual and the community. Such practices have at least a subtle effect on the gender roles of the kibbutz.

The Threat of War.   Another factor in the wider environment of the kibbutz which has negatively affected the position of women has been the impact of war and the constant threat of war. In the years of struggle preceding the founding of the Israeli state, females often participated in combat duties. Several female soldiers are national heroines. Today, females continue to serve in the Israeli army and are subject to the draft just as males are, but they are not given combat training. Instead, females are given clerical jobs and other non-combatant tasks which free men for combat. These practices apply to kibbutz members as well as to other Israeli citizens. Thus, kibbutzniks are placed at the age of eighteen into the highly sex-segregated military setting and are introduced to the male dominant values which underly it. A great deal of prestige accrues to the brave fighting man who defends his country. Women are not so honored for their contributions to the war effort. Kibbutz males have been especially prominent among the lists of war heroes and war casualties. This has increased their prestige within the kibbutz as well as outside it and given males a further advantage over females.

The constant threat of war has also led to an increased emphasis on the maternal role for women. Throughout Israel, including on the kibbutz, mothers of sons in combat are expected to play important supportive roles for their sons. They are to keep in close touch with their soldier sons and provide emotional support in their letters and telephone calls. They should send food packages and other homemade luxuries to comfort the soldiers. They should also follow the war-related news closely as a demonstration of their concern for their sons' welfare. Again, this serves to emphasize male importance in society and females as supporters of the more important males.

The war threat has increased the emphasis on the maternal role and the family in another way as well. It has led many parents, especially mothers, to insist on keeping their children in their own quarters at night.[23] In response to the tensions engendered by terrorist raids, parents often feel more secure with their children nearby when in fact taking the children from the children's houses makes their collective protection more difficult. The wartime situation has exacerbated the trend for second- and third-generation kibbutz women to demand greater maternal involvement. But this increases the emphasis on the family unit at the expense of collectivity and contributes to an increased emphasis on women's familial roles at the expense of public roles.

Industrialization. The kibbutz has now, however, entered a third stage of development. Recent increased involvement in industrial production may help bring women back into the productive sector. Industrialization and automation have been more fully implemented in the service sector, thus freeing many women from these jobs. Automation has also eliminated some of the work in the kitchens and laundries which women found particularly oppressive. Industrialization has also created more opportunities for women to engage in profitable labor. Blumberg notes that kibbutz industry is more profitable than agriculture and that profitability lends the work and workers prestige in the kibbutz.[24] According to Blumberg, if the kibbutz can keep industry sexually integrated and avoid developing a pattern of male managers and higher-level technical staff and female factory operatives, there may be a rise in sexual egalitarianism.

Sexual equality may also be promoted by demographic factors. Blumberg points out that immigration is no longer an important source of new labor on the kibbutz. In addition, the kibbutzim have suffered higher male casualty rates in war, thus reducing the proportion of males in the labor force. Shortages in male labor may force a fuller integration of females into previously male-dominated occupations.

Another factor promoting greater sexual equality is the rebirth of the international feminist movement. The new wave of feminism affects the kibbutz just as the demise of feminism hampered sexual egalitarianism on the kibbutz in the twenties. The feminist movement in Israel is still small, but it does provide women with an explanation for their frustration and an ideological basis for resisting male dominance.

Some writers have argued that innate biological and psychological factors account for the failure of the kibbutz to achieve sexual equality.[25] The foregoing discussion indicates that factors inherent in the social structure are likely to be of greatest importance. The kibbutz never really undertook the social structural changes necessary to free women and men from traditional gender roles. The communal kitchens, laundries, child care, and economic support system freed women from their ties to domestic tasks and economic dependency only within private family units. The sex-segregated division of labor which locked women into the domestic-oriented service sectors and allowed men to dominate the productive sectors re-created the traditional situation at the community level. Women were left as the housekeepers and mothers for the collective and this inhibited their self-esteem, prestige, political participation, economic power, and satisfaction with kibbutz life.

SUMMARY

The socialist experiments undertaken by the Soviet Union and the Israeli kibbutz movement have not been successful in achieving sexual equality. The primary reasons for this appear to be the persistence of the domestic/public dichotomy and the absence of an organized, articulate, and active feminist movement to act as a watchdog on women's issues.

In the Soviet Union little progress has been made toward the socialization or industrialization of housework or child care. Early ideological support for such programs were dropped in the face of economic scarcity and political opposition. Women have been integrated into the public sphere on a much larger scale than in other countries. However, the double burden of housework and child care inhibits women's ability to devote themselves to work in the public sphere. Thus they are unable and often unwilling to compete successfully with men for the more prestigious, powerful, and better-paying political and economic positions. Women remain at the lower levels of the economic, political, and social structures of the Soviet Union. Little organized resistance to this situation has existed since Stalin's purges of feminist leaders in the thirties.

On the kibbutz the original ideological commitment to communal housework and child care has been realized. However, women still remain tied to domestic tasks. The domestic sphere has been made part of the public sphere, but the sexual division of labor between male economically productive work and female service work remains unchanged. Women still do the laundry, the dishes, the cooking, and the child rearing, but they do it as professionals for the entire community instead of for one family unit.

Because communal domestic work is not as highly valued as the communal agricultural work done by men, women's self-confidence and self esteem are undermined and their participation in the decision-making of the kibbutz and in the more powerful and prestigious elective offices is inhibited. The trend toward industrialization on the kibbutz may, however, increase sexual equality by bringing women more fully into work in an economically productive and prestigious sector. The revival of international feminism may also be a force in support of sexual equality on the kibbutz.

Notes

1. See, for example, Shulamith Firestone, *The Dialectic of Sex* (New York: Bantam Books, 1971); Charnie Buettel, *Marxism and Feminism* (Toronto: The Women's Press, 1974); Linda Jenness, ed., *Feminism and Socialism* (New York: Pathfinder, 1972); Evelyn

Reed, *Problems of Women's Liberation* (New York: Pathfinder Press, 1971).

2. Frederick Engels, *The Origin of the Family, Private Property and the State* (1880; New York: International Publishers, 1972); August Bebel, *Woman Under Socialism* (1904; New York: Schocken Books, 1971).

3. See, for example, Hilda Scott, *Does Socialism Liberate Women?* (Boston: Beacon Press, 1974).

4. This discussion of the Soviet Union relies on Gail Lapidus, *Women in Soviet Society: Equality, Development, and Social Change* (Berkeley: U. of California Press, 1978); Dorothy Atkinson, Alexander Dallin, and Gail Lapidus ed., *Women in Russia* (Stanford, Cal.: Stanford U. Press, 1977); William Mandel, *Soviet Women* (Garden City, N. Y.: Anchor Books, 1975); Richard Stites, *The Women's Liberation Movement in Russia: Feminism, Nihilism, and Bolshevism 1860–1930* (Princeton: Princeton U. Press, 1978); Michael Sacks, *Women's Work in Soviet Russia: Continuity in the Midst of Change* (New York: Praeger 1976).

5. Lapidus, 1978, p. 37.

6. Engels, 1880; Bebel, 1904.

7. Rose Glickman, "The Russian Factory Woman, 1880–1914," in Atkinson, Dallin, and Lapidus, p. 81.

8. Sacks, p. 15.

9. Sacks, pp. 7, 23

10. Lapidus, 1978, p. 49.

11. Marlis Allendorf, *Woman in Socialist Society* (New York: International Publishers, 1975), p. 59.

12. Michael Swafford, "Sex Differences in Soviet Earnings," *American Sociological Review,* 43 (October, 1978), 657.

13. Mandel, 1975, p. 107.

14. Lapidus, 1978, p. 188.

15. Lapidus, 1978, p. 216.

16. Lapidus, 1978, p. 210.

17. Mollie Schwartz Rosenhan, "Images of Male and Female in Children's Readers," In Atkinson, Dallin, and Lapidus, ed., 1977, pp. 293–305.

18. Lapidus, 1978, p. 344.

19. This discussion of the Israeli kibbutzim relies on Rae Lesser Blumberg, "Kibbutz Women: From the Fields of Revolution to the Laundries of Discontent," in Lynne B. Iglitzin and Ruth Ross, eds., *Women in the World: A Comparative Study* (Santa Barbara, Cal.: Clio Books, 1976), pp. 319–344; Blumberg, *Stratification: Socioeconomic and Sexual Inequality* (Dubuque, Iowa: Wm. C. Brown, 1978), pp. 112–116; Blumberg, "The Women of the Israeli Kibbutz," *The Center Magazine,* 7 (May–June 1974), 70–72; Elaine Soloway, "Kibbutz Women: In Transition," *Communities,* 23 (November–December 1976), 8–9; Hyman Mariampolski, "The Decline of Sexual Egalitarianism on the Kibbutz," East Lafayette, Ind.: Purdue University, Institute for the Study of Social Change, Working Paper No. 89, April 1975; Yehuda Don, "Industrialization in Advanced Rural Communities: The Israeli Kibbutz," Madison, Wis.: University of Wisconsin, Land Tenure Center, Paper No. 112, January 1977; A. I. Rabin, "The Sexes: Ideology and Reality in the Israeli Kibbutz," in Georgene H. Seward and Robert C. Williamson, eds., *Sex Roles in Changing Society* (New York: Random House, 1970), pp. 285–307; Melford E. Spiro, *Kibbutz: Venture in Utopia* (3rd ed.; New York: Schocken Books, 1970).

20. Blumberg, 1974, p. 70.

21. Blumberg, 1976, p. 329.

22. Blumberg, 1974, p. 71.

23. Shimon S. Camiel, "Some Observations about the Effect of War on Kibbutz Family Structure," *The Family Coordinator,* 27 (January, 1978), 43–46.
24. Blumberg, 1976, p. 335.
25. Lionel Tiger and Joseph Shepher, *Women in the Kibbutz* (New York: Harcourt Brace Jovanovich, 1975).

11

Conclusion

But the creative changes now required in our social structure also entail a leveling of old power structures and a shift
in basic priorities and values. Outsiders must be brought into
the establishment and at the same time infuse the whole
society with new life. Thus will the interests of women and
the interests of all then be joined together. If sex role change
does constitute a true revolution, it will reorder the whole
society and its place in the world.

Janet Zollinger Giele, *Women and the Future*

Now that the positions of women and men in different types of societies and at different points in history have been examined, what implications are there for the future of gender roles and sexual stratification systems? One conclusion that can be drawn from this analysis of cross-cultural and historical data is that no specific types of gender roles or sexual stratification are universal or inevitable. Diversity and change are hallmarks of the social positions of the sexes.

But it is nonetheless impossible to select the type of gender roles we would like from the many possible ones. Gender roles cannot be borrowed from one context and adopted into a quite different context. For example, the communal egalitarianism of foragers may be appealing. But a society cannot implement these gender roles without simultaneously adopting their system of economic production and distribution and the social and cultural systems associated with their mode of production. This would not, of course, be feasible for the large-scale, densely populated nation states that characterize most of the world today.

Gender roles are part of the wider evolutionary changes in society and therefore are constrained by environmental imperatives. Gender roles change with the environment. Thus what we have found in the past and present does not necessarily tell us what we can or shall have in the future. The social, cultural, economic, political, and ecological conditions of the future will undoubtedly differ from those of the past. Yet for those interested in directing social change—in particular for those interested in working for liberation from the constraints of gender roles and the inequities of sexual stratification—knowledge of the factors giving rise to, supporting, and destroying past systems can help in attempts to discover what must be done to dismantle such systems and to prevent their reemergence. Human beings can affect the direction of social change, but they do so only within the limits imposed by the conditions of their time and place. Individuals and organized groups can change the course of history, but they do not always achieve the results they desire. Some changes are impossible in specific social settings. Understanding the influence of wide social forces can help us understand what aspects of gender roles and stratification may be altered and under what circumstances such changes may be achieved.

For example, it is true in various societies that a sharp division between the domestic and public spheres isolates one sex in the domestic sphere and contributes substantially to the subordination of that sex. Not all societies have isolated women into the domestic sphere, and in the modern context it is probably unnecessary to continue to do so. Functional alternatives to the full-time housewife now exist. Many of the burdens of the domestic sphere have been taken over by other institutions such as the school system and the food-processing industry. Bottle-feeding has freed many women from the necessity of breast-feeding and made possible a much greater participation in early child care by fathers. But this technological advance has not resulted in much change in women's roles because women have continued to be assigned the tasks associated with bottle-feeding. Therefore women are no less limited than they were with breast-feeding.

Thus far, the sex subordinated within the domestic context has always been the female, and females have consequently exercised less power in society than have males. However, if males were systematically isolated in the domestic sphere and cut off from participation in political, economic, and social institutions, we could expect males to be less powerful than females. Such reversal of traditional roles is within the realm of possibility if the technology associated with childbirth and child care continues to remove these processes farther from biological constraints. Test-tube babies may sound dehumanizing and frightening now, but they could become the accepted mode of reproduction in the future. Such a technological change could be used to free women from the limitations of their reproductive role, but it would not necessarily do so. To avoid sexual stratification based on the isolating effects of child care, both men and women must participate in this sphere as well as in public spheres.

With or without such technological changes in reproduction, the domestic/public dichotomy as we know it today will probably be altered. With the current problems of population growth and limited global resources, the full-time housewife and full-time breadwinner roles are in many respects dysfunctional.* Full-time housewifery seems to encourage women to have more children, thus further increasing population problems. It also encourages consumerism and thereby exacerbates the problem of wasting scarce resources. One of the housewife's main tasks in modern society is directing family consumption. Freeing large numbers of women to pursue this task full-time has been one of the effects of industrialization and has vastly increased the amounts of goods and services consumed by residents of the developed countries. Similarly, the full-time breadwinner role for males cuts men off from the satisfactions of child rearing and encourages men to fulfill themselves through wasteful materialistic consumption. It also encourages men to value mastery of the environment over a more ecologically adaptive or conservationist approach. These consumption and production practices have in turn created

---

* For a further discussion of this topic see Janet Zollinger Giele, *Women and the Future* (New York: Free Press, 1978); Elise Boulding, *Women in the Twentieth-Century World* (New York: Halstead Press, 1977); and Rosemary Radford Ruether, *New Woman: New Earth: Sexist Ideologies and Human Liberation* (New York: The Seabury Press, 1975), pp. 186–214.

disastrous problems with pollution and the depletion of finite resources. The excessive consumption habits of the developed world have also increased the problem of the worldwide maldistribution of resources and have thereby contributed to the problems of international inequality and the resulting international tensions. This way of life cannot continue unchanged.

Changes in the domestic/public dichotomy may also be related to future problems of population pressure. Population pressure has been an important variable affecting gender roles in technologically less advanced societies. It may reemerge as a relevant factor in the future. By tremendously expanding productivity, industrialization rendered population pressure relatively unimportant in the developed world. It is becoming apparent, however, that there are limits to such expanding productivity, again because of pollution and scarce resources. For example, overcrowding may in the long run make the isolated nuclear family dwelling unit impossible. The small-scale, reduplicative, kin-based production and consumption units for domestic tasks may be too wasteful of space and other resources to be maintained for the masses in the future. The domestic role for women associated with the single-family house or apartment may not be able to survive.

However, in the short run, the domestic role may again become the only respectable role for women. Periods of economic decline have in the past led to a backlash against women's fuller participation in the public sphere. Current problems with high unemployment and economic recession in the developed world as well as in underdeveloped countries may lead to attacks on feminism as the scapegoat and a return to the "cult of domesticity" among those who can manage to afford it.

The study of contemporary and past societies points out the importance of warfare and competition in the subordination of women. Women have, in general, fared better in peaceful, noncompetitive environments. If the future is one of greater population pressure, competition over scarce resources, high crime rates, and other forms of internal feuding and endemic warfare, female subordination will probably increase. Controlling population, competition, fighting, and warfare may be of the utmost importance for women's liberation.

Economic roles and economic control are important variables for an understanding of variations in women's and men's positions in society. Economically dependent people tend to be subordinated people. To free women as well as other oppressed groups, it is necessary for them to gain some degree of economic independence or an equal measure of economic interdependence with others. Women and men, as well as slaves and masters and the lower class and the upper class, have traditionally been economically interdependent: men as breadwinners have needed the services of their wives, slave owners have depended on the work of their slaves, and the upper class has depended on the labor of the lower class. However, the bargaining positions of the groups have been unequal. The two groups' control over resources must be roughly equal to avoid the inequities of a stratification system, whether sexual, economic, or racial. One group cannot be allowed to monopolize important resources of wealth, education, jobs, political power, or the instruments of coercion.

The current feminist movement has attacked this type of sexual inequality. But it is not sufficient merely to integrate a few women into the predominantly male elite that now controls these important resources. Liberation from the inequalities of class and racial stratification is relevant to achieving liberation from the inequities of sexual stratification. Having elite women share power with elite men does not liberate either the women or the men of non-elite groups, although it may benefit women of the elite relative to men of the elite. It will require a radical restructuring of most modern societies' social, economic, and political structures to equalize the bargaining positions of most of their members. It will also require a radical restructuring of the international situation to equalize the bargaining positions of individuals in poor countries relative to individuals in rich countries. All of this is probably necessary if we are to avoid the negative effects on women and on human freedom in general of population pressure, warfare, and competition.

To achieve this egalitarian future will probably require action among many different groups of subordinated peoples. Feminist movements, both reformist and radical, can contribute to this process. But the problems of women's liberation cannot be separated from wider issues of human liberation, which will require active, committed persons willing to work and sacrifice for these goals. The forces arrayed against such liberation are many and powerful. Revolutionary changes to advance human freedom cannot be brought about easily, but this difficulty is insufficient reason to accept defeat.

Selective Bibliography

This listing includes only those books that deal with the general study of women and men in society in cross-cultural and historical perspective. Articles have been excluded, but the women's studies journal *Signs* is highly recommended as a source of numerous articles on cross-cultural and historical topics. The large number of books that deal only with one specific country have also been excluded. The following list should, however, provide the student with sufficient bibliographic material to begin the pursuit of further study of specific countries or other specific topics within the area of the comparative analysis of sexual stratification.

Agonito, Rosemary. *History of Ideas on Women: A Source Book.* New York: Putnam, 1977.

Ardener, Shirley, ed. *Defining Females: The Nature of Women in Society.* New York: Halstead Press, 1978.

Beck, Lois and Nikki Keddie, eds. *Women in the Muslim World.* Cambridge, Mass.: Harvard U. Press, 1978.

Blumberg, Rae Lesser. *Stratification: Socioeconomic and Sexual Inequality.* Dubuque, Iowa: Wm. C. Brown, 1978.

Boserup, Ester. *Woman's Role in Economic Development.* New York: St. Martin's Press, 1970.

Boulding, Elise. *The Underside of History: A View of Women Through Time.* Boulder, Col.: Westview Press, 1976.

———. *Women in the Twentieth Century World.* New York: Halstead Press, 1977.

Branca, Patricia. *Women in Europe since 1750.* New York: St. Martin's Press, 1978.

Bridenthal, Renate and Claudia Koontz, eds. *Becoming Visible: Women in European History.* Boston: Houghton Mifflin, 1977.

Bullough, Vern L. *The Subordinate Sex: A History of Attitudes toward Women.* Baltimore: Penguin, 1973.

Carroll, Berenice A., ed. *Liberating Women's History: Theoretical and Critical Essays.* Chicago: U. of Illinois Press, 1976.

Davis, Elizabeth Gould. *The First Sex.* Baltimore: Penguin, 1972.

de Riencourt, Amaury. *Sex and Power in History.* New York: D. McKay Co., 1974.

Fernea, Elizabeth Warnock and Basia Quattan Bexirgan, eds. *Middle Eastern Women Speak.* Austin: U. of Texas Press, 1977.

Figes, Eva. *Patriarchal Attitudes.* New York: Stein and Day, 1970.

Friedl, Ernestine. *Women and Men: An Anthropologist's View.* New York: Holt, Rinehart and Winston, 1975.

Giele, Janet Zollinger and Audey Chapman Smock, eds. *Women: Roles and Statuses in Eight Countries.* New York: Wiley–Interscience, 1977.

Gies, Frances and Joseph Gies. *Women in the Middle Ages.* New York: Crowell, 1978.

Glazer, Nona and Helen Youngelson Waehrer, eds. *Woman in a Man-Made World: A Socioeconomic Handbook.* 2nd ed.; Chicago: McNally, 1977.

Goodwater, Leanna. *Women in Antiquity: An Annotated Bibliography.* Metuchen N.J.: Scarecrow Press, 1975.

Griffiths, Naomi. *Penelope's Web: Some Perceptions of Women in European and Canadian Society.* Toronto: Oxford U. Press, 1976.

Hafkin, Nancy J. and Edna G. Bay, eds. *Women in Africa: Studies in Social and Economic Change.* Stanford, Cal.: Stanford U. Press, 1976.

Hahner, June E., ed. *Women in Latin American History.* Los Angeles: UCLA Latin American Center Publications, U. of California, Los Angeles, 1976.

Hamilton, Roberta. *The Liberation of Women: A Study of Patriarchy and Capitalism.* London: George Allen and Unwin, 1978.

Hammond, Dorothy and Alta Jablow. *Women in Cultures of the World.* Menlo Park, Cal.: Cummings Publishing Co., 1976.

Hartman, Mary S. and Lois Banner, eds. *Clio's Consciousness Raised: New Perspectives on the History of Women.* New York: Harper and Row, 1974.

Iglitzin, Lynne B. and Ruth Ross, eds. *Women in the World: A Comparative Study.* Santa Barbara, Cal.: Clio Books, 1976.

Jacobs, Sue Ellen. *Women in Perspective: A Guide for Cross-Cultural Studies.* Chicago: U. of Illinois Press, 1974.

Kelly-Gadol, Joan. *Bibliography in the History of European Women.* 4th rev. ed.; New York: Sarah Lawrence College, 1976.

Kessler, Evelyn S. *Women: An Anthropological View.* New York: Holt, Rinehart and Winston, 1976.

Knaster, Meri. *Women in Spanish America: An Annotated Bibliography from Pre-Conquest to Contemporary Times.* Boston: G. K. Hall, 1977.

Kuhn, Annette and AnnMarie Wolpe. *Feminism and Materialism: Women and Modes of Production.* Boston: Routledge and Kegan Paul, 1973.

Lefkowitz, Mary R. and Maureen B. Fant, compilers. *Women in Greece and Rome.* Toronto: Samuel-Stevens, 1977.

Little, Kenneth. *African Women in Towns: An Aspect of Africa's Social Revolution.* New York: Cambridge U. Press, 1973.

Martin, M. Kay, and Barbara Voorhies. *Female of the Species.* New York: Columbia U. Press, 1975.

Matthiasson, Carolyn J., ed. *Many Sisters: Women in Cross-Cultural Perspective.* New York: Free Press, 1974.

Mead, Margaret. *Male and Female: A Study of the Sexes in a Changing World.* New York: Morrow, 1949.

Mednick, Martha, Sandra Tangri, and Lois Hoffman, eds. *Women and Achievement: Social and Motivational Analyses.* New York: Halstead Press, 1975.

Mickelwait, Donald R., Mary Ann Riegelman, and Charles F. Sweet. *Women in Rural Development: A Survey of the Roles of Women in Ghana, Lesotho, Kenya, Nigeria, Bolivia, Paraguay, and Peru.* Boulder, Col.: Westview Press, 1976.

Nash, June and Helen Ickin Safa, eds. *Sex and Class in Latin America.* New York: Praeger, 1976.

O'Barr, Jean. *Third World Women: Factors in their Changing Status.* Durham, N.C.: Center for International Studies, Duke University, 1976.

O'Faolain, Julia and Lauro Martines, eds. *Not in God's Image: Women in History from the Greeks to the Victorians.* New York: Harper, 1973.

Parveen, Shaukat Ali. *Status of Women in the Muslim World: A Study in the Feminist Movements in Turkey, Egypt, Iran, and Pakistan.* Lahore: Aziz Publishers, 1975.

Patai, Raphael, ed. *Women in the Modern World.* New York: Free Press, 1967.

Paulme, Denise, ed. *Women in Tropical Africa.* Trans. H. M. Wright. Berkeley, Cal.: U. of California Press, 1974.

Pescatello, Ann, ed. *Female and Male in Latin America: Essays.* Pittsburgh: U. of Pittsburgh Press, 1973.

———. *Power and Pawn: The Female in Iberian Families, Societies, and Cultures.* Westport, Conn.: Greenwood Press, 1976.

Pomeroy, Sarah B. *Goddesses, Whores, Wives, and Slaves: Women in Classical Antiquity.* New York: Schocken Books, 1975.

Putnam, Emily J. *The Lady: Studies of Certain Significant Phases of Her History.* 1910; Chicago: U. of Chicago Press, 1970.

Raccagni, Michelle. *The Modern Arab Woman: A Bibliography.* Metuchen, N.J.: Scarecrow Press, 1978,

Raphael, Dana, ed. *Being Female: Reproduction, Power, and Change.* The Hague: Mouton, 1975.

Reed, Evelyn. *Woman's Evolution: From Matriarchal Clan to Patriarchal Family.* New York: Pathfinder Press, 1975.

Reische, Diana L., ed. *Women and Society.* New York: H. W. Wilson, 1972.

Reiter, Rayna, ed. *Toward an Anthropology of Women.* New York: Monthly Review Press, 1975.

Rohrlich-Leavitt, Ruby, ed. *Women Cross-Culturally: Change and Challenge.* The Hague: Mouton, 1975.

Rosaldo, Michelle Zimbalist and Louise Lamphere, eds. *Woman, Culture, and Society.* Stanford, Cal.: Stanford U. Press, 1974.

Rosenberg, Marie Bauvic and Len U. Bergstrom. *Women and Society: A Critical Review of the Literature with a Selected Annotated Bibliography.* Beverly Hills, Cal.: Sage Publications, 1975.

Rowbotham, Sheila. *Hidden from History: Rediscovering Women in History from* the Seventeenth Century to the Present. New York: Pantheon Books, 1975.

Saffioti, Heleieth I. B. Women in Class Society. Trans. Michael Vale. New York: Monthly Review Press, 1978.

Saulniere, Suzanne S. and Cathy A. Rakowski. Women in the Development Process: A Select Bibliography on Women in Sub-Saharan Africa and Latin America. Austin: Institute of Latin American Studies, U. of Texas Press, 1977.

Schlegel, Alice, ed. Sexual Stratification: A Cross-Cultural View. New York: Columbia U. Press, 1977.

Seltman, Charles. Women in Antiquity. New York: St. Martin's Press, 1955.

Seward, Georgene H. and Robert C. Williamson, eds. Sex Roles in Changing Society. New York: Random House, 1970.

Steiner, Shari. The Female Factor: A Study of Women in Five Western European Societies. New York: G. P. Putnam's Sons, 1977.

Sullerot, Evelyn. Woman, Society and Change. Trans. Margaret Scotford Archer. New York: McGraw-Hill, 1971.

Tinker, Irene, Michele Bo Bransen, and Mayra Burinic, eds. Women and World Development: With an Annotated Bibliography. New York: Praeger, 1976.

United Nations. Status of Women: A Select Bibliography. White Plains, N.Y.: UNIFO Publishers, 1975.

Ward, Barbara, ed. Women in the New Asia. Paris: UNESCO, 1963.

Whyte, Martin King. The Status of Women in Preindustrial Societies. Princeton, N.J.: Princeton U. Press, 1978.

Women Workers and Society: International Perspectives. Geneva: International Labour Office, 1976.

Woodsmall, Ruth Frances. Women and the New East. Washington, D.C.: Middle East Institute, 1960.

Youssef, Nadia Haggag. Women and Work in Developing Societies. 1974; Westport, Conn.: Greenwood Press, 1976.

Index of Names

327

Index of Subjects

Abayah, 220, 221
Abolitionists, 242
Abortion, 64, 80, 255, 275–276, 280–281, 297, 300, 301, 304
Absolutist monarchies, 110
Academy, Greek, 171
Achaeans, 163
Achievement motivation, 28
Adriatic city-state, 187
Adultery, 54, 57–58, 97, 121, 146, 165, 181, 234
Advanced industrial society, 59–60, 259–316. See also Capitalism; Industrial societies
Advanced market economy, 55–57, 231
Affirmative Action Plan, 277, 283
Africa, 111–112, 127, 144, 146, 153–154. See also Bushmen; Fulani; Ganda; Ghana; Hadza; Lovedu; Nigeria; Nuer; Pondo; Pygmies; The Sudan
Aggression, 48, 50–51, 54–57, 65–66, 72, 78, 91, 119–121, 125, 148; in agrarian society, 160–161, 163–164, 169–171, 184; in children, 97–99, 148; as a gender role stereotype, 3, 13, 14, 21, 27, 28, 29, 30; among hunters and gatherers, 78, 97–99; among pastoralists, 138, 140–142, 148–149; and testosterone, 2
Agrarian society, 152–192, 218, 219, 220, 227, 293; in ancient Greece, 162–173, 190; in ancient Rome, 173–180, 190; in medieval Europe, 180–190
Agriculture, 43, 49, 52, 57–59, 63, 77, 96, 102, 135–136, 146, 149, 152–156, 189, 194–195, 200–201. See also Agrarian society
Ainu of Japan, 155
Alienation, 17, 204, 229
Alimony, 209
Alliances, 52, 145, 158–159
Ambruina relationship, 93–94
America: Central, 110; Latin, 198–208; South, 110
American Federation of Labor (AFL), 263
Anal stage, 10
Anarchism, 261
Androcentrism, 24–26
Androgyny, 28
Anthropology, 5, 6, 24–26
Arabs. See Bedouins; Marri Baluch
Archaic period: of Greece, 164–167; of Rome, 173–174

dustrial society; Advanced market economy; Capitalism; Industrial society
Market relationships, 50, 60, 76, 109, 133, 227
Markets of sexual exchange, 51–52
Market systems, 71, 111
Marriage, 4, 32, 42–46, 51–56, 58, 72, 136; in agrarian societies, 158, 164–168, 172, 174–175, 177, 180, 182–183, 186; and capitalism, 8, 14; in capitalist society, 234, 238, 240, 243, 245–246, 263–266, 284, 286, 288; child, 93, 96, 208, 213; group, 7, 42–46; in horticultural societies, 112–120, 122–125; among hunters and gatherers, 79, 85, 92–97; on the kibbutz, 311–312; manuals, 29; among the Marri Baluch, 147; and the Nuer, 146, 148; pairing, 44–45; among pastoralists, 145–148; serial, 92; sociology of, 23, 24; in the Soviet Union, 293–294, 297, 299–300, 303–304; among the Tiwi, 92–95; in underdeveloped peasant societies, 197, 201, 203–205, 209, 213, 214, 216, 217, 219, 221, 222
Marriage and Divorce Bill, 252
Marri Baluch Arabs, 147
Marxists, 294–296
Masculinity, 19, 264, 271–272
Masochism, 11, 29
Masturbation, 240
Materialism, 41–42
Maternal deprivation, 17
Maternal instinct, 4, 8, 9, 14, 34, 238, 256
Maternity leave, 17
Matriarchy, 5, 6, 25, 26, 67, 113, 267–268
Matricentric kinship, 115
Matrifocality, 197
Matrilineality, 5, 6, 7, 8, 46–48, 67; and agrarian society, 163, 164; and communal households, 44–48;

"debate" about, 47; and the Greeks, 164; and horticultural society, 113–129; and hunters and gatherers, 97; and inheritance, 46–47
Matrilineal principle, 7
Matrilocality: and the Greeks, 164; and horticultural societies, 114–118, 121, 128; and the Iroquois, 116–117; and the Truk, 117–118
Matron, Iroquois, 116
Mayans, 110, 198
Mayordomo, 203, 204
Mbuti Pygmies. *See* Pygmies
Medicine: sexual stratification within, 302; views of women, 239–240
Medical sociology, 21, 22
Mediterranean pastoralists, 132, 141–146
Men's clubs, 15
Men's house, 25, 112
Men's spaces, 136
Menstruation, 68, 80, 124, 126; in capitalist society, 238; as the "curse," 14; as a focus of ritual, 25; in India, 214, 215; and the Marri Baluch Arabs, 147
Merchant class, 155, 187–188; 227, 236–237
Mesopotamia, 153
Mestizo, 200
Mexican revolution, 200
Mexico, 198–208
Military, 52–53, 65–68
Minoan civilization, 162–163
Misogyny, 169–171, 177, 185–186, 282
Missionaries, 25
Mithras, 172
Mobility, 15
Mode of production, 41–42
Mohammedism. *See* Moslems
Molimo, 102
Monasteries in medieval Europe, 180, 183–185
Monastic movement, 180
Mongols, 139